Sarah M. (Sarah Micolena) Brownson

Life of Demetrius Augustine Gallitzin, prince and priest

Sarah M. (Sarah Micolena) Brownson
Life of Demetrius Augustine Gallitzin, prince and priest
ISBN/EAN: 9783741182228

Manufactured in Europe, USA, Canada, Australia, Japa

Cover: Foto ©Andreas Hilbeck / pixelio.de

Manufactured and distributed by brebook publishing software (www.brebook.com)

Sarah M. (Sarah Micolena) Brownson

Life of Demetrius Augustine Gallitzin, prince and priest

Published by Fr. Pustet & Cº Newyork & Cincinnati, O.

LIFE

OF

DEMETRIUS AUGUSTINE GALLITZIN,

PRINCE AND PRIEST,

BY SARAH M. BROWNSON,

WITH AN

INTRODUCTION BY O. A. BROWNSON, LL. D.

. Behold a great Priest who in his time pleased God and was found just; and in time of wrath became an atonement. Who was beloved of God and men; whose memory is in benediction.—[ECCL. XLIV. XLV.]

NEW YORK:
FR. PUSTET & CO., 52 BARCLAY STREET.
AND
204 VINE STREET, CINCINNATI, O.
1873.

1804

TO MY

Dear Mother

WHO DID NOT STAY FOR THE END
OF THE WORK SHE LOVED SO WELL, SO LONG
GUIDED AND SUSTAINED BY HER VIVID INTEREST, HER
ADMIRABLE JUDGEMENT, PERFECT TASTE AND DE-
VOTED FAITH, THIS ACCOUNT OF A SAINTLY
LIFE NOT UNLIKE HER OWN, IS
INSCRIBED BY THE

Author.

1872

CONTENTS.

PREFACE.. I
INTRODUCTION... V

CHAPTER I.
THE GALLITZIN FAMILY.

PAGE

Its antiquity.—Origin.—Poland's prisoner.—Prince Vasilii Gallitzin.—Plans for the Greek Church.—Field Marshall Gallitzin.—The ice palace.—Prince Dmitri Gallitzin.—Russian ambassador to Paris.—Visits Aachen. — His marriage.—The wedding journey.—Appointed ambassador to Holland.................... 1

CHAPTER II.
THE PRINCESS GALLITZIN, née VON SCHMETTAU.
(1748—1778.)

Early days.—At the convent at Breslau.—Her persistency, affection and loyalty as a child.—Her home education.—At a fashionable French boarding-school.—At court.—Perplexities.—Desire for knowledge.—An old gentleman's wisdom.—Mental confusion.—Observations during her wedding tour.—Birth of Marianna Gallitzin. — Of Demetrius. — Life at the Hague.—The Star of Holland.—Diderot's visit.—Mimi and Mitri in the nursery.—Hemsterhuys' influence.—Final retirement from society....... 11

CHAPTER III.
AT MUENSTER.
(1779—1783.)

Nithuys insufficient.—Advantages of Geneva.—Fuerstenberg's public school system.—Muenster.—Foundation of the university.—The princess' observations.—Decides to remain in Muenster.—Regulates her household.—Home pleasures.—Freedom and enjoyment of her reunions. Distinguished visitors.—Baron von Fuerstenberg.—Hamann.—Travels.—At Halle.—Effect of her method of education.—Mitri's timidity, sensitiveness and reserve......... 24

CHAPTER IV.
A NEW LIFE.
(1783—1789.)

Spiritual necessities. — Example of Catholic friends. — A critical moment.— Dr. Overberg. — Recovery.—Investigation.—Confusion.—The study of the Scriptures. — Love of metaphysics.—Light.—Embarrassment in regard to the children.—Uneasiness about Mitri.—His character.—Travels.—Happiness of the princess.—Her devotion to the Church.—Her zeal.—Her friendship for Overberg..... 38

CHAPTER V.
PRINCE DEMETRIUS AND WHAT TO DO WITH HIM.
(1787—1792.)

His views on religion.—Enters the Catholic Church.—Plans of travel.—Influence of the French Revolution.—Appointed aide to the Austrian General von Lillien.—Death of Leopold II. — Fuerstenberg's opinion of a trip to America.—Mr. Brosius.—Mr. Schmet. — Sails from Rotterdam for the United States.... 54

CHAPTER VI.
PRINCE DEMETRIUS ARRIVES IN MARYLAND, DECIDES HIS OWN FUTURE, AND ENTERS THE SEMINARY OF SAINT SUPLICE.
(1792.)

First Catholic colony in the United States.—Appointment of Bishop Carroll.—Arrival of Mr. Nagot and the French Sulpicians.—Mr. Brosius and Mitri in Baltimore.—Mitri's choice.............. 67

CHAPTER VII.
WHAT THE WORLD SAID.
(1792—1795.)

Opinion of Rev. Fr. Schnoesenberg.—Vexation of the princess.—Confidence of Mr. Nagot and the bishop in Mitri's vocation.—Views and letters of Rev. Dr. Overberg, Baron von Fuerstenberg, General von Schmettau, and Prince Gallitzin.—Their effect upon Demetrius....................................... 76

CHAPTER VIII.
ORDINATIONS AND FIRST MISSIONS.
(1795—1799.)

Characteristics of his seminary life.—Receives minor orders.—Joins the Society of Saint Sulpice.—Is ordained by Bishop Carroll.—Mission at Port Tobacco.—Stationed at Baltimore.—At Conewago.—Visits the Alleghany mountains.—Spirit manifestations.—Visits Cliptown, Va. — Difficulties with his congregations.—Accepts the call to McGuire's Settlement.................... 92

CHAPTER IX.
SETTLES ON THE MOUNTAINS.
(1799.)

Catholic Missions in Pennsylvania.—Philadelphia.—Conewago.—Goshenhoppen. — Lancaster.—O'Neill's Victory.—Sportsman's Hall.—McGuire's Settlement.—Reception of missionaries by the early settlers.—Poverty of the missions.—Pastoral residence at McGuire's Settlement.—Midnight Mass in the new church.. 112

CHAPTER X.
DISAPPOINTMENTS AND ENCOURAGEMENTS.
(1800—1802.)

Early trials.—Lack of sympathy in his projects.—His austerities.—Growth of the Settlement.—Lancaster.—Rev. Louis de Barth—Concerning the Russian property. — Prince Gallitzin becomes an American citizen.—Conversion of Count von Stollberg..... 125

CHAPTER XI.
DEATH OF PRINCE DMITRI GALLITZIN, AND CONSEQUENT PROJECTS.
(1803—1804.)

Plans for a return to Europe.—Bishop Carroll's advice.—Last years of the prince.—The Russian property.—The princess' affection.. 142

CHAPTER XII.
RESPONSIBILITIES AND CARES.
(1804—1805.)

Clerical influence.—Duties of a missionary.—Some small troubles.—Loretto.—Beulah.—Ebensburg.—Formation of Cambria County.—Sunday in Loretto.—Father Gallitzin's Regulations.—Father Gallitzin as a preacher.—As a confessor.—His isolation.—Rev. Mr. Fitzsimmons... 160

CONTENTS.

CHAPTER XIII.
THE FIRST PERSECUTION.
(1804.)

PAGE

The false brother—Confusion of Gallitzin and Smith.—His mistakes, faults, and peculiarities of temper.—A boy's quarrel.—An injured friend.—Gallitzin as a physician.—Adopts a family of orphans.—Hopes of a religious order of teachers.—Consequent opposition and calumniation.................................. 179

CHAPTER XIV.
THE SECOND PERSECUTION.
(1804—1806.)

Peculiar trials.—Hatred of evil.—The restraints of Loretto.-Munster.—Appeals to the bishop.—Continued opposition.—His life in danger.—Charges of interference in private affairs.—Rebellion in the church.. 196

CHAPTER XV.
DEATH OF THE PRINCESS.
(1806.)

How the news was received.—Consolations.—The princess' last illness and death.—Some traits of her character.—Effect of his sorrow upon Father Gallitzin................................. 212

CHAPTER XVI.
THE FINAL PERSECUTION.
(1806—1807.)

Renewal of trouble.—Mr. Phelan again.—The Westmoreland conspiracy.—Jacob.—E. V. J.'s retraction.—The committee visit Bishop Carroll.—John Weakland's argument.—Broken down.—End of the slander.................................... 230

CHAPTER XVII.
FINANCIAL AND DOMESTIC MATTERS.
(1807—1808)

Settlement of the Russian law-suit.—Computation of the estates.—His sister's regard and solicitude.—Building in Loretto.—Effect of Gallitzin's persecutions upon the Protestants of the neighborhood.—His severe rule of life.—Appointment of new bishops.. 255

CONTENTS.

CHAPTER XVIII.
FINANCIAL EMBARRASSMENTS.
(1808—1809.)

Poverty of the Church.—Gallitzin's appeals fruitless.—Continual disappointments and losses.—Visits Philadelphia.—Bitter trials. — A last offering. — "Entertaining angels unawares." — His buildings and farms. — Views on temperance.—An act of the Pennsylvania Legislature 275

CHAPTER XIX.
STILL AGAINST WIND AND TIDE.
(1810—1814.)

Princess Mimi's explanations.—Troubles in Europe. — Pius VII. at Fontainebleau.—On the way to Italy.—His reception at Rome.—Rejoicing throughout the Christian world.—Loss by the invasion of Russia and Prussia.—A famous speculation.—F.'Gallitzin's care of the altar.—His love of books...................... 292

CHAPTER XX.
DEFENDER OF THE FAITH.
(1814—1825.)

The war of 1812—Captain Richard McGuire.—The Loretto recruits. —A national fast.—A war sermon.—DEFENCE OF CATHOLIC PRINCIPLES.—Mr. Hayden Smith.—Mr. Douglas.—The minister's vindication.—LETTER ON THE HOLY SCRIPTURES.—Personal influence.—A spirited woman.—Mixed marriages.—A public announcement 307

CHAPTER XXI.
AT HOME AND ABROAD.
(1815—1823)

Death of Archbishop Carroll.—Of Mr. Nagot.—Whithdrawal from the Society of Saint Sulpice.—Bishop Egan.—Philadelphia difficulties.—Bishop Conwell.—Father Gallitzin's plan for a diocese in Western Pennsylvania. — Bishoprics refused by him.—Death of Rev. Mr. Heilbron, — Appointment of Rev. F. X. O'Brien.—Irish laborers.—Rev. C. B. Maguire.—Rev. T. McGirr.—European Affairs and marriage of the princess........ 328

CONTENTS.

CHAPTER XXII.
FINAL SETTLEMENT OF THE EUROPEAN PROPERTY.
(1817—1828.)

PAGE

The Prince of Orange.—King of the Netherlands.—His affection for Gallitzin.—Dr. Overberg comes to the rescue.—The collection of antique stones. — Count de Merveldt's intervention. — Death of Princess Mimi. — Her will. — Death of Overberg.—Father Gallitzin's position.—His statement of business matters.—Visits Blairsville and the Irish laborers on the canal. The Russian minister.. 348

CHAPTER XXIII.
AS VICAR GENERAL.
(1827—1830.)

F. Gallitzin and Bishop Conwell.—F. Gallitzin as a mediator.—Extent of his jurisdiction.—Rev. Mr. Heyden.—Rev. Mr. O'Rielly. —Mr. McGirr and Mr. Maguire.—F. Gallitzin uses his authority. —Mr. McGirr's idiosyncracies. — F. Gallitzin's patience...... 360

CHAPTER XXIV.
UNDER BISHOP KENRICK.
(1830—1831.)

Rev. Mr. Mathews resigns.—Rev. Mr. Kenrick appointed coadjutor. —F. Gallitzin's anxieties in regard to Rev. Mr. McGirr.—His counsels to Bishop Kenrick.—Pleads for his reverend brethren. —Confirmation at Loretto.—The missing mitre.—Mr. Heyden's disappointments.. 376

CHAPTER XXV.
SETTLEMENT OF NEW PRIESTS.
(1830—1834.)

Changes.—Rev. James A. Stillinger.—Rev. James Bradley.—A singular call. — Ebensburg. — Rev. P. H. Lemcke. — His first impressions of Dr. Gallitzin. -- The chapel at Loretto. — Carrolltown.—St. Augustine.—Summit.—Gallitzin................. 390

CHAPTER XXVI.
DR. GALLITZIN AND THE PRESBYTERIAN PARSONS.
(1834.)

Tranquility of the present.—Peace in Loretto.—The outside battle. —The Presbyterian Synod.—Dr. Gallitzin's reply............ 406

CONTENTS.

CHAPTER XXVII.
AT EVENING TIME.
(1834—1840.)

PAGE

In 1834.—First signs of failing strength.—The winter of 1839-40.—Lenten duties.—Easter Sunday.—His last sermon.—Mr. Bradley, Mr. Lemcke, and Mr. Heyden called to Loretto.—Wednesday, May 6th, 1840.................................... 431

CONCLUSION.

ERRATA.

PAGE III. For Rev. Charles Lee read Rev. Thomas S. Lee.

PAGES 160—65. For Belah and Berelah read Beulah.

PAGE 361. The last line should read: Spirit to which he trusted all his decisions.

PAGE 411. First line *the* is misplaced, read: Leave the pure light of the Gospel.

PAGE 411. Second line for onr read our.

other great and holy men, he was beyond his age, misrepresented and misunderstood; the best strove to compass his designs, bad men reviled and opposed him, common-place people ridiculed and persecuted him, the "timid good" deprecated his rashness, bewailed his want of prudence, and in their own way, and with the best of intentions, did their utmost to paralyze him, but the God of armies was his protector,

PREFACE.

In the following pages will be found the account of a young prince, wealthy, brilliantly educated, of splendid appearance, fascinating address, and full of genius, who, from the purest and highest motives, became a Catholic priest, devoting his life, and all it contained, to the salvation of souls.

Disgusted with the irreligion, the immorality, the laxity of discipline, and the universal rising against lawful authority of his time, in Europe, he conceived the idea of founding a purely Catholic community in the unbroken forests of the New World, wherein the true religion and correct discipline should be taught and wrought into action untrammelled and unimpaired; he chose the highest point of the Alleghany Mountains, in Pennsylvania, for his project, founded the village of Loretto, and spent forty-two years of incessant labor in evangelizing Western and Central Pennsylvania, converting its wild forests into a smiling garden. He formed his character, or it formed itself, according to the commands of the Church, the precepts of the Gospel, the counsels of the saints, and measured all his undertakings and all his motives by the highest standard of Christian perfection, so that like other great and holy men, he was beyond his age, misrepresented and misunderstood; the best strove to compass his designs, bad men reviled and opposed him, common-place people ridiculed and persecuted him, the "timid good" deprecated his rashness, bewailed his want of prudence, and in their own way, and with the best of intentions, did their utmost to paralyze him, but the God of armies was his protector, and he passed on in spite of all the world or the devil, open foes or doubting friends could do, to a most successful and blessed end.

The history of his exterior life has been often outlined and faintly sketched, but always with errors, inaccuracies, and misrepresentations, invariably failing to support by the incidents related the universal opinion of his saintly character, his heroic life, and the charming, cheerful, delightful traditions of his fiery, but admirable disposition. In the present volume the aim has been to be accurate and exact, to present not certain special phases of his character, but to show it, as far as possible, in its completeness, for it was one of marked originality, of rare consistency, and of unusual gracefulness, growing lovelier and richer and more harmonious the more its details are brought to light, showing him, if possible, even greater in what he was than in what he did.

The greatest difficulty has been experienced in obtaining these details. The obstacles with which every biographer has to contend even under the most favorable circumstances, have been multiplied in this case. The most valuable papers have been mutilated, destroyed, or placed beyond reach; those who remember him are, for the most part, very old people, born and bred in the mountains, who were still young when he was long past his prime, and who had never in all their lives the habit of close observation; uncontested facts have been improperly interpreted and perverted by incompetent or careless commentators, until it has become almost impossible to place them in their true light with their original significance. A nobleman surrounded by the ignorant and the lowly, the heir to princely wealth living in actual want, a pastor the servant of his people, a man who realized what it meant to be fashioned in the image and likeness of God, a priest who knew what it was to enter into an *eternal covenant* with the Most High, a holy missionary whose life was hidden in Christ with God, not every eye could penetrate the veil of his humility, not every hand unfold the mantle of simplicity in which true greatness is ever clothed, and those who stood the closest to him, sometimes knew him the least. "When a servant of God passes, God passes with him," and in the near light of the heavenly radiance which surrounded him, men knew not to analyse and question by what means it was brought.

Every doubtful circumstance or unauthorized statement has been carefully excluded from the present account, and no pains nor study spared to obtain reliable information and a true insight into his noble life and lovely character; and though there was certainly a deeper life, known only to God, which underlay and moulded all, not here displayed, since it would be sacrilege to unveil it, it is to be hoped it will be suggested to the good heart and honest mind of every God-fearing reader, and that the result of that continual sacred communion with God,—a result which plainly manifested itself in the life here related, however imperfectly told,—may bring with it for all an influence and an inspiration like that silent and unexplained spirit which, in days gone by, turned so many souls to God, and uplifted to the heavenly gates so many weary hearts fainting by the way.

The warmest and most respectful thanks for prompt and generous assistance in the preparation of this work, are due to Right Rev. M. Domenec, D. D., Bishop of Pittsburg, Right Rev. Boniface Wimmer, O. S. B., Abbot of St. Vincent's, Very Rev. James A. Stillinger of Blairsville, (Pa.) who to the use of reliable papers, have added most welcome encouragement and kindly interest. Also, to Rev. Charles Lee, Secretary of the Archbishop of Baltimore, for letters belonging to the archepiscopal archives, Very Rev. Mr. Dubreuil of Baltimore, for recollections of Dr. Gallitzin's seminary life, to Rev. James Bradley of Newry, (Pa.) for accounts of early days in Pennsylvania, and especially to Rev. Gerard M. Pilz, O. S. B., for the first introduction to the subject, continual encouragement and advice, for the greater part of the translations from the German used in this work, and, finally, for the frontispiece which sheds light upon all that is to come. The other translations from the German are due to the kindness of Rev. Mr. Lachermaier and Rev. Mr. May, who from veneration for the saintly subject of this memoir, willingly employed their few leisure hours in helping on the account of his life. Sincere thanks are rendered as well to John G. Shea, Esq., and to the Hon. Simon Cameron, for assistance in procuring materials; as to the very many dear and venerated friends who have so kindly followed this work through its course of preparation, with the fervent prayer, that in learning somewhat of the saintly Gallitzin, they may be amply repaid for their unfailing encouragement.

THE AUTHOR

Elizabeth, New Jersey, May 6, 1872.

INDRODUCTION.

My daughter, very unnecessarily, has asked me to write a few words by way of introduction to the work she now offers the public on the Life and Character of the late Reverend, the Prince Demetrius Augustine Gallitzin, the Russian missionary in America, and founder of the interesting colony of Loretto in Western Pennsylvania. Of the merits or demerits of her work it does not become me to speak, but I may be permitted to say that she has labored conscientiously at her task, and has spared neither time nor pains in collecting and arranging the facts of the life and labors of the illustrious missionary and humble priest, as far as they are now recoverable, or in ascertaining and appreciating his character alike as a man and as a missionary.

There are few personages connected with the history of the Church in this country more interesting, or more worthy to be remembered, than the subject of this memoir, or whose faith and devotion, whose charity and untiring labors in the cause of Christ and the souls of men, are better fitted to inspire us with gratitude to Almighty God who gave him to us, or to confirm our trust in the power of divine grace to overcome every obstacle the world here or elsewhere may interpose to prevent its victory. Few when Prince Demetrius was born could have foreseen that he would ever become a Catholic, far less a Catholic priest, far less still that he would live and die a devoted Catholic missionary in the wilds of the Alleghanies in Pennsylvania. He was born of parents who had practically lost their faith, or scorned to profess it, like so many of the princes and nobles of the latter part of the eighteenth century, and was brought up in early childhood and youth in profound ignorance of religion, and the chances were that he would grow up like his father a Voltairian, an unbeliever, if not a scoffer. That the son of such a father, and of a mother in whom faith was dead, born to high rank and great wealth, and educated in the *enlightened*, or as now said, the "advanced" ideas of the age, which regarded the Church as dead and only waiting its obsequies, should become a Catholic, a zealous priest, and laborious missionary could be no less than a miracle of grace, a striking proof that miracles have not ceased, and that God has not abandoned the world, or ceased to care for the Church, which he has purchased with his own blood.

The circumstances of his conversion, and the providential influences that led to it, will be found detailed in the memoir itself; but a point of no little interest is the fact that his conversion was that of a Russian of high rank, and belonging to a family highly and honorably distinguished in the annals of the Russian Empire. His personal connection with Russia was indeed very slight, yet he was born a Russian subject, and whatever is related in any degree to Russia, between which and our own country there has always been, and it is to be hoped there always will be good understanding, cemented by the interchange of mutual good offices, is of itself of deep interest to us Americans. Russia is really the youngest and freshest of the nations of the Old World, and while she is sometimes their dread, she, perhaps, should be looked upon as their hope. The so-called Latin races at this moment seem to have become effete, and the Germanic races, for the moment apparently possessing the hegemony of Europe, have to a fearful extent lost their faith, and become almost as unbelieving and as misbelieving as when they overran and supplanted the Roman Empire, or as they were before St. Boniface carried them the Gospel and civilization with it.

Unless the German people, especially their princes and nobles return to the communion of the Holy See, and resume the work of Karl the Great and his Austrasian Franks and

Allemani, the newly reconstructed German Empire will fall as rapidly as it has risen; for it has no support in religion or in the traditions of the German people. According to all human foresight the hegemony of the Old World is destined to pass from the Teutonic to the Sclavic race, from Germany to Russia. Russia has not lost her religiosity, and there are no people in the Old World among whom there is found so much religious sentiment as the Russian, or that are so capable of being moved by religious or Christian motives. The late Emperor Nicholas may have had his faults, but let people say what they will of his cruelty, tyranny, and despotism, he was the wisest, the ablest, and the most beneficent secular sovereign in Europe in his day, and the world lost in him one of its greatest and noblest men. His son is not equal to him, and I fear is too much influenced by the desire of the applause of the West, and to be regarded as a liberal and enlightened prince, as was the case with Katharine II.

The Russian Church, too, is the best of all the churches not in communion with the See of Rome. The Sclavonians and even the Russian branch of the Sclavonian family, were converted from idolatry to Christianity by missionaries from Constantinople indeed, but before the schism between the East and the West, and the Russian Church was an integral part of the one holy Catholic and Apostolic Church during many centuries. The Metropolitan of Muscovy assisted at the Council of Florence in 1439, and gave in his adhesion with the other Oriental prelates, to the reunion of the East and West effected in that Council, convoked and its acts approved by Pope Eugenius IV. The long dominion exercised over the Russias by the Tartars under Gengiskhan and his successors, had a disastrous effect on Russia in general and on the Russian Church in particular, and for a long time after that dominion was thrown off, the schools remained in sad condition, and the great body of the clergy in extreme ignorance, and it was not till the seventeenth century that any important efforts were made to provide for their instruction, and then chiefly by professors from the West, and mainly through a prince of the Gallitzin family.

But the Revolution of Peter, called the Great, against the Empress Sophia, chiefly through the bigotry of the Protestantizing Archbishop of Moscow, and the effort of Peter, after his successful usurpation of the throne, to introduce the material civilization of the West, and to subject the Church to the crown as in all Protestant nations, interrupted the schools and the education of the clergy, and prevented the Russian Church from resuming her original and normal relations with the Roman See. Alexander I. did something after the defeat of Napoleon, to root out Protestantism from the national church, and would have done more, if he had not been in the last years of his reign too much influenced by the mysticism of that extraordinary woman, Madame Krudener. Still more was done to purify the Russian Church from heresy, which had crept in under Peter I. and was more or less tolerated in the national clergy down to the accession of Alexander I., by the late Emperor Nicholas. Since then the Russian Church has been steadily recovering its orthodoxy, and almost in spite of the Holy Synod by which it is governed.

When I speak of heresies that crept into the Russian Church, I must not be understood to mean that these heresies, borrowed from Protestantism, ever found admission into the official teaching of the Russian Church. They were entertained not by the Church, but by individual churchmen. As a church the Russian Church claims to be and always to have been orthodox, and since the reunion of the East and the West in the Council of Florence already referred to, I am aware of no official act of the supreme Ecclesiastical authority pronouncing it, as a church, either heretical or schismatical, consequently the sin of heresy or schism does not, unless I am in error, attach to the communion, but solely to the individuals who personally and voluntarily make themselves heretics or schismatics. In this respect there is a marked difference between the Russian Church, and the several Protestant Churches so-called, and which are simply establishments and no Churches at all. In the case of these the sect or establishment is under anathema; with the Russian Church, the communion, as far as I am aware, is not under anathema, but only the individuals in that communion, as elsewhere, who make themselves guilty of heresy and schism, by refusing due obedience to the supreme authority of the Catholic Church.

The points of difference between the Russians and ourselves are the supremacy of the Pope and the Procession of the Holy Ghost. As to the first point, I know not what change in their attitude the recent definition of the Council of the Vatican may have effected, but previously their attitude was less that of denial of the papal supremacy than that of wilful refusal to submit to it. They admit the authority of the Greek Fathers from the first, prior to Photius, as fully as we do, and the supremacy of the Pope by divine authority is plainly taught in them, and was so admitted by their prelates at the Council of Florence, which asserts the supremacy of the Pope in language as clear, as positive as it is possible to use, both in teaching and governing the universal Church, and by undeniable implication his infallibility, otherwise he might by divine authority lead the whole Church into error, which cannot be admitted, for God can neither teach error nor authorize any one to teach it. To me the Orientals have seemed always to persist in the act of disobedience rather than in the denial of the authority itself or their obligation to obey it.

With regard to the second point, on which there have been so many and such violent disputes, the Russian Church and the Western really agree, and there is only a purely verbal difference between them. The Russians accuse the Latins of having added the words *Filioque*, "and from the son," to the Creed, and inserted with it by so doing a heresy. The Latins accuse the Greeks of teaching that the Holy Ghost proceeds from the Father alone, which is a heresy, yet it was found at Florence when each party explained its meaning, that neither was right in its accusation against the other. The Latins thought the Greeks excluded the Son from all share in the procession; and the Greeks thought the Latins by their *Filioque* made the Holy Ghost proceed from two principles instead of one; but the fact is the Greek holds that the Holy Ghost proceeds from the Father as principle through the Son as medium, which is strictly orthodox, and the Latin holds that though the Holy Ghost proceeds from the Father and the Son, yet not as from two principles, but as from one principle only, which obviates the objection of the Greeks, and is orthodox. So there is really no difference between the two parties.

The Filioque when proposed by the Synod of Frankfort to be inserted in the Creed was objected to by Pope St. Leo III., not because he did not hold the doctrine it was intended to assert, but because the Fathers of Constantinople, probably for good reasons, had omitted the phrase, and because its insertion would give the Greeks a pretext for a schism, as we see subsequently it actually did. The Holy Pope refused to sanction its insertion, and reaped a rich harvest of obloquy and abuse, some individuals going even so far as to accuse him of heresy. The phrase was first inserted, I believe, by Spanish and Gallic prelates who could ill appreciate the Greek mind, and thought the Greeks must be heretics because they did not accept it. It became very extensively inserted in the Creed in Spain and Gaul, and as it expressed what was undoubtedly of faith, the popes were finally obliged to sanction its insertion in order to guard against the heresy which it was alleged its omission favored, but which the Greeks in reality were as far from holding as were the Latins themselves. In point of fact the phrase unless explained, would to a Greek mind imply that the Holy Ghost proceeds from the Father and the Son as from two primordial principles, for the Greek always understands by *principle* what the Latins understand by *primordial* or *first principle*, and never a medial principle. The true doctrine is expressed by St. John Damascene, if my memory serves me, and as both Greek and Latin theologians hold it, namely: "The Holy Spirit proceeds from the Father through the Son," or from the Father as principle and from the Son as medium, or the medium of the procession. This accords with the view that in the Blessed Trinity the Father is principle, the Son is the medium, and the Holy Ghost is the end, the completion, the consummator.

On all other points there is no controversy that I am aware

of, between the East and West on matters that either holds to be of faith. The Russian Church has valid orders, real bishops and priests, who offer really the unbloody sacrifice, who really consecrate the body and blood of our Lord in the sacrament, and can give valid absolution. It has not only sound doctrine which Anglicans might have, but the seven sacraments, and all the constituent elements of a church, though out of its normal relations with the Church Universal, which Anglicans have not, whatever their pretensions, for they have neither orders nor jurisdiction.

The causes which separated, and which keep separate the East and the West ought not to prevent a solid and permanent reunion. The obstacles to be overcome seem to me to grow less and less every day. The original causes of separation such as the rivalry of new Rome with old Rome, the ambition of the bishops or patriarchs of Constantinople, and the intermeddling of the Byzantine Emperors with Catholic dogma and ecclesiastical government, have passed away, and the ignorance of the great body of the Oriental clergy of Christian antiquity, and the real merits of the controversy between the East and West, occasioned by the Tartar invasion and conquest of Russia, and the Ottoman conquest of the Greek Empire, is passing away in Russia, and will pass away with the Christians under Turkish rule, when Russia is permitted to fulfil what seems to be her providential mission in putting an end to the Ottoman Empire, and the Mahometan power, hitherto upheld by the Western powers both Catholic and Protestant, to the scandal of Christendom, in the interests of trade and the so-called balance of power. Yet signal vengeance seems already to have overtaken the powers that waged, or favored it without engaging in it, the unprovoked Crimean war against Russia in support of Turkey, and the subjection of the Christians of the East to a Mahometan despotism. Napoleon is a fugitive, and France lies prostrate under the armed heel of the Prussian conqueror, and convulsed and torn by intestine divisions; Austria has lost her Italian provinces, been driven out of Germany, rent asunder by the Dualism which renders Hungary practically an independent kingdom, while her Sclavonic provinces are ill-at-ease under a Germanic rule, which is no longer German; England is no longer a power in Continental Europe, and she has fallen so low that nobody fears or heeds her threats; only Sardinia has escaped, but her day of reckoning will come when the measure of her iniquity is full.

In the Ottoman Empire, the great obstacles to the reunion are the civil as well as ecclesiastical power exercised by the bishops over their Christian flocks, which they would lose, or find greatly restricted if the reunion were effected, and the opposition of the Porte which prefers to deal with a chief who is its subject and within its power, than with a spiritual chief who is independent of it, and beyond its reach. In Russia there are some old prejudices created in former times by quarrels between the Russians and the Poles, and some fears of the Russian people that if the reunion were effected their beautiful and gorgeous Greek Liturgy, to which they are very much attached, would be abolished, and the briefer and simpler Latin Liturgy be substituted in its place. But these are not insuperable, and the chief obstacles are probably in the Czar, who fears he would lose his control over the Church in his dominions, and the Russian bishops who fear that they would lose their spiritual independence by being subjected to the See of Rome. This fear on the part of the bishops is idle, and even absurd; for they have already lost their spiritual independence, not to the Pope indeed, but to the civil power. Ivan IV. very nearly destroyed the independence of the Russian Church, and subjected it to the imperial power; what he left undone, Peter I. completed, when he supressed the metropolitical power of the Archbishop of Moscow, and organized a Synod with himself at its head, and usually presided over by a member of the Emperor's staff, for its government. The bishops would regain their spiritual independence by the reunion, and find in the Supreme Head of the Universal Church on earth a powerful and steady defender of their ecclesiastical rights and authority. The Russian bishops and prelates have everything to gain and nothing to lose by reunion.

The real interests of the Czar or Emperor, the Autocrat of all the Russias, demand the reunion. His Imperial Majesty holding his crown as his sacred and inviolable inheritance, is necessarily a conservative, and the uncompromising foe of revolutions and revolutionists. And yet the existing order of things in Russia is not free from peril. The Church being his slave can add nothing to his power, and give his government no aid against a revolution. Large numbers of the Episcopacy sigh for independence, and there is the whole party of Old Russians amounting to many millions, who absolutely refuse to be governed by the Holy Synod instituted by Peter I., and demand the restoration of the metropolitical power he suppressed. Dangerous sects are, also, springing up in various parts of the Empire, which neither the national Church, nor the national government is able to suppress, and these will make common cause with attempted revolution against the government.

Russia is open to revolutionary ideas through her Baltic provinces, Courland, Esthonia and Livonia, as also in Finland in which Protestantism is the prevailing religion, and Protestantism is the very consecration of the revolutionary principle. She is open to them on the side of Poland, which has not ceased to regret her lost national independence, and which it will require many generations to Russianize completely. Western ideas, that is, the ideas of the heretical and unbelieving West, find their way in spite of the police, into the Russian universities, and young Russia already aspires to imitate young Germany or young France, and already Russia is covered over with a network of secret revolutionary societies. The only reliance of the government against the revolution when it breaks out, is the army; but the army may be infected with the revolutionary fever, and join the rebels, as we have seen more than once in France and elsewhere. A national Church can afford no assistance to the government; for the national Church will itself be carried away by the national sentiment, and be able to offer it no effective resistance. No: the interest of the Czar is not in having a Church that he controls, but a Church that has an independent existence, holds not from him but from God, that governs men's consciences by the law of God, and whenever he is in the right, can bring the consciences of the people to his support and against his foes.

His real interest then is in reunion with Rome; for the firmest and only real support of civil governments in their rights, as well as the people in their liberties, is the papacy, which is catholic, dependent on no nationality, but present in the precise respect needed in all nations. The papacy has not, indeed, prevented revolutions in Catholic nations, but precisely because the sovereigns of these nations have tried each to make the papacy national, and subject to the national authority, as the Czar must know from the history in modern times of Austria, France, Italy and Spain. The papacy if allowed its freedom and independence, and sincerely coöperated with by the secular authorities, would have saved Europe from its century of bloody and devastating revolutions. The fault was not in the papacy, nor indeed in the people, for the era of modern revolutions was opened by the sovereigns themselves; chiefly by Frederic II. of Prussia, Catharine II. of Russia, and by Joseph II. of Austria. They set the people the example of rebelling against the laws by trampling on the laws of nations, Frederic in his invasion and annexation of Silesia, and all of them in the first and second partition of Poland.

The Czar using his power and influence to reunite the Russian Church with the universal Church, and coöperating with the papacy in the effort to reorganize the now disorganized nations of Europe, would prove himself a benefactor of his race for ages to come, place Russia at the head of the civilized world, and deserve well of the Church of God. Events have removed from his path the political rivalries that might have deterred him from any action of the sort. Were he to do so now the realization of the dream of Pansclavism would be then not a thing to be dreaded, but welcomed as the harbinger of a new and better era under the hegemony of a newer, fresher, and more vigorous race than the worn out Latin races, or the misbelieving and unbelieving Teutonic races. It is because I firmly believe the reunion of the Russian Church with the Universal Church will be effected, and that Russia is destined to make an end of the Ottoman power, and take her turn as the future leader of the civilized world, that I regard with such deep interest everything connected with her.

O. A. BROWNSON.

LIFE OF
Demetrius Augustine Gallitzin,
PRINCE AND PRIEST.

---o---

CHAPTER I.
THE GALLITZIN FAMILY.

Its antiquity.—Origin.—Poland's Prisoner.—Prince Vasilii Gallitzin.—Plans for the Greek Church.—Field Marshall Gallitzin.—The Ice Palace.—Prince Dmitri Gallitzin.—Russian Ambassador to Paris.—Visits Aachen.—His Marriage.—The Wedding Journey.—Appointed Ambassador to Holland.

A hundred years ago, before there were any railroads or steamboats, American Republics or French Revolutions to perplex mankind, a little child with shy, dark eyes, played unconcernedly in his father's palace at the Hague, or sore against his rapidly developing desires, was carried about in state by the grandest of nurses, to be coaxed, petted clasped, kissed and exclaimed over by lovely ladies in gorgeous brocades, with powdered hair, hoops, laces, jewelled fans, and little high-heeled satin shoes; and, as the bravest of men may be discomposed by the feeblest of babies, addressed with trepidation by famous gentlemen in knee breeches, silk and velvet coats and perfect ruffles, whom our imagination represents to us as dancing a perpetual minuet, or forever taking perfumed snuff from gem encrusted boxes.

The child's name was Demetrius Gallitzin, afterwards called Augustine, and he was the only son and heir of one of the oldest and most famous families of the Old World; a Russian family with a pedigree longer than that of the reigning czar, which has always influenced, often controlled, and at times all but filled the throne of Russia, numbering in its ranks men of every talent and all renown. A family so old and so famous that one must go backward into the remotest past to trace its issuing from some forgotten forest or rocky cavern, a thousand years or so ago, whence it presses onward, like an ever-broadening river, through the changing centuries; onward past barren wastes, by prosperous lands, leaping palace walls, encircling imperial thrones, channelling historic battle fields, through gloomy forests, by castled homes, in many lands; a stream, a cataract, a surging river, dividing re-uniting, branching into half a hundred ways, some in light and some in shade, and one, fretted for a moment by the world's barriers flung close across its course, but the next sweeping aside the bars of human pride and sin, hurries onward, swift and strong, until the angels swing wide the gates, and it flows straight and free into the Vineyard of the Lord.

This is ours. First of all, ages ago, there was in Lithuania, one Mikhail Ivanovitch Bulgark, a famous fighter, surnamed *Goliza*, which signifies a leather glove or gauntlet, suggested by a rough mitten, made from the skin of an animal with the hair left on it, with which this redoubtable warrior covered his mighty hand, dealing with it, undoubtedly, many a stinging blow, which fixed his hairy glove in the memory of the men of his time.

In nearer days there appears another Prince Goliza, or Galiza, who serves as a landmark. He lived in the sixteenth century, commanded an army sent by the Grand Duke Basil in 1514 against the Poles, was defeated through the treachery and cowardice of an officer jealous of his power and fame, taken prisoner and held for thirty-eight long years in painful captivity, although the richest ransoms were freely offered for him. When Sigismund II. became king of Poland he, of his own good will, broke the prisoner's chains, saying to the Czar Ivan II., that "As I believe it to be our duty to reward fidelity not only in our own subjects, but also in those foreigners who have shown devotion to their sovereigns, I have set at liberty the general of your father's army."

Upon this welcome news the czar hastened to embrace the venerable prince, to load him with honors and presents, and to invite him to dinner; but so broken that even the imperial favor could not revive him, the once erect and haughty commander asked but to end his days in the seclusion of a monastery, which was granted him.

Another famous hero and statesman, named Vassilii (Basil) Vasiliievitch Gallitzin, (as the name had now come to be known,) was born in 1633, towards the close of the reign of Michael, first czar of the Romanoff lineage, and received an education rare at that time not only in his own country, but elsewhere, including the Greek, Latin, and German languages. He passed his youth at court, entered the army when of suitable age, and made himself so famous in fighting the Turks, the Tartars of the Crimea, and the Cossacks of the Dnieper, that the Emperor Alexis, son and successor of Michael, promoted him to the command of the Cossacks, and afterwards raised him to the great dignity of a Boyar. Alexis was very much annoyed by the pride of the nobles, who refused to obey the command of a military or civil superior whose title could not be proved older than their own; in this emergency the Boyar Gallitzin counselled and carried into execution a remarkable way of securing their allegiance; by command of the emperor the nobles were required to bring forward all the documents proving or relating to their rank and birth, and in this case they obeyed. When all these papers were gathered together, instead of examining them and pronouncing their force as was expected, Alexis and Gallitzin made a bonfire of them, together with the old nobiliar record of the empire.

The Czar Alexis was twice married, and though he had in all twelve children, only two of his sons by his first wife, survived him; of these Fedor died after a very short reign, and should have been succeeded by the other, Ivan, but the powerful family of the second wife set him aside as imbecile, and succeeded in bringing forward her son Peter, who was then but ten years of age, but these were resolutely met by her step-daughter Sophia, who took the reins of power into her own strong hand, and governed firmly in the name of her brother Ivan and her half-brother Peter, with Prince Vasili Gallitzin for her prime minister. His position included the Government of Novgorod, giving him great wealth, power and influence, which he used to embellish Moscow with many splendid buildings, to bring men of learning into the empire, and to induce the nobles to send their children abroad, to receive the education not possible in Russia. When the pope encouraged John Sobieski to resist the Turks, the prince took advantage of Poland's fear of them to obtain a most advantageous treaty of peace with her, and, later, leagued with her and Venice against the infidels, sending ambassadors to the courts of Versailles, Madrid, Amsterdam, Stockholm, and Copenhagen, to invite the sovereigns of these countries to join the league. In all these courts a Russian ambassador was at that time a novelty; the monarchs were all very polite, but not inclined to take part in the proposed crusade; Sophia kept firm to the plan, and the prince received command of the expedition sent by the original signers of the league: Venice, Poland and Russia.

So far from being hostile to Catholics this far sighted statesman counselled the return of the Greek Church, and labored with the greatest earnestness to effect a reunion, which he regarded of vast importance for the interests of his country from a temporal point of view, while his strong religious feelings and his freedom from the blinding mists of narrow national prejudice, enabled him to see the question in clearer spiritual light than perhaps any other nobleman in the empire. But the sudden uprising, in his absence with the expedition against the Turks, which ended in the overthrow of Sophia and the accession of Peter, surnamed the Great, put an end to his hopes. But though unsuccessful, the mere desire appears to have been a good seed for future years to develop into abundant fruit for his noble house. We may owe it to him, "building better than he knew," that the first impulse to Catholicity was imparted to his family, and the Gallitzins in the Vineyard may perhaps regard him as the founder of their line. He died in exile in the district of Mezen.

Two of his cousins were in great favor with the new emperor, one of them, Prince Boris Alexeivitch having been the tutor, and the other Prince Mikhail Mikhailovitch Gallitzin, the playmate of the youthful Peter. Prince Boris was a man of great learning and very pious, so much so that he was surnamed *the Baptist;* he filled the position of governor of Astrachan until, borne down by age and infirmities, he resigned the trust, and ended his days in a monastery. Prince Mikhail renounced his position at court that he might enter the army as a simple soldier, and win his honors at the point of his sword. In 1709, after many heroic deeds, he contributed greatly to the success of the famous battle of Pultowa, if indeed he did not actually win it, and three days afterwards forced the surrender of the remnant of the Swedish army. He was appointed a few years later, governor of Finland, and general in chief. Besides all these military exploits he won great honors as a naval officer, receiving, upon one occasion a present from Czar Peter of a sword and cane richly mounted with diamonds.

The peace of Nystadt (1721) ended his work in Finland, and as Peter was about to depart for the Persian wars he confided St. Petersburg to his governorship. Catharine I. made him field marshall, and Peter II. placed him over the military college at Moscow, where he died in 1730.*

Upon the death of Peter II., in 1730, the crown was offered to Anna Ivanovna, Duchess of Courland, daughter of Peter the Great's half-brother, Ivan, whose promises of a more liberal form of government caused her to be preferred to her aunts, the daughters of Peter the Great. Prince Mikhail's brother was one of the plenipotentaries sent to make the offer, which was accepted; during her reign of ten years she loaded him with honors, but she exiled another Gallitzin, and played a memorable part towards still another.

This took place in the winter of 1740 in the last year of her reign, when to amuse her flagging spirits the infamous Biron got up a palace and a wedding on a novel plan.

---

* *Nouvelle Biographie Universelle,* vol. XIX *Gallitzine; Etudes de Théologie,* vol. I, *Un document inedit.*

It was a most terrible winter even for Russia. Upon the proposition of the chamberlain, Fatischef, her majesty graciously permitted the construction between her palace and the Admirality of a house of ice. Accordingly great blocks of choice ice were hewn out in the form of immense stones, which were placed one upon another, and cemented by throwing warm water, which instantly froze, upon them. This house of many rooms presented a most charming aspect, and was built according to all the rules of architecture: all its decorations, inside and out, were wrought out of ice as pure as the rock crystal. The entrance was defended by six ice cannons, which by being drawn backwards a few steps, were made to throw out two cannon balls, also of ice. Two dauphin guns, by means of an ingenious contrivance, vomited fire. The trees planted around the house with different birds perched on their branches, the windows, a bed draped with curtains, the tables, chairs, vases, glasses, a toilette with its mirror, a multitude of other objects, and even the plates with meats artistically imitated, all were of ice. The logs in the fireplace, the wax lights in the ice candlesticks covered with naphte, shone in the evening as in a luxurious drawing room. Near the house was an elephant (always ice) of life size, upon which a Persian was seated; this elephant in the daytime threw out water from his trunk, and at night lighted naphte; a man concealed inside imitated the animal's cry. There was also a bath chamber attached to the house which, although entirely of ice, was heated to such a point that a bath could be taken. All its constructions remained without injury from the first days of January until March, the winter was so steadily severe.

This new kind of a wonder was built for the wedding of a nobleman, of illustrious birth, forced to become the buffoon of the court in punishment for having, while in foreign lands, embraced the Catholic faith. Past fifty years of age he was, in derision, made a page; widowed husband of a Narichkin, father of a young man who was already an officer of the guards, the empress forced him to remarry, promising to generously defray all the expenses of the wedding. They claimed that he had *chosen* for his bride a Bohemian octogenarian.

While amusing herself with this wedding Anna desired to manifest by it her immense power. She ordered the governor of each of the provinces of the empire to send her two persons from every different race in Russia. On their arrival in St. Petersburg each couple was dressed, at the imperial expense, in the costume of their province. The organization of the festival was entrusted to the grand huntsman, Volinsky (who was hung in the June following, after having had his tongue torn out and his right wrist severed). On the appointed day the guests to the number of more than three hundred, met at his house, presenting themselves with grotesque ceremony before the empress' windows, and parading the streets of the capital in procession. The newly married pair shut up in a cage on the back of an elephant led the march. The guests were arranged by couples in sledges drawn by reindeers, dogs, oxen, and goats; some were perched on camels. A repast was prepared for them in the Duke of Courland's riding school. For each representative of a province the favorite dish of his district was provided. After the banquet there was a grand ball, at which each couple had its own distinctive music, and danced its national dance. Finally, after the ball, the newly married pair were carried to their ice palace, forced to lie on the bed of ice, which had been prepared for them, and that they might not leave it, armed sentinels were placed at the door of the nuptial chamber. *

"This torture," says Prince Augustin Gallitzin, "which still more rends the heart by its burlesque etiquette, is confirmed by eye witnesses, I shall only cite those upon which it is easiest to place the hand.

"'Prince Gallitzin,' says General Manstein †, 'although of one of the first houses of the empire, was forced to become a buffoon. This employment was given him as punishment for having embraced the Catholic religion.' And, having without

---

* *Un Missionaire Russe en Amerique* by Prince Augustin Gallitzin.

† "MEMOIRES HISTORIQUES SUR LA RUSSIE, *par le general comte de Manstein, traduits de l'allemand, Lyons* 1772 *tom. II, p. 72.*"

any emotion related this event at which he had assisted in gala dress, the Lutheran Manstein certifies that the newly married were conducted to the house of ice, stretched upon the cold bed, on which the next day there were, undoubtedly, two dead bodies.

"A pious tradition recounts that Prince Gallitzin, in expiring, made this touching prayer to the God for whom he had sacrificed all: 'O Jesus! vouchsafe to grant me one grace; it is that conversions may never cease in the Gallitzin family!'"

Such were the ancestors in the spiritual and natural order of the little prince at the Dutch capital. His father, Prince Dmitri Alexeievitch Gallitzin, son of Prince Alexis Ivanovitch Gallitzin and his beautiful wife, *née* Princess Gagarin, was born in 1728, commencing his career with the reign of the Empress Elizabeth, who had succeeded, after a short interval, the cruel and despotic Anna. He preferred to emulate the glory of his illustrious ancestors in the paths of science and diplomacy, rather than on the battle field, and early in life occupied positions of great importance at the court, and in foreign negociations, and while yet very young was made minister to Paris, in which office he was retained by Catharine, with whom he was in high favor, both on account of his diplomatic talent and his great literary attainments. It was at his representation that she purchased his friend Diderot's library, when that airy philosopher had succeeded in dissipating money faster than he could make it, and was in great need; she generously made as the condition of her purchase that the late owner should take care of it for her, at an excellent salary, a great part of which she paid in advance.

In 1768 after fourteen years residence in Paris, as Russian ambassador, where he had been the generous friend of Diderot, Voltaire, D'Alembert and others whose names are only remembered now as belonging to the froth and fermentation, the folly and wickedness, which led to the Reign of Terror, the prince was recalled to Russia to receive a new appointment.

On his way to St. Petersburg he rested for a few days at Aachen (Aix-la-Chapelle) where the season had already commenced, and very soon attached himself to the train of Princess Ferdinand (wife of Ferdinand, brother of Frederick the Great), who with several ladies of her court was sojourning at the baths; the pleasure the prince appeared to find there caused him to remain longer than he originally intended, and it soon became evident that he was detained by special regard for a lady of her suite, Countess Amalia von Schmettau, only daughter of the celebrated Prussian Field Marshall von Schmettau, a bright, fresh, vivacious yet thoughtful and high-minded girl of nineteen, whose beautiful dark blue eyes, had aroused many an affection which her unaffected dignity, and freedom from all coquetry, had never permitted to manifest itself. The prince, however, had rare advantages; the splendid suppers he gave, the numerous schemes for amusement which he devised and executed, made him very popular with the pleasure seekers, while his high literary attainments, his great culture, his familiarity with all the new ideas and glittering names of the day, rendered his companionship most delightful to a young girl of noble nature, who felt herself made for something better than the mere routine of fashionable life.

When he made known his wishes to her she found the princess in whose care she was placed, and her own brother, General von Schmettau, entirely in favor of his proposals; the time of his stay was rapidly drawing to a close, as he had to be in St. Petersburg at a fixed date, a special messenger was dispatched in all haste to Berlin to procure her mother's consent, and on Amalia's twentieth birthday, August 28th, 1768, they were married in a chapel at Aix-la-Chapelle, setting out immediately after the wedding for St. Petersburg, accompanied part of the way by Princess Ferdinand, and travelling in the most magnificent manner possible, resting at the principal cities, where they were entertained by the most distinguished residents, until they finally reached St. Petersburg. The young wife was presented to the "Semiramis of the North", the rather unprincipled Catharine II., and won all hearts by her exquisite womanliness, her very finished manners, the fascination of her conversation, and her rare musical acquirements.

After a short sojourn in the capital the prince received his appointment as ambassador to Holland, where they arrived about two years after their marriage, and took up their residence at the beautiful city of the Hague.

CHAPTER II.

(1748—1778.)

THE PRINCESS GALLITZIN, née VON SCHMETTAU*.

Early days. — At the convent at Breslau. — Her persistency, affection and loyalty as a child. — Her home education. — At a fashionable French boarding-school. — At court. — Perplexities. — Desire for knowledge. — An old gentleman's wisdom. — Mental confusion. — Observations during her wedding tour. — Birth of Marianna Gallitzin. — Of Demetrius. — Life at the Hague. — The Star of Holland. — Diderot's visit. — Mimi and Mitri in the nursery. — Hemsterhuys' influence. — Final retirement from society.

Amalia von Schmettau, who after so short a courtship had consented to become the beloved wife of Prince Dmitri Gallitzin, had lost her father when quite young, and when only four or five years old was placed by her mother, formerly Baroness von Rüffert, at a convent school in Breslau, where she remained for several years, learning little, but exhibiting many marked traits of character, which were afterwards lovingly recalled by the good nuns, and in the charming narrative of a maternal aunt, who was very fond of her: "I received word from my dear sister," says this lady†, "that she would send her daughter, my beloved niece, in care of a maid and groom to be placed at a convent for education, and wished me to meet her in Breslau at a stated time.... She was four years old, knew not one word of German, embraced me, and her first words were full of exultation: '*O ma chère tante! j'ai un grand panier!*' (O my dear aunt! I've got a big

---

* *Denkwuerdigkeiten aus dem Leben der Fuerstin von Gallitzin*, von Dr. Katercamp. Muenster, 1828.

† *Tagebuch und Briefwechsel der Fuerstin Adelheid Amalia von Gallitzin*. Stuttgart.

basket!)" After she had been sometime in the convent her mother visited her, and was quite shocked to find her fingers frost bitten, but the nuns assured her it was not their fault, for the child persisted in sitting by the window at dawn and twilight, working at her "sums", instead of keeping warm by the fire as the others did. She was taken to stay a while with her aunt at Breslau, where she made so many friends that when she went away, she said: "This is indeed the earthly paradise." Politics ran high at the convent, as the waves of the war between Frederick the Great and Maria Theresa for Silesia dashed over the playground. "We had better tea and sugar," argued the adherents of the fair Queen of Hungary, "when the Austrians were in town. Long life to Maria Theresa!"

"My father was a Prussian field marshall," cried Amalia, "and I must be a Prussian too. Long life to my king!"

When she was nine or ten years old, Amalia was taken home to Berlin, and placed under private teachers. She had a natural talent for music which the nuns had carefully cultivated, and in her other studies she was thought to have made some progress. It was intended she should be brought up a Catholic, that being her mother's religion, while her two brothers, according to their parents' marriage contract, were to be as their father, Protestants, but Amalia's religion at this time appears to have been developed only in one phase: she had an excessive fear of the devil; she was so much afraid of him and of hell, that it made her almost morbid and very gloomy, at times. She had been to confession, but it is not likely she had had any preparation for her first communion, as she was so very young when she left school, and in her mother's house, which was perhaps the gayest and most hospitable in all Berlin, her religious instruction probably never gave any one a moment's thought. She was, however, a very good little girl, and very watchful over herself, anxious to do nothing she knew to be wrong, and very desirous of acting bravely and truthfully in everything. When about fourteen or fifteen years of age the honest, natural German manner was thought to need French polish and gilding; the rage for everything French being than at its height in all European society, an infidel Frenchman, Mr. Premoval, found no difficulty in establishing himself in Berlin for the finishing of the daughters of the nobility, Amalia was sent to his school, and after two years returned home with charming manners, various accomplishments, and in spite of Mr. Premoval, a true heart and a clear head. She was duly introduced into society, was greatly admired, and so esteemed by the Princess Ferdinand that she invited her to become one of her maids of honor.

At that time it was the fashion, brought over with upholstery and costly apparel from France, to discuss everything, the more sacred the better, and all manner of new ideas buzzed about Amalia's ears; she was told how the world had waked up, was coming out of its barbarous state, was throwing aside its superstitions, learning how to eat, drink, dress, be merry and, above all, to reason. It was clear, nobody any longer believed in anything; Christianity especially was out of date, and its absurd restraints altogether unfashionable. The speculations, the philosophy so called, the brilliant flights of rhetoric in which humanity and liberty rode on golden and purple clouds, confused the young girl; she listened, she tried to understand what all the rest seem to know thoroughly, she felt awkward and constrained when she discovered that, in spite of all her hard thinking, she could not in the least comprehend what every body was talking about. This mortified her and distressed her so much that, believing it to be on account of her defective education, she threw herself heart and soul into study and reading; but having no one to guide her or advise her what to read, and nothing in herself by which to fix a standard, she made but little progress; she found in whatever she read something understood by the writers of which she knew nothing. Once she ventured to ask a venerable gentleman of her acquaintance for advice, begging him to send her something suitable; he complied at once, most gallantly, by giving her a quantity of novels, French novels at that, which she took in good faith and devoured with eagerness. They, too, were beyond her intellect, but they aroused her emotional nature, until she herself became wise enough to cast them aside. In this way a thirst for knowledge took possession of her mind, and a morbid craving for she knew not what, her whole nature; she became restless, sometimes wildly, brilliantly gay, at others depressed to the verge of despair, her whole soul in a ferment. Fortunately, one should rather say, by special Providence, her heart remained untouched, and her intellect kept pace if it did not outstrip her sensibilities, but at any moment it might give up the contest and she would be at the mercy of the other. Prince Gallitzin attracted her mind from the first; when she became engaged to him the brightest vision that allured her was that he would become her teacher, fill up for her the gaps in her education, advise her in her studies, and clear up all obscure passages and unintelligible allusions in her reading. But the prince was very well satisfied with his wife as she was, and being thoroughly informed of the thousand events, theories, and so on, of which she knew little if anything, he could not, in the full maturity of his intellect, at all understand the restless desires of the young, unformed mind that looked to him so wistfully; he knew that by observation, social converse, and in various inperceptible ways all that she wished would come to her in time, and made little account of the feverish impatience of youth. At the same time, her evident admiration of his superior intellect and knowledge of the world, by no means lessened his affection for his girlish wife, whom he introduced to his friends, wherever they visited, with a proud satisfaction in her beauty, her fascinating manners, her lively intelligence and her womanly self respect. When her hopes of a teacher in her husband became somewhat clouded by finding herself always in the midst of society, she listened, considered, and judged for herself, not always, as formerly, accepting everything she heard for unquestionable truth. Soon she became fairly roused, was at last on the alert, quick, observant, sympathetic, full of nice perception and keen discrimination, so susceptible, in the best sense, to affection and admiration, which are to woman as the June sunshine to the roses, that it was a real pleasure for those who met her to unfold their thoughts to her. Her unselfish nature called upon her in return to make every effort, whatever might be her mood, to please and entertain all with whom she was thrown; but this cost her many heartaches and after-exhaustion, even in the beginning, for she could not fail to see that the conversation and society which had at first dazzled, awed, and delighted her, really led to very lame results, that though the great men all talked the grandest philosophy, the noblest sentiments, their brilliant ideas revolved in a very small circle, always returning to the place whence they started; and though in society every one gave utterance only to the most wonderful and original ideas, it really seemed to her that even in Paris there was hardly one man who could truly he called great, scarcely learned. In the midst of all she felt as one who fears to scrutinize the play too closely, lest the stage efiects should reveal themselves too glaringly, and once in a while she asked herself if there was no rest on earth save in stagnation and passive indifference.

At Berlin the travellers rested upon their return from St. Petersburg, and while there the Princess Marianna was born, Dec. 7th 1769. After remaining some time at the Prussian capital, they journeyed to the Hague, where the Prince Demetrius, subject of this memoir, was born, Dec. 22. 1770.

Whatever hopes of intellectual improvement, and companionship the princess may have still cherished for the time when she and her husband would be settled in their own home, no sign of them appeared when she became acquainted with the life considered necessary in the prince's position. Every one will recollect the ever encreasing splendors of the eighteenth century, the wild years of luxury, extravagance, unbelief and depravity, gilded and glittering, of the upper classes, which are supposed to have prepared the way for the French revolution, shaking the whole wide world, and crumbling the labors of centuries into rubbish and dust. With the magnificent Catharine, the "Northern Cleopatra", petting Diderot; Frederick the Great resting on his laurels, and proud of his intimacy with Voltaire; Marie Antoinette just coming to the throne of France; Maria Theresa giving place to Joseph II., worst friend of religion and the pope, and the rich Holland merchants intent upon still further gain, and only one old man among all the sovereigns of Europe to raise his voice for virtue and truth, and the fear of the Lord, it was clearly every one's duty to eat, drink, and be merry while the day lasted. Prince Gallitzin, thoroughly in harmony with the age in which he lived, made his residence at the Hague the centre of all that there was of wise, witty, and illustrious in the city, receiving his friends from other lands with true princely hospitality, and when the Empress Catharine visited the Hague, the part of the Russian ambassador in her reception was magnificently performed. She, on her side, hastened to show her regard for the prince by having his little son, then about two years old, brought to her, even placed in the imperial arms; as he was a most lovable little one, slight and delicately formed, with bright, bird like eyes, she even caressed him tenderly, while commissioning him, then and there, officer of the guard. Little Mitri did not much appreciate the honor which filled his father's heart with so much satisfaction, but, released from the imperial embrace, shook out his curls, as a bird its ruffled plumage, and gladly trotted to the nearest place of safety, probably behind his nurse's gown, without ceremony.

This mark of imperial favor, which was intended to shape the future of the child upon whom it was bestowed, by no means calmed the unrest which troubled all the princess' days. It but entangled her the more in the life already becoming most distasteful to her. Balls, parties, *réunions* of all kinds, followed each other in rapid succession; magnificent dresses and lustrous jewels made the nights brilliant, while the days were crowded with the conventional round of receptions, visits, state dinners and the innumerable claims of social life. Once a week, or so, she would steal a moment to visit her children, and they would wake to see her bending over them like a fairy queen out of the story books, her slender figure arrayed in rustling brocade and exquisite lace; her luxuriant hair, the admiration of all beholders, curled and rolled, powdered and puffed, and wreathed with pearls, her dark-blue eyes but glowing the brighter for contrast with the gems she wore. She endeavored to stifle the voice within her crying for a nobler life, by submitting to the inevitable, even to make the best of it, and by her extraordinary gaiety of disposition, her bouyant and joyous nature, she was led to please all, and seek to become a leader, a queen in society, in which she succeeded so admirably that she was called the Star of Holland.

But the position she so easily commanded, and with no apparent effort fully sustained, only brought her weariness and disgust; false friendships, selfish advantage taken of her generous nature, base ingratitude, petty intrigues, and contemptible arts to which she could not close her eyes, and which gave her many a cruel sting, assured her there was nothing the world could give worth having; she had tried to believe there was something higher and better in it than she had found at first, but when she came to know it well, had seen all it had to offer, her heart sank, and she was almost in despair. She had no one to whom she could confide a single wish. "I seldom went to sleep," she said afterwards, "without tears. I was like those actors on the stage who amuse others while their own hearts are breaking." For whatever her grief and depression, she never felt free to let a shadow pass over her face in presence of others.

At the time when her disgust had become so great as to be almost beyond concealment, her husband's friend, Diderot, who had accepted Catharine's invitation to Russia, and was on his way to her court, stopped for a few months at the prince's house in Holland where with the sharp eyes of a shrewd man of the world, he saw that the princess however truly a queen in her circle, was altogether different from those who among the *"philosophes"* aspired to the title, her woman's mind holding nothing in common with the "vehement female intellect" of the time, which, "with metaphysics and flirtation, system of nature, fashion of dress caps, vanity, curiosity, jealousy, atheism, rheumatism, *traités, boutines*, noble sentiments and rouge pots,",was "sailing on a chaos where a wiser might have wavered, if not foundered*." Whether she took his *sentimens nobles* for honest truth, for he had indeed a "gilded tongue", or was no longer able to hide her trouble, she confided to him, of all people in the world, the longing for a better life, the thirst for knowledge, the ardent desire for a simple, natural way of living which consumed her. He did not doubt her sincerity; no hoary headed father confessor could have more quickly pronounced the absence of the world's stamp on that restless and impatient nature, than did this "vehement, volatile", infidel Frenchman. He entered entirely into her views, sympathized with her wholly, fully recognizing her mental and moral unfitness for her present mode of life, urged her to throw it aside, obey the desires of her heart, — Diderot and his clique always counsel obedience to the desires of the heart, whatever they may be, — and devote herself to study and the care of her children. He even undertook to break the subject, which she dared not hint, to the prince, who saw in his wife only a loving, brilliant, light hearted woman, scarcely more than a vivacious girl. Diderot was quite at home on all subjects, never more so, perhaps, than when descanting upon the following of one's own inclinations, liberty to perfect (or degrade) one's self as one's humor might be; the princess, he said, showed a remarkable intellect, a great love for knowledge, and a willingness to acquire it; with her natural inclination for a quiet and studious life, she would undoubtedly make great progress, and in consideration of the brilliant but responsible future of the young prince, what could be more fortunate than that he should be trained under the eye of a thoroughly cultivated mother? On this text a Frenchman is irresistible; the prince so far from being displeased at the suggestion, put with due tact more as his wish than hers, saw in it much that was desirable. It was decided that he would permit her withdrawal from society, and to occupy a certain portion of the house free from all visitors, and to have what teachers she pleased. She received the news with joy, immediately

---

* *Carlyle's Miscellanies*, Vol. III, p. 303.

clouded by the fear that she was too old, she was in her twenty fifth year, to accomplish anything, for in all her life she had never learned anything systematically; she seemed to herself to have only scraps, odds and ends of knowledge, acquired she knew not how, belonging she knew not where, but her husband encouraged her by his confidence, encouraged in his turn by Diderot's praise of her talents, and nerved and inspired by the thought of her children and their need of her, she lost not a day in starting upon her new life. She immediately put aside all her beautiful dresses, and wore a plain and simple one which took but little time in its adjustment, and first of all prepared to have the children under her own eyes. Good natured Mimi (Marianna) and wilful Mitri (Demetrius) had so far in life had things pretty much their own way, having their own carriage and servants, over whom they tyrannized with the largest Russian despotism, but all at once, as so often happens in Russian history, they woke up one morning under a new sovereign, the servants and the carriage and innumerable playthings were confiscated, and the little autocrats exiled to a land of sudden lessons, self discipline, cold baths, and general good behavior.

The princess had often envied the peasant women whose brown and hardy children tumbled about their doorstep, and when once she began to make her children's closer acquaintance, she wondered at herself that she had endured the life, now happily ended, for so long. She had not commenced a day too soon; Mitri had already fine beginnings of temper, and, little despot that he was, like all other tyrants, was sorely afraid of a mightier than himself; though but four years old he was master of all the nursery arts, screams, disobedience, and persistence, as means of obtaining instant fulfillment of his desires. Mimi who had lived a little longer in this world, was much wiser; studying the nursery-powers with much natural shrewdness, she came to have no very high respect for domestic government, and issued her orders, without ado, but as one certain of obedience. Their mother had herself to discipline no less than them, and found the task well worthy of her energy and determination.

She intended to study everything which her children should ever be required to learn, and in advance, so that when she could not herself give all their lessons, she might be able to direct them; but where to begin she could not tell, until her husband's thoughtful care aided in procuring her a guide beyond her brightest hopes in Franz Hemsterhuys, a very learned man, whom she had met at times in society, but who, supposing her to be what she seemed, a mere woman of the world, had never sought her acquaintance. When he heard her retirement from society mentioned, and rumors of her devotion to her children and to study, his admiration of her heroism in daring to do so, led him to seek to know her better. His own favorite study was ancient philosophy and the Greek language, and as their acquaintance ripened he never wearied of talking to her of the virtue and wisdom of the ancients, which so interested her that, advised and encouraged by the prince, she resolved to apply herself under his professorship to the study of Greek, as a beginning. Hemsterhuys was gifted with a gentle nature, with great truthfulness and simplicity of character; he cared nothing for fame, though a great student published little, and that in small editions for his own friends and a small circle of refined and thoughtful readers; his natural uprightness, his love for every thing really beautiful, had kept him free from the prevailing errors of the day, and his life was an emulation of the ideal of a pagan philosopher. Amalia's straightforwardness charmed him, and her quick perceptions, her real desire for knowledge, won his whole sympathy, and he placed himself at her service to assist her in any way she desired. She soon looked up to him as to a devoted parent, he was twenty eight years her senior, receiving his advice on all subjects, especially in regard to the discipline of her children, with filial reverence; he read with her, explained all the obscure passages, made so to her for want of fuller information, and with the greatest tact and judgment aimed to develop her mind without crowding it, or taking away any of its freedom.

Meantime many comments upon her change of pursuits came to her ears, and as she was sensitive as well as high spirited, she was often deeply pained; some laughed, some sneered, all considered it a whim of which she would soon tire, and she felt that while she remained in her husband's house, she could not be secure from intrusive visits and remarks, but she expected to be obliged to endure them, as there seemed no way of evading them.

After a year in Russia Diderot again visited the prince, and announced, with exultation, that the princess had justified his judgment, she had made wonderful progress; he advocated complete retirement from the world, and to his eloquence, and that peculiar power by which he could make his listener always entirely of his opinion, for the moment, the princess owed it, that her husband consented that she should occupy one of his country houses, as her own exclusive property, to live and study just as she pleased. She chose one between the Hague and Schevelingen, which was far enough from the city for quiet, but within easy and pleasant reach of her husband's palace. The city of the Hague was formerly the summer residence of the Holland nobility, who had there the most beautiful summer houses and parks, so that the streets were more like walks or drives through private landscape gardens, than the thoroughfares of a city, therefore the prince would be put to no unpleasant journey in visiting his family and throwing off the "cares of state", in the house she longed to make a HOME. Hemsterhuys would also find it easy to continue his lessons, the children would have entire freedom, and she would be beyond the reach of criticism, though it grieved both her and her husband that the claims of his position necessitated even so slight a separation.

She furnished her new house with great simplicity, and named it NITHUYS (*Not at home*), conveying the idea that the bird had flown to her nest, the world was shut out, and that she was no longer AT HOME in social phrase; in the language of the heart she had never been at home before. That no one might say she was still trifling and would soon return to society, and still more because it occupied so much of her time to attend to it, she cut off her beautiful hair, and wore a *peruke,* like a judge's wig, and dressed with the utmost plainness; her children, in easy, comfortable clothes, were always under her eyes, playing as freely as the envied peasants' little ones, in their short hours of recreation; her venerable guide, Hemsterhuys, came almost every day to her cottage, her few friends entered without any ceremony, for they were all of her own way of thinking, those whose chief happiness in life was in the pleasures of the mind. Of these the Princess of Nassau-Orange, wife of William V., reigning stadtholder of the Netherlands, was her warmest and most intimate friend, who often visited Nithuys bringing with her the little Frederick William, her son, two years younger than Mitri. While the Princess of Orange fully sustained Amalia in her course, she did not fail to lament her own incapacity to follow her example, any further than to direct her son's education as fully as her duties, as wife of the sovereign, permitted; a resolution she carried out with great thoroughness. Other ladies of note were encouraged to do the same, and more than one nobleman in after years owed it to the courage of his mother's training, that he escaped the prejudices which dragged his friends into all kinds of misfortune in the years of universal revolution.

The princess now devoted herself to her own and her children's education more systematically than before; she read Socrates and of the Stoics, and endeavored to bring up her children upon their principles; Mimi and Mitri were obliged to be their own maid and valet, to take cold baths every morning, and go to sleep in the dark every night; Mimi took it philosophically, but Mitri protested lustily; the moment the light was put out his screams were fearful to hear, and when the princess, unable to endure them, would go back to reason with him, she would find him trembling and convulsed with terror, which would be under control while she staid, but the moment she left him alone would break out into frantic shrieks as before. She argued with him each time, forcing him to give a reason for every answer he made to her questions, for every objection to her propositions; but though she dealt with him most logically he grew every day more timid and nervous, and she had to devise many ways of overcoming what she regarded as his cowardice, and try to make him brave and manly.

"I soon found such a happiness in my new life", she wrote in her journal, "in the society of my children, in my own gradually increasing knowledge, and in the peace of soul in which I lay down at night, that still higher capabilities began to appear; God and my own soul began to form the main subject of my thoughts and inquiries."

CHAPTER III.
(1779—1783.)
AT MUENSTER.

Nithuys insufficient. — Advantages of Geneva. — Fuerstenberg's public school system. — Muenster. — Foundation of the university. — The princess' observations. — Decides to remain in Muenster. — Regulates her household. — Home pleasures. — Freedom and enjoyment of her reunions. Distinguished visitors. — Baron von Fuerstenberg. Hamann. — Travels. — At Halle. — Effect of her method of education. — Mitri's timidity, sensitiveness and reserve.

When four or five tranquil years had thus passed in the seclusion of *Nithuys*, it became evident to the princess, as to her husband, that they could not procure in Holland the thorough and brilliant education demanded by Mitri's illustrious birth and position. As he was now eight or nine years old, it was considered the time had come for deciding what course of training to adopt, that the princess might at once enter upon it, in accordance with her intention of studying everything in advance. Assisted by her own little circle of thoughtful men and women, and by correspondence and consultation with her husband's distinguished friends in different cities, she carefully examined the most commended systems of education in Europe, that her choice might be deliberate and just; even keeping herself informed of less noted theories, plans, and institutions. An illustrious man of learning, visiting the prince, finally decided her in favor of Geneva, where, she was assured, she would find the most perfect system, and the most profoundly wise professors in the world. This plan was rendered more feasible and alluring by the prince's owning a handsome residence near the beautiful Geneva lake, where her eyes would constantly enjoy the vision of nature in all her loveliness. It did not matter to her in the least that the shadow of stern and loveless Calvinism, the awfullest cloud unhappy man has ever known to place between the blue, smiling heavens, and fond, up-looking earth, rested above the beautiful land she longed to see; she had never looked upward since her early childhood, and knew nothing of light.

But as all was arranged for the journey, her attention was arrested by an account sent her of a new theory, just being put into practice in the staid old city of Muenster, already famous for its intellectual advantages. There were phases in it new to her, and very suggestive, which would not permit her to pursue the Geneva plan until she had learned something further of this. She, therefore, considered it her duty to visit Muenster and judge for herself of the truth of what she heard; she arrived there in May 1779, and spent nineteen days in close examination of its schools, and in making the acquaintance of their founder, Baron Francis von Fuerstenberg; so much was she pleased with all that she saw, that she believed it would be unjust to her purpose of securing the best the world could offer to settle in Switzerland, before obtaining some of the benefits of the baron's system. She therefore decided, with the prince's concurrence, to postpone the journey to Switzerland for a year, when Mitri would still be quite young enough to enter upon the Geneva course, and to spend the intervening time in Muenster with her children, to become more fully acquainted with its advantages and resources; a resolution she promptly carried into effect.

Muenster, capital of the Prussian province of Westphalia, is a quaint old Catholic city, distinguished for the number of its churches, the piety and learning of its inhabitants, and and for its famous university, established by Fuerstenberg. At this time it was a bishopric, under the civil and spiritual government of a bishop, who was also Elector of Cologne. About ten years previous to the princess' first visit, Maximilian Frederic, a prince of the ducal house of Bavaria, Archbishop and Elector of Cologne as well as Bishop of Muenster, conceived the idea of founding a seminary and university in the latter city, for the education of Catholic youth, especially those who might wish to enter the priesthood. There was no Catholic university within reach, for that of the Jesuits at Paderborn was entirely theological, and one was desired at which history, higher philosophy, classical literature, the languages, botany, law, medicine, and all the branches of a superior education should be taught, thus placing the Catholic sciences on their plane of ancient glory and olden splendor, especially needed at that time when rationalism and unbelief, by the deep root they had taken in all Germany, increased the danger to which young Catholics are always exposed at non-Catholic schools, colleges, or universities.

By various plans the elector saw means for securing buildings, and a reasonable revenue for the university which was to "renew among the ministers of religion," he said in his circular to his clergy upon the subject, "the ancient splendor of the sciences, of discipline, and other advantages required for them.... Thus will the olden love and zeal for religion and its ministers be revived among the people, and the sacred lines of church and state, upon which depend the welfare of the clergy and people, be consolidated."

Baron Frederic von Droste-Vischering, canon of Muenster and Paderborn, of a noble family and noble character, was chosen to advocate the plan at Rome, the permission of the Pope, Clement XIV, being, of course, necessary for its establishment. It was not deemed advisable, however, that so vast a plan should be at once undertaken in the manner proposed, and the whole idea would, perhaps, have been abandoned, or at least postponed, had not the elector possessed in his coadjutor and vicar-general, Baron von Fuerstenberg, an executive officer of extraordinary ability, who was just suited to carry out the project, when the objections to it should have been removed, and, in the meantime, to prepare the way for it, by drawing men of science to the bishopric under his charge, and establishing preliminary schools and academies*.

Baron von Fuerstenberg belonged to a princely family, dating as far back as the thirteenth century, distinguished for its love of learning, a quality with which he was himself highly gifted, as also a rare power of organization. When placed over the bishopric of Muenster he put a whole new life into its affairs, reëstablished its credit, encouraged agriculture and all branches of industry, reformed the internal administration, obtained the clergy new facilities for solid studies, opened a military academy for the education of officers, armed a *"landwehr"*, set the gymnasium†, on a new footing, and finally established the famous university to which Clement XIV. gave his hearty consent (1773) for he had the highest idea of the mission of such institutions: "'The unanimous opinion of the wise," said the Holy Father in the document conveying this sanction‡, "and the experience of all times.... unite in attesting that public universities, in which the young are taught the principles of *belles lettres* and the sciences, have always been of great usefulness in the perfect administration of the Christian Republic. It is, indeed, by means of the learned and those whose minds have been cultivated, that darkness is dispelled, and the clouds which surrounded mankind, inheritors of the original fault, are dissipated; it is through them that errors, for the most part born of ignorance and often sullying the purity of sound doctrine, are confounded; finally, it is through them that other men learn to regulate their lives on the principles of equity and justice, that private and public interests can be administered justly and wisely." The Pope desired that besides all the sciences, such as philosophy, theology, jurisprudence, and medicine, with all their

---

* *Histoire du Pontificat de Clement XIV.*, translated from the German, vol. I, p. 297.

† An institution for instruction which comes between an academy and a college.

‡ *Histoire du Pontificat de Clement XIV*, vol. II, p. 275.

ramifications, international law, Oriental languages, profane history, etc., taught at the university, there should be a seminary attached to it, for the better preservation of the faith.

It was the report of these educational reforms and establishments, which reached the princess, and when, on her first visit, she saw the provisions made for every branch of study, from its elementary foundation to its highest perfection, she was filled with astonishment at the genius which could devise and put into practice such an admirable method. Her surprise and satisfaction constantly increased upon her second visit, when she quietly took an unpretending residence in the city, which seemed to her like one vast college, so orderly, regular, and calm, where the students and professors went about freely, grave and thoughtful, and where everything she could wish was at her hand. That all was Catholic, from foundation stones to observatory tower on Catholic principles, inspired by Catholic faith, breathing only Catholic thought, she did not consider worth a passing remark. She was willing to accept Catholic Muenster as previously Calvinistic Geneva, and if need were, infidel or pagan professors. She lived for this world, her only end and aim to acquire all possible knowledge by the most direct means, not for its own sake only, but for the sake of her children's education. She had obeyed the voice which called her out of the life of society and she was no longer unhappy, for though she still craved an unknown something, she was contented, for she doubted not she was on the right road to it, and that what she desired and needed would be found at the goal of mental development.

The year in Muenster passed away almost as quietly as if at *Nithuys*, but with such perceptible profit, and such clear advance in her own and the children's studies, that she found it a difficult task to break away from all that had absorbed her so completely, and commence in a new way. She compared that which she knew of the city with the most favorable accounts of Geneva, the judgment of her mind and heart assured her she could gain nothing by the change, and after

due deliberation, she decided to remain. The Geneva plan
was not postponed but abandoned, and she prepared to consider Muenster her home for several years, at least, until
Mitri's education should be completed. She retained her
pleasant city residence, procuring a country house at the
village of Angelmodde, about five miles distant, for the summers, where her children could enjoy the full freedom of out-of-door life, and she could receive the prince and her friends
with all the charms of country life about her.

From the first days at *Nithuys* Mimi and Mitri had been
trained in a rather severe school of athletics, everything
that could be devised for their physical development had
been carefully and thoroughly tried; they were taught to
ride and swim, made to take long walks, to run, jump, and
practise gymnastics to the full extent of their strength, they
kept regular hours, ate the simplest food, and were freed
from all the torture of fashionable over dressing, being kept
always neatly, but plainly and comfortably clothed. To this
fencing was added for Mitri, and a full course of reasoning
as mental development, for both; they were called upon at
all times to assign a cause for every sensation, a motive for
every action, an opinion on every occurence. She now procured them tutors of the wisest and best in Muenster, and
arranged her house and time with entire reference to study.
All rose early, every hour had its alloted duties, one thing
was never allowed to crowd another, there was plenty of
open air exercise, whatever was done, taught, or learned was
filled with life and spirit by her interest in it, and the care
she took that no dead weight should be laid on the mind.
She herself would often sit up the greater part of the night,
and in the daytime forget to eat, if she became absorbed in
any especially interesting subject, or involved in conflict
with an unusually stubborn idea, until some one of her servants would venture to ask her to take the chocolate or biscuit, previously placed uncalled for at her hand, and long
unnoticed, which request she would pleasantly comply with,
for she was of most amiable disposition, grateful for little
attentions many would resent as intrusions.

In the afternoons and evenings certain hours were kept free for conversation, when she gave herself up to the amusement and entertainment of her children, with the same zest and abandonment with which she pursued her most serious studies. Besides her own children she had with her for education her niece and adopted daughter, Countess Amalia von Schmettau*, daughter of a brother of the princess who died when quite young, and George Jacobi. After some years there were intimately associated with these the children of a noble Westphalian family, one of the few with whom she kept up acquaintance, that of Baron von Droste-Vischering, whom she loved almost as her own and delighted to have join in all her lessons, expeditions and amusements; they came nearly every day to her house, with their tutor, Dr. Theodore Katercamp, to enjoy the hours of conversational reunion, which increased in interest as they grew in years. In these talks all that they had learned from books was applied, illustrated, and kindled into reality, so that the tutors and friends, who dropped in to take part or to listen as inclination led, considered these conversations as useful to the young students as a university course, while for themselves the dry bones of dull routine seemed clothed with living flesh by the spirit she infused into them. As time passed on the little circle enlarged yet drew ever closer together; the reunions, which took place in the garden or in the drawing room, according to the season, and were informal home-gatherings, became famous, and were awaited from day to day with impatience; grave professors, hard worked and care-laden men came to them as unceremoniously as did the children; distinguished strangers in the city sought admittance; she had often one or more of her "philosophes" friends with their wives or sisters visiting her house, and venerable priests with childlike hearts met there infidels and unbelievers, lingering to hear old lessons revived for eager youth. Whatever form the conversation took, the princess was always its leader and inspirer, whether she spoke or was silent.

---

* Afterwards a Catholic and member of a religious house in Vienna.

Among these visitors Baron von Fuerstenberg, whom the princess called *le grand homme*, held, as if by the tacit consent of all, the most distinguished place; his advice guided her in all her undertakings, and he was accustomed to discuss with her his plans and theories in regard to the great subject which was common ground to both ; she entered with all her soul into every detail, every branch of it, perceiving with woman's ready wit, many a little matter in connection with his projects, overlooked by his broader vision, which she contrived, no easy matter, to bring to his notice, without appropriating to herself the merit of discovery. His assistance in developing and guiding her splendid intellect was immense, as she recognized with thorough gratitude; she admired his noble character while she accepted his foibles, the peculiarities of genius, with all affection; he liked to state his own side of a matter in full, as she knew very well, but seldom permitted his opponent the same privilege: "I nearly choked with laughter," she wrote in her journal, "when after a long argument with Hamann in which he himself had done nearly all the talking, he said to me, 'I shall not enter into another discussion with Hamann, *he does not allow me to say one word.*'" When, shortly after her settlement in Muenster, various influences working in favor of political ambition against him, it was feared that he would lose his position as administrator or prime-minister of the elector, to the great loss of the district in his charge, she took up his cause with immense devotion, and exerted a wide influence in his favor among the ambassadors or ministers from various courts, who would have voice in the decision, but without success: "On the 18th inst.," she writes to Thulemeier, Prussian minister at the Hague*, Sept. 20. 1780, "Mr. de Fuerstenberg received.... a courier with a letter in which the elector made known to him that he was well satisfied and grateful for his service to the state, but in view of the present condition of affairs he prayed him to tender his resignation," which request he calmly complied with,

---

* *Tagebuch und Briefwechsel*, p. 87.

sending in his resignation of his position as administrator, but as to the direction of the educational establishments, the seminaries, convents, civil and military schools, not holding it from his ministry (in the civil sense), but from his vicariat, he should not resign it, he said, but contentedly continue to serve his country in that department, the more so, that though other affairs could go on without him, he did not foresee that education could sustain itself without his care."

This change, while it grieved his friends and roused their indignation at the ingratitude to him, enabled *le grand homme* to devote himself exclusively to the direction and development of education in Muenster, to the great advantage of Germany. The princess was filled with admiration of his noble character thus brought out, and said of him: "If ever I should have an itching to write, it would be to portray his life and character, not with the intention of pronouncing his panegyric but for the good of men.... He is so strong without effort, with so much simplicity of manner that three fourths of the people pass him by without suspecting it, and without being arrested by it. I freely compare him to the immense dome of St. Peters' church at Rome. All those who have seen it tell me that, having looked at this collossal dome from the outside, without calculating its dimensions, they have always been surprised at the slight impression received of its immensity when inside, which proves the perfection of harmony in its prodigious proportions."*

"Mr. de Fuerstenberg," wrote her distinguished correspondent in prophetic reply, "is a great man, but not of our age, he is of the brilliant days of Greece and Rome.... We shall not have long to wait to see in the country you inhabit, a revolution fatal to the welfare of its people, too happy, however, in this that the public acts and all the establishments formed under Mr. de Fuerstenberg's auspices, continue under his direction."†

---

* *Tagebuch*, p. 89.
† Same, p. 96.

After this the princess' reverence never abated, but increased with further acquaintance and the revelations of a noble friendship. Next to Hemsterhuys, her *Socrates*, as she delighted to call him, and Fuerstenberg, may be mentioned as her friends at this time Jacobi, Johannes von Mueller, the historian, who sent his manuscripts to her for her criticism and opinion, and Hamann, who also was a philosopher, and in rather straightened circumstances; her house was for him as a beautiful and welcoming home; she provided him many comforts and pleasures, above all, to an unappreciated intellect the dearest and best, that of a thorough and evident faith in him; attended him, as a devoted daughter, in his last illness, and finally buried him in her own garden. "For it was an inexpressibly sweet thought to me," she said*, "that I might preserve the ashes of the blessed one — that great one — so little known — in my own garden; at his grave, perhaps, in time, to infuse into my children some portion of his spirit, — and for myself a continual inspiration."

As the children grew older, she travelled with them the greater part of each summer, visiting the principal cities of Germany, making a little circle of illustrious friends wherever they staid, and endeavoring to impress upon the minds of her young travelling companions the history, geography, every important or distinctive feature of whatever they saw. She visited with especial interest all the noted schools and academies, to converse with the professors upon the great subject which still occupied her thoughts. She was quite competent to do so, for she had rounded into a truly intellectual woman, while retaining the naturalness and vivacity of her youth, duly subdued and elevated as became her maturer years; she had learned Latin, Greek, and mounted beyond reach of ordinary intelligences in mathematics, and appeared to have read with understanding all the ancient and modern literature considered worth naming. In her journeys she was often accompanied by parties of friends, by Fuerstenberg, and others, and nearly always by one or

---
* *Tagebuch*, p. 29.

more of the children's tutors, to whom in those days of expensive travelling, such journeys were of the greatest and most prized advantage; on the way either Mimi or Mitri, who were always kept in the carriage with her, would be required to read aloud from some book relating to the country through which they were passing, which gave a vivid reality, never to be forgotten, to the account of battles, invasions, or other events once taking place there; and when this whole wise and actively intelligent party visited the schools, it may be believed their examination was neither listless nor flimsy. "At Halle," a professor relates[*], "they visited the Normal school, and as the school hours were about over, the princess asked for some mathematical exhibition, that she might have an illustration of their manner of teaching. While one of the pupils, with much fluency, was proving the Pythagorean theorem, she followed him with an expression of great interest, questioning him in regard to other methods, and finding these unknown to the teachers, went to the blackboard herself, and illustrated them with such clearness that the listeners forgot to wonder at the singular spectacle of a princess with a piece of chalk in her hand, and hung eagerly upon every word she spoke." They visited the military academies, where Mitri was called upon to exhibit his skill in all military exercises, in which he had been trained with the greatest care by private masters, as well as in the military school at Muenster; no museum of science or art was left unexplored, and nothing examined carelessly or superficially.

Such a course of education by books and by travels, by constant and familiar intercourse with the greatest and most cultivated minds of the country, pursued by every art or device to be imagined, which would gather from it the most value for their intellectual development, formed, moulded, and inspired the children to an immense degree, while the vigorous exercise and simple life which they led, the con-

---

[*] *Leben und Wirken des Prinzen Demetrius Augustin Gallitzin*, von P. Heinrich Lemcke, Muenster, 1861; p. 72.

stant and almost overpowering presence of their mother's mature and powerful intellect, prevented any appearance of precocity or undue subordination of the health and spirits of youth to grave and mighty thoughts. They were delightful children, full of life, spirit, and individuality, winning friends wherever they went.

Mimi was the more forward, frank, and outspoken, Mitri the more reserved, simple, and timid; Mimi may have made friends more readily, but Mitri kept his longer; indeed, this was a most remarkable trait of his character, that the friends of his childhood were never estranged or forgotten, although he was rather inclined to excess of affection, without being demonstrative, when giving at all. In the eyes of the mother they were full of faults. "Mimi," she said to one of the teachers, urging him to severest discipline, and to have no mercy upon the children's vices, as she named them, "Mimi is talkative, quarrelsome, and full of mischief; Amalia fibs like a printed book, and Mitri prepares many miseries for me by his uncontrollable indolence, and absurd timidity."

This accusation had been brought against the child from the days when he screamed at being alone in the dark, and no efforts could reason him out of his nervousness. He announced one morning at Angelmödde, when he was a pretty big boy, that he had heard a noise in the garden the night before; that the first time he heard it, he would not give up to his fright, but the second time the noise came, he was overwhelmed with fear and jumped into bed as quick as he could, pulling the coverlid over his head. At this the princess refrained from reproaching him or laughing at him, but after the manner of Socrates, as her custom was, undertook to get him over it by sound instruction: "What was the use of hiding?" she asked.

He admitted that was not very clear to him.

"Well, then," she went on, "we must try to make it clear. What did you think caused the noise?"

"Robbers."

"What did you suppose the robbers wanted?"

4*

"To break into the house."

"And supposing the robbers had got into the house, is it not true that one of two things would happen, either the robbers would have overpowered us, in which case they would probably have killed us, or we should have overpowered them? Now, fancy, if the thieves had killed us, what would you have done all alone in the world? And if we had put out the thieves, would'nt you feel ashamed, a young fellow, to have your life saved by women, while you were hiding yourself?"

This made him very much ashamed*, but so far from conquering his fright at future noises must have greatly accelerated it, for imagination is an easier faculty to rouse in a child than pure reason; here there was presented to his nervous, and easily excited temperament, the dreadful prospect of being left alone in the world, and the scarcely less painful shame of being protected by his mother and sister. A more commonplace mother, knowing nothing of Socrates, would have given him some assurance of safety, which would have put his mind at rest, and given his boyish courage time to outgrow his childhood's fears, now raised to the greatest importance. It is probable he was more careful, afterwards, about acknowledging his terrors, the surest way for a child to double them, for besides the shame felt at the exposure of his timidity, he knew very well he would always get the worst of a discussion with his mother, finding it beyond his power to give satisfactory reasons for his thoughts and actions, however convinced he might be of his own view; he became very sensitive, dreaded any investigation of his inner nature, and with instinctive defence of his own weakness against her keen perceptions, retreated into his shell the instant she turned her eyes upon him; he did not leave the least opening, for by instinct rather than any conscious thought, he felt his own weakness, and that if she obtained the slightest hold, he would be at her mercy, incapable of any resistance. His reserve towards her grieved the prin-

---

* Dr. Katercamp's life of the princess, p. 89.

cess beyond all things, and she did her utmost to make however small a breach in it, for she, too, felt confident if she once could do that she could break the wall of his reticence with utmost ease, and his whole heart and soul be open to her unobstructed inspection; but if she was watchful, fully conscious of what she sought, he was no less wary, unconscious that he was hiding himself from her. She loved him with a boundless devotion, and he knew there was no woman like her, but perfect love cannot exist where fear is, there must be some equality before it can cast out the fear.

CHAPTER IV.

(1783—1789.)

A NEW LIFE.

Spiritual necessities. — Example of Catholic friends. — A critical moment. — Dr. Overberg. — Recovery. — Investigation. — Confusion. The study of the Scriptures. — Love of metaphysics. — Light. — Embarrassment in regard to the children. — Uneasiness about Mitri. — His character. — Travels. — Happiness of the princess. — Her devotion to the Church. — Her zeal. — Her friendship for Overberg.

Even in her most confused and inexperienced days, before her mind was sufficiently cultivated to be able to reason clearly and judge impartially, the princess had refused to surrender, even to the wittiest and most subtle of those men who have been called the apostles of the religion of Anti-Christ, her belief in the existence of God, and her own immortal soul. Though she knew it not, it was spiritual development she craved far more than mental expansion; she was well aware that the existence and needs of her physical nature were not more real than those of her mind, the luxuries, which other women of her rank and dainty tastes regarded as necessary to their physical being as food and drink, she could easily renounce, but for her intellect she sought everything the world could offer, and when all was gained she was as dissatisfied as any spoiled child of fashion or ambitious queen, who could find nothing more to ask for. While she had been studying and increasing in human wisdom, far higher capabilities were developing, and when she seemed to have reached the end of her journey, she found she had but passed, by a dark and narrow passage, to the boundary land of spiritual life, and, much as she tried to do so, she could not content herself to lie down upon the outer edge, and live upon what she had learned.

This came to her gradually, and much against her will; she desired to keep apart from all connected with the thought, to stifle the voice crying for it in herself, and to turn aside with indifference all that came from outside to warn or to persuade her. In Muenster she was entirely surrounded by Catholics, whose lives she could not but admire and whose principles, as now and then they appeared to her, seemed to her good and beautiful, but as the whole theory of religion was to her thinking absurd and out of date, any little details of it failed to move her. She freely admitted that she was impressed by the virtue and greatness of her friends, *le grand homme* Fuerstenberg, and others, whom she knew to be firm believers in Christ, but she looked upon their religion as accidental, and those things in them which excited her admiration, as entirely independent of their peculiar faith, merely the result of natural gifts thoroughly cultivated. In regard to the pious Catholic family of the Von Drostes, she was not so satisfied, for she was obliged to acknowledge that the religious sentiments which united them in a most charming family life, really added great attractions to each individual member, and that she could never have loved the children so tenderly had that element been lacking; she also saw too clearly to be denied, that though far less efforts were made for their education than she was compelled to use, their progress was most remarkable; she could only ascribe this to the faith of their parents, for she was too honorable and high-minded to refuse justice, and even in the secresy of her own thoughts scorned to attempt self-deception, or to turn coward to her own perceptions. Crying for light, for spiritual health and understanding, it would seem as if the noble examples under her constant observation would at once have shown her the way to truth; but she implored her friends to leave her to herself, to make no effort to convert her, to use no influence over her. She wished, she said, to know of God only that which he himself should impart to her; her soul was open to the light, and she would wait for him to send it to her, not knowing that God reveals himself in his own way, as indirectly as he pleases, and through what instruments he wills.

In the meantime nothing was said to the children, except such conversational remarks in their presence as were unavoidable. Mitri's future was settled, and whatever conclusions she might arrive at, she could no more permit herself to shape his thoughts in any mould prejudicial to his position, than she would undertake to train him for any other than the military career to which he was destined. Even if she were free to teach him what she would, there was little that could be said while she rejected all systems of religion, and was very much dissatisfied with the theory of happiness which she had built up for herself. There were professors, generally Catholic clergymen, whom she chose as most competent, for every branch, but she gave the greater part of the lessons herself, and was present and directed all, careful that no one of the teachers should transgress her instructions to avoid all mention of religion or revelation, however indirectly. Still, Christianity was a fact in the world's history, and could no more be passed over in a polite education than the pyramids of Egypt, or the palmy days of pagan Rome, and she could not for some time see any escape from the dilemma, but she had too much cleverness to remain long penned up, by any such matter, and finally found a middle course: Christianity should be mentioned as any other historical fact, but without comment, or investigation into its undercurrents.

In 1783, as she was becoming more troubled and uncertain, she was taken very ill, with what would now be regarded as a nervous fever, in connection with other diseases, which soon placed her life in danger, and brought a day when all hope was abandoned, and her friends were told that every hour might be her last. In agony of grief at her eternal peril, and rendered desperate by the need, they could no longer forbear; at Baron von Fuerstenberg's request, his confessor, Dr. Overberg, a gentle, holy priest, whose nature, by the vastness of its charity, held something of a woman's tenderness and skilful devotion, and was therefore best suited for the task, went to her and spoke of her approaching end, with such incentives to profess the faith in Christ, save by whom no man can see the Father, as the fleeting moments upon which eternity depended, required. The princess was perfectly conscious, and Overberg as one inspired; it was a moment of breathless interest, when all the angels of heaven might seem to listen motionless, to hear her answer. All she would say was that if God permitted her to recover, she would hear all they had to say, and conscientiously examine and seek the truth. God knows the heart, and words do not deceive him; where a fuller promise might have been rejected, hers was accepted, the crisis passed happily, hope returned, and she recovered. In conformity with her promise, she listened to their arguments, though she still preferred to avoid discussion, in which her friends seldom thwarted her, for they would not force her, and as a preliminary step, she commenced the reading of the Bible.

Its pages were fresh for her, free from all the prejudices of early education, from the distortions and contentions of the sects, which have made its words of sweetness bitter to the taste, its glowing, glorious, wonderful language commonplace and meaningless. It had never been forced upon her in youth, when it was impossible for her to understand it, and she went to it as to the new history of an unknown country. She was carried on from Gospel to Gospel, she lingered over the exquisite words, the joyous outbursts, and the keen insight of the Old Testament, her ears entranced by the sound of sentences the meaning of which escaped her; the New filled her with conflicting emotions, human nature of itself could not bear the majesty and tenderness of its pages. Its precepts she wished to regard as the sublime perfection of human wisdom only. "I resolved to follow the doctrine of Christ faithfully", she said, "that I might know if it were divine, to act in all things as if I did believe in him. I began at once to compare my religion," for her theories of life and its duties were a religion to her, "and principles with his, and how much I found to be altered where I had previously seen no defect! I had prayed but seldom, now I prayed frequently, and I was so often answered that I had no doubts of prayer, and many doubts of Christianity were dispelled."

She gave up her doubts but slowly, and accepted the inevitable conclusion of her investigations with deliberation, painful to the impatient lookers-on, who feared lest she should lose the truth in this apparent dallying; but she was in earnest, and if she had been blind was now willing to see, but light must come gradually to eyes used only to darkness, and our Lord is the most prudent, the most noble, and the most tender of physicians. If he is asked for, he comes without delay to the palace, or to the hovel; he never puts his patient off, or bids him come another day, or demands his fee in advance. If others have sought his aid for an unwilling one, he may reason and persuade, but he will not force the will to receive him. Once he comes he takes no anger at the nervous fears, patient and amiable even with foolish fancies, but he demands obedience, exact and prompt, to his orders. Tenderly and swiftly with a hand that yields nothing to the tears that bathe it, he cuts and probes, till the work is done, then prudently witholds the light, though the patient pleads for perfect day even while the quivering eyelids fall before the shaded candle-light.

For three years the princess read, studied, and cried for light in vain. It was a time of bitterest trial for her, there were things her intellect could not straighten and compass, all seemed confusion and uncertainty; that which one day appeared clear and settled, the next would find overthrown, and to be all set up again; faith which she had received in baptism, was with her, but belief mocked and played with her. At last she realized that she had thought and examined too much, she had tried to follow all roads at once, she endeavored to banish useless speculation and follow a simpler course, as she wrote in a pleasant way to her friend Hemsterhuys*: "You know that I have always had a passion for metaphysics.... but alas! I see that my poor head does not suffice to contain at the same time the numberless speculations to which this passion lures me, and the constant practice of the more pressing duties imposed upon me. Thus I have the hard task of sacrificing several years of this delicate nourishment for food coarser, but necessary for my mental sustenance, and this task brings me, if not delight, at least a certain peace, or rather an interior truce, but you see how for a year past, questions and quarrels have arisen in Germany, from which I have labored, up to now with success, to abstract myself; at last the demon tempter has seized me afresh, he has won the victory and leaves me, in no condition to resist him further, to the study of these quarrels. Kant, Herder, Jacobi, and by their diabolical magic, Spinoza, Descartes, Leibnitz, etc. etc. (the others are not worth mentioning), make in my head a fintamare, which prevents me from hearing myself. Oh, St. Socrates, *ora pro nobis!* Jacobi, in part the unfortunate cause of my fall, is still here."

In the same letter she relates an anecdote characteristic of the times:

"Jacobi's sister writes to him by the last post, that a dispute arose between her and Le C*** on this question: Ought one to give the idea of God to a child, and permit it to invoke him, in which Le C*** strongly and forcibly maintained the negative by a thousand reasons worthy of his robust philosophy. In the course of the dispute Le C*** made it felt, as he often has in the last two years (I don't know why), that he believes in God, and declared that there were no atheists, saying: 'For my part, I have never known one, and if any exist, they must be stupid creatures or very vain people, who have watched for thirty years to make a name;' an assertion which resulted in two little embarrassements, for in the first place, his host, Count de N***, who was present at this conversation, is an atheist, neither dull

---

* *Tagebuch*, p. 71.

nor vain, a circumstance unknown to the *corps;* according to Mlle. Jacobi, he did not know where to put his hands and eyes during the fulmination of this anathema, while Countess de N***, who is not an atheist, hid her head behind the door, like Sarah, and laughed."

At last, all became clear and certain to her, and her only marvel was that she could ever have avoided seeing it. Once she acknowledged that Christ was God, her way was clear, she had always known that the Catholic Church was his Church, that she alone held his doctrine and his promises; that she alone had remained unchanged through all the centuries; that many a prodigal son had turned his back upon her, and many an ambitious one had claimed something of her glory, but she had kept the old homestead and the keys. Recognizing his right to command the way by which all should come to him, she had never to doubt which was the way, but obeyed his orders, and entered the Church he had established. She made her first communion on the 28th of August 1786, the feast of St. Augustine, for whom she ever afterwards cherished unbounded devotion.

There now commenced for her a life, such as her fondest imaginings could never have pictured, for although the Church appeared to her from the first complete, perfect in all its parts, its succession a line unbroken, its army of saints and martyrs, regiment after regiment, marching in perfect order with all their colors flying; though each doctrine stretched wide and far, meeting, following, upholding the rest, she could never enough wonder at the mosaic variety of its marvellous symmetry; in every smallest detail there was a beautiful meaning, an ever glowing spark of divine light. It was not enough that she had found a heaven to live for, but already upon earth a world of heavenly delights to learn and to love, every day something lovelier and more entrancing than before.

But at the outset great trials accompanied her new found happiness; while she grieved for every human being outside of the Father's house, her distress at the position in which she was placed in regard to her children, cannot be described.

The prince would permit no thought of Catholicity to his son, whatever might be allowed to Mimi, and it was Mitri who aroused all her anxieties, for he alone seemed beyond her reach in all things, and gave her, as she read him, daily cause for fears. Long before her conversion, she had been weighed down by the sense of responsibility in his regard, the more so that she mistook his reserve and avoidance of discussion, for lack of candor and earnestness of purpose, and exerted herself to the utmost to rouse him, to appeal irresistibly to his affections, to his manly spirit, not understanding that these were already too much excited, so that he had to conceal and control all, or be overwhelmed by them.

"Mitri! Mitri! my beloved child! Child of my inmost heart," she would cry to him in passionate entreaty, "a thousand deaths would be too little to suffer for your good! Why am I not the confident of your thoughts, why are your simplest desires hidden from me? Am I strict with you, do I require more of you than you can give? Believe me, my darling child, I am so only for your good. I know the world, and some day you will bless me for the severity that keeps you from it."

"I am filled with alternate joy and terror," she wrote him on his fourteenth birthday, 22nd Dec. 1784*, "on this day. My first thought on awaking this morning was one of joy and thanksgiving that God had given you to me; given to me, perhaps, to have brought into this world a great, good man. But that PERHAPS! Here a second thought came to frighten me. 'To day,' I said to myself, 'fourteen years have passed for him, and, oh God! he is still entirely without will or energy, creeping about under the influence of others!' This painful thought brought on another, more terrible still, the doubt if this being whom I had carried under my heart, would finally be acceptable to God, and eternally blessed, or whether he would continue to run to perdition, in spite of the excellent gifts which the Almighty has given that he might

---

* *Leben und Wirken*, Rev. P. H. Lemcke, p. 60.

become the best and happiest of men, in spite of all my prayers, warnings, and entreaties... At times during the last months I have been filled with better hopes, and these, I freely admit, have not now altogether deserted me, only they are depressed and clouded by the worse times of late, and by the ever recurring signs of the slavish submission, with which you again give yourself up to your frightful laziness and inactivity.... Beloved Mitri, oh! would to God that to day, being your birthday, reading this letter, you would begin anew with this: that, feeling for your slavish, effeminate, and indolent inertness the disgust which it merits, because of its ruin of your happiness, you might be filled with dread in reviewing the past, and fall on your knees to invoke him for the coming time, with the consciousness that you have now at least resolved with your whole soul to act in future as a free being, who knows that though no man sees him, God sees him, and calls him to an eternal destiny. O Mitri mine, in this expectation dearest child, I throw myself with you at the feet of our Father (kneeling I write it), and cry from the depths of my heart: Have mercy on him and me!"

His father understood him differently: "Mitri, I fear, will yet cause us much trouble, if not anxiety and vexation," he said, when his son was fifteen years old. "Still waters run deep. I think you mistake his disposition, he is always running against wind and tide." (*Il est toujour contre vent et marée.*)

Still more after her conversion did the princess feel the burden of responsibility for his welfare, and stood aghast at the years of impressible childhood lost to all religious principle or even religious sentiment. She saw, the splendid education she had procured by long years of unremitting labor, had been built on sand, the first wave from the outside world which should break upon their shore, might easily sweep it away, leaving hardly so much as the stranded remains of a principle or noble thought, to mark the wreck. With Mimi this might be remedied, for she would be, for a few years at least, under her mother's eye, but how could she hope to repair the loss for Mitri, so soon to be sent out upon the great ocean of temptation? Now religion could not be longer put out of the question, and whatever influence it might have upon his worldly prosperity, she knew he was bound to seek the truth, to cleave to it when found, and that it was her sacred duty to assist him in his search. She blamed him for his submission to others, for he would rather yield than make a contest about minor affairs, and no others had met him yet; she wished to see him acting independently of all outside influences, at the same time that she expected, or hoped for him to enter without delay into the true fold; she feared to have him linger in his decision, lest it should prove him obdurate and irreligious, and she feared to see him enter readily, lest he should do so from a too easy compliance with the views of those around him. Undoubtedly, also, Mitri had his own interior combats, at this time, when his father upon one side, and his mother upon the other, made him the constant object of their care and watchfulness, when the creed of his country and his intended future was the Greek, that of his education no-belief, of his earliest and ever dear friend, the Prince of Orange, Protestant, and of his present most intimate associates, the young Von Drostes, Catholicity; it was a difficult thing for a boy of sixteen to steer manfully, and with straight, unerring course, through such strong, conflicting currents. Young people seldom know themselves, and it is in mercy to themselves, that they involuntarily and unconsciously know how to guard their inconsistencies and contradictions, at least to some extent, from the eager, scrutinizing gaze of their more logical elders. Mitri would not have been human if, in these circumstances, he had not been of a hundred different minds in a week. That it was so his mother suspected with dismay, for she called vacillation that which to another might have seemed but the luxuriance of youthful thoughts and imaginings. She was restless and anxious, doubtful of his sincerity, even when he expressed himself most as she desired, uncertain whether he was replying to her, or to the voice of truth, fearing to hurry him, unable to let him alone, a position rendered the more vexatious to herself, because she could not but contrast it with the quiet and cheerful patience of other mothers, who having far more apparent reason for anxiety, did all that could be done calmly, and left the rest, with delicious Catholic faith, to God; as yet the princess wore her religion as a new garment, as converts must, and having all her life relied upon herself, feeling that whatever fell to her lot to do, must be done by her alone, and forced to its end with unceasing labor, knew not how to sow the seed, leave it time to grow, and remember that *it is God who giveth the increase;* thus by the very efforts she made to leave Mitri free to develop, she overpowered, and in a measure crushed him, withdrawing all kindly shade, so necessary for the protection of the delicate roots of youthful thoughts, pouring upon him a flood of glaring, dazzling sunlight, so that he could not but shrink, and hang listless and wilted in her sight.

To continue all efforts to prepare him for his great part in the world, the princess resumed her travels after her conversion, often remaining for some time in one place, that Mitri might receive instruction from some famous preceptor, or observe fully some exhibition of military tactics, storing up everything which might of possibility be of use to him as a student, a courtier, a statesman, a savant, a man of the world, if he should desire, at some future day, to add to his profession of arms the honors of any of these; he accepted all dutifully and with apparently equal pleasure, endeavoring to keep up the lively interest required of him; in the art-galleries he had sometimes as much difficulty to repress his enthusiasm as at other times to arouse it, and had he given away to his desires, as he afterwards admitted, he would never have left the famous Dresden Madonna, which was one of the first, if not the very first thing, which came to suggest to him that he had a soul not wholly incapable of action. As he was no longer a child he made friends for his own sake, though he opened to but few, whom he remembered with affection as long as he lived; these were the poet Claudius, Herder, Count von Stolberg, and especially Hamann, who was very fond of him, and several wise and mature women, whose learning was not too apparent, who took a gentle and soothing interest in him, delighted by his natural, simple disposition; he received from these friends books of their own writing, with autographs and suitable inscriptions; others wished him to correspond with them, and all prophesied great things for their boyish friend and guest; but his mother would not be comforted by their assurances, she dreaded lest the good they discerned in him was a mere superficial quality, or, perhaps, a reflection of their own excellence. When one sees a youth start and turn pale, like any foolish girl, at a sudden step, and trembling at the most improbable danger, it is difficult to imagine him, springing up a rampart, with flashing eyes, in the midst of shot and shell, or leading a forlorn hope, in terrible silence, through a dark defile, past countless foes in ambush.

The princess herself was full of life and energy, her enthusiasm, spirit and intelligence seemed, by comparison, to have been before but faint and half awake. Her gratitude, her joy in the gift of faith she had so lately received were almost more than she could bear; it was like David's transports before the Ark; had it not been for the inspired outbursts of the prophets and the Psalmist, which she could make her own, her very heart would have rent itself in the effort at expression. A convert is like one who has grown to manhood, homeless, and with at best an adopted name, the unconscious, unrecognized son of a royal house, the title of which falls on his ear with indifference, or, perhaps, for some reason he cannot divine (in reality the natural love for it, turned backward into the bitter waters of ignorance), with disgust and hatred, who all at once is taken from his obscurity, and proclaimed son and heir of the noblest line in all the land. The bells are rung, the flags fly up, and with all the pomp and splendor of joy and pride, he is welcomed to his father's house, wherein all is his. To him it is a world of wonder, the endless galleries, the gathered treasures of ages of color and form, of painting and statuary, of marbles and bronzes, wondrous exotics, old manuscript books, the swords, the armorial bearings, the battered shields of a thousand fights, the antique cups, the swinging tapestry, the yellow lace, the history of the house, its thousand legends and traditions all burst upon him at once, each in its place, and each worth the study of a life time; it is impossible for him to settle into the easy attitude, the light, uncaring mirth of the children of the house, who have never known another; their easy comfort shocks his sense of responsibility, their satisfaction in common trifles seems unworthy their glorious origin and the surrounding grandeur.

So with Amalia; she would have every Catholic a hero and a saint, and the whole world drummed into the Church forthwith; she prayed day and night for those unhappy ones who knew not the truth, and if she had had a thousand lives, she would have worn them all away in pleading, instructing, arguing, and announcing the joys of truth. When she thought or spoke of what her life had been and what it was, it seemed to her as if no one could hear and refuse to believe. She no longer tried to keep out of discussions, but wherever she went, at home and abroad, with Herder, Jacobi, Goethe, with downright infidels, and wavering sinners, she was strong as an army, and for the rest of her life the zeal for the house of God might well be said to have *eaten her up.*

"I believe firmly," she wrote in her journal, in unconscious excuse, it may be, for her impetuous zeal*, "that in two persons of equal abilities, of whom one in order to secure his salvation, most carefully avoids temptations, and therefore seldom transgresses, and the other, out of love and confidence in the divine mercy, exposes himself more and falls oftener, the latter is nearer to Christ, more like him, than the former. How could it be that the God of love in tender mercy, would not store up forgiveness for him, who for his love takes a great burden upon himself, and drags it onward, though he stumbles, even falls under it, if he but rises readily, and so carries it to the end? A faithful and watchful servant, who at the merest glance of his master hastens to him, comes here, goes there, brings and takes away, though he oftener breaks something or makes a mistake

---

* *Tagebuch,* p. 9.

than his fellow servant, who is more careful of his own honor than his master's, who would rather let one wait than take any risk by hurrying, who rather keeps back, when there is a critical errand, in which one might easily make a mistake, and lets it go to another; — now, master of both, lay your hand upon your heart, and if you have feeling, — though, it may be, there is no complaint to be made of the second who, perhaps, fulfills his *duty* the more faithfully and faultlessly, — which of the two do you love best?"

These words may come back to the princess some day in connection with another than herself.

Amalia did not content herself with rousing up all the lukewarm Catholics, and, no doubt, they were plenty, whom she met, and endeavoring to bring outsiders into the knowledge of the Church, but in a thousand ways proved her devotion and gratitude. Her charity was boundless, the love which accompanied the charity an ever flowing crystal stream; God's poor were to her as direct messengers of his love, whom she cherished and recompensed as messengers of glad tidings from an infinitely dear one; it was her joy to lay her gifts on the altars where he rested, and those who served them she served with reverence and readiness, as those whom the king delights to honor, and this above all for Dr. Overberg, not only on account of his beautiful character and sacred profession, but because he had been the special, chosen ambassador to her; had he, at the risk of his own life, drawn her out of deathly peril, she would have counted it as nothing in comparison with the spiritual death from which he had rescued her, and the eternal joys to which he led her. Most women have, or persuade themselves to have, the same ideal of loving guidance, of a nature with heart and mind so large and great that their own is ever sheltered in its lordly rooms, yet never lost in dreary, unused, and unfurnished chambers, which they seek in the usual way of romance and sentiment, but the princess's ideal had ever been a friend who would be to her as a true father, to walk by her side, over roads not unknown to him, however unfamiliar to herself. It was this desire which led her to prefer the mature mind of the prince to her more youthful admirers; it was this, gathering strength from disappointment, which inspired her reverence for Hemsterhuys, but though their friendship continued its first warmth until his death, in 1788, it was more because of the womanly submission of her intellect than the commanding manliness of his, for her keen intelligence often shot far ahead of his calm philosophy. Again she thought she had found the guide she sought in Hamann, but though she would not permit herself to own it, she did not find the satisfaction and reliance of which her soul was capable. After she became a Catholic, a new light was shed upon the dim desire which had kept her groping through the labyrinths of human weaknesses for so long. She saw now that what she needed was the submission of her own will to another, not for the gratification of a natural inclination to confidence and veneration, but for her advance in perfection. Still, although she perceived the absolute necessity, she said, of perfect obedience under another's direction, she had after a long conflict with herself, continued to imagine the giving up of her own will to be too great a sacrifice, despairing of finding a person to whom she could submit herself with thorough confidence. But she had become more and more convinced that guidance of this kind was a real necessity for her, that she had need of "a friend, a father, to whom she might lay open her whole heart, to whom she might freely confide the good as well as the evil in it, for him to judge and manage it", from whom she might obtain directions for her conduct, and who from Christian zeal, without being questioned, would observe, examine, correct, console, exhort, and care for her soul as if it were his own. "This man, full of fervor and love," she said, "who for a long time has vividly represented to me, in his meekness and holy simplicity, the most striking features of my Saviour's character, who appears to answer all the wants of my heart, I have found." This was Overberg, and at her earnest but timid entreaties, he took the direction and care of the soul he had been the instrument of bringing to the faith. He took up his residence in her house, and was not only her guide and confessor, but a friend and companion who strove with her for perfection. She submitted to him with the ready humility of which only a great nature is capable, following his advice with eagerness, recognizing in him far more than friend or brother, a true spiritual father to whom she owed, under God, her soul's life, for whom all her desires in the past had been tried and disappointed, that they might be freed from all dross of earth. His humility insisted that she also should aid him, and it was agreed that each should candidly and fully warn the other of any imperfection which might appear. He was her almoner, and in all his undertakings was as sure of her interest and aid as of his own. Their mutual striving for perfection led to a friendship seldom reached in this world, the exclusive gift of specially chosen souls. It was a friendship absolutely free from human doubts or fears, death had for it no terrors, absence no dread, for life was their probation time, eternity their union. Other affections, like ships at anchor, are bound to earth, close to the shifting sands of time, restless in the daily ebb and flow of earth's smaller joys and cares, tossed by the waves they no longer rule or ride, but upon such a friendship as this earth has no hold, it is far out at sea with sunshine on its sails; the fathomless ocean of spiritual knowledge, with pearly caves and coral deeps, its white-crested waves of thought leaping to the blue heaven that alone bounds the vision, surrounds them, while virtue and faith guide the good ship to the eternal haven.

The good she did the princess never knew nor counted; there was no woman of her time and country to rival her in influence and veneration; friends gathered about her from every land, attracted by the blended charms of her learning, her beautiful womanliness, and, in spite of themselves, by the faith which illumined her. They were honored by her interest or criticism, and *carried her on their hands*, as the Germans say, when she visited them, for her presence in a house brought blessings with it. The simplest mannered of women, as soon as religion came to give light and grace to her nature and acquirements, she became the most loved and honored.

CHAPTER V.

PRINCE DEMETRIUS AND WHAT TO DO WITH HIM.
(1787—1792.)

> "*O poor little one, tossed with tempest, without all comfort, behold I will lay thy stones in order, and will lay thy foundations with sapphires.*" (Isaias, LV, 11.)

His views on religion. — Enters the Catholic Church. — Plans of travel. — Influence of the French Revolution. — Appointed aide to the Austrian General von Lillien. — Death of Leopold II. — Fuerstenberg's opinion of a trip to America. — Mr. Brosius. — Mr. Schmet. — Sails from Rotterdam for the United States.

Now all these journeys, reunions, conversations, and discussions, undertaken for the most part for Mitri's improvement and enlightenment, could not well be without effect. He heard all the arguments between his mother and the Catholics on one side, his father and the non-Catholics, infidels, unbelievers, reformers, Greeks, Protestants, theorists of every shade and degree, on the other, and the time came when his own mind showed him the necessity of choice. "Raised in prejudices against revelation," he said afterwards[*], "I felt every disposition to ridicule those very principles and practices which I have adopted since.... I soon felt convinced of the necessity of investigating the different religious systems, in order to find the true one. Although I was born a member of the Greek Church, and although all my male relatives were either Greeks or Protestants, yet did I resolve to embrace that religion only which, upon impartial inquiry,

---

[*] *Letter to a Protestant Friend on the Holy Scriptures*, p. 19.

should appear to me to be the pure religion of Jesus Christ. My choice fell upon the Catholic Church." This occured when he was about seventeen years old; he took the name of Augustine in confirmation to please his mother, whose devotion to the great doctor was constantly increasing, and because of the similarity of the maternal love with which she wept and prayed for her son, to that of St. Monica, of which her friends delighted to remind her; he heard Mass every day with his mother and sister, there were frequent communions of the little group, and he even went so far as to mention a desire to become a priest, an idea instantly frowned down by his indignant father, and passed over by his mother as the caprice or enthusiasm of an inconstant boy, whose resolves were traced on sand; indeed she could hardly help seeing in it another proof of his submission to the influence of others, for such was the desire and intention of his friends, Caspar Maximilian* and Clement Augustus† von Droste, who undoubtedly learned more, in the freedom of their boyish confidences, of the inner life of the young prince than his mother could divine. She naturally regarded the expression of such an idea a proof of his thoughtlessness, making no account of the gravity and greatness of the office he was so willing to enter, and of his lightness of purpose which could imagine such a thing possible for a young Russian, a commissioned officer of the guard. He was daily exhibiting such signs of simplicity and superficial observation. However, the wish appeared to vanish as lightly as it came, and no more was heard about it, as his mother feared, and his father hoped, would be the case with his Catholicity. The princess did not allow herself to reckon with any security upon his constancy, and wept and prayed that he might persevere, as formerly that he might embrace the truth; while the prince argued, and vexed at his boyish obstinacy, comforted himself with the thought that he would soon be taken from his mo-

---

* Afterwards Bishop of Muenster.

† Who became Archbishop of Cologne in 1835, and was imprisoned for the faith by the King of Prussia, in 1837.

ther's influence, and, of course, when he put on the uniform of an officer of the guard, he would put the state religion on with it, and there would be an end of all this vexatious talk.

Both parents were otherwise much embarrassed in regard to the next step to be taken. Mitri was approaching his majority, and, consequently, the time when he would be required to take his place in the world, according to his rank and the empress' favorable designs. All that the universities and military academies could teach him, all that the most accomplished tutors could do to form his mind and perfect him in knowledge, was done; he had visited the principal cities of Germany and Holland, but no young nobleman's education was at that time considered complete until he had spent a year or two in travel, not as a school boy, but in manly style; there were yet two years before he would be expected to enter the service, which should have been devoted to a European tour, but just then the French Revolution broke out to deluge the earth with horrors, showing the world what crimes could be committed in the name of Liberty, and to what the fine sentiments of the "philosophers" so logically lead; disorder let loose upon the nations held high carnival at Paris, Paris the beautiful, at whose shrine every tourist bent the knee, without which no tour could be thought worth undertaking, Paris was given over to vengeance, and the world shunned it with terror. The storms which gathering in unhappy France thundered about every throne in Europe, had not passed lightly over the prince's own aristocratic head, and many a dark foreboding of gloomier days to come reached him in the midst of the gay life he still led; he saw nothing that could be gained, and too much that would be risked by the usual travels; it was a dangerous time, depravity, anarchy, and wickedness, sometimes gilded and glittering, at others in undisguised deformity, ran riot in greater or less degree in every city and fashionable circle. No man was safe from suspicion or pollution, least of all a young nobleman, whose position could not be concealed. The only safe plan seemed to be to send him at once to St. Petersburg, — Catharine had petted the last of the French philosophers, and at the first alarm had shut down the iron gates of absolute authority against the once cherished "liberalism".

The princess was hardly less distressed at this decision than she had been at the prospect of two years of travel in the midst of European convulsions. She knew very well that though he might escape political danger in St. Petersburg, that it had in reality little religion to boast of even by the side of Paris; she was terrified at the idea of taking a young man directly from his home studies, the influence of the family circle, to cast him with all the temptations of wealth, youth, rank, accomplishments, and utter inexperience into the whirlpool of society, of court-life, of military habits. But as the prince had so settled it, she saw nothing she could do, unless she herself removed to Russia and made her home in St. Petersburg, there to guide, warn, and watch over him until the wisdom of manhood should render him more capable of resisting the snares of the world, but the very thought of her feeble health, of the tedious journey, the loss of the beloved circle at Muenster, the arrival in a city to the ways and customs of which she would be entirely a stranger, the change in her way of living, overpowered her, and with all her firm sense of duty she shrank from such an effort, feeling with all her courage that she should die in an atmosphere so foreign to all her thoughts and aims, especially as she would be deprived of that which was the very breath of life to her, the free and open practice of her religion. She pleaded with her husband once again, and after much consultation between parents and friends, in which it does not appear that Mitri had any voice, the prince conceded that there being no likelihood of any active service for Mitri at present, as Russia was taking no part in the war just declared by Austria and Prussia against the French Revolutionists, there was no urgent need of his immediate entrance into the army, and professed himself willing to accede to any feasible plan which could be devised for the gradual preparation for the career eventually to be his.

The princess thought if he could serve as a volunteer in some service nearer home, under the command of her brother, if possible, it would be some modification of the Russian sentence, and in this view laid her perplexities before her brother, General von Schmettau, through whose influence, and that of Austrian friends of high position, Mitri received an appointment in the early part of the year 1792 as aide de camp to the Austrian General von Lillien, who commanded an army in Brabant, at the opening of the first campaign against the French Jacobins, who had declared war against all kings as against all religions.

Mitri was the very beau ideal of a stately young officer; he was rather tall, being about five feet nine or ten inches high, with that peculiar reticent, dignified, high bred air, which has the effect of the most imposing height; he had a slender and lithe, yet compact figure, a fine clear complexion, not too fair for manliness, and the handsomest dark eyes that ever glanced love or anger from the shadow of a military cap, eyes "dark splendid", fathomless in their tenderness, flashing fire at the slightest contradiction, full of mischief and merriment the instant anything amusing crossed their outer or inner vision; masses of shining black hair clustered around a delicately formed, haughtily set head, while a long, large nose, very prominent and slightly acquiline, gave that character, force, and dignity to his countenance, which seldom if ever accompany features of perfect regularity. He had been trained from boyhood in all manly exercises, he handled a sword as dexterously and with as many bewildering evolutions as a Spanish coquette her fan. He was a superb rider, and looked nobly when on horseback; there was no feat of horsemanship not easy to him; he would often before mounting amuse himself by putting one hand on his horse and springing over him to the other side, and, changing hands, spring back again, with lightness and rapidity, an instant afterwards he would be in the saddle, raising his hat with laughing ceremony, as horse and rider passed out of sight. Gold lace, military buttons, and all the brilliant paraphernalia of epaulettes and gold embroidery seemed to belong to his slender figure and dark eyes by every right of fitness. His mother, who only knew him under the restraint which he always felt in her presence, was not quite so sure of his coolness and steadiness on the battle field, nor could she tell how much or how little of the soldier spirit of obedience and discipline he had imbibed in his military drills and fencing lessons, but she resigned herself to the trial of a courage in him of which she had as yet seen no sign.

It was not to be in this way, however, for just as he was about to join his general, the Emperor of Austria, Leopold II., died very suddenly (March 1st 1792), from the effects of poison it was thought, administered by a member of the *illuminati* in the interest of the French revolutionists; this, taken in connection with the murder of the king of Sweden by Ankerstrom for the same purpose, caused a very stringent order to be at once issued by the Austrian and Prussian commanders, that no foreigners should hold office in either army. General von Schmettau at once apprised his sister that Mitri was thus excluded, as no exceptions whatever could be made to the rule, and either in this letter or one written somewhat later, suggested that a journey to the young republic over the sea, where all that was good and simple, orderly and honorable appeared to have taken refuge, might fill up Mitri's transition year with profit. This was an entirely new idea, and the princess hardly knew whether her husband would regard it as a wild scheme not to be thought of for a moment, or as a relief from the embarrassment felt by all concerned in regard to the disposal of the young prince. She knew that her husband, who kept himself thoroughly informed of all political affairs, signs, and changes, had always spoken with great respect of Washington, and the new nation which had just come out from its war for independence without stain upon its honor, and settling down in calmness to repair the ravages of battle and lay a solid foundation for future prosperity, offered a white and shining contrast to red-handed France, rending her garments in the frenzy of uncontrolled revolt, and, perhaps, it was not impossible that the proposal to entrust his son to such excellent and novel influences, would strike the prince favorably, although, as a general thing, a voyage to America in those times was regarded about as a journey to the interior of Africa, or up to the North Pole is in ours. The princess before submitting the plan to her husband, sought to obtain a clearer idea of its advantages and disadvantages for herself, and to give it weight as well, she consulted Fuerstenberg on the subject, receiving from him, probably at her special request, a written answer to her questions. General von Schmettau had proposed introducing Mitri to Washington and placing him under the special care of the Great President; this part of the plan did not meet with the baron's approbation, for the reasons given in his written opinion, which were legitimate enough, for the world's history, especially the history of his own time, could not conceive of a man like our Washington, loyal and faithful to the last.

THE BARON VON FUERSTENBERG TO THE PRINCESS GALLITZIN*.

In this, Madame, you will see my views concerning Mitri's travels, which I submit to your judgment. I have maturely considered them.

I look upon a journey to America as highly desirable for Mitri. His mind by well grounded instruction and discipline is now well cultivated. His energy must become aroused by travelling, for we all know the influence exerted by a long journey, a journey across the sea, in developing a youth, in arousing his energies and forcing him into activity.

For one who will travel with a mind open to observation, America now will prove a most interesting land. If only politically considered, the first trial of an entirely theoretical, perfectly unique constitution, with its good and its evil effects, its influence upon the energies, the lower propensities, and the moral tone of its people, as well as upon industry and commerce, makes the present undoubtedly the most favorable moment for studying all that is there in commotion, and is, therefore, a rich field for the politico-philosophical.

---

* *Tagebuch*, p. 174.

observer. Mitri has considerable knowledge of pure mathematics, knows something of astronomy, mechanics, physics; is psychologically versed in ancient and in German history, understands psychology, is very practical, and, consequently, as far as his education is concerned, is well fitted for travelling. It remains for him, if he goes to America, to learn to judge for himself as much as possible, to observe facts and define for himself the connection between causes and effects; to accomplish this he should have for a companion one who will be of use to him in arousing thought, but whose judgment or prejudices will not have undue influence over him, for there Mitri must learn to think for himself. His companion should be at the same time a sensible and moral man, who will look after the prince's health, etc., and send us all necessary information concerning him.

The proposal to send Mitri to Washington appears to me hazardous. It is true, we have aimed throughout Mitri's whole education, to secure him against the blind following of strange views or prejudices, but he is young, weak, and vain, the fame of Washington is dazzling for him; he would very likely accept his opinions, even his manners, perhaps, out of veneration for him, and to please him. We know the impression a famous man makes upon a youth, and who of us has any knowledge of Washington's religious and moral principles, of his political honesty? The idea requires consideration; a journey to America is an excellent and promising *debut* in the world; whatever career Mitri may adopt he may there have had occasion to notice the original arrangements, but to be looked upon as a pupil of Washington in times like these, would be only a hindrance to a young man just entering the world. I retain my first impression. However, if General von Schmettau decides us, it will be best for him to speak out plainly, approve our plan unequivocally, then the prince will probably be satisfied also.

The guide desired for Mitri, in case his father should decide to send him to America, was already at hand in the person of a young priest, Felix Brosius, at one time professor of mathemathics in the gymnasium at Düren, who while tutor in the Droste-Vischering family, had formed the resolution of going as a missionary to the United States, for which purpose he had spent two years studying English, at the Seminary for Foreign Missions in Lüttich, where the languages were taught to those who desired to go as missionaries to foreign lands. Mr. Brosius had come to Muenster to take leave of his friends, just at the time the consultation was going on in regard to Mitri's travels, and was, of course, much pleased at the prospect of having the young prince whom he knew well, for his travelling companion, for whom he was perfectly willing to act a friendly tutor's part, and anxiously to carry out the princess' views, which were, that Mitri should continue to improve in the sciences, and to use them in his observations in the new land.

The more the American plan was considered, the more reasonable it appeared, and seems to have perfectly satisfied the prince from the first, for he decided in its favor, and entered cordially into it, charging his son to send him minute and precise accounts of politics there, besides full descriptions of the country, its domestic, social, and scientific character, and by all means to cultivate the acquaintance and listen attentively to the views of its leading men, with whose names and general character the prince was remarkably well acquainted, owing, perhaps, to the residence of John Adams, the "clearest head and firmest heart of the Continental Congress", as American Minister at the Hague, where, it is hardly to be doubted, he and the prince had often met. Mr. Adams had succeeded by the resolute energy of his character in forcing the States General to accept and receive him in 1782, on that day which appears so often in American annals, April 19th, as ambassador of the new nation, which had not quite yet completed its war for independence. He had written a great deal for the Dutch papers concerning the causes and motives of the American revolution, which had done an immense deal towards the enlightenment of the Dutch and Germans in regard to it. Ambassadors from two widely different nations, differing hardly less in their individual characters, the Russian prince and the republican lawyer had yet certain sympathies and thoughts in common, which must have drawn them enough to each other to have made their other views, so very opposite, most interesting in their clashing. At all events, the very high regard and deep interest which the Russian ambassador then had in our struggle for existence, was but the beginning of a friendly feeling, which still continues unabated between the two nations. Up to the time of his leaving, the prince took the liveliest interest in talking to his son about the United States, impressing upon him all that he himself knew of its affairs, and mentioning the special points on which he desired Mitri to obtain him precise information. The princess for her part procured him a letter of introduction from the Prince-bishop of Hildesheim and Paderborn to Bishop Carroll, to whose care and guardianship she desired to confide her beloved son, as the general had advised his being confided to Washington, wherein the princess had not chosen unwisely even for this world, and far better even than she knew for the next, for if one was the Father of his Country, the other was the Father of its Church, and both were fine specimens of republican virtue, in one case exalted and purified by circumstances, in the other refined and sustained by grace. The princess felt much of her anxiety would be relieved if the bishop took interest in her son, as he would thus secure, she thought, some Catholic and worthy acquaintances to whom the bishop would make him known, who would prove, she trusted, to have some influence in keeping him firm in his religion, and regular in the observance of its duties. With all her buoyancy and cheerfulness the princess' nature admitted the gloomiest forebodings, and her heart was full of fears, lest, once away from her influence, Mitri would fall from his faith and his duties. Over and over again she besought him to perseverance and to firmness, and entreated Mr. Broslus to do the same. She had some comfort in this that it had been decided by the prince, the general, and their friends, that it would be much better for Mitri to travel as a simple gentleman, as young men of his position occasionally did, without his title, and the state, the publicity, and the enormous expense which the etiquette of the day would require to keep it up, and in accordance with the custom of those who desired to avoid the inconveniences of rank, he took an unpretending name, that of Schmet, from his mother's family, the whole name, Schmettau, having been rejected as hardly less conspicuous than that of his father. The princess trusted that as Mr. Augustine Schmet he would escape much of the adulation, and many of the temptations which would beset the path of Prince Demetrius Gallitzin. The voyage to America was in itself a long and hazardous affair, made in sailing vessels, with few comforts and many dangers, still, no one allowed himself to be disheartened in Mitri's presence, at least. He said good bye to Muenster, August 8th, but not to his mother so soon, as she with some friends was to accompany him to Rotterdam, and see him on board the ship. Every one did his utmost to make the last days pleasant, and it is said that the young prince told afterwards, that the night before sailing, or else the night before leaving Muenster, report is not clear which, he attended a grand ball given for him, at which he danced from dark to daylight, from sun-down to sun-up, for Mitri was young and enjoyed the luxuries of wealth, and the pleasures of life, with a light heart, and to the utmost. But when the hour came to say his last good bye, he was completely discouraged, and had no heart for the work. His mother had kept close to him, hardly leaving him through all the last days, and the spirit and strength of purpose upon which he had always relied, appeared to be forsaking her; her weakness, while it more and more unnerved him who had never used any strength of his own where she was concerned, but made her appear less distant and more dear to him. All at once the whole journey looked very unnecessary to him; he was always timid before commencing any undertaking, as many people are who are as brave as a lion, and persistence itself, once it is entered upon; he had little if any love for adventure or desire for change, no wild craving for romance, for which partly his education, and partly his repose-loving nature were responsible; even at that moment, though his baggage and attendants were on board, though they saw, as they walked along the pier, that the boat sent to take him to the ship was coming near, he would gladly have turned back and given it all up; with the simplicity of his character he made no concealment of his dread and fears, eagerly begging his mother, whose grief increasing as the moments passed, restrained and controlled as it was, showed her more yielding, more tender than he had ever seen her, to let him stay, and as she, who had always led him, now clung silently to him, her eyes soft with unshed tears, he looked at her, and impulsively declared he could not go, he would die away from home, he was afraid of the ocean dashing up to his feet, afraid of the strange people beyond. "Mitri! Mitri!" exclaimed his mother, shocked into sudden action, and turning instantly with flashing eyes, upon him, "Mitri! I am ashamed of you!" He was between her and the water, on the very edge of the pier, and her sudden and unexpected movement, at a moment when he was absorbed in his own entreaties, caused him to lose his balance, and fall over. But the boat sent out for him was close at hand and he was an excellent swimmer, so he was very quickly rescued, and with one last look at his mother standing on the pier, he was swiftly rowed to the ship.

What new life was born in him in that moment's conflict with death under the waves, one cannot say, but it must have been as the first taste of glory to a youth who had never heard a bugle call, nor seen a standard fly upon the battlefield, for in the moment's struggle he felt his own strength, unknown before, battling with the strength of the elements, life, hardly awake until then, springing up armed and desperate at the sudden approach of death. Old Neptune gave him a short but hard tussle, and when the young prince, with all the evidences of his singular baptism about him, walked across the deck, it was with an exultation new to him, and a truly princely spirit in his soul as in his bearing.

They sailed from Rotterdam August 18th, and did not arrive at Baltimore until the 28th of October; in the meantime

Mitri, the Herr Schmet, or Mr. Smith, as the Americans would call him, had ample time for meditation, and self examination; germs of thought dropped long ago upon his heart took root and blossomed in those long days and nights at sea, when the clumsiest sailor that climbs the giddy masthead reaches to a sublimity of thought, broken and confused though it be, inconceivable to him on land. Those exquisite days, those marvellous nights at sea, the long monotonous swell of the green ocean, the starlit sky, the sunny heavens, the glow of sunset, the flush of sunrise to him who was so sensitive to all things béautiful, were days of grace indeed; nature, then, was his Moses and spoke to him the word of God, in language which would soon be made clear to him.

CHAPTER VI.

PRINCE DEMETRIUS ARRIVES IN MARYLAND, DECIDES HIS OWN FUTURE, AND ENTERS THE SEMINARY OF SAINT SULPICE.

(1792.)

First Catholic colony of the United States. — Appointment of Bishop Carroll. — Arrival of Mr. Nagot and the French Sulpicians. — Mr. Brosius and Mitri in Baltimore. — Mitri's choice.

The first Catholic settlement of the original United States was made in Maryland, by English Catholics, who entered the Potomac in two little vessels, the *Dove* and the *Ark*, on the morning of the 25th of March 1634, and after hearing Mass by Father Andrew White, a Jesuit priest who had accompanied them from England, cut a cross from a tree, carried it in solemn procession to a place marked out for it, where they planted it, a veritable "Cross in the Wilderness," as a witness to their faith and a pledge of protection from the Saviour it commemorated. Under its shelter they built their villages, which became in time the headquarters of the Church in the United States.

In 1774, two years before the Declaration of Independence, Baltimore was a station visited once a month by a priest from White Marsh, who brought with him his vestments and altar-service, as that pleasant little village could not furnish the necessities for the celebration of the Holy Sacrifice. All the Catholics, priests and laity, in the country, were under the spiritual jurisdiction of the Vicar General of London, who, perhaps, on account of the rebellious attitude of the Colonies towards England, held no communication whatever with the Colonial Catholics during the war for Independence. When this was decided in our favor it was seen that it would not be wise for the Catholics of the United States, few as they were, and insignificant and despised their position, to remain under the charge of an English vicar, which might very naturally, however unjustly, give occasion to the government to question their loyalty. But they were so thoroughly aware of their inability to support a bishop in a manner in the least suitable to his position, that they by no means desired one to be placed over them in their present condition. In July 1784 the Holy See met their case by appointing Rev. John Carroll, a native of Maryland, brother of one of the signers of the Declaration of Independence, and of known devotion to his country, superior of the clergy of the United States, with many of the powers of a bishop. But on account of the heterogeneous character of the people, even of the clergy, who were from all parts of the world, some of them entirely ignorant of the English language, and others in no very good repute at home, it was soon found that ampler powers were needed for him who would hold these tangled reins with proper firmness, and the Holy See, therefore, erected the country into a bishopric with Father Carroll for its bishop and Baltimore as his episcopal see. This was in the year of the breaking out of the French Revolution (1789) whose upheavals cast a number of zealous priests upon our shores, to the great comfort and relief of the newly appointed bishop, for his mitre was set thick with thorns, of which the lack of priests to share his burden was by no means the least painful. His jurisdiction extended over an immense extent of country, newly settled, agitated by a seven years' war, with most uncertain and uncomfortable means of travelling, when there were any means at all; his people ignorant and undisciplined, always misjudged, sometimes bitterly persecuted, often hated and despised; the priests who were the captains of his scattered army, were sometimes the most faithless and incompetent of officers, others, zealous and fervent as heart could wish, were, for various reasons, such as foreign education obtained, often, at great sacrifices and without regularity, ignorance of the language and customs of the country, a serious annoyance instead of assistance, while again one filled with the true Catholic spirit, devoted to his religion with absorbing veneration, reverencing it in spirit and truth, would find himself transplanted from the cultured and pious circle in which he had lived from childhood, to a wild settlement,-to take charge of a rough congregation, rude, untaught, unteachable, victims of cruellest oppression and hopeless poverty, to whom their religion was scarcely more than a name, and so mixed and mingled with the fancies and superstitions of ignorance that it was hardly recognizable, where he would be attacked as madly as by a wild animal battling for her young, should he attempt, as religion and conscience command, to separate the truth from its network of falsehood, and wash the dirt of superstition from the face of religion, so that the bitterer torments of the mind, the crushing burdens of the spirit were added to the physical pangs to which he was constantly exposed, hunger and cold, lonely and defenceless nights in the howling wilderness, the countless trials and terrors of a missionary's life. The surest hope for any country, most of all for a new world like ours, native priests, the bishop could hardly hope for in his own day, but knowing the inestimable necessity he caught at the first prospect of providing for them in the future, which was held out to him in letters received while in England to be consecrated, from Mr. Emery, Superior-General of the Society of Saint Sulpice of France, who, anxious to secure a shelter for his Society, which he foresaw would not escape the fury of the revolutionists, wished to know what refuge could be offered by the young republic. "This correspondence resulted in the arrival at Baltimore in 1791 of Mr. Nagot with three Sulpician priests and several seminarians, with some means towards establishing a seminary to educate priests for the United States. They had in their charge a young nobleman of France, Viscomte François de Chateaubriand, who like the young Prince Gallitzin, alarmed by the excesses of the French revolution which made European tours unpleasant, even dangerous, had decided to finish his education by a visit to the United States, hoping to make himself famous by the discovery of a Northwest passage to the Polar Sea, and, having spent a few days in Baltimore, hastened to present introductions to Washington and the leading statesmen of the day. Mr. Nagot and his clerical companions set themselves at work with all earnestness to fulfill their far greater ambition, purchasing a house as quickly as possible, and preparing it as well as circumstances permitted, for the opening of the college and seminary. They were soon joined by a little band of French priests, whose names are set in such shining letters in our history, that we can hardly imagine their first coming, heart heavy exiles from the beloved land of France, their sunny youth clouded by their country's dissensions, their own persecutions, and the gloomy parting from home and friends, and national customs, to seek a home in a far land, where poverty and toil alone awaited them. But poverty and toil were not their only welcome, for, as they were about calling upon Bishop Carroll, immediately after their arrival, they were met by him, "on foot", as they noticed with intense surprise, coming to call on them; and when with all deference, they disclaimed the high honor, the noble answer of the bishop: "Gentlemen, you have come thousands of miles to see me, shall I not walk a few squares to see you?" was an earnest of the greeting of the whole American heart to them for all time.

These were Rev. John Dubois, a young priest of peculiarly energetic character, joined to most gentle and winning manners, Rev. Messrs. Benedict Flaget, John B. David, Francis Matignon, Ambrose Maréchal, Gabriel Richard, and Francis Ciquard. The Abbé Stephen Badin, who was not yet ordained, but had received all the other orders in France, arrived with the first, the Rev. Messrs. Louis Dubourg, John Moranville, John Lefevre Cheverus, and others, came a year or so later. All placed themselves with utmost willingness at Bishop Carroll's disposal, remained for longer or shorter periods in Baltimore and its vicinity, studying English, laboring faithfully at every priestly duty, attending missions, aiding the bishop, teaching for Mr. Nagot, then separated, some for far distant missions, North, South, East, and West, where their names are in benediction.

Thus it was far from being a princely palace to which Mr. Brosius and Mitri directed their steps, when hastening to present their letters to the bishop, and to be made acquainted with his little band of laborers, but Mitri's heart was won at once by the kindness of the stately bishop, while he felt by no means among strangers with the rest, for French was the language of his home, as it was at that time of many European families. With these young Frenchmen he could converse on subjects familiar to him, but the bishop did not fail to make his young guest acquainted with society supposed to be more congenial to his youth and his high ambition, and procured him cordial welcome in many of the most charming Baltimore families, regretting greatly that he could not permit Mr. Brosius to accompany his young charge through the country, as the princess desired and expected. In the great lack of priests, at that time, each had the work of ten, sometimes of more, and not one could be spared from active service, nor could the bishop expose Mitri to the delays and uncertainties which would be inevitable if he followed Mr. Brosius to his mission, for in those days when all our priests were missionaries, no one could be said to be stationary; each had many congregations to attend, scattered far apart, seldom with any roads between, and what roads there were terrible ones to travel; no argument of course could be needed to show that it was out of the question for the delicate young prince to be exposed to the dangers, the fatigue, the poor lodging and plain fare of the best of these missions. In compensation the bishop offered him letters to families in Washington, Philadelphia, and other cities, who would delight in extending all courtesies to him, and in their turn would make his visits elsewhere easy and agreeable. So Mitri remained a little while looking about Baltimore, "having," as he said himself, "nothing in view but to pursue his journey through the States, and to qualify himself for his original vocation." He was treated with the utmost kindness and confidence, and, with true American frankness, politics, religion, the welfare and the embarrassments of the country and of the Church, were freely discussed in his presence, although his boyish reserve and the gravity which he felt it necessary to assume, now that he was thrown upon himself in a strange land, might sometimes have chilled the speakers, but for the earnest deference with which he took part in every discussion, as a matter of politeness, as well as of intellectual duty. There was no guide near to prevent him from receiving other people's impressions, or to mould his own, for Mr. Brosius either could not or would not attempt the dominion over his mind which had been exercised, often unconsciously, by the princess and her advisers; in a few days he had seen and heard enough to enable him to observe the peace of the people he was now with, in contrast with the tumult of old world troubles, too painfully familiar to him, and then the purpose of his life came to him in plain shape, and he lost no time in telling the bishop that he had no desire for further travels, no wish to return to Europe, save, perhaps, as a visitor, at some future day, for his heart had found its resting place, *even Thy altars, O Lord of Hosts*, if the bishop would accept him for their service.

He had been led to this decision, he said, because "the unexpected and incredible progress of the Jacobins, the subversion of social order and religion, and the dreadful convulsions in all the countries of Europe on one side, compared with the tranquil, peaceable and happy situation of the United States, together with some considerations, naturally suggested by these events, on the vanity of worldly grandeur and preferment.... caused him.... to renounce his schemes of pride and ambition and to embrace the clerical profession for the benefit of the American mission."

There was undoubtedly much in this decision to embarrass the bishop. Through the letter of the Prince-bishop of Hildesheim as well as from Mr. Brosius and other sources, he must have known, though very little was said about it, that "Mr. Schmet's" parents had far other designs for him, and it was not likely his father, at least, would willingly consent to his becoming a priest, at all events not in the humble American Church, and unquestionably he knew the set accusations which the world always brings against the Church, when one from whose rank or wealth it hopes much for its own selfish ends, leaves it for God. Still, there was but one question he had a right to consider in regard to the young candidate, was it his vocation? If so, rich or poor, prince or peasant, all the same must be his reception. But the Church is never hasty in admitting any one into her sanctuary, for well she knows that one traitor, coward, or laggard in her camp is more dangerous than a regiment of open enemies in battle array; and the more they bring to her which gives them wider influence or higher place, the more careful must she be in putting into their hands the sword which may be made as powerful against her own children as against her enemies.

The bishop, therefore, thought best in Mr. Brosius' necessary absence, to invite the young prince to make his home at the seminary, there to reflect well upon his future career, while with Mr. Nagot he himself maturely considered the application he had made to enter the service of the Church, and knowing well the charges given the young man by his father, the bishop desired him, at the same time, to apply himself carefully to the study of the constitution, laws, manners, and geography of the country, and to assist him in doing so, took him with him when visiting different parts of his diocese, taking him into the home circle of the most distinguished American families; in the books of the Sulpician seminary at Baltimore it is recorded that the frank and "honest manners of the young Prince Gallitzin, and his excellent education gave Bishop Carroll the liveliest pleasure during this journey, but he was astonished to find that he travelled only with reluctance, and that nothing could make him forget his beloved seminary; a most precious disposition which the prelate considered a certain sign of his vocation to the ecclesiastical state, as was indeed the opinion of all who knew him." In truth it was soon apparent that Mitri had

" no other ambition than to acquire the science of the saints, and every day to die to himself and the world."

"That which I have learned of you, Madame, from Mr. Brosius and from your son," wrote Bishop Carroll, in French, to the princess, Dec. 13th, 1792, "adds to my veneration for your virtues, and binds me to interest myself still more in the welfare of Mr. Gallitzin. I believed the best thing I could do, to respond to the confidence with which you have honored me, was to place him here under my own eyes, at the seminary which is just being formed in this city. This establishment is well furnished with excellent professors: piety, the greatest regularity, the love of study and seclusion are its characteristics. It is under the presidency of a French priest of the highest virtue, Mr. Nagot, late first director of the grand Seminary of Saint Sulpice at Paris, but by the changes in France forced to seek an asylum here. I have put your son in his hands for the direction of his conscience, and surely he could not be better placed in order to respond to the views which Providence seems to have for him. I have the pleasure of telling you that so far his conduct is all that the virtuous and saintly Monica could desire in her dear Augustine, and I am persuaded that his future conduct will not belie its present beautiful presages."

In Mitri's own mind there had never been a moment's hesitation; scarcely had he stepped upon American soil than he felt through all his frame the thrilling sense of a work upon it awaiting him, and the psychological, politico-philosophical observations he was to make, according to Fuerstenberg's programme, all rounded and met in this that he saw the *harvest indeed is great but the laborers few.* He saw the young priests, born to ease and wealth, enter with light hearts upon their toilsome life, and though often, as he knew, hard pressed for the necessities of the rudest existence, adapting themselves to their work with even more than the " gentle courtesies and nameless grace of France," regarding their own heroism as worth no more than the point of a merry story, and he knew that these were they whom the world holds *in derision and for a parable of reproach,* whose life was esteemed *madness and their end without honor;* he saw the poverty, the need of the Church, the hungry souls crying in vain for the bread of life, and the hours were too long, the days went by too slowly until he could hasten to their relief.

Thus Mitri Gallitzin, at twenty two years of age, in full possession of all his faculties, knowing well what world he threw behind him, and what world was before him, made his deliberate choice, *choosing rather to be an abject in the house of the Lord than to dwell in the tabernacles of sinners,* and striving day and night so to live that the Lord would give him to *dwell in that house all the days of his life.*

CHAPTER VII.
WHAT THE WORLD SAID.
(1792—1795.)

Opinion of Rev. Fr. Schnoesenberg. — Vexation of the princess. — Confidence of Mr. Nagot and the bishop in Mitri's vocation. — Views and letters of Rev. Dr. Overberg, Baron von Fuerstenberg, General von Schmettau, and Prince Gallitzin. — Their effect upon Demetrius.

The one great thing in choosing our state in life is to know the will of God, and for what he designed, fitted, and now calls us, the first persons to be consulted in regard to it, are those whom God has ordained his representatives, and to whom we have confided the direction of our conscience. Therefore, as soon as Mitri felt that God called him to the priestly state, he asked counsel not only of the bishop and of his present director, Mr. Nagot, but wrote at once to his former confessor, Rev. Mr. Schnoesenberg, a Franciscan, in Muenster, opening to him the desire which had taken possession of his soul, explaining the need of missionaries in the United States, asking advice from him who had so long known his interior life, and requesting the reverend gentleman to break the news to the princess, telling her that he had "devoted himself heart and soul, mind and strength to the service of God and the salvation of his fellow-men in America; a resolution made because of the urgent need of workmen in the vineyard of the Lord; for the priests of this country," he wrote, "have often to travel forty and fifty miles and more, to carry the Last Sacraments to the sick. It was to be hoped that the severe labor which such a life demanded would cause them to acknowledge the truth of his vocation." Mitri, in his humility, and the restraint which he had ever felt in his mother's presence, had little doubt that the reverend father, who had himself vowed to leave the world, father and mother and all for God, would be much better able than he to place before her the spiritual advantages to be gained, which should soothe her loving heart for the temporal ones renounced by this decision, and encourage her noble mind, with all the experience and authority of his mature years and holy habit, to bear for her beloved son the bitter trials of a poor missionary's life, in consideration of the inexpressible delights which God showers upon those who serve him.

Confident that the wisdom and piety of his confessor would present his case in the most spiritual and consoling manner, and knowing how slowly letters travelled in those days, and how often, long before a letter was received, nearly all it contained might be changed and forgotten, Mitri quietly settled to his new life, applying himself in all earnestness to test and prove the truth of his vocation, shutting out the world, thinking, speaking, living, only in spiritual things.

It happened that this letter to his confessor, Mr. Schnoesenberg, arrived in good time at Muenster, and was not falsified before being read. It caused the good Franciscan great perplexity; it appears he had not quite taken off the old man before putting on the new, an omission which often gives trouble even when, as in this case, a compromise appears to be effected between God and Mammon. He congratulated himself, however, upon the absence of the princess from Muenster which excused him, he thought, from any explanation to her. He modestly forbore giving the young seminarian any advice whatsoever, feeling himself released from any expression of opinion by the knowledge that Mr. Nagot, "a man of great merit and high spiritual distinction, and even Bishop Carroll were fully convinced of his penitent's vocation and fitness for the life chosen," and careful not to say anything which might displease the princess and her distinguished husband, not considering, as Gallitzin told him later, "that I did not address you as my mother's friend, but as my confessor," he put the young man's letter out of sight, and said not a word about it to any one, not even to the writer.

In the meantime the bishop and Mr. Nagot wrote to the princess to assure her of her son's health and contentment, alluding to the designs God appeared to have in his regard, not saying what they were, however, for they supposed her already acquainted with them through Rev. Mr. Schnoesenberg to whom Mitri had confided all. As time passed and no answer arrived, the young prince, who easily took fire when he considered himself or another wronged, and in his hot headed zeal could understand nothing that took the form of passive religion or spiritual neutrality, wrote again and this time with considerable vigor and sharpness, repeating that which he had said before concerning his vocation, and insisting upon an opinion of some kind, heading the letter: *sub sigillo confessionis* — under the seal of confession.

This letter also reached Muenster in course of time, and was sent with some others under cover to the princess, as the reverend gentleman relates*.

Rev. Mr. Schnoesenberg to Prince D. A. Gallitzin.

"Instead of sending your letter to me at the monastery, she (the princess) sent for me to come to her. I went at once. As soon as I entered the room where she was, she said, with sadness and depression, if I mistake not, "Here are letters from my son, one short and of no importance to me, a much heavier one for you; it is here on the table, will you open it and see what it is he desires?" I did as she requested, unhesitatingly, and was about to read it when Baron von Fuerstenberg entered the room; as I found I had forgotten

---

* See *Leben und Wirken des Prinzen Demetrius Augustin Gallitzin*, von P. Heinrich Lemcke, p. 96. — This is one of the letters which Rev. Mr. Lemcke found among Prince Gallitzin's papers, carried away with him from Loretto, and translated from Latin and French into German for his "*Leben*", from which, as the originals cannot be recovered, they are of necessity retranslated for this work.

my spectacles I asked Mr. Overberg, who was also present, to read it aloud. How I felt during that reading, in what embarrassment the reader found himself, you may imagine. I cannot express the sorrow which filled my heart when I saw your mother so deeply dejected. Baron von Fuerstenberg maintained a profound silence, and I fully realized that I, though entirely without fault of mine, was the cause of this distressing scene."

It is not to be wondered at, after this, that the diplomatic friar entreated to be spared any further confidences from his late penitent. But he was in every way inexcusable, because he knew the state of affairs with the writer before the arrival of this letter, and that it was not likely to be one well to read aloud.

In consequence of this second letter from the young prince to Rev. Mr. Schnoesenberg, the news of Mitri's singular purpose became known to all his mother's circle at once, and was the all absorbing theme of conversation. The princess soon wrote to Mr. Nagot, very plainly intimating that she had no faith in Mitri's vocation, and not much, if the truth were told, in the disinterestedness of his advisers. Mitri to her was a straw blown about by every wind; she was terrified at the thought of being the mother of an incompetent or unworthy priest, thoroughly vexed at those who had, either consciously or unconsciously, deceived themselves into a belief that he was fitted for the great duties which would devolve upon him, and, foreseeing with morbid fears the storm certain to burst upon her own head on account of it, could hardly help attributing unworthy motives, and undue influence on the part of those to whom she had confided her child, who had, probably, been dazzled by his position and prospective wealth.

Mr. Nagot and the bishop, both did their utmost to disabuse her of this idea, by endeavoring to convince her, as they were themselves convinced, that Mitri was a chosen one of God, upon whom the Lord would bestow a great priesthood indeed. "If his is not a true vocation," wrote

Mr. Nagot, "then there is no standard by which a true vocation can be tested." "Never have I led to the altar a young man of whose vocation I was more certain," he assured her upon another occasion, and that he might not be considered partial, he added the testimony of the bishop and of all who knew Prince Demetrius, to the same effect. To Mitri she wrote asking him to tell her honestly if on account of having resided at the seminary, he had felt himself bound to accede to the wishes of those who controlled it, to which Mitri replied that his resolve had been taken at once, that he was in no ways influenced, and was free to leave at any time he pleased. She represented to him the bitter disappointment this would cause his father, who she believed would certainly disinherit him, and would never forgive her; she expatiated on the terrible responsibilities of the state he intended embracing, and warned him of the faightful account he would have to render, if he should force himself into a place to which God's grace had not called him. It was full a year after hearing of his choice before, becoming at last convinced that he knew what he was about, she wrote him a word of sympathy or consolation, which, on account of the great delays in sending letters, brought it to him about the time of his ordination, but having once accepted his vocation as a real one, her fears and gloomy forebodings subsided, and she threw herself heart and soul into his new interests, and rejoiced with her whole heart, at having a son capable of a choice so pure, and a perseverance so rare.

Dr. Overberg, at the princess' request, also wrote to Mitri immediately after the announcement of his choice, which had fallen like a thunderbolt upon the circle at Muenster; his letter was kind, but undecided. He was a good and amiable man, devoted to his duties, which ran along quietly enough, and was taken entirely by surprise by the new world ideas so suddenly bursting upon the stillness of Muenster life. The old world had rolled on in its own ruts for so long, that it was just then rather difficult, even for a good old priest, whose life had been one of loving regularity, all in the usual way, whose humble parents thanked God every day for his position, which was, even in the eyes of the world, a most honorable one, to take in, at a glance, the fiery longing of a young heart, long chafing under old chains, for the open field, for real sacrifices, earnest toil, and apostolic labor. He was devotedly attached to the princess, had known Mitri from childhood, and disliked very much to see either of them unhappy. He commended patience and passiveness for a time, thought it better to take no decided step just yet, and remarked to him, as Gamaliel to the Jews: *If this counsel or this work be of men, it will come to naught, but if it be of God ye cannot overthrow it.*

Baron von Fuerstenberg wrote less affectionately and more decidedly; he evidently was very much of General von Schmettau's opinion, although he expressed it more mildly than suited the old soldier's temperament, that the young man had fallen into the hands of a set of enthusiasts, — the general called them bigots and fanatics, — who had beguiled him into forgetfulness of his rank, his family, all the comforts and honors of life. If he must needs become a priest, the very reverend and greatly distinguished baron advised him to return at once to Europe, where his friends would endeavor to procure him a position worthy of his exalted station.

Before entering the seminary, while the matter of his vocation was yet under consideration, Mitri went to Philadelphia, probably by the bishop's advice, for his own mind was made up, to consult with Mr. Brosius, and knowing the great interest his father would take in all concerning the country, he took pains, with real filial affection, to write him a full and complete description of the journey, no short one in those days, but, of course, as they were not yet settled, he said nothing about his future plans, and the prince naturally fancied he was pursuing his travels through the Union, as so much desired. He was very much mortified, afterwards, at this reticence, and considered his son had not been altogether frank with him, but before receiving any of the minor orders Mitri wrote, formally announcing to his father what choice in life he had made.

7

Previous to the reception of this letter the prince wrote to his wife:

.   PRINCE GALLITZIN TO THE PRINCESS*.

At the Hague, Jan. 20th 1794.

At a moment when I did not dream of such a thing, Mr. C. sends me an Order, which he was directed to deliver to me; an Order for Mitri to join his regiment within six months, as by seniority of rank, he should receive his commission on the first of this month. I send the Order in a literal translation. I wrote at once to the First Major, stating that I had sent my son to America to travel for his further improvement, as I had not ventured to allow him to go over Europe, on account of the lawlessness and immorality everywhere rampant; that he was to have come back this year, but I could not hasten his return, as, since his departure, crossing the ocean has become very dangerous, the French having declared war against England, Holland, and Spain. I wrote at the same time to my brother requesting him to see about it. As the Count von Romanzow is in your neighborhood, I beg you, my dear friend, to seek his advice, and put the settling of the affair into his hands. I have also written to day to C*** asking him to do what he can for us; he probably can do much through his friends at court. He tells me he would have visited you, the other day, but you were not in Muenster. Adieu, my love, I love and embrace you with all my heart.

In the Order, accompanying this letter, it was stated that if the young ensign to whom it was addressed, did not appear to receive his commission as higher officer of the guard, within the time stated, he would be altogether excluded from his regiment. By means of his father's influence, and that of his distinguished friends, an extension of his leave was obtained, or some modification of the order, and the prince anxiously awaited his son's return, urging the princess to insist upon it.

---

* *Leben und Wirken*, by Rev. P. H. Lemcke, p. 113.

PRINCE GALLITZIN TO THE PRINCESS*.

At the Hague, Feb. 16th, 1794.

I have not said anything to you, my dearest, concerning my special intentions in regard to Mitri, because, in the first place, I have none, except to have him come back as soon as possible; after that, I do not see how we can avoid sending him to Russia. My brother, from whom I have a letter dated Jan. 3rd, tells me that it is absolutely necessary for him to go to Petersburg, where, he says, he will be at once commissioned officer of the guard. Should he have no inclination for military service, he could receive a civil appointment besides, probably in the diplomatic line, in which, on account of his military rank, he would be placed higher than could otherwise be expected. But nothing can be done until he reports himself in person at St. Petersburg.

The testimony of the Bishop of Baltimore to his excellent conduct gives me great satisfaction. God grant he may find in my native land people to judge him as justly! Simplicity and naturalness are not prized so highly there as in America, I fear that he will be judged by the outer bark, which, perhaps, is not so rough and knotty as it was before he left us, travelling often makes great changes in the manners of young people, and, after all, in the end, every thing depends upon the tailor and the hair dresser. When once he sees the necessity of being well got up, and befrizzled like other people, he will have no difficulty in showing himself off to the best advantage.

The princess hastened to enclose both these letters, and the Order, to her son, accompanying them with a very earnest letter of her own, under date of March 20th, 1794.

PRINCESS GALLITZIN TO HER SON†.

My dear son,

The decisive moment of your whole life on earth, which, it is true, should serve you only as a preparation for eternity,

---

* Lemcke, p. 115.
† Same, p. 109.

has now come, as you will see from the letters of your father which I enclose. They leave only two courses open to you.

First, if you intend to remain in the world, you must go at once to Russia, as the empress orders, and enter upon the career for which your father has always intended you.

Secondly: If you are really determined to enter the sacerdotal state, you must at once inform your father of your intention, in a respectful manner, but so decidedly that there shall be no room left for doubt of your intention, or for hope of changing it, either by flatteries, or by threats of disinheritance, the only ones he can use against you; but even the law will prevent him from taking everything from you.

She even enclosed him a formula, made out by the astute Fuerstenberg, which he was to copy and send to his father, lest, by his own want of tact, he might not make his purpose clear enough, or so clear as to arouse the prince's anger, and peril his inheritance. In the meantime she herself devised all possible means of averting her husband's wrath, when the American choice could no longer be concealed.

The news reached the prince, at last, at a time when the princess was quite ill, and very much depressed by her physical sufferings, as well as by her mental anxiety.

Prince Gallitzin to the Princess*.

Jan. 12th, 1795.

Above all things, I pray you, my dear friend, to try to unite with me as friends, reasonably and coolly to discuss that which is properly our common trouble, and by what means to get out of it. I entreat you to put aside every idea which could tempt you to believe that I would willingly cause you vexation or annoyance. I protest on my honor, before God, that I have no wish to do so, and if, here and there, an expression in this letter should remotely suggest such a thing, believe me it is rather because I lack the

---

* Lemcke, p. 126.

power to express myself better, than because I would intentionally grieve you. Alas! why should I, when I know that whatever befals us grieves you even more than it does me! But to the subject.

First, what do you wish me to write to Mitri? I beg you to tell me and advise me. It appears to me that on his side everything is settled, and he does not wait for our letters before deciding whether he will return to Europe or not, and that by his conduct he cares neither for my consent nor for my opinion; but I pledge you my word that if I were to see him again, I would receive him in the kindest manner, and would not permit one harsh word to pass my lips, much less ever to act towards him in anger or in an imperious way. I have already exhausted all arguments in his regard, and it is now his turn to give me better reasons than I have given him.. In regard to his writing me I see in his letters only an enthusiast who, in his overstrained mind, abuses the laws of the gospel, and derives conclusions from them which are thoroughly false and unworthy of the Deity; for instance, "Christ says, who loves father and mother more than me is not worthy of me." Be it so, I find that entirely reasonable, but how conclude from this that one must become a priest? To follow Christ, to be worthy of him, says no more, and can imply no more, than that we should follow the religion he has given us, and exactly fulfill our duties. Nowhere does this religion tell us that in order to fulfill the duties it imposes upon us, we must become priests, and I should like to ask Mitri if he who throws his father and mother and sister into despair is worthy of Christ. But all our arguments, as I believe, are of no avail, and you will see that everything is already settled.

Tell me, therefore, I beg you, in the second place, should I not now inform my brother? He never writes to me now without asking when Mitri will be back, and adds that he will not be dismissed from his regiment before the first of January, and that he will try to keep him in even longer. Now that we know what we are to believe in regard to Mitri, if seems to me I should look like an intriguer, if I put off my brother, even the court, any longer, to await his arrival in St. Petersburg. This might bring me into even greater difficulties than those in which I am now involved, in consequence of this odd vocation, and especially this singular intention, if it be not already an accomplished fact.

Thirdly, Mitri intimates that he voluntarily resigns his inheritance. He does not know that by entering the clerical profession he is already disinherited, not by me indeed (for I assure you I have never had such an idea), but by the laws of our country. There is no instance in our annals of one of his rank becoming a priest; some have become monks, it is true, and in this case the first thing is a vow of poverty, by which all is renounced, and if the new brother has not first given every thing to the monastery, the family immediately takes possession of it. But Mitri can do nothing of the kind, for all is mine and will, therefore, go to Mimi. I know she is honest and magnanimous, and would be too conscientious to deprive a brother that she might enrich herself. Still, she could not save the estates for him, if she were to renounce them the family would at once take possession of them without any difficulty, you know I have several nephews.

If you think best you can send him this letter, and thus relieve me from the painful necessity of writing him. However, I think when a nobleman unconditionally renounces the military service, for which his birth destines him, he has no choice but to become a missionary, or to lock himself up in a monastery, if he would prove to the world that he abandons his proper station, neither from cowardice nor from ambitious motives.

The princess, not being able to write herself, requested Dr. Overberg to enclose this letter, and write to Mitri, which he did, giving many interesting details, and an account of the final conclusion into which his parents and their circle had settled for the present.

Rev. Bernard Overberg to Prince D. A. Gallitzin.*

Beloved in our Lord Jesus Christ,

"I have not written to you in a long time, but I have not on that account ceased to remember you in my prayers. And how could I forget you when I have daily before my eyes a mother who loves you so much, and sacrifices herself for your welfare, who has already suffered greatly on your account, and has to bear constantly sufferings of a different character, which are, in part, at least, the consequence of the loving sacrifices she has made for you? You may have learned from your father's letters somewhat of the trials which afflict her body, but you would know nothing of her love if you judged only from those letters; it is of such a degree that your father could not possibly comprehend it. How disinterested, how persevering, how active, how like, therefore, to the divine love, is her love for her Augustine! How much she has borne, through this love, during your absence, seems known neither to Augustine nor to the reverend president. I would wish above all things to bring this love before your eyes, for I doubt not it would be pleasing and salutary to you in many respects, and I would love to lay it upon your heart, but I feel I am not capable of doing it as I would desire. I should have to write a book if I were to undertake to say all that could be said of it. I mention it, however, in order to accompany your father's letter, as your mother is too ill to write herself, and to give you some news of her, which she herself would probably not write you.

I said you seemed not to understand the sufferings she has endured in your absence, on your account. Her fortitude in them shows her love, so I design giving you an outline of them. They were indeed terrible. All, except our little circle, were opposed to your purpose of becoming a priest, and in America. Some who heard of it cried out against it as if it were something contemptible, others regarded it as a sign of cowardice and of indolence; the better-natured

---

* Rev. H. Lemcke, p. 131.

looked upon it as boyish enthusiam, as recklessness and thoughtlessness; all turned with their public or private reproaches to your mother, who, in their eyes, was to blame for this monstrous wrong, as they called it; your father at the head, your uncle following, but more gently, out of love for his sister; then came the part of the public which was more or less interested in your choice. She had to defend against these not only her Augustine but herself, and, consequently, there was many a sharp contest. But there was more to come; our friends who kept behind at first, murmured more and more loudly, when letters from America seemed more and more to indicate, that not only were your friends disregarded, but even your mother, and such a mother, from which they inferred that the vocation was a doubtful one, for the example of St. Francis Xavier, and of many other saints, shows the true call to the apostolic profession, does not dissolve the ties of spiritual friendship, but only draws them the closer. Here again she had her Augustine and herself to defend. All these contests but served as an accompaniment, so to speak, of the severest conflict, and of the heart-breaking suffering she experienced when she felt herself bound to reveal to the president the past and present faults of her Augustine, in order that his vocation might be fully tested, and in this her distress was the more overpowering because every answer showed that the purity of her motives was questioned, which would not have been the case had her son made his mother's character known to the president, as it was he even treated her as one who, for temporal satisfaction, would tear her son from the Lord. But even this she endured for the love of God and of Augustine. She sought only to find in each letter from America, clearer proofs of the vocation, to know if Augustine persevered, and she thanked God with tears when new indications of this came. How could she do otherwise when it was the deepest wish of her heart, that the son who had cost her so many tears, might work out his own salvation, and become, in the hands of God, a useful instrument for the salvation of other souls, redeemed by the blood of Jesus?

She has already begun to see in part the consequences of her faithful perseverance, for God has turned the whole matter in a manner truly wonderful, so that not only your father, but all for whom during the first two years of your absence, everything heard of you, was food for scandal, are since last spring, as entirely in favor of Augustine's choice, as they were in the beginning opposed to it. For the glory of Divine Providence I will briefly relate how this came to pass.

We were in the greatest anxiety, as you may imagine, lest there should come a tremendous storm, when your father should receive news that his son was to become a priest in America. This dread was the less unfounded, because, as you know, there had been a great outburst when once before, while here, you intimated to him that you would like to be a priest. We all prayed, therefore, for a good result, and your mother made use of all natural means in her power to further it. She knew that he was coming to Berlin, and she let the news rest until then, and informed her brother of it, begging him to influence Princess Ferdinand to help him in moderating the anger with which your father would probably receive the tidings, and to induce her to attempt to avert, if possible, the disinheritance which was feared. As we knew the influence exercised upon him by the opinion of the great of this world, we hoped much, through God's grace, from the combined assistance of your uncle and the princess. The result far exceeded our expectations, for which God willed an advantageous circumstance, even did not prevent an error, but one by no means as great as that by which Joseph was led from a prison to the throne. The circumstance was this: Your mother feeling too ill to write had been obliged to dictate to Mimi, and your uncle was asked to give the letter, which contained the news of your becoming a priest, to your father. When he read it, and your uncle and the princess saw the storm pictured in his face, they hastened to represent the affair as not only not dishonoring his family, but even honorable, at least in this, that such a step showed energy. All the princess' court united in expressing the same opinion, and thus his anger was moderated; the idea, however, remained hateful to him, as you may have seen from your uncle's letter to your mother, which has already been sent you. It was hateful to him, because he looked upon it as the grave in which was forever buried the splendor of his family, and his hopes of bringing that family to the highest dignity in the Russian court, and this was all the more painful the less he knew, or sought, any other dignity. The opinion of the great people, as I have said, moderated his wrath, but there had been no judgment passed on your mother, and as she in his opinion, was the cause of it all, his whole rage would have turned upon her, and would have caused terrible scenes, had not God permitted your uncle to make a mistake, which she would by no means have permitted if she had known it; he made use of her illness, saying it was the consequence of trouble and fright at Augustine's decision, and that it would be dangerous for her life for any one to dare let her know the father's dissatisfaction, etc. This falsehood led your father, glad to find her agreeing with him in the affair, to write her a letter of consolation, and when he came to see her afterwards he said not a word about Mitri, fearing to trouble her mind again. He continued, however, to complain of you, until a second circumstance changed all to congratulation.

The Empress of Russia died. On this your father rested all his hopes. The present emperor* had, as your father believed, a very great regard for him, having even treated him as an intimate friend. As he was now raised to the throne, your father believed the highest place of honor at the

---

* It will be remembered that Catharine died in 1796 after a reign of thirty four years, and was succeeded by her son Paul, whom she detested, regarded as an imbecile, and meant should never come to the throne, which she destined for her grandson Alexander. But Paul succeeding her, banished her friends, showered favors upon her enemies, and altogether conducted himself in a most tyrannical manner, with even more than the usual eccentricity of uncontrolled passions and unlimited despotism. He was assassinated in 1801, and succeeded by his son, Alexander I.

imperial court was awaiting him. In this expectation he wrote the emperor, not to ask anything of him for that, indeed, he considered altogether superfluous, but because he thought it proper to offer his services and congratulations; he was not even honored with an answer! From that moment his language in regard to courts and court-life underwent as great a change as about religion, for it was evident to him that with the disregard of religion was connected the disregard of the nobility, and its persecution. The once stupid and simple Mitri was now commended as wise and happy, because by the step he had taken he had saved himself from the slavery of court-life, from the ingratitude of the great, etc.

You would often wonder, dear Augustine, even be astounded, if you could see with us the change that has come over the aristocrats who have no religion, since the French Revolution.

These were not tranquillizing letters to be sent to a young seminarian, whose heart and soul were absorbed in preparation for the sacred office of priesthood, who was seeking in seclusion, to forget the world for a while, that he might try on his armor, and in most intimate communion with God learn all his desires, and receive his commands, as the knights of old kept their vigil before receiving their spurs. The writers could by no means put themselves in his place, and it was even more impossible for him to open the deep recesses of his heart, just now wrapt in stillness, and lighted with soft gleams of sacred fire from the Holy Spirit Himself, for discussion even by his own mother and her pious friends. But so far from interfering with his resolution, they but made him cling the firmer to it, and shut him still more closely into the retirement of the spiritual life he had chosen.

CHAPTER VIII.

ORDINATION AND FIRST MISSIONS.

(1795—1799.)

Characteristics of his seminary life. — Receives minor orders. — Joins the Society of Saint Sulpice. — Is ordained by Bishop Carroll. — Mission at Port Tobacco. — Stationed at Baltimore. — At Conewago. —Visits the Alleghany mountains. — Spirit manifestations. — Visits Cliptown, Va. — Difficulties with his congregations. — Accepts the call to McGuire's Settlement.

Notwithstanding the opposition of his friends, the sneers of his enemies, the doubts even of his own mother, Prince Demetrius persevered in the choice he had made. His seminary life was most beautiful and edifying, glimpses of it still preserved are most touching, and, to worldly eyes, possibly a little overstrained; the exquisite delicacy of his conscience under the severe rule of the seminary, filled him with the greatest remorse, and caused him to rejoice when his confessor permitted him to resort to more than the usual penance and mortification whenever a sudden temptation to vexation at a reproof, a quick, sarcastic word when nettled, a delight in ridicule, or a momentary glance at some fair face in the chapel, or passing his window, showed him his predominant failings. If under the rigid watch which he kept over himself to mould every thought in the way of perfection, one could find any special characteristics more marked them others, they would be, a tendency to intensity in whatever he undertook, to absorption in his work, a readiness of speech and to form decided opinions, a lively sense of the ridiculous and the stupid, and a mind more active than contemplative, "But the good God," says his last entry in his seminary note book, "but the good God gives me many graces, notwithstanding my faithlessness. Among others, on the day when I should have gone to the Adoration of the Blessed Sacrament, I felt an extreme reluctance for this Adoration, so much so that I did not know how I could endure to spend half an hour in prayer; but little by little this dryness was, by the goodness of God, changed into the very sweetest consolation."

These were the crisis days of his interior life, and if he permitted himself little freedom, it was because he was as one passing from one precipitous mountain to another, crossing upon a single plank, over the most frightful abyss, who knows that the swerving of an eyelid, or one heart-throb the more, may cause him to lose his steadiness, and whirl him into the terrible depths beneath. It is not until long after such a one has gone well over the broad fields, and up the gentle slopes of the safer side, that he breathes freely, relaxes his muscles, or ventures to look

"at even
A pretty child, or God's blue heaven."

On account of his rare proficiency in other branches, he was able, as soon as the bishop released him from the study of the American geography, history, and form of government, which were so distasteful to him at that time, to devote himself to his theological course, in which he made such clear and rapid advance that in the summer of 1794, he was found fully prepared to receive the minor orders, and on the twenty-first of November, of the same year, feast of the Presentation of the Blessed Virgin, he was made subdeacon.

"At the commencement of January," says his little French note book, "God gave me the desire to unite myself to the Society of the Sulpicians. Communicating this to Mr. Nagot, he advised me to refer it to our Lord; this desire continues as if it were already accomplished." The members of this Society are bound together by no special vows or obligations of conscience, but by mutual good will and affection, and as Mitri more and more desired to be received as one of them, its superiors, having a loving regard for his many virtues, his charming character, his straightforward piety, and the many marks of sanctity which he already unconsciously manifested, convinced, by its steady continuance, that the desire was from God, cordially accepted it, after a year's trial, and with the approval of Bishop Carroll, enrolled him a member of their admirable society, on the 13th of February 1795, while he was yet only a deacon.

On the 18th of March 1795, one of the Spring Ember days, in less than three years from the time of his leaving Europe, the desire of the young prince's heart was fulfilled, and with the most fervent dispositions, he received the Ordination which Bishop Carroll administered with a solemnity and emotion beyond all power of description. For though the second priest ordained by Bishop Carroll, and in the United States, Prince Gallitzin could truly be considered the firstborn of the American Church; Rev. Stephen Badin, ordained some time previously, had been made a deacon before leaving his native land, France, and the United States gave him only the final consecration and commission, but Father Gallitzin was all our own. Ours from the first page of his theology to the moment he arose from the consecrating hands of the bishop, forever and forever to bear the seal of the Lord's Anointed. He had not come to us for a day or an hour, in an interval of trial or trouble, but in the brightest hour of his prosperity, for all the days of his life, to know no country but our country, no work but our work, no home but our home. He had drifted to us by no chance, or accident, or passing whim, he had been driven to us by no exile, poverty, alienation of friends, by no clouding of his earthly prospects, no uncertainty of wordly power or place; he came to us because he loved us better than all these things, and because our poverty and desolation were dearer to him than all the pomp and magnificence of Europe.

Not unlike other young seminarians, Mitri began sometime before his ordination, to show in his inelastic, almost languid step, his lack of color, strength, and vigor, the effects of his sedentary life and many mortifications, and Bishop Carroll, with the watchful care which made him ever a true father to his priests, decided, almost immediately after his ordination, to send him to a pleasant country place, where, it was thought, he would at once recruit his health, and recover his vigor, which however, was with him less the result of physical health, for his constitution was not a strong one, than of great nervous energy, and an indomitable will which held the body as the absolute slave of the soul. The place chosen was called Port Tobacco, or the Manor, part of the Conewago mission, a settlement on the Susquehanna, not far from Lancaster, a very mild and pleasant climate, where the bishop desired him to remain a few weeks, before proceeding to the headquarters of the mission, Conewago, where Mr. Brosius and Rev. James Pellentz very much needed his assistance.

At Port Tobacco, so far from recruiting his health, the young priest, the natural impetuosity of his temperament, heightened by the rash and inconsiderate zeal of a youth bound to be a saint, forgot that he could no longer bear exposure, after the seclusion of the seminary life, with the same safety as when, under his mother's spirited training, he was accustomed to be out in all weathers; and used to all kinds of exercise, and the bishop was filled with distress at his impatience of confinement, his indifference to the changes of our ever changing climate. He hastened to urge him to take up his residence at Conewago, where he could be of the greatest use, and would be, the bishop no doubt considered, somewhat restrained by the advice of older and cooler heads.

Conewago, on Conewago Creek, in York County, Pennsylvania, a few miles north-east of Gettysburg, was one of the most promising missions in the United States, having been established as early as 1741 by the Jesuit father, William Wappeler, and fortunate in afterwards coming under the charge of Rev. James Pellentz, of the same order, a native of Germany, an excellent man and a noble missionary, whose name is lovingly remembered all through Pennsylvania. It was the centre of many little missions, scattered far apart, too small and poor to support a resident priest even had there been, which there certainly was not, one in the whole country to spare for them. Whether because he already saw work which he felt he could do at the Manor or in its vicinity, or because he, as young men will, rather disliked the idea of being placed again under the tutelage of his former guide, Mr. Brosius, or because, frightened at the outset of his labors, his heart longed to return to the peace, the quiet, and regularity of the beloved seminary, it is certain that Mitri was very unwilling to be permanently placed at Conewago, and urged his objections in a letter to the Rev. Mr. David, one of the professors at the seminary, to whom as to a friend he felt he could speak with more frankness, and probably force, than would be suitable in adressing his bishop. Mr. David thought proper to show the letter to the bishop, to whom the young priest also wrote mentioning his wishes, to which the bishop immediately replied.

RIGHT REV. BISHOP CARROLL TO REV. D. A. GALLITZIN*.

April 17th, 1795.

Rev. and dear Sir,

The arrival of Rev. Mr. Napier and your messenger yesterday evening, relieved our minds from much uncertainty and many fears concerning you. You ought to have given us early notice of your delay and where you were. Though the account of your health, as expressed in your letter, gave me much concern, I feel much more in observing how unsettled your mind is, and how often you vary your projects. If you would have given yourself time for reflection, it would have been evident to you that your last proposal cannot be complied with: for if even there were not sufficient cause for not adhering to my plan of sending you to Conewago, yet you could not be left at Zachariah, but must be placed at Baltimore, otherwise the Germans here, who are now much displeased with me without any good reason [for the bishop really had no priest able to speak German, except Gallitzin,

---

* This letter, like all the rest in this book, when not otherwise stated. is copied directly from the original.

whom he could possibly give them.] would then be justifiable in their dissatisfaction. Till very lately you attributed your indisposition to a sedentary life in the seminary, and expressed a wish of living in the exercise and wholesome climate of Conewago; which, it is my full conviction, would soon restore your health, if, as I would direct, you should not be employed in hard service till you recovered your strength. Mr. Brosius, who leaves me to day, and is exceedingly mortified at your proposal (with which he became acquainted as soon as I read Mr. David's letter, and before I saw your request that it should remain secret), tells me that you may afford him and his companions very great relief, without having any hard work that could distress your health; and I cannot think that you are either so much attached to other places of residence, or so regardless of the consequences which will ensue to Mr. Brosius, by your continued objections to sharing his labors, as to leave him and Mr. Pellentz under their present distress. It is true that you always express a determination to submit to my orders; but it is painful to a superior to lay on orders, when after a full manifestation of his will, he finds difficulties continually thrown in his way. You say that I may send Mr. Eden to Conewago, and he may be replaced by Mr. Maréchal. But if I had the power to compel Mr. Eden to leave his place and accept of Conewago, would it become me to require this of a priest who, for several years, has been laboring in all the hardships of long rides, and the service of many congregations, merely for the sake of freeing a young man, who has not yet commenced his career, from the burthen of duty?

You cannot infer from your present state of health that it will not improve at Conewago. In my opinion your present weakness was brought on by your undertaking the long rides from Baltimore to Georgetown, and thence to Port Tobacco, during Lent, and with the risk of meeting poor diet on your journey, and above all, by your great imprudence in persisting to leave St. Tho's manor on such a day as you parted from it. To me it would be a wonder if after it you had not a severe spell of sickness. I am sorry to be so averse to your wishes; I wish to be much more the father than the superior of the clergy under my jurisdiction; but I must not be partial in my favors, and forget a paternal care over those who have been and are laboring for the good of souls, that I may gratify the wishes of younger men. I am likewise to consider myself the father of the faithful in my diocese, and distribute the assistance which can be afforded them, in the best manner which my judgment can direct and conscience approve. Under the influence of these, I persist in requesting you to acquiesce in your appointment to Conewago, and, consequently, of coming hither as soon as can be consistent with your strength and convenience. As I shall leave town in eight or ten days, it is of importance that you be here before that. I am, with esteem and with great affection,

  Rev. and dear Sir,
    Yours most sincerely,
        † J. Bishop of Baltimore.

Upon this summons Mr. Gallitzin, or Rev. Mr. Schmet, or Smith, as he was generally called, went up to Baltimore, as quickly as he could, and, probably because he had very good reasons to urge, which he could better present in a personal interview, remained there, with the bishop's sanction, attending the Germans, and faithfully fulfilling his priestly duties through many trials and annoyances. In the summer following his ordination, Mrs. John Burgoons, a Protestant woman, living beyond the limits of civilization, a week's journey from Baltimore, by unbroken forests, and now and then an Indian path, far up the Alleghany mountains, was taken very ill, and begged so hard to see a Catholic priest, that Mrs. Luke McGuire, a good Catholic neighbor, in company with another person, undertook the long and dangerous journey to Conewago to find one who would be able and willing to visit her. The message came to Mr. Gallitzin, and he hastened to join the good Samaritans, and carry the strengthening sacraments of the Church, to the stranger in the wilderness. Mrs. McGuire fretted very much at the many delays necessarily incident to the journey, fearing the woman would die before they could reach her, but she was comforted and made confident by the priest's assurance that if Mrs. Burgoons so desired to see a priest, as they said, God, who had certainly given her the desire, would not permit her to die until it was fulfilled. His words were so far made good that she recovered her health, after being instructed and received into the Church, and lived a good Catholic life for many years afterwards. His coming was hailed with joy by the few families scattered in that unbroken country, to which only at long intervals a priest had ever penetrated. He said Mass in the principal loghouse of the settlement, administered baptism to a number of children, and even one or two grown persons, exhorted them all to faith, prayer, courage, and perseverance, and, having a liberal allowance from his mother, his father since he had chosen to be a priest did not interest himself in furthering his temporal affairs, he considered it not a bad investment, and, perhaps, a kindly act, to purchase a quantity of land on the mountain for himself.

Returning, he remained in Baltimore until sometime in the year 1796, when he fulfilled the bishop's original design by taking an active part in what was called the Conewago mission, visiting from this central point Taneytown, Pipe Creek, Hagarstown, and Cumberland in Maryland, not far from the Pennsylvania border; Chambersburg, Path and Shade Valley, Huntingdon, and even the Alleghany mountains in Pennsylvania. In Maryland his congregations were mainly English speaking people, which forced him to a greater fluency in the English language. In Pennsylvania, especially in the neighborhood of Chambersburg, the greatest ignorance prevailed, accompanied, as usual, by prejudice, bigotry, and persecution. Mr. Brosius attending the same mission, was looked upon with such horror, being known to be a Catholic priest, that he was in danger of his life, at one time, and only saved himself from a party of pursuing bigots, by the superior speed of an excellent horse, which enabled him to take refuge at the house of Mr. Michael Stillinger, a good Catholic, residing at Chambersburg, in whose home the priests often said Mass before a church could be built, and Mr. Gallitzin, "timid Mitri," accustomed to the quiet and orderly vicinity of Muenster and Angelmodde had many a dangerous journey to face upon his missions.

In the summer of 1797 reports having accumulated at Conewago of mysterious, perhaps diabolical performances in Virginia, he was relieved for a time of his laborious mission, and deputed to visit the scene and investigate the truth of the reports. He did so with readiness, not having the least faith in them, and no belief whatever in any but a natural cause for all that, since then, has become familiar to us under the general head of Spiritism. He remained in Virginia from September until Christmas, dividing his time between the houses of Mr. Livingston and Mr. Richard McSherry, and "no lawyer in a court of justice," he wrote, years afterwards, to Mrs. Doll, daughter of Mr. McSherry, "did ever examine and cross-examine witnesses [more] than I did all the witnesses I could procure. I spent several days in penning down the whole account, which, on my return to Conewago, was read with the greatest interest, and handed down from one to another, till, at last (when I wanted it back), it could no longer be found."

These things caused the greatest excitement at the time, and many accounts, more or less mingled with reports and recollections of those who knew the original persons concerned, have since been published. Father Gallitzin spent many happy days in the pious and agreeable society of the Catholic families mentioned, and bore witness to these manifestations. He very soon came to a full belief in the presence of the evil spirit, and possibly it was from this early contest with the devil in such material form, that he received, and never afterwards could overcome, a nervous dislike of ever again encountering him.

This occured in Jefferson County, at a village called Middleway, since changed, on account of what there took place, to Cliptown, near Martinsburg, Virginia. Some seven or eight years previously, Mr. Adam Livingston, a Pennsylvanian by birth, of Dutch descent, and a Lutheran in religion, an honest, industrious farmer, moved with his large family from Pennsylvania to Middleway, and soon acquired a handsome property there. He was kind, generous, and hospitable; it was said that a poor Irish traveller, a Catholic, being ill while in Livingston's neighborhood, was taken into his house, carefully nursed and attended through his last sickness, and properly buried. The only thing Mr. Livingston refused to do for the sick man, was to send for a priest for him; he had never seen one, and in common with the generality of his class, had probably very extraordinary ideas of Catholic priests, many actually believing they were the living emissaires of Satan, that they had horns, like their master, and various other equally enlightened fancies; nothing, therefore, could induce any of the Livingstons to accede to the dying man's entreaty; and this through no hardness of heart, it must be understood, for they were all of kindly disposition, but because to them the request was absurd, of no consequence, and a great deal better disregarded.

Soon after this death, and this refusal, Mr. Livingston appeared to be given over to the buffetings of Satan in good earnest; his barns got on fire and burned down, nobody knew how; his horses and cattle died; his clothing and those of his family, their beds and bedding were either burnt up, or cut into strips so small they could never be mended or put together again, generally in little pieces in the shape of a crescent. Boots, saddles, harness, all shared the same fate; chunks of fire rolled over the floors without any apparent cause; all conceivable noises tormented their ears; their furniture was banged about at the most inconvenient times, their crockery dashed to the floor, and broken to atoms. These things depriving them of sleep, torturing their nerves, and terrifying their very souls, very soon reduced the family to the depths of physical and mental distress, while they aroused the whole neighborhood to horror and sympathetic advice. Livingston sent far and wide for ministers of all persuasions, for conjurors of all kinds, to come and lay the devil, but the evil one gave them most inhospitable reception, mingled with a malice so minute, and yet so overpowering, that it actually seemed as if he and all his imps were laughing at them. The ministers' tracts and the conjurors' riddles were flung about the house, and treated one with as little respect as the other, and when it was thought the reverend gentlemen had talked long enough, a great stone, apparently kicked down the fireplace, brought their exhortations to a sudden end, and so terrified them that they unceremoniously departed. Less meddlesome visitors, as they might have been considered, were hardly any better treated, one old Presbyterian lady, says Father Gallitzin*, told a company at a tea-party that "having heard of the clipping, to satisfy her curiosity she went to Livingston's house; however, before entering it, she took her new black silk cap off her head, wrapped it up in her silk handkerchief, and put it in her pocket, to save it from being clipped. After a while she stepped out again to go home, and having drawn the handkerchief out of her pocket, and opened it, she found her cap cut into ribbands."

In this hopeless misery Mr. Livingston was permitted, we may, perhaps, be allowed to fancy on account of his hospitality to the poor traveller, to have a dream so remarkable and so vivid that it was more like a vision: he dreamed he had toiled up a rugged mountain, climbing it with the greatest difficulty; at the top of the mountain he saw a beautiful church, and in the church, a man dressed in a style he had never seen before; while he was gazing upon this person, a voice said to him: "This is the man who will bring you relief." He related this dream to his wife and many other persons, one of whom told him that the dress he described as worn by the minister of his dream, was precisely like that worn by the Catholic priests, and advised him to try one of them. But Livingston, discouraged at so many failures, paid little attention to this advice, until importuned by his wife he made enquiries to learn where one could be found; somebody knew of a Catholic family, named McSherry, living near

---

* *Letter to Mrs. Doll.*

Lectown, where he would be likely to find one. His troubles increasing, his wife entreating, and the conviction forcing itself into his own head that a Catholic priest could not work him much more evil than he was already enduring, induced him to go to Mr. McSherry's, and try. Mrs. McSherry met him at the gate of her residence, and asked him his errand, he told her he would like to see the priest, to which she replied that there was no priest there, but one would be at Shepherdstown to say Mass the next Sunday. Mr. Livingston went to Shepherdstown at the time she told him, and the moment the priest, Rev. Dennis Cahill, came out upon the altar to say Mass, Mr. Livingston was so affected that he cried out before the people: "The very man I saw in my dream!" He remained during the service in the greatest agitation, and as soon as the priest had retired into the sacristy followed him, accompanied by Mr. Richard McSherry, and an Italian gentleman, Mr. Minghini, who kept a boarding house at Sulphur Springs, who were among the most prominent men of Mr. Cahill's mission, had heard the exclamation, and knew somewhat of the circumstances. But no sooner had Mr. Livingston, with tears in his eyes, and choking in his throat, made known his errand, than the bluff and hearty priest laughed at him, and told him his neighbors were teasing him; to go home, to watch them closely, and they would soon get tired of the amusement. The other gentlemen, however, took up his case most earnestly, and insisted upon the priest's compliance; he very reluctantly yielded to them, at last, assured that it was all nonsense, loss of time, and a very unnecessary journey.

When he reached the house, heard and saw pretty clear proofs of Livingston's story, he sprinkled the house with holy water, at which the disturbances ceased, for a time, and at the moment the priest was leaving, having one foot over the door-sill, a purse of money, which had disappeared sometime before, was laid between his feet.

When Father Gallitzin was there, the disturbances having recommenced, he intended, as he related afterwards to Rev. Mr. Bradley, to exorcise the evil spirits for good and all, but as he commenced, the rattling and rumbling, as of innumerable wagons, with which they filled the house, worked so upon his nerves that he could not command himself sufficiently to read the exorcism, so that he was obliged to go for Rev. Mr. Cahill, a man of powerful nerve, and hearty faith, who returned with him to Livingston's, and bidding all to kneel down, commanded the evil spirits to leave the house, without doing any injury to any one there; after a stubborn resistance on the part of the devil, they were finally conquered and compelled to obey the priest. Afterwards, Mr. Cahill said Mass there, and there was no more trouble. Father Gallitzin carried a trunk full of clothing, which had been cut to pieces during this period of destruction, back to Conewago, where they have been seen, even of late years, by eminent priests, who have added their testimony to the truth of these occurences.

Among these clothes, however, are said to have been one or two garments marked in quite a different manner, one bearing the impress as of a hand burnt in the cloth, the other an I. H. S. made in the same manner. For scarcely had the Livingston family been relieved from the torments of the devil than they were visited by a consoling voice, which remained with them for seventeen years. It has been supposed that this voice came from some soul suffering in purgatory, for some reason permitted to visit, console, and, finally, to instruct the family. This may, perhaps, have been in return for the hospitality shown the poor Catholic, who died at their house. In gratitude, perhaps, for the relief he had received at the hands of a Catholic priest, and with perfect submission of his will to the truth of the Church which alone could cast out devils, Mr. Livingston desired, with a portion of his family, to be made a member of it, and after giving them the rudiments of instruction which were absolutely necessary, Mr. Cahill received them into the Church. Mrs. Livingston complied with this, but she was never sincerely converted, and always said she was Judas. They had scarcely made their profession of faith, and heard one or two Masses, before a bright light awoke Mr. Livingston, one night, and a clear, sweet voice told him to arise, call his family together and to pray. He did so, the hours passed as a moment, for the voice prayed with them leading their prayers. Then it spoke to them, in the most simple yet eloquent manner, of all the great mysteries of the Catholic faith to which they had assented, and which as far as they could, vaguely understanding them, they sincerely and firmly believed. But now these truths, dimly guessed at before, and accepted because the Church gave them, became clear, intelligible, fascinating, ever and ever more plain and more beautiful. Among other things which they could remember to repeat to others, the voice said that all the sighs and tears of the whole world were worth nothing in comparison with one Mass in which a God is offered to a God. It exhorted to boundless devotion to the Blessed Virgin Mary, continually implored them to pray for the suffering souls in purgatory, whose agony the voice could never weary of describing, and once, in illustration of their pains, a burning hand was impressed upon some article of clothing, directly under the eyes of the family, while it was speaking. It also urged to hospitality, to simplicity in dress, it would reprove the least extravagance in which any of them might indulge, and induced them to many voluntary penances, to long, strict fasts, to unbounded charity and to continual prayer. Mr. Livingston, to whom the voice more particularly addressed itself, was made its agent for innumerable good works; he would be called up at night to undertake long journeys to persons taken suddenly ill, or in affliction miles away; he would receive messages without any explanation, which he was enjoined to give at once to different people, to whom they would prove of immense relief, of amazing prophecy, of timely warning. It foretold events, which were always verified, and explained the meaning of many others.

It is said that while Father Gallitzin was investigating these matters, and was much concerned if they were of God or a delusive spirit, that startling proofs were given him that, at least, they were not of man, and that he was told of terrible trials, of slander, persecution, denunciation, of bitterest deception and desertion in store for him, even circumstantial details, so far from anything he was likely to meet, that he could hardly understand, but did not fail to remember them, and, afterwards, they were verified to the letter. As the evil spirits cannot foresee the future, it evidently was from this voice that he received the communication.

Upon one occasion Mr. Livingston and his family were together in one room, when there appeared among them a young man very poorly clad, and, though it was a bitterly cold day, barefooted. They asked him where he came from, he answered: "From my father."

"Where are you going?"

"I am going to my father," he said, "and I have come to you to teach you the way to him."

He staid with them three days and three nights, instructing them on all points of Christian doctrine. They asked him if he was not cold, offering him a pair of shoes, he replied that in his country there was neither heat nor cold. When he left the house the same idea occurred to each of them, that, as they had not noticed when he came in, they would watch and see what direction he took when going away. They saw him go into a lot in the front of the house and then disappear.

At that time there was no priest settled in the neighborhood, and very few Catholic books to be had even in the large cities, but Bishop Carroll, Mr. Gallitzin, Mr. Brosius, Mr. Cahill, and Father Pellentz, and other clergymen who conversed with Mr. Livingston, were astonished at his knowledge of the Catholic religion, and were all convinced that he had been instructed from above.

Mrs. Livingston heard the voice oftener than the others, and endeavored by every means in her power to falsify it. Among other things, it had said she would die in her own house; she was so often rebuked by it that she would not stay at home, but went to the house of a quaker family; while there she became ill, and to prove the voice wrong, positively refused to be taken home, but, afterwards, she was forced to beg to be carried back, and died in her own house, as predicted.

Fourteen persons were converted in one winter by these things, which were well known and widely discussed; others, influenced by the account of them, received clearer impressions of the reality of another world, of the close proximity of the evil one, and of the intimate union between the Church militant and the Church suffering, from which they were moved to the serious practice of virtue, and to endeavor to live as they would wish to die.

Prince Gallitzin, having fully and thoroughly satisfied himself of the nature of these different manifestations, returned to Conewago, and took up again the burden of his missions. There had been from the first much to dishearten him in these, and to tempt him to despair of ever effecting any good among them, especially those in Maryland. All seemed to him started on a false basis, and in the spirit of the world, not of Christ; how to "make all things new," would have been a problem hard enough to solve if he had been left to do it his own way. But this he by no means could do, and he had many an affront to bear from those who, instead of placing obstacles in his way, should have shown themselves gentle and docile children of the Church, eager to second all his efforts to bring a better-soul life among them, as well as a temporal one more in consonance with spiritual ordering. In his Maryland congregations were men of little education, of no refinement, and often of immensurable conceit, fully imbued with the idea that independence for America meant license for all who, by fair means or by foul, could get a hold upon her soil; men who believed that not to have borne arms against America entitled them to own and to rule her, who fancied that to read, possibly to write, gave them the pronouncing voice upon all the sciences, who having a few phrases of the letter of the law, cared nothing for its spirit, and seemed to consider that loudly trumpeting themselves Catholics, constituted them the main body of the Church. One or two of these in one place is always quite enough to leaven the whole community.

Now, Father Gallitzin was intensely Catholic; the whole order of his mind, the deepest recesses of his soul, the very moulding of his spirit, all was thoroughly, strictly Catholic; he had also, as if by natural instinct, cultivated to the perfection of a science, a clear conception of what a Catholic community should be, and no idea nor place for an idea of the concession of right to expediency; he had fixed opinions of organization, of regularity and thorough-searching discipline,. the confused, slovenly, slip-shod way in which communities came together at that early and drifting period, was a positive torture to him, the more so that all attempts to bring order among them were readily resented as out of his province; the interference of laymen and their dictation in Church matters was an abomination to him, to which he would never yield, not only because of its momentary hatefulness, but because he saw in it the germ of that system which has since borne such bitter fruit of schism and scandal, has weighed priests, even bishops, to the dust, imperilled, if it has not lost many an immortal soul, and even then was beginning to vex the heart of many a struggling missionary, already overburdened with the charge of his weak and fickle flock. When all these things culminated, as they naturally must, in indifference to religion, in lack of reverence for the sacredness of its ministers and sacraments, in disregard of all authority spiritual or temporal, then he who had seen what such irreverence and insubordination had done for Europe, deluging it in blood and tears, turned sick at heart, and felt overpowered by his responsibility; but when this evil spirit manifested itself, with more or less consciousness, in the House of God, his wrath knew no bounds. If that House were no more elegant than a stable, he demanded in it the reverence, the hush the decorum and ceremony of the king's palace. In all things pertaining to religion and his own sacred office, he was unbending, all exacting, superbly just, making no allowance for natures lame and twisted, coarse and crooked; for him there was but one thing to think of: the surest way to get to heaven; he would not take into consideration that everybody else was not so much absorbed in that thought as himself.

Thus he was very unhappy, and, burning to bring the whole world to the feet of his Master, had no mercy on the faint-hearted or irresolute, and was inclined to class all who did not run with him, as laggards, cowards, and traitors ; to them his rules seemed arbitrary, and they soon made their opinion known to the bishop who, perhaps, favored them more than he would have done, had he seen as clearly as the young priest the overtopping evils that spring from an irregular foundation ; at the same time his long experience, his patience, and kindly heart were certainly justified in admonishing Father Gallitzin to gentler measures.

RIGHT REV. BISHOP CARROLL TO REV. D. A. GALLITZIN*.

October 20. 1798.

As I see both sides of my people, I understood the whole affair (of their complaints) at once, and gave them no hearing, but sent them home with the admonition to do their duty and be obedient to their pastor ; however, I will soon, during my visitation, come to Taneytown, and investigate the matter. Of my own personal views in your regard, I said nothing to them, I will mention them to you. I have already often admonished you, and others in whom you have perhaps placed more confidence, have urged you to try more to win the affections of your congregations, to lead them by mildness, even here and there, to overlook things which are not precisely as they should be, that afterwards you may correct them by gentle persuasion, instead of at once making use of your authority, and to carry that authority to its utmost limits. I repeat this exhortation, and assure you that I have generally found this the best and most effectual way of doing, although the opposite course might for the moment create more excitement, and more noisy applause, especially from those who are not for the moment the immediate objects of a hot and impatient zeal. And then, what a doctrine it is that all who are under your charge, should be bound also to yield to every opinion you may have, to every proposal you make, without being permitted a question ! If this were intended to be so, why should there be bishops placed over priests, arch-bishops

---

* Rev. Mr. Lemcke's *Leben und Wirken*, p. 147.

and patriarchs over bishops, and over all the pope? Do not these degrees of the hierarchy show plainly an admission that each may judge wrongly, and his decision be subject to revision?

Evidently Mitri had inbibed a little of his mother's method.

There was nothing that Father Gallitzin more desired than to fulfill the bishop's instructions and guide his people by mildness and affection, but the task seemed to him hopeless, for everything was wrong, according to his thinking, and although he continued to do his utmost, it was only by the strongest effort of duty, for he despaired of accomplishing anything among them, and when one is but twenty-five or so, one does not like to throw one's life away. But he, too, had to learn that no life is thrown away that is used as God appoints; the evils he contended with and could not master, actually broke open the door for the good he longed for, and was some day to do. He had first to learn what to reject before he could be be taught what to secure.

Deliverance came to him at last. The scattered settlers on the mountains, amounting to ten or twelve families forming the settlement, generally known as McGuire's, sometimes called Clearfield, where he had visited the sick woman, to which he had since made several journeys, in conjunction with others in their neighborhood, sent a petition to the bishop, begging that a priest might be appointed to reside among them, trusting that with the aid of some land previously given to Bishop Carroll for church property, and such tithes as they could give him, the priest might be able to provide for his physical subsistance, while he cared-for their spiritual needs. Several of the petitioners had come from Maryland, having been within Mr. Gallitzin's mission previous to their removal to the mountains, and, therefore, sent their petition through him, entreating that, if comformable to his own wishes, he might be the pastor chosen for them.

He made this request his own and the bishop cordially acceded to it.

RIGHT REV. BISHOP CARROLL TO REV. D. A. GALLITZIN.

Washington City, March 1. 1799.

Rev. and Dear Sir,

I fear you have been disappointed in not receiving an earlier answer to your letter which covered a list of subscribers in Clearfield, Frankstown, and Sinking Valley. I had come hither on business immediately before the arrival of yours at Baltimore. Your request is granted. I readily consent to your proposal to take charge of the congregations detailed in yours, and hope that you will have a house built on the land granted by Mr. McGuire and already settled [cleared?] or if more convenient on your own, if you intend to keep it.
.... Before I received yours my intention was to advise you of the notice lately given me by Mr. Egan, that he would return to Ireland in the spring or summer. I meant to have offered to you with your present congregations that of Emmetsburg and the mountain (now Mount St. Mary's) united in one. ....

† John Bsp. Baltimore.

Thus sanctioned by his bishop, called by the people, and urged on by a voice higher than all, with renewed hope and burning desire to be at his life's work, the young priest lost no time in making preparations, but packed up his few possessions, mounted his horse, and turned his face northwestward, "over the hills and far away," to found a Catholic community on the lasting basis of Catholic virtue and true religious simplicity.

He was succeeded at Taneytown by Rev. Nicholas Zocchi, a zealous, active priest, born and educated in Rome, who served the Maryland and Pennsylvania missions with untiring devotion and faithfulness for forty-one years, through the greatest trials, which he met with unfailing cheerfulnes. He died in 1845.

CHAPTER IX.

SETTLES ON THE MOUNTAINS.

(1799.)

Catholic missions in Pennsylvania. — Philadelphia. — Conewago. — Goshenhoppen. — Lancaster. — O'Neill's Victory. — Sportsman's Hall. — McGuire's Settlement. — Reception of missionaries by the early settlers. — Poverty of the missions. — Pastoral residence at McGuire's Settlement. — Midnight Mass in the new church.

From Maryland, the headquarters of the Church in America, an English Jesuit, Rev. Josiah Greaton, went, in 1730, to Philadelphia, the colonial capital, to which there had previously been irregular visits from different clergymen, to effect a permanent church organization there. From Philadelphia, in 1741, the Jesuits sent out two priests, one, Rev. William Wappeler, a Westphalian, to minister to the Catholics at Conewago, a settlement considerably west of Philadelphia, and north of Baltimore, the other, Rev. Theodore Schneider, of Bavaria, to officiate for the German emigrants at Goshenhoppen, about forty-five miles west of the city. Midway between these new missions Father Wappeler bought some land at Lancaster, looking to a future church there. From these two mission-headquarters, as they might be styled, the two priests, their rare clerical visitors, and later, their assistants and successors, made excursions, at long intervals, some distance into the wild country beyond civilization, to carry the consolations of religion to such as they could reach among the hardy pioneers, who, the axe and the rifle their almost sole protection and support, were striving to earn their bread with the sweat of their brow, hardly surmising even, that far to the east, and north, and south of them, drums were beating a battle call to the colonists, and an army, small and scantily provisioned, was making a nation for them, unfurling over their toil worn heads a flag of protection before which the oldest tyrants of earth should be made mute, while another army, scantier still, with no roll of drums or blare of trumpets, silently closing up its ever-gaping ranks, was marching to their eternal rescue, to plant side by side with the Banner of Freedom the Standard of the Cross. †

Some time after the close of the Revolutionary war, a small number of families from the vicinity of Philadelphia, thinking they could thus improve their worldly fortunes, crossed the Alleghany mountains, and settled in Westmoreland County, near the present town of Greensburg, having first obtained a promise that they should not be forsaken in their spiritual needs, but that a priest should now and then be sent to them. Almost their first act was to obtain (March 1789), at the cost of a few shillings, something over an acre of land, to be used, some day, for church ground, and a graveyard. Shortly afterwards, in accordance with the promise made them, Rev. John Causey came and remained a while with them; he is believed to have been the first priest to officiate in Western Pennsylvania*. Mr. Causey was succeeded in the autumn of 1789 by Rev. Theodore Brauers, a Dutch Franciscan, possessed of some considerable means, which desiring to use for the poor who were without a church decided him to cast his lot with the little band of pioneers, notwithstanding. the entreaties of the trustees of St. Mary's church in Philadelphia, whose pastor, Rev. Mr. Heilbron, he was visiting, to remain in the city.

---

* There were French chaplains, however, attached to the forts erected by the French in 1753—1754 to guard the Valley of the Ohio, which they claimed as their own, who undoubtedly celebrated Mass on the western borders of the state, for the few years the French retained possession. Of these forts, Fort Presqu'isle stood on the site of the present city of Erie, and Fort Duquesne, afterwards, when it came into the possession of the English, called Fort Pitt, has now given place to Pittsburg. See Shea's *History of the Catholic Church in the United States*, p. 275.

Mr. Brauers made two land purchases, one of one hundred and sixty two acres on the east side of the Loyalhanna, known as "O'Neill's Victory", and the other of something over three hundred acres, not very far from Greensburg, which as it had been used as a hunting ground by a gentleman from Harrisburg, was rather grandly styled "SPORTSMAN'S HALL". His great dream and desire in regard to the latter purchase was that it might become a second Conewago, the residence of devoted priests, the headquarters of an army of religious who from it would attend the surrounding missionary stations, which would, he hoped, sometime arise in the then unbroken country. He wished to bequeath the land to his spiritual successors, duly appointed, with the desire that they should every year say one Mass for the repose of his soul and three for his intention; but his will was so worded by the person who drew it up, as to leave room for confusion, until its was finally settled with much clearness and force by the Pennsylvania courts, in accordance with its real meaning*. His desire after many years of trial and distress, has at last, in God's own time, been abundantly fulfilled, with *good measure and pressed down and shaken together and running over*, for "O'Neill's Victory", is now well supplied and cared for, and "Sportsman's Hall" is covered by the Abbey of St. Vincent, from which in twenty-five years many priests have gone forth to carry the blessings of the faith, far and wide into the surrounding country.

After the death of Mr. Brauers (Oct. 29th 1790) his flock was a fold without a shepherd, into which wolves and hirelings easily penetrated, and remained in great spiritual destitution until 1799, when trouble apppeared, for a time, to be at an end.

Some years before these few families left the neighborhood of Philadelphia, to seek a home in the unbroken wilderness

---

* A fuller account of this famous will, and of the extremely interesting litigation in regard to it, with some details of events and places which can properly be only touched upon in passing, in this book, is reserved for a sketch of Catholicity in Western Pennsylvania with which the writer trusts to follow the present volume at some future day.

beyond the mountains, an officer of the Revolutionary army, Captain Michael McGuire, a Catholic residing in Taneytown, Maryland, being a great hunter, and fond of making expeditions far into the interior of Pennsylvania, took up land on the very summit of the Alleghanies, to which, in 1788, he went with his family to live. The journey alone was enough to have dismayed the stoutest heart; hitherto Conewago had been the extreme limit of travel, from it to the spot chosen by the hunter for his new residence, one hundred and thirty miles, or so, had to be made through wild forests, on horseback, with no resemblance of a road, and the brush so thick that he would have to cut a passage as he went, only now and then encountering an Indian path over which the moss had by no means grown, suggestive of terrible possibilities.

Four or five years afterwards, the captain's brother, Peter, with his bride, followed him from Maryland, and before a great while six log huts, with roofs of evergreen, standing on the little patches of land cleared by the stout arms of half a dozen stalwart men, formed McGuire's settlement. Their first, and for many years their only near neighbors were the settlers at Blairs Mill's, twelve miles away, with a dense forest between. Captain McGuire lost no time in providing for the church, for which his wonderful faith alone could have given him hopes, and took up four hundred acres of land which he made over to Bishop Carroll, who had just been consecrated, and returned to the United States. During the troubles attending Father Brauer's will, many families intending to join the first settlement at the present Greensburg, discouraged at the religious situation there, disheartened perhaps by the fearful trials of the journey, or induced by the advantages of climate and abundance of land, scattered themselves in the woods all along from Conewago to Greensburg, toiling away with little hope of ever beholding the shining cross of a church-spire above the dark immeasurable forests closing about them, like a great sea, on every side. Only a brave and resolute priest could venture to seek them out in their scattered and isolated homes, but when one did so, he was received as an emperor by his subjects, a long lost father by his children. Long before the most experienced vision could descry the faintest sign of a human habitation, even of human existence, in any direction, it would already be known, as if by magic, that a priest was coming ; some uncouthly arrayed, shy and curious child would dart like a squirrel from the thicket, admonished to show him the way, and suddenly, in the midst of frowning woods there would be seen the chips of a tree newly cut, and the slow smoke from a little log cabin, where, wiping tears of joy from her eyes, some lonely woman was hastening to prepare such a meal as the limited resources of the wilderness would permit, while her husband, tramping in from his toil, added his welcome. How the news would travel for miles through the woods was always a mystery, but it never lagged. Soon, children who had never seen a priest were gathered and brought for baptism, starting long before daybreak, and in the morning by dangerous passes, over unbroken ways, the pioneers would come, once again to roll off the burden of their sins and sorrows, and, in the one room of the cabin which served all purposes, an altar would be constructed of rudest materials, the priest's saddlebags unpacked, and Mass said with the same ceremony, and the same efficacy, as if the tall trees, standing straight and stern about the door, were marble columns, and the blue sky far over-head, were an old time Gothic arch. No happier day for them until the far away time, when the ring of the axe upon the happy logs that promise a house for the Lord in their midst, shall fill their hearts with exultation, a thrilling sense of His nearness and protection.

Thus Mr. Brosius once or twice made the pilgrimage from Conewago to McGuire's settlement, and Father Pellentz even to the settlers at Greensburg, after Father Brauer's death. During the years of troubles consequent upon the famous will, the bishop requested the Rev. Mr. Lanigan to make some investigations about it, which would be useful in his suit against the intruding priest, Mr Fromm, who persisted in remaining on Father Brauer's estate, and, later, desired Rev. Mr. Wheeling, or Whelan, to attend to the spiritual necessities of this poor little flock, which he did for a short time, living in the greatest destitution, and most miserable poverty, until the bishop permitted him to go to another mission. When Mr. Brosius visited McGuire's Settlement, he set apart a portion of the ground donated by Captain McGuire, and consecrated it for a cemetery, although as yet unneeded. When Mr. Lanigan visited "Sportsman's Hall" and "O'Neill's Victory," he, too, staid a few days at the Settlement, said Mass in the captain's cabin, and, distressed at seeing cattle on consecrated ground, had the men and boys band together to enclose it.

Too soon afterwards, November 17. 1796, Captain McGuire like Father Brauers, found a final resting place in the land he had given the Church.

"Their good swords rust,
  Their souls are with the saints, we trust."

Priest and layman, each did his best; they were the first in Western Pennsylvania to provide means for the Church to plant herself there, and right royally has she availed herself of those means.

After these, Mr. Gallitzin came, received the sick woman into the Church, said Mass in the old chief's house, and bore back with him, whether he knew it or not, the germ of the thought, over which the sun shone, and the winds blew, until, four years later, it ripened into the purpose of his life.

Thus, in 1799, the bishop had the happiness of seeing these two remote settlements provided for, for in this same year Mr. Heilbron, a staid old campaigner who had been a soldier in Europe, who now always rode on his missions with his pistols in his belt, his rifle over his shoulder, and his stole, it may be, pressed close to the heart that at any moment might be called upon to defend the insignia of his office with the last drop of its blood, and Prince Gallitzin, the young recruit, full of fire and vigor, went out into the wilderness, and divided between them a wild and inhospitable region, which now rich and beautiful, fair as a garden of the Lord, teems with pleasant homes and happy harvest fields, with churches, monasteries, and convents, and boasts of three well worn mitres and a corps of most admirable priests and religious.

Father Gallitzin reached his mission in the latter part of the summer. He found about a dozen families in the settlement who, with a few persons who had come up from Maryland and Conewago with him at about the same time, formed his immediate parish, but his labors were by no means to be confined to them, for all who were out of reasonable reach of Conewago, or had strayed away from the Greensburg settlement were under his charge. At McGuire's Settlement he commenced at once to put things in order, thankful enough that as yet the field was unploughed, consequently, free from the tares, which had so choked up the wheat, and tortured him, in the older and more important stations he had attended. He at once divided his own land, which cost him about four dollars an acre, into lots which he sold to them for a mere trifle on long credit, credit so long that much of it still lasts, and he held out the same inducements for all, who, unable to procure the first means for subsistance, would wish to join him, and make a home for themselves and their children in his neighborhood, providing always that they were honest, industrious or desirous of becoming so ; he wanted no wolves in sheep's clothing in his fold. No words could describe the poverty of all the early missions, especially in Pennsylvania; Conewago and Goshenhoppen, even, would have had to be given up, but for the little assistance which the more comfortable Marylanders could afford them when they were in great straits, and the aid which came at times from the legacy of an English Catholic, Sir John James. Mr. Whelan wrote letters to the bishop which would be piteous if the misery they describe were not so abject, and others from other places speak of continual hunger, of almost starvation, and inconceivable hardships. There was not a single rich Catholic, perhaps hardly a well to do man of any creed, in that part of the state, to ease in the least the terrible pressure of want. Bears and wolves and wild Indians surrounded them, keeping them always on the watch ; the winters were long and severe, but somehow they kept heart and hope, and when Rev. Mr. Gallitzin came to share with them such remittances as he would from time to time receive from his mother, they had reason to be wonderfully cheered. It was not long, indeed, before it was seen that a whole new life had come,— not only to McGuire's Settlement, which was in comparative ease, but to all the settlers within sixty miles at least,—with this frail young priest, whose rapid ringing step once heard could never be forgotten, and whose flashing dark eyes were at once the delight, the terror, and the inspiration of every man, woman, and child of his congregation. His gravity and reserve, often mistaken for coldness and haughtiness, gradually gave way before the joy of his heart in having at last cast aside the trammels of all false societies, and his tender love for these great men, giants in strength and stature many of them, to whom his look was a law, his least word a treasure, added a peculiar sweetness to his natural dignity. He was everywhere, saw everything at a glance, planned and acted without an instant's hesitation; young, handsome, with most soldierly bearing, with a bright smile, and a cheerful word for every laborer, he would go from one to another, as they worked, making any toil light by his very presence. partaking of whatever they gave him, with real thanks, and perfect courtesey, attentive to their least trouble, the very ideal of a prince-priest.

When he arrived he found that Captain McGuire had very thoughtfully given a few animals as stock for the farm to be prepared for the use of the priest who should live on the church property, and had placed a man in charge of it and them, hoping thus to have a portion cleared, and made some what productive while awaiting its reverend occupant. Father Gallitzin gave some of these to the tenant whom he displaced, and lived in the houses of the settlers until his own log cabin could be built. This was put up on the slope of the hill, on the church land, which was about two miles from the chief McGuire farm, was made of round logs, and covered a space of some sixteen by fourteen feet, and for the first time in all his life the princely heir to grand old castles and entire villages, set foot upon his own threshold; and if "every man's house is his castle," truly, his was his palace and his kingdom.

With uncontrollable eagerness he watched the progress of the log church, which fast took size and shape under the strong and willing arms of his parishioners, his own inspiration and generosity. As soon as the harvest was gathered he gave employment to them all upon the church, and even had the women occupied in making a great number of candles for it, and on Christmas Eve of that year it was finished, placed under the protection of St. Michael, and ready for Midnight Mass, the only house of God from Lancaster to St. Louis. The snow lay waist-deep beside it, and far as the eye could reach around it; the stars shone over it bright, and cold, and pure, as on that other December night over the scarcely poorer stable at Bethlehem. He had instructed the men to bring in branches of the beautiful evergreen trees, which grew thick upon the mountains and at their very doors, the women set their candles amongst the dark green foliage, covering the rude walls, and just at midnight, when the people who had gathered from immense distances through the wilderness of snow, were hushed in wrapt expectation, he came out upon the altar, with all the ceremony of the grandest cathedral, and intoned the Mass; he was a magnificent singer, those who remember wipe their eyes when they speak of it, and never did the GLORIA IN EXCELSIS come more joyously and exultingly from his heart, or lips, than when he now, for the first time, opened and gave to the Holy Family a shelter from the storms, a refuge in the wilderness, a home on the mountains. Oh, Father Gallitzin, much has been said of your sacrifices, your renunciation of princely rank, fortune, fame, comfort and ease, but with all the world at your feet, what could it offer you to compare with that magnificent, triumphant GLORIA!

The church was small, yet the band of worshippers did not overcrowd it, even though, besides all the Catholics, men women, and children, living within twenty and thirty miles, there were present, that night, old hunters, trappers, and Indian traders, who knew of heaven and of God no more than the savages of the forests, with whom they dealt, and to whom they bore wild and terrifying ressemblance. Dressed in the untanned hide of the animals they had killed, they looked on, wondering, staring in mute amazement, not unlike the dumb creatures at Bethlehem, only vaguely surmising something in themselves not known before, until the priest turning announced in stirring, ringing words, that God had come to his people, that the heavens had opened and rained down the Just One; that earth was his cradle, our hearts his resting place, and thus battered down the thrice plated iron doors of ignorance, poured sudden light into the close and swarming cavern of the flesh, and showed a soiled and starving soul, shivering, trembling, crouching with wild, terrified, hungry eyes, in its farthest corner; a soul the Child had come to cleanse, to dress, to adorn, to give food and nourishment, to raise to its feet, with head erect, strong and comely before the eyes of angels and of men.

Shortly after the holidays Father Gallitzin had occasion to go to Conewago, for he was now full of business, so many were coming into the neighborhood of the "Clear Fields" or McGuire's Settlement, most of them very poor, every one of whom he held in his thoughts, anxious to provide for the spring planting on which their whole dependence was placed. From there he wrote to Bishop Carroll, mentioning very simply the completion of his house and church.

Rev. D. A. Gallitzin to Right Rev. Bishop Carroll.

Conewago, Feb. the 9th 1800.

My Lord,

Being just now returned from the backwoods, and hearing of James Driscoll's going to Baltimore, I cannot let this favourable opportunity slip to give your Lordship some brief account of the state of that part of the spiritual vineyard entrusted to my care. I am sorry that I cannot be so diffuse as the importance of the subject seems to require; but the shortness of the time does not allow of it.

Our church which was only begun in harvest, got finished fit for service the night before Christmas; it is about forty-four feet long by twenty-five, built of white pine logs, with a very good shingle roof. I kept service in it at Christmas for the first time, to the very great satisfaction of the whole congregation, who seemed very much moved at a sight which they never beheld before. There is also a house built for me, sixteen feet by fourteen, besides a little kitchen and a stable. I have now, thanks be to God, a little home of my own, for the first time since I came to this country, and God grant that I may be able to keep it. The prospect of forming a lasting establishment for promoting the cause of religion is very great; the country is amazing fertile, almost entirely inhabited by Roman-Catholics, and so advantageously situated with regard to market that there is no doubt but it will be a place of refuge for a great many Catholics; a great many have bought property there in the course of these three months passed, and a good many more are expected. The congregation consists at present of about forty families, but there is no end to the Catholics in all the settlements round about me; what will become of them all, if we do not soon receive a new supply of priests, I do not know. I try as much as I can to persuade them to settle around me.

I am at present in a tolerable state of health, though weak, but with the help of God, I hope from the healthfulness of the country, and the quality of the provisions it affords, that I shall get stronger and abler to undergo hardships. If the proximity of lent did not oblige me to return soon, and the season was more favourable, I would give myself the pleasure of paying your Lordship a visit; however, I shall go to Baltimore in May to receive my contingent in money, which will afford me an opportunity of acquainting you with every other circumstance relating to the above subjects.

* * *

....Fearing to importune your Lordship any longer, I break off, and recommend myself to your prayers, begging that you would receive the assurance of the most profound respect with which I am,

      My Lord,
       Yr. most hble. and obt. Servt.
        Augustine de Gallitzin.

P. S. Your Lordship has very likely been informed of the miraculous conversion of Mrs. Minghini in Virginia, to which I was called on a Thursday, January the 18th and who departed this life the next Monday, Jan. the 22nd, provided with all the rites of the Church. The particulars of it I shall relate to your Lordship when I come to Baltimore.

Rev. Mr. Cahill resides this winter at Cumberland. I should be very happy to receive a few lines from your Lordship before I start, which will be, I believe, to-morrow week.

Mrs. Minghini was the Protestant wife of the Italian gentleman who, it will be recollected, was the proprietor of a boarding-house at Sulphur Springs, Virginia. She had been ill for a long time, and troubled in mind on the subject of religion; the voice at Livingston's sent word to her husband to have a Catholic priest visit her, but as he would have to send forty or fifty miles for one, he actually refused, saying she could send for her own preacher, when, as a Catholic, he must have known perfectly well the eternal consequences to him and herself if she died outside the Catholic Church, and that through his fault. A Presbyterian minister was accordingly sent for, and talked with her; but he only still more confused her. Mrs. McSherry then visited her, and found her very well disposed, perfectly ready and willing to do whatever was right; she repeated an act of contrition with Mrs. McSherry, with every appearance of sincerity and penitence. When Mrs. McSherry was at home again her mind was full of the matter, and she could think of nothing else, being very uneasy about the woman, distressed at the thought of her dying outside the Church when evidently so willing to enter it. In the night she dreamt she saw a puny child strike an immense rock with a little stick, and the rock instantly crumbled away. The dream made a great impression upon her, but supposing it only a dream, to which she had no right to pay any attention, she said nothing about it, and tried to put it out of her mind, but quite early in the day Livingston (having heard nothing of the visit and dream), sent his daughter to Mrs. McSherry to say that the voice had told him the child in her dream was the act of contrition Mrs. Minghini had repeated, and that her sins had crumbled away on account of it; the voice desired her to go again to Mr. Minghini, and try to induce him to send for a priest; that he would make many objections, but she must still urge it; at last he would say he had no one to send, and she was to answer that one of Mr. Livingston's sons would go; it also said that the messenger would meet two priests, Mr. Cahill and Mr. Smith (Gallitzin), but he was to procure Mr. Smith, he being the one intended for her, as having a gentler nature. All took place as the voice foretold; Mrs. McSherry went to Mr. Minghini and the messenger was finally sent for the priest, met two, and gave the word to Father Gallitzin who went to Mrs. Minghini at once, received her into the Church, and gave her the sacraments, so that her mind was at last at rest and her soul at peace.

CHAPTER X.

DISAPPOINTMENTS AND ENCOURAGEMENTS.

(1800—1802.)

Early trials. — Lack of sympathy in his projects. — His austerities. — Growth of the settlement. — Lancaster. — Rev. Louis de Barth. — Concerning the Russian property. — Prince Gallitzin becomes an American citizen. — Conversion of Count von Stolberg.

It is of no sort of use to expect to find, or to make a garden of Eden upon earth; "the trail of the serpent is over it all." Disappointments and annoyances of the smallest and therefore most vexatious kind beset Father Gallitzin at the very outset of his career, and he had not yet advanced far enough in the way of perfection to be careless of their sting. It is possible he even shrank from the point at which no man's word would have power to hurt him; for when we are crying our eyes out over our broken playthings, it is a dreary thought that a day may come when our toys will be chipped to nothing before our very eyes, exciting in us no regret. It is so hard for us children of earth, clinging to our idols of to-day as if we had not flung aside as dear ones of yesterday, to realize that when we become, at last, indifferent to mere earthly things, it is because we have outgrown them, and all our energies, and all our affections, every faculty we possess is absorbed in something far dearer and greater than they. But as yet Gallitzin had scarcely entered upon the unsheltered highway, out of which led the lone and narrow path which was to be his veritable *Via Dolorosa*. The scorching ground beneath his weary feet, the glaring light, the choking dust oppressing him, won no pity from the gay world riding swiftly by, small recognition from the good world seated, calm and stately, in the old familiar coach.

He had gone up to the mountains with a noble project undertaken from the purest motives, a project replete with homeliest details, but of vital importance, in his estimation, not alone for those directly concerned in it, but for the whole church struggling in poverty and greatest spiritual destitution for a foothold in the United States. "Let us have but one spot for our own," he cried, "one single place wherein the true Catholic spirit can have room to grow and manifest itself, and it will leaven the whole country. Let us be careful what seeds we drop in the furrows of this rich land; let us keep the faith incontaminate here; let us own one place wherein a man can live a hearty, vigorous, joyous-hearted Catholic life. Elsewhere the ground is choked with weeds that must be suffered to grow with the wheat until harvest time, the air thin, vitiated, foggy, and enervating, here let us keep the moral atmosphere, with God's help, as fresh and invigorating as the air of our mountains."

Good people listened to him attentively, sometimes carried away by his earnestness, sometimes amused by his enthusiasm; they had had enthusiasms, too, some of them, and so they would not be too hard on his; they gave assent, — it is so much easier to run with the stream than to pull against it, — made promises which he took in full faith, and which they gave up as soon as he passed out of sight, and left them to drop into their old routine of thought. No one seemed to grasp the deeper meaning, to get hold of the great principle which was all in all to him, and it is in the superficial response of such as these that the evil one conceals his most dangerous and subtle temptations, when he would break down a noble warrior, or undermine a noble work.

Though warm, intense, even a little enthusiastic at times, Mitri Gallitzin was no dreamer, no visionary; he set about his work in the most practical spirit, with the most reasonable demands and with regard to the most ordinary and least heroic details; he understood that he was to provide the temporal, natural body for his project, and so care for it that the Holy Spirit would freely breathe into it the breath of life.

The place chosen could not have been more favorable. It was at the very summit of the mountains, where the air is wonderfully clear, elastic, and renovating, the land good, the surrounding scenery most entrancing; the soft lines of the Alleghanies, which are remarkable for their symmetry among all the mountains of the earth, undulate into innumerable hills and valleys, making ever varied and ever charming views in all directions, while the luxuriance of the varied foliage forms a world of color, ever delicious and ever new; nature was there unstained by the wrongs of man, the world with its bustle and hurry, its sins and its shame, was far away; there in that mountain nest there need be only harmony and peace, love of the good God and kindness to each other; with proper industry the earth would yield them all that was necessary for their wants, and already the Cross, with its promises, had been placed in their midst.

This was the wish, the theory into which Father Gallitzin threw himself heart and soul, striving to work it into reality by every means in his power. Wherever he found a family, in whatever rank, pressed for a home, discontented, or unable to uphold itself in the position in which it found itself in the older communities, he eagerly unfolded the advantages to be gained by joining the band of simple, contented settlers on the mountains, and with the princely generosity of his nature, justified by the great wealth of his family, never hesitated to offer them assistance out of his own resources, and to soften for them by every means in his power the privations of the wilderness. In return the most solemn promises were broken, every conceivable advantage taken of his charity, his generous and trusting nature, which he felt the more keenly that he considered the means God had given him, as a trust placed in his hands for the use of the poor and the good of the Church, while repeated disappointments and the difficulties of transmission from Europe to America, often left him without the means for supplying his own most urgent necessities. But with it all he kept up heart and hope, full of faith in God's help, and willing to bear any mortification if by so doing the divine help could be made more secure for his little band. He, luxurious, indolent Mitri, slept on a bundle of straw spread upon the floor of his cabin, with a book for his pillow, eat but little and of the simplest food, and when he replaced the clothes he brought from Conewago, it was with the coarse, ill fitting homespun worn by the farmers. Unrelenting in his austerities, ever cheerful with his people, he pointed every word and act towards the one great aim he had in view : to make every life within his reach loyally, practically, fervently Catholic. He knew well that for a few years, at least, his colony could do little more than struggle with the earth for the bare necessities of life, but he never permitted them on that account to hold the salvation of their souls as a separate thing; he blessed their harvest fields, and called unceasingly for the sun and rain of God's grace to enrich their souls, with such results that he was able in the summer to write encouragingly to the bishop:

REV. D. A. GALLITZIN TO RIGHT REV. BISHOP CARROLL.

My Lord,

It is with the greatest pleasure I embrace the present opportunity to acquaint your Lordship with the happy success that seems to crown my weak endeavors in establishing the kingdom of Christ in this part of the country. The congregation is considerably increased since the time I moved hither; and I feel the greatest satisfaction in seeing the most unequivocal signs of the sincerest repentance and conversion in some of the most inveterate sinners. The church which I got built last August is very often almost full, and will have to be enlarged in a couple of years. I live at my own cabin ever since Christmas last, though in a very poor style yet, as your Lordship may expect. The moving to a country where I had to begin in the woods, the furnishing myself with everything necessary for housekeeping, when I had nothing of the kind, the great improvements I have made in order to put the place in such a state as to afford a maintenance for a priest, in fine, the great disappointments of last summer mentioned in a former letter to your Lordship, have exhausted my finances.

All these different circumstances make it necessary for me to apply to your Lordship for a little help; I understood that your Lordship has to dispose of a certain sum of money [probably the legacy of Sir John James] that is sent here (for the support of missionaries), every year from England. I trust you will not forget me for the next year, or even for a couple of years, in the distribution of the said money, especially as I have spent all my own, improving the church place, neglecting to improve my place. It is very likely that I shall see your Lordship in Baltimore next October, when I send my wagon down.

I beg your Lordship's blessing, and remain with the most profound respect,

    My Lord,
        Yr. most hble. and obt. Servant,
            Augustinus Demetrius Gallitzin.

Clearfield, July the 15th 1800.

Some months later he was very much distressed at receiving intimations, even the direct announcement that he was to be removed from his present position, and placed at Lancaster, where there was now a large congregation in need of a resident pastor, and appeared to the bishop of much more importance than the remote mountain settlement, in which he was considered to have buried himself.

Lancaster had been laid out as a town by Governor Hamilton in 1730; in 1745 a little log chapel, called St. Mary's, had been put up on the land bought by Father Wappeler, a few years before, and the congregation which was mainly German, attended by Fathers Pellentz, Schneider, Brosius, and other missionaries from Philadelphia, Conewago, and Goshenhoppen, until in 1751 Father Ferdinand Steenmeyer, a Swabian, known to us by the English version of his name,

Farmer, undertook to reside there, and attend to the congregation. He lived in the greatest poverty and piety, devoting himself with fervor to his missionary duties for seven or eight years, until called to other fields; he was a most exemplary religious, and saintly priest, who later as assistant to the Rev. Mr. Carroll, afterwards bishop, had superintendence of the missions, and rendered the greatest assistance to the American Church. He died in 1786. Father Molyneaux, and Mr. Heilbron, among others, attended Lancaster after Father Farmer left, and at the beginning of the century the bishop found it of such increasing importance that he wished to place an able priest there, anxious at the same time to put Father Gallitzin in a position where his talents, his education, and his great personal influence would be made manifest, as they could not be in an isolated mountain settlement, in the midst of the woods, where illiterate farmers and rude pioneers formed his only society. But Father Gallitzin felt that he was burying no talent in a napkin, by undertaking the work to which he believed God decidedly called him, and he was so wrapped in that work, bound by every tie of religious zeal and charity to it, that nothing could grieve him so much as the fear of having it taken from him. He found use for all he had learned in all the schools, even there, among those unlettered country-people; in silence and solitude, in the physical activity and mental energy required to meet the constant calls upon him,—for he had often to ride fifty and sixty miles on a sick call, and a walk of a dozen miles through the woods was a short promenade for him, while at home and abroad, he was the arbitrator, the father, and the servant of his people,—his mind had leisure to digest, arrange and work into practical shape, ready for use, that which he had learned or had forced upon it in his early youth. In this respect his isolation was of great service; he had learned too fast at home, and when his mother complained that his mind was inactive, she should have seen that it was overloaded; as it was now, Father Gallitzin walking about the settlement, his hands behind him, stopping now and then to watch the haymakers, or the sowers going out to sow their seed, gravely considering the boundary of a new field, and making queer mistakes in planting it, was by no means letting his intellect run to waste, but, on the contrary, ordering, arranging, freshening and leisurely enlarging it, breaking down useless barriers, lighting up dark and narrow passages. When in his sermons, which were plain doctrinal instructions, he made clear to those untutored minds the great truths over which the schoolmen are still fighting, like King Arthur's knights in the fog and mist wherein none knows if he strikes friend or foe, when step by step he led them through the labyrinths, the *depths of the riches, of the wisdom, and of the knowledge of God*, uniting those unlettered backwoodsmen in heart and mind to the glorious band of apostles, confessors, and martyrs, teaching them how to infuse the light of the mysteries of religion into their simple daily life, he showed a force and breadth of thought, a rare word power, which only constant study, continual mental activity, aided by the Holy Spirit, could give, and found fuller employment for his learning and ability, than though he had been placed before a congregation of greater culture, able to come half way to meet his thought. And if it had not been so, it would have made no difference, for when he renounced all claims to worldly grandeur, he gave up all claims to wordly distinctions, and sought no more to shine before the world as a famous writer, preacher, pastor, or confessor, than as prince or soldier; when he gave himself to the service of God he kept back no talent, no accomplishment. It is true he was not contented until he found the work to which the voice of grace continually called him, but once that work was found, through all obstacles and discouragements, though it proved a cross under which he often nearly fainted, he was never willing to give it up, or regretted the day he took it upon his shoulders. If you had asked him if he were not losing himself, as was thought, in isolation and obscurity, he would have answered that a servant of God is never lost where there is any of God's work to be done, and he least of all, for where could there be harder work, or fewer hands to do it?

Fortunately, by some delay in receiving the announcement,

10*

he was spared long uneasiness, for the permission of the bishop to remain with his charge soon followed to quiet his fears.

In his reply he mentions a clergyman expected from Muenster, probably Rev. Louis de Barth, a native of that city, educated at Bellay and Strasburg, who found himself, soon after his ordination, forced, on account of the persecution of religion, to leave France, even Muenster and resolved to seek refuge in America, encouraged to the step by the princess who understood from Mitri's letters the need of priests in the United States. She had already made it her special duty to induce and assist as many young priests in putting themselves at the bishop's disposal as possible, and to her energy and zeal, her glowing faith and unfailing charity, we are indebted for some of the most valued missionaries of our annals. Mr. de Barth remained at Lancaster, assisted by Rev. Michael Egan, afterwards Bishop of Philadelphia, until appointed vicar general and administrator of the diocese of Philadelphia in 1814.

Rev. D. A. Gallitzin to Right Rev. Bishop Carroll.

Clearfield Settlement, February 5. 1801.

My Lord,

Your Lordship's letter of Nov. 19. 1800, I only received last night, about half an hour before Michael Byrne's return from Baltimore. As much as the contents of the first letter seemed to disappoint me in my expectations, as much was I rejoiced at the contents of the second, which Michael Byrne fetched. I am happy to see that your Lordship has altered the resolution of removing me from here, which removal would be attended with the destruction of this new establishment. Catholics are gathering in from all quarters, upon the promise that I made not to forsake them, in as far as I had it in my power to make such a promise. The plantation will hardly be able in two years to maintain a priest, unless there is yearly as much money spent in the improving of it, as the congregation's salary amounts to*. How then could a priest subsist here, during that time, except it be one that has some permanent income to depend upon, independent of what the congregation could make up?

Between clearing of land, building and purchasing all the necessary furniture of the church, the house, and the place, I have sunk in about sixteen months almost four hundred pounds, tho' I could not accuse myself of a great many useless expenses. Your Lordship knows, besides, that I have always had a permanent inclination to the backwoods, ever since the first time the Rev. Mr. Pellentz, deceased, sent me there, which was about five years ago, last September; from all which circumstances Your Lordship may judge, that the disappointement would be very great if I had to exchange this place for Lancaster. It will be, perhaps, a matter of great pleasure to your Lordship to hear that there is a German priest, (who knows both German and English) coming, some time next spring, from Muenster to this country. From the acquaintance I had with him, when I lived in Germany, I judge him to be an edifying priest, tho' the Rev. Mr. Brosius having had more acquaintance with him than I, I believe, will be able to give him better recommendation. Having no time to translate his letter to my mother, which is in the German language, (for my wagon starts early to-morrow morning,) I send the original which some of your German acquaintances (Mr. Cheginere, for instance,) could translate into English.

Yr. Lordship will be kind enough to accept of my grateful thanks for the charitable advice given me in your last, and also for the chocolate which came to hands very safe. I have the honor to remain with the most profound respect,

My Lord,
Your most hble. and obdt. Servt.
Augustine Demetrius Gallitzin,
Parish priest of Clearfield.

---

*This means the salary, which the congregation would be able to give; Father Gallitzin never received any salary, either from the bishop, or any of his congregations.

P. S. I wrote a letter to my father about six months ago, in order to undeceive him from his expectation that I had renounced all claims to the succession to his temporal estate, and sent the duplicate of the same letter to my mother. This I expect will be sufficient.

The letter to his father here mentioned, was called forth by a passage in one of the prince's letters, in which it is taken for granted that Mitri had no thought for the property, except to assist his parents in securing it to his sister, when, in reality, Father Gallitzin was every day more anxious to make sure of his own portion, for he relied upon it as the great, and necessary instrument in forming a "lasting establishment for promoting the cause of religion" in the United States.

"We are both," wrote the prince*, alluding to the princess and himself, "we are both well advanced in years; your mother, moreover, is laden with infirmities, and I begin, especially since the past severe winter, to feel my age; there is, then, no time to be lost if you wish to see us again.... Indeed, your return is absolutely necessary in order to arrange matters in regard to my estates in your sister's favor, for although you have renounced them by your choice of profession, as well as by your repeated declarations to me, there are certain formalities to be attended to, otherwise the property would go to the side heirs."

Whatever Father Gallitzin may have felt in regard to this matter in the first moments of his choice, he very soon saw that his was not a case in which it would be allowable, if it ever is allowable, for the means rightfully his to be given up to the world's use without a word of remonstrance; the Scripture command, *Go sell all thou hast and give to the poor*, seemed especially designed for him, and he longed to fulfill it. What he did renounce, and so delared to his father, was his position in the world as a *grand seigneur*, his rank,

---

* Rev. Mr. Lemcke's *Leben und Wirken*, p. 186.

his titles, all honors and luxuries, never to use his wealth for himself or for the world. Prince Gallitzin was not just the man to see the distinction, and naturally he did not feel desirous of having the estates which had passed from generation to generation of Gallitzins go out of their hands now, at any price. The princess understood the matter very differently, and continual anxiety about it greatly troubled the last years of her life, but such was the Russian law that the prince could not have left the property to his son, even if he had desired, for it regarded him as in disfavor, he having remained away from his regiment, and his country, without the imperial permission. The prince could have disposed of some of his property, and bequeathed the money to his son, but that was rather too much to ask of a man devoted to the world, intensely aristocratic, proud of his name and wealth, which he considered it his greatest duty to preserve as he had received them. He probably hoped, if Mitri would return to Europe, he could, at least, induce him to remain there, even if he did not receive the imperial pardon and permission to reside in Russia, and could occupy in France or Germany some high position, perhaps, as prince-bishop. The princess, although she knew her husband so well, may also have had hopes of some compromise between them, if Mitri and he should meet, for the prince was kindly disposed, and, perhaps, in his disgust at the state of affairs in the Old World, might not look upon the idea of colonizing the New, as such a very childish scheme as it now appeared. She could not hope he would ever give it a moment's serious consideration as a plan for saving souls, but there might, perhaps, arise some human aspect of the matter, which would strike him favorably. But Father Gallitzin saw no way open to him to think of a return to Europe, and in writing that he did not renounce his share in his father's wealth, he did all that could be done, and the result must be left to God.

So far from intending to leave the United States, at any future time, unless for a short visit, all Father Gallitzin's affections, as well as his absorbing interests, centred in the young republic, of whose character, opportunities and mission, he had a clear appreciation, which showed he inherited the statesman character of his father, and his ancestors, who made the sovereigns for whom they did the thinking, famous for foresight and judgment. The carelessness, the short-sighted views of many who were shaping its destinies, aroused him to a degree of indignation, incomprehensible to those who saw nothing of the importance of their acts, at a moment when the country, like clay in the mould was taking shape and form, sensitive to the faintest touch. There was a great deal of loud boasting then, as now, in which Father Gallitzin took no part, but the fondest dream of our Fathers did not pass the calm and well considered hopes he had for us, and in his own small sphere set about to realize, for with him, of course, true Catholic principle was the adamantine foundation on which to build true political rights. The great charm of his views, and that which gave them their greatest force, was that they never lost themselves in visionary projects; you could only deduct his theories from observation of his practice, and learn his whole plan from the precision of its details.

It was, therefore, an important event for him when Congress having shortened the period of probation, he found himself, in 1802, qualified to become an American citizen, and in August of that year applied to the courts of Huntingdon county in which his residence was then included, for naturalization*.

He was naturalized as Augustine Smith, the name which had become fixed upon him at the seminary, and had so clung to him since, that he was probably advised by his lawyer to use it, as he was known by no other either socially or in his business transactions, and to prevent the confusion and the misunderstanding which would arise from any attempt to resume his family name. At the time of first taking that name he had little dream that he would ever become a citizen and

---

*From unpublished notes of Richard B. McCabe, Esq., a distinguished lawyer of Pennsylvania, who knew Dr. Gallitzin personally and intended writing his life, but died before accomplishing his purpose.

landowner in this country, and when he was ready to become such he found it almost impossible to make any change. Except so far as it might possibly involve him in legal difficulties at some future time, he liked this well enough, for he had no ambition to make his true name known, indeed was very careless by what one he was called.

But much as he rejoiced in his new found citizenship, it cannot be supposed he thus renounced in legal form, his country and his hereditary rank without a pang. No thoughtful man, with manly instincts, can turn his back upon his native land, and place his hand in the stranger's, without an effort, and never can a Russian divest himself of the last lingering tenderness for his own land, even when it banishes him from its sight forever, and with a nature so intense as his, a character in which there were no radicalisms of any sort, nothing but the pure desire to serve God as he seemed to wish could have given him strength so often to renew the sacrifice. Indeed if a sacrifice were made when made, we might all be heroes and many of us saints ; but the renouncing of one thing to take up another, is but the beginning of the sacrifice ; every hour of our lives it must be renewed ; renewed when the feet are sore, the soul fainting, no less inexorably than when we run towards it, elastic and bouyant; in the long days of inaction, no less than in the thickest of the battle; as well when the colors drop and the day is lost, as when the standards fly and all the bells ring victory. It must not become a habit, put on from custom, but a uniform embraced every day as if worn for the first time ; it must not be suffered to grow mechanical as a farmer sows his field, but a loving labor, fresh as the bride's first household care. Such was the sacrifice Mitri made, such the sacrifice Father Gallitzin continued, with God's grace, to carry on. His iron will could have made him a stoic or a puritan, but only God's truth and grace could make him the light-hearted, steadfast priest he was fast becoming.

It was a great comfort to him when still more closely binding himself to his new home, to know that the ties between himself and his old friends were being drawn the closer,

as time passed on, and each became more absorbed in the
great work of salvation, that work which reaching over the
great ocean, united the Pennsylvania mountains to the Westphalian plains, and bound noble and peasant in the chains of
grateful affection. It is rather a peculiar circumstance that
while his greatest success was with the unlearned and poor,
the princess, his mother, was the means of leading some of
the greatest minds, and men of noblest birth to the light of
truth. First and brightest on the list of those whom she
could number among her converts was Count von Stolberg,
his wife, *née* Sophia von Redern and nearly all the members
of his large and charming family, whom she had visited
shortly after Mitri left her for America, and while she was
much prostrated with fears and grief for his absence. After
seven years of inclination to the Church, and the severest and
most searching investigation of its history and its doctrines,
in which the princess assisted him with glowing zeal, the
count and his wife made profession of Catholic faith in the
princess' private chapel, on June 1. 1800, feast of Pentecost.
When Father Gallitzin heard from his mother of their conversion, he rejoiced greatly, not only because of his affection for
them, because of the inestimable value of one soul seeking
salvation at the only fountain of life, not only for his mother's
part therein, but also on account of the influence for good
which the amiable character, the great talents, and the wide
reputation of the count would place in his hands, expectations which have been fully justified, for his conversion,
while it threw his late associates, Klopstock, Voss, Claudius,
Goethe, Lavater, and others, mostly infidels and philosophers,
into great indignation and distress, led others to look again
at that temple which they had thought fallen, and, in time, to
seek a shelter therein themselves; prominent among these
was Frederick Schlegel, the philosopher, who, in his turn,
made the truth known to many more, and thus, the conversion of Count von Stolberg might be said to commence a new
era in German thought, and that he is rightfully considered
the father and pioneer who cut the way for those illustrious
German Catholics who have since arisen in their strength as

true philosophers and real thinkers*. After his conversion he gave up his high position under the government, and removed from Eutin to Muenster to enjoy the constant society of the princess, and the circle of which she was the vivifying centre, to whom he owed, under God, the gift of faith, as he gratefully expressed to his well remembered friend, Mitri.

COUNT VON STOLBERG TO REV. D. A. GALLITZIN.†

Muenster, March 27. 1802

I have often wished, dearest Mitri, to write you, even while I was in Eutin. I have received from your mother so much never to be forgotten pleasure, and she has so attached me, after God, to her with a love for which I hope to praise him forever, and in which I hope ever to rejoice, that I longed to speak to you of her, and I could not bear the thought of being as a stranger to the son of that dear mother, but a certain feeling of shyness has kept me back. . . In my inmost thoughts a certain hope spoke to me in accents more or less distinct: perhaps as a child of that great and holy mother, who now invites you to her bosom, to whom he in the new world brings more children, you may be able to speak of her and beg him to thank the beloved, Heavenly Father for the mercy that he has shown to me. This, dearest Mitri, I now do, though late. Yet, even before your dear mother informed me, last spring, of that which you had written in the fulness of your heart, of your affection for my wife and me, when you heard we had entered the Church, I knew what you felt for us, and I rejoiced in your joy at the blessing God has bestowed upon us, and this all the more that he has given it through the instrumentality of your blessed mother. For this was his intention when he brought me eleven years ago to Muenster, and attached me to her as he only can bind soul to soul.

---

*Stolberg was a prolific writer, he was widely known as a poet, a traveller, and a novelist, before he became a Catholic, afterwards he published a great deal; his main work was THE HISTORY OF THE RELIGION OF JESUS CHRIST, of which he lived to complete fifteen volumes. This was taken up and carried on by others after his death in 1819.

†Lemcke, p. 192.

Through her, beloved Mitri, we are nearly related, are bound together in heartfelt love by her. And when I hear her speak of you, when, as she speaks of you, through her mother's tears there shines at once love, joy and praise to God, then, dearest Mitri, I feel near to you, closely connected with you. .

Pray for me, for my Sophia. for my children. Think of us sometimes at the Holy Sacrifice, and recommend to the heart . of the great, all-merciful High Priest, my oldest daughter, who by the time you receive this letter will be not only not a Catholic, but probably the wife of a Protestant, to whom she was engaged when the Church opened her arms to us. I cannot, nor do I desire to touch this chord, for it agonizes me, so much I have said that you may intercede for this my very dear child.

I reach you my hand, beloved Mitri, over land and sea, I feel myself near to you in that love which neither time nor space can disturb. In this love I press you to my heart.

Fr. L. Gr. z. Stolberg.

Letters also arrived frequently from his friends Baron Caspar Maximilian von Droste, and his brothers*, which informed him of home matters, the great changes in Muenster, which was secularized in 1803, and many things of historical as well as personal interest. The tie that was so long lacking, without which his education would have remained barren, now united his mother and himself in the loving confidence, which each had so vainly sought before religion opened her heart, and awoke the slumbering forces of his soul, and gave life and endurance to his boyish friendships, which had never been complete until all were on the same ground of eternal hope and trust. There was no incident of his homely surroundings too trivial to be related to his mother, and she poured out the treasures of her love and charity to him and his charge, without a thought or remnant of the restlessness which had

---

*Rev. Mr. Lemcke in his *Leben* alludes to these letters which he obtained at Loretto, but does not give their contents, and the originals cannot now be recovered.

devoured her in the cold and loveless days they had spent apart in the desert land of mere intellect. At the same time there was no plan too lofty, no aspiration too unworldly or impracticable for him to fear to mention it to her. Thousands and thousands of miles apart mother and son were together as they were not even when under the same roof, and her sympathy, her intelligent understanding of the highest and deepest matters he could wish to mention followed him, and sustained him in many a dark and friendless hour, when puny minds steeped in ignorance and self-conceit pronounced upon his master-words. Mother and son and friends, all were now at home in one house, working freely and cheerfully, with many a pleasant interchange of thought, as they passed back and forth at their appointed tasks. Perfect love had cast out fear.

CHAPTER XI.

DEATH OF PRINCE DMITRI GALLITZIN, AND CONSEQUENT PROJECTS.

(1803—1804.)

Plans for a return to Europe. — Bishop Carroll's advice. — Last years of the prince. — The Russian property. — The princess' affection.

Although Father Gallitzin saw no way of acceding to his father's often repeated request, and the desire of his own heart to visit his parents once more, they could by no means give up the hope of seeing him. His mother followed his father in making the same request, and urged it with all the tenderness of her heart, pointing out to him the great advantages he could procure for his mission, by an understanding with his father, and the assistance which his wealthy friends would be only too glad to send to the young church of America, could they but once understand its needs, and become interested in it, for arguments like these would be, she knew, the ones most likely to decide him to undertake the journey. What a coming home that would have been for him! As he thought of it more he began to have hopes that it was not out of the range of possibilities; the only obstacle in the way was the lack of a priest to take his place, for though he were to bring back to his people all the gold in the Russian treasury, he knew well it could not weigh a feather in the balance against the spiritual loss to them, if left without a pastor. In 1803 he felt so much encouraged by the prospect of a faithful priest to attend his congregation during his absence, that he set his temporal affairs in order, and did not write to his mother for sometime, expecting to see her instead, but the promises, like so many others made him, could not be fulfilled, and that bright wish of his heart had also to be set aside.

Rev. D. A. Gallitzin to the Princess.*

I dare not think of it. My heart trembles with love; it seems to me as if I absolutely must see you once more in order to leave the world in peace. God knows what is best in this, and what would tend most to his honor; but according to all appearances it does not seem as if it would soon be possible. The number of priests is becoming smaller instead of greater and the Catholics increasing. I know that you are entirely satisfied with God's will, far more than I am, and that you ask to see me only on the other side of the grave in the bosom of the Heavenly Father. But it would do me good to lie down at your feet, to bathe them with my tears, to receive your blessing, and hear from your own lips that you have forgiven me everything; I would rather have this than all the treasures of earth. I feel as if the hand of God were heavy upon me, on account of my olden disobedience, and indifference to your admonitions.

I have never felt this more intensely than since I have seen, with my own eyes, how this damning freedom, this reckless disobedience, and false shame lead so many souls to perdition. It seems as if I could not remain all my life as now, one has so many temptations here, that I should be glad to end my days in some place, where I should have no other responsibility than the care of my own soul.

The letter from which this is an extract, is dated June 26th, 1803, and crossed on its way to Muenster one written on the 26th of March by his sister, at his mother's dictation, but retained until the 16th of May, in order to have an enclosure which could not be got ready sooner. This letter, which, as it took about three months for one from home to reach him, was probably received in August, contained the announcement of his father's death.

---

* Dr. Katercamp's *Life of the Princess Gallitzin*, p. 234.

PRINCESS GALLITZIN TO HER SON.*

My dear Child,

I inform you in haste that it pleased the dear God to call your father from us on the 16th of March. He died from hemorrhage, which lasted only three hours, having that very day, and only a few hours before, written us that he was well. He left no will, so it is very urgent that if you cannot come at once, you should send me power-of-attorney, because not even the personal property, which is at Brunswick, can be had (for the Brunswick government put a seal on everything immediately after his death), unless we three, you, Mimi, and I can show ourselves living and claiming it, either in person or by power-of-attorney. I must, in any event, produce a power-of-attorney in Russia. In fact, I am, by my marriage contract, the usufractory of the whole of your father's wealth, and after my death you two shall inherit it; but this contract was not made in Russia, and it is therefore very possible that your father's brother and nephews, may discover something in the Russian law to put obstacles in the way of your inheriting it, especially as so many believe you have become a monk, and therefore cannot inherit property. To secure your interest for you, I must have a power-of-attorney from you as soon as possible. I enclose a model of the way in which it is to be drawn up.

Do not be negligent this time, my son, for though your small estimate of the value of this world's good gives me joy, I must confess, for that very reason I desire to save them for you, you are called to use them well, and you owe them to your mission and your parishioners. As your father's affairs have always been unknown to me, you can easily imagine how hard it now is for me to learn about them. Hasten, then, my dear child, to send the power-of-attorney; even if you expect to start the very next day for Europe yourself, do not fail to send it, for the ship that brought you might be longer on its way than the ship carrying the letter. Remember that if I should die you would lose all....

* Rev. H. Lemcke, p. 207.

A postscript, dated May 16th, urged him still more to be prompt and exact, and added that, since writing, she had found something in his father's papers, leading her to fear that by the Russian law, he was disqualified by his clerical profession from inheriting or receiving an inherited estate. If this should prove to be the case then she would strive to find some way, by which he could have the benefit of the property, after her death.

Immediately upon receiving this letter Father Gallitzin had full power-of-attorney prepared with all due legal flourish, which he sent to his mother, writing her as before that it was not possible for him to leave his congregation, even though a princely fortune at stake was now added to the longing to embrace her once more, and soon after received from Mr. Overberg and herself, answers to his letter of June 26th, in which his coming back is still further urged, as of the greatest necessity, on account of the state of his father's affairs.

REV. DR. OVERBERG TO REV. D. A. GALLITZIN[*].

Beloved in Our Lord,

So it was not the will of God that we should see our dear Augustine in the summer, as we wished, and had, indeed, so much reason to expect! I believe the Right Reverend Bishop will make a way for you to pay us a visit, when he learns how necessary your coming is in regard to the matter of your father's property, in which the American mission is also interested.

I assured you, my beloved, in the lines which I wrote you on your birthday, that I thought of you often, especially in my prayers. But never except in my prayers, have I thought oftener of you, and of your happiness in your vocation, than since we have had for our evening readings the *Lettres edifiantes et curieuses des missionaires*. This is a collection of letters, filling several volumes, a splendid work, which you also would read with great pleasure, if time and circumstances permitted. How often, in reading them, have I

---

[*] Lemcke, p. 196.

become convinced anew that a missionary's vocation is the holiest, and most to be venerated to which a priest of Christ can be called! He himself followed it, and the apostles succeeded him in it; who, therefore, more justly merits to be regarded a successor of the apostles, a priest of Christ, than a missionary? It is of him alone, properly speaking, of whom the Scripture says: *How beautiful upon the mountains are the feet of him that bringeth good tidings, and that preacheth peace: of him that sheweth forth good, that preacheth salvation!* (ROMANS X, 15, ISAIAS LII, 7.)

During the French revolution we became acquainted with the Trappists who were entirely unknown to me previously. They have a monastery at Darfeld, and when any of them come to Muenster, which happens quite often, they always call to see us. At first I looked upon their vocation as the *ne plus ultra* of sanctity to which a man could reach in this world, but when by reading these *Lettres Edifiantes* I became better acquainted with the missions, I changed my opinion; I still respect the Trappists, but I must admit that the missionaries hold precedence, because they conform more to the life of Christ and his apostles, and also because they unite to work out through various ways (not only by prayer and good example, but by sowing the seed of the divine word,) the salvation of souls redeemed by the blood of Christ, while subjected to no fewer mortifications, though not always of the same kind, than those by which the Trappists seek to sanctify themselves. It is undoubtedly true, as you say, dear Mitri, that a missionary is exposed to many temptations, but this would not alarm me, if God had given me the grace to enter that state, for nowhere could I be more certain that I was following Christ in all his works, and should I not have the strongest confidence that he would hold me in his care? As a missionary I think I should with full reliance apply to myself the Ninetieth psalm, and fear no attacks of the infernal enemy, should walk with courage *upon the asp and the basilisk,* and *trample under foot the lion and the dragon,* for I could not doubt that he whose work I was endeavoring to do, precisely as he had set me the model, would cover me with his strong wings. I would fear it still less, it being a penance for my sins, because as the Holy Spirit tells us in Holy Writ: *If any of you err from the truth, and one convert him: He must know, that he who causeth a sinner to be converted from the error of his way, shall save his soul from death and shall cover a multitude of sins.* (James v. 19, 20.). How could the offence to God of having soiled and defiled His image in ourself be better repaired, and the honor taken from him be better restored, than by striving to purify and make beautiful this image, not only in ourself, but in others? As regards the responsibility resting on those who have the care of souls, it is great, I know, but to my thinking, it would be still greater if we should seek to shake off the charge of souls confided to us by God, because of the strict socount which He demands of us. I have long thought, as seen in my "Directions for Teachers" (*Anweisung für Schullerher,*) p.37, that those who for fear of the strict account they will have to render, let their talent for assisting in their neighbor's salvation, lie unused, will greatly offen d God, like the servant in the gospel, who buried his talent because he feared the strictness of his Lord. If one having the care of souls is zealous, but not so much so as he could or should be, it may be said to him: Thou hast often been careless and unfaithful in thy Master's service, but he cannot be called an entirely idle and unprofitable servant, like him who buried his talent. Should not the former hope for mercy more than the latter? And here seems appropriate the words of St. Paul to Timothy, in his First Epistle iv. 16: *Attend to thyself and to doctrine: be earnest in them. For in doing this thou shalt both save thyself and them that hear thee.* Paul found both things necessary for salvation, attention to ourself, and not to ourself only, but to the doctrine also. If ever it was necessary to attend both to ourselves and to the doctrine, it is necessary in these times in which we live. With thoughts like these I often seek to calm myself, and I wish that they might also serve you for the same purpose.

You know your dear mother, you know her extraordinary love for her Mitri, you will therefore, believe me without any proofs, when I tell you that her affection has increased in devotion, (by which I understand the meeting and union of two souls which love each other,) since her dearly loved son has chosen the same end as she, and ardently strives to attain it. Although she has schooled herself to give herself to God's will, it costs her not a little so to moderate the desire to see her Mitri, that it shall not destroy her peace of mind,—it costs her tears. She probably can write but little to you this time, as she has written to the Rt. Rev. Bishop, and Mr. Nagot, to arrange with them that your coming here, which we hold necessary, may be hastened as much as possible in the season when a sea voyage is the least dangerous; besides her health does not permit her to write much at one time. In August we went on account of her ill health, to the baths at Dryburg; as long as we were there she felt easier, and not so weak, but upon our return the old troubles came back. It is evident that God intends to purify her like gold in furnace, for he loves her.

The grace of our Lord and Redeemer be and remain with us.

Oremus pro invicem, ut salvemur.

B. OVERBERG.

On the day on which you received your first holy orders, 1803.

The princess accompanied this with a letter of her own, written not in French, as usual, but in German:—

PRINCESS GALLITZIN TO HER SON*.

Tenderly loved son of my heart,

I will not make the short time left from the dictating and writing of other letters concerning your arrival among us, and your affairs, still shorter by descriptions of the long and delightful expectations, and of the hopes of seeing you, wrecked by your letter of June 26. Your own heart so good by

---

Lemcke, p. 202.

nature, so purified by grace, will by its sympathy, give you the best idea of it. I, too can gather from your letter, what feelings you surrendered to the best will of our Heavenly Father. It has seemed to me, from the first, as if our hearts were enough in unison, for one to know the other without exposing ourselves to misjudgments, although in matters of intellect, or rather of the lower will, we have not always agreed. It cannot be denied that it was often your fault, for you had to be a child, and then a youth, before you could be a man. But my part of the wrong, which is not the smallest has not this excuse and yet, my darling, I am so fully convinced that so far as you are concerned you readily forgive me, that, indifferent to it, I reach my arms out to you; all the more that the infinite mercy of God, remembering my weakness and infirmity, has undertaken, and this I ascribe to your prayers and hearty clinging to God's will,— to purify me, in my age, from the heavy stains of sin accumulating for years. Pray, therefore, fervently that I may bear this purification as God wills, and unless you wish to sadden me, grieve no more, as if you had yet to receive pardon for your faults. As far as I can look back on my useless, sinful life, I cannot find a time when anything in you would so have affected my heart that pardon would be necessary. For some years, by God's grace, I have been enabled to see in that sort of blindness and coldness which for a time, appeared to close your heart to me, that which I now see in the present persecutions from both sides of the family,— a merciful fire which, (if I faithfully persevere) may consume so much of my load of sins that when I go hence I may have the hope of embracing you, my dearest, in the bosom of God, and forever sing praises and adoration to him, in union with all the saints Allelluia. Now, judge for yourself, if I can possibly have anything to forgive when I see in you my Augustine, and since I firmly believe that you have given yourself for ever to God, in humility and faithfulness.

I have written to the Right Rev. Bishop of Baltimore, and to Mr Nagot, everything which may help or be necessary for your journey, because they receive letters sooner than you, and besides, you must have permission, and means of conveyance from them. I only repeat the request that you will not sail at a dangerous season, and that you let me know what is decided; this I ask for my own peace of mind, and in order to give directions, in conformity with this information, for your interests, and in regard to the Russian business.

I send you with this the answer received from Mr. Vogt of Hamburg, concerning your money matters, for I called him to account last January.

Upon receiving these letters, and others from the bishop and Mr. Nagot, urging his compliance with the desire expressed in them, Father Gallitzin went to Baltimore, where he had not been for two years, to convince them by a personal interview, as he could not by letter that, as he was situated, it was quite impossible for him to leave the country, and to discuss with them any plans which their great anxiety to further the princess' wish, might suggest to them. Mr. Nagot was about visiting France, and was very desirous of having Father Gallitzin accompany him on the voyage. It was not until he laid before them the many phases of the work in which he was engaged, that they began to have any real conception of the breadth, and importance of the remote mountain settlements, united in one by his pastoral affection, and as they obtained somewhat of an idea of what might come from them, they became only the more earnest in urging him to go abroad, and spare no exertions to secure the inheritance, which would be of inestimable value, was, indeed, absolutely necessary to the completion of his work. But the already toil-worn missionary was eminently a practical man, by grace and self-discipline, if not actually by nature, who saw his present duty always clearly, and could not be drawn from it by any prospects, however alluring, of future advantage, even though every fibre of his heart was strained to meet it, and every impulse of his soul leaped to grasp it. Still more in this case for, as he had said, in simple truthfulness, he would rather have heard from the lips of his mother, that she forgave him his youthful thoughtlessness, and childish errors, than to receive all the treasures of earth. But for no earthly consideration could he justify himself to his own conscience, if he left his post, now there being no one to whom he could entrust it, who would be able to exercise the vigilance, the forethought, the ever-active care which it every day needed more. The comparative peace of the Church in Europe, as well as the great hopes which the friends of religion built upon the first acts of Bonaparte, who was now First Consul and, apparently, the great protector of the papacy, put a stop to the emigration of the clergy, even induced many who had come to us in the days of terror, to return to France, while several of the Irish clergy, who had also taken refuge here in the times of the troubles in Ireland, at the close of the last century, gave up the thankless task of guarding the isolated and almost unmanageable missions which tried the patience of all our early priests, and joyously set sail for the ever dear land of their birth; it was too soon to expect much from our own extremely limited resources, and as Catholics were constantly arriving from almost all parts of Europe, every day increased the burden of the remaining priests. As Bishop Kenrick well and truly said, years later, these missions often "required the gift of tongues and a health of iron," Gallitzin who knew this better even than Bishop Carroll and Mr. Nagot, for there is no teacher like experience, who was well aware that half a dozen assistant priests, could he have had them, would hardly have sufficed to lighten his own burden, was not the man to lay it for a day upon another, already weighed down by his own charge. It was not to be thought of; facts like these, heartbreaking though they were, could not be evaded, and when he detailed them to his superiors it was with no hope of having them argued away; undoubtedly if the bishop and Mr. Nagot had actually laid their commands upon him to leave his responsibility to them, he would have done so, for a quiet unobstrusive obedience to orders, even to advice or suggestions from those empowered to give them, is very noticeable throughout his correspondence with Bishop

Carroll, but this neither the bishop nor the Sulpician president would think of doing, even though it is hardly likely they felt as keenly as he did himself, the full import of his reasons, and the all but crushing sense of responsibility from which escape grew every day less possible. Their last argument was drawn from his mother's letter to the bishop, in which she had written that it was absolutely necessary for him to come, but he showed that the word *absolutely* had been crossed out, and that over it she had written *held*; it was held necessary that he should come; he understood from this that his mother gave him no commands, but left the decision to his own conscience.

Perhaps when Father Gallitzin turned away from Baltimore, after this, and rode back to that lonely mountain village for which he had given all hope of seeing kith or kin again, of holding his dear mother to his heart once more on this side of the grave, the sacrifice of his life reached its supremest height, from which through all years to come, he was bound not to let it recede for one moment.

The princess in her reply, dated July 24. 1804, proved herself a true Christian woman, worthy to be his mother:

PRINCESS AMALIA GALLITZIN TO REV. D. A. GALLITZIN*.

Hard as it comes to my mother-heart to renounce the hope, so near to it, of embracing its beloved son, I can say with truth that your letter which gives me the information, bestows upon me the greatest consolation I can desire upon earth. Every line of it is in unison with my own sentiments and wishes. You understood me perfectly in regard to my intention in the word crossed out, in which I expressed the unconditional in my letter to the bishop, and wrote above it the conditional. In business matters for which I care little and understand less, I must take counsel of those who understand them, and follow their advice, in so far as nothing higher or better suffers by it, because they concern the in-

---

* Katercamp, p. 266.

terests of my children. This seemed possibly the case here when I had to write, according to their advice, to the bishop of the absolute necessity of your presence. But as I had not even the security that your personal presence would aid in saving our fortune, the possibility on the contrary, of your mission suffering by your sudden departure, came so vividly before my eyes, that the fear of it forced me, as it were, to change the *il est absolument nécessaire*, to *on dit* or *on croit qu'il est nécessaire*. Praise to the Lord who has ordered all for the best, and who will continue to do so if we desire the best only, His honor and glory in all things, and, so far as our shortsightedness permits, have it in view in all our actions. The whole earth cries to us so loudly and so forcibly: "All below is vain," that I am growing timid and fearful for all who cling to anything transitory, which the infinite mercy of God permits to burst assunder, with startling, terrible thunderpeals, before our very eyes, like an exploded soapbubble. Oh, the power of blindness, born of pride! But with God's grace, the hypocrite will come out last at the end. The excesses to which the children of the deceiver are giving themselves up, apparently in triumph, are already preparing their own downfall and the triumph of the holy Church. The times before this universal world-revolution were far more dangerous, for then pride worked through an all pervading wavering in the faith, of all classes of people, even among the innocent, all the more that it had to be careful everywhere to conceal its claws under the outer garb of virtue, philanthropy, and a glittering outside shell of religion. But since the mask has been thrown off, and the terrible results not only stand there, but even attack the greater part of men of all conditions, the world everywhere seems to be on guard and observant, as if the Angel of the Lord was here with the winnowing sheaf in his hand, and the separation of the wheat from the cockle had begun. The race of the lukewarm is daily dying out. Some are found who plainly belong to the stragglers (who do not know whether they should go on or stand still) who are calmly satisfied that they have Abraham for their father. The greater number is divided into two sorts: the rude, blindfolded mass, and the penitents who hasten on. You would be amazed if I could talk with you for one short hour, and tell you what changes are going on among individuals, and whole families, even in this part of the country, many of whom are known to you.

At the same time the princess wrote to the bishop her full approval of her son's decision, painful as it was to her and him:

Princess Gallitzin to Bishop Carroll.*

July 31th, 1804. (Written at Amsterdam.)

Monseigneur,

As the precarious condition of our property does not permit me to pass the season, as usual, at the baths, and as my physician, moreover, finds it absolutely necessary for my health that I should make a carriage journey of, at least, ten or twelve days, I chose coming to Amsterdam to see and to speak with the missionaries, who are to have the honor of receiving your blessing, and are to see my dear son face to face. God, to whom I have entirely, and with a free heart, devoted him, knows that never has the happiness of clasping him in my arms approached that caused by the dispositions which attach him to his post, and make him prefer his lambs to his fortune. God has given him a great grace in permitting him willingly to resign a fortune, which would equally have escaped him, even could he have been able to make the journey to Russia, without any risk to the parishioners whom Providence, and your goodness, Monseigneur, have confided to him.

I have found, independently of Mr. Charles Nerinx, whom I have already had the honor of announcing to you, in a letter dated at Muenster, which, without doubt, has reached

---

* From the original in French belonging to the Archepiscopal archives of Baltimore.

you long before this, Mr. François Malavé, another candidate perfectly recommended by all that there is of most pure in Brabant; he had come intending to accompany Mr. Nerinx to Baltimore, to put himself under your orders, but it happened that the Jesuit, Father Becker, *curé* here, authorized by the Father General, Gruber, to receive persons eligible for the Society, showed him a letter he had just received from the Father General, in which it was mentioned that you, Monseigneur, had presented thirteen of your missionaries for admission into the Society of Jesus*. This letter joined to the representations of Rev. Father Halnath, whom to name suffices to say all, and who it may be remarked, in passing, has contributed no little towards attracting me here, — determined Mr. Malavé to commence by passing several months at Dunebourg, at the Jesuit novitiate, whence he begs you to have the goodness to re-claim him from the Superior General Gruber, as belonging to you, for he feels himself in the most special manner called to America, and only goes to Dunebourg in order to make himself more capable of fulfilling your orders, and intentions, in whatever you may deign to use him.

You will see in this, Monseigneur, what he has entreated me to say to you, — he is not yet entirely decided himself how it will be, — just as I am about leaving Amsterdam, where I have spent only three days, for and with the saintly personages who drew me here; — I have not even an entire

---

* It will be recollected that the Society of Jesus, which Clement XIV. had reluctantly suppressed in 1773, had been permitted, at the earnest request of the Emperor Paul, by a brief of Pope Pius VII., dated March 7th, 1801, to unite together in Russia as the *Company of Jesus*, with the rule of St. Ignatius for their guide. As Russia was the only country in which this privilege was then allowed, many ex-Jesuits from all parts of Europe, and even some from the United States, availed themselves of it. In 1806, two years after the date of the princess'. letter, the permission was extended to this country, and a novitiate established at Georgetown College with Rev. Robert Molyneux, for superior, subject, however, to the superior general in Russia. In August 1814, the Society was completely reestablished, everywhere, with all its ancient privileges.

sheet of paper at hand, but I must still mention to you, Monseigneur, Mr. Charles Guny, *curé* near Brabasçon, who accompanies Mr. Nerinx to Baltimore, undecided as yet whether he will there join the order of La Trappe, or whether God will call him to the missionary life, for which he now believes himself incapable; he has the same recommendations in his favor, and I do not think he will lose anything in your estimation by his own opinion of himself.

I venture to entreat you, Monseigneur, to write me a few words concerning these earnest men, who interest so many saintly souls here, and whom I hope you will like.

I do not speak of the excellent news which Father Halnath brings us from St. Petersburg, whence he has just returned. The bearers of this letter with give you all the interesting details. God be blessed that His mercy deigns thus to repair the losses, which we have every day in the larger part of Europe, and to prepare us the missionaries of which we shall soon have more need than the countries beyond the sea.

I am with the most respectful attachment,

   Monseigneur,

     Your most humble and obedient servant,.

      Augustine's Mother.

P. S. Having been so prolix I flatter myself, Monseigneur, that your charity will pardon me, if I venture to add my most affectionate regards to the President, Mr. Nagot, and embrace my son, leaning with him on the heart of my Saviour.

With this letter ends the correspondence, so far as it is now obtainable, consequent upon the sad and sudden death of the prince, and the immediate effects of his having died without a will. He had been in political life from his early youth, and had only left it upon the conquest of Holland by the French, under Pichegru (1795), with the intention of soon returning to it, but the conduct of the Emperor Paul, having entirely disgusted him, he never after sought any public position, but retired to Brunswick, where he devoted himself to-science. He was a member of the Academies of St. Petersburg, Stockholm, Berlin and Brussels, and president of the Mineralogical Society of Jena, which received his cabinet of natural history. He wrote a *Description physique de la Tauride, relativement aux trois règnes de la nature,* published at the Hague in 1788, and a *Traité de Minéralogie, ou description abrégée et méthodique des minéraux,* published at Maestricht in 1792 and afterwards with additions at Helmstaedt in 1796. He was, perhaps, as manly, honorable, and fine a type as could be found of a man sustained only by material, earthly things, without faith, without fixed religious principle or feeling who believed in nothing not plain to his senses, yet never sank his gifted nature and noble intellect into the degrading depths which appear to have been the natural element of the men of his order of thinking in those days. The excesses of the French Revolution, and its effects, opened his eyes to the evil of much he had previously accepted as manly and reasonable, and in the matter of Mitri's choice of life showed less severity than could have been expected after such a crushing blow to all his hopes. He never overcame his distaste for the act, but it cannot be doubted he felt in his heart great affection for his only son, whose constant prayers during the years of his priesthood, while the prince was yet living, must have won grace for him, which, it is to be hoped, as no one knows what passes between a soul and its God at the last moment, he did not wholly reject. Father Gallitzin grieved greatly for him, and long afterwards was discovered practising the greatest and severest penances upon himself, for his father's sake.

Immediately upon the prince's death, his relatives in Russia took possession of his estates as his heirs, considering Mitri as thrown out altogether on account of his profession, as the prince had always expected; the princess Mimi was by the laws of Russia, only entitled to one fourteenth of the real estate, and to one eighth of the personal property. By the advice of his mother, Father Gallitzin appointed Baron von Fuerstenberg, Count Frederic Leopold von Stolberg, and Count Clement Augustus von Merveldt, his agents, with full power-of-attorney to bring a suit against his relatives who claimed the estates, while the princess took every possible step to secure the property for him, or if that could not be, for herself, through her marriage contract, which resulted in an expensive litigation, of which Father Gallitzin from time to time received some reports.

He had the satisfaction, at the time of the arrival of several of the reverend gentlemen mentioned in the princess' letter, — who afterwards, especially Mr. Nerinx, or Nerinckx[*], rendered us great service, of receiving a large box which they had brought from his mother, containing useful and valuable presents of all kinds for his church and his parishioners. Among them was an entire and beautiful set of vestments to be worn at Mass, which she and Countess von Stolberg had worked for him, hoping, perhaps, herself to place them in his hands, even to see him wear them, it may be; but for such a mother to have such a privilege was too much happiness for earth, and they were packed up with tenderest care, with moist eyes and trembling hands assuredly, to be worn in a strange land, thousands of miles away, where the barefooted peasant would have the blessing for which the highborn, princess-mother would freely have yielded up her life. There were, besides, rosaries, prayer-books, pictures, household linen, relics set under precious stones, in gold and silver crosses, accompanied by the papers establishing their authenticity, even baby-trousseaux for him to give away when the little things were brought to him for baptism, and, finally, a cheque for an unusually large amount. In preparing this box, the princess showed more than by any words she could have used, the fulness of her happiness in being the mother of a priest, and the contentment with which she felt justified in giving herself up to an absorbing love for her son, at which under other circumstances she might almost have scrupled, for now every act of love for him was an act of faith in the religion for which he lived, an

---

[*] An interesting account of this noble missionary is found in *Sketches of Kentucky*, by M. J. Spaulding. D. D. Chapters VII, XII.

act of charity, and an act of adoration of the God whose priest he was; every expression of affection for one included the other, and, unlike other women, she had never to fear that she loved too well. For Father Gallitzin, it may be that, after all he had not climbed to the saddest point of his sacrifice when he turned away from Baltimore, hopeless of ever seeing her again, but then, when he bent over the box upon which she had spent so many hours.

CHAPTER XII.

RESPONSIBILITIES AND CARES.

(1804—1805.)

In journeying often, in labour and painfulness, in hunger and thirst, in fastings often, and solicitude for all the churches. (II. Con. xi. 27, 28.)

Clerical influence. — Duties of a missionary. — Some small troubles. — Loretto. — Belah. — Ebensburg. — Formation of Cambria County. — Sunday in Loretto. — Father Gallitzin's Regulations. — Father Gallitzin as a preacher. — As a confessor. — His isolation. — Rev. Mr. Fitzsimmons.

In remote settlements where the people are almost beyond the reach of the laws of the country, often ignorant or careless of the amenities of social life, and where all tongues and tempers meet, all tribes and nations are represented, if they would be at peace among themselves, and work their mutual dependence into order and the common good, they turn instinctively to the minister of religion, if there be one among them, for guidance and assistance in all their affairs, temporal as well as spiritual. Thus Father Gallitzin, like the ministers in the rigid but honest old days of the New England colonies, found himself at the same time servant and ruler, prince, priest, and counsellor, lawgiver and law-enforcer, not, as they, however, over a band united by all the ties of religion, race, and caste, but one containing in itself all possible elements of discord, antagonism, bickerings and strife. A man of stern integrity, severely just, rigidly upright in all his dealings, speaking honestly, according to the light given him, might win their respect, but respect, even fear alone, would snap in a moment at the first outbreak among them; something more than mere natural force and virtue, though of the most winning and the most unbending character, was evidently necessary to acquire any influence, or control, or have any power to harmonize such diverse interests into any kind of order, and Father Gallitzin with his slender-frame, and complete self-abnegation, with an iron will, and a loving heart, with all the light and grace of the Church, all the strength and power of the truth, found himself as time advanced and the settlements increased, by no means the father of a fond and docile family, the pastor of an humble and submissive flock. Only slowly and reluctantly, after the first effusion of joy at having a priest among them had subsided, did many even of the earlier settlers, incited to rebellion by the new spirits of discord continually arriving, give up to his influence, while every inch of his way as priest and benefactor, guide and parent, was contested with new comers and old, with a brave and cheerful exterior, but many a heartache within ; with many a bold and determined act before the world, and many a hard and pitiless austerity known to none.

To rise long before the light and sit, fasting, for hours in the church that never knew a fire, hearing confessions before Mass on Sundays, to preach to them in English and in German, explaining their religion to them from its first precept to its sublimest result, to baptize their children, to comfort their dying, to bury their dead, this for one little parish alone, would have taxed his strength, never great, but duties like these are but a small part of a missionary's life. The missions are many and widely scattered, they must be reached at the appointed time, let the weather be what it will, the perils what they may ; the priest must ride and ride though the rain falls in torrents, or comes crashing over the mountains, in rage and fury; though in stillness, more dreadful, often, than any storm, the dead-leaves rustle under his horse's feet, like the sound of stealthy Indian, or sly panther, or approaching tramp of bear or wolf from the mysterious depths of the surrounding forests; when the long day is thus passed and night comes on, shutting out the last hope of a human face, or thin cloud of smoke curling from some human fireside, it can bring no better promise for the morrow. When a shelter is reached, how cold and poor and crowded it is! There is no warmth, no repose, no seclusion in which to prepare for the round of duties soon to press fast and close upon each other; Mass, confessions, baptisms, marriages, funerals, exhortations, advice, consolations, and then the long journey, to some other crowded log hut, where the people will gather to meet him with all their accumulated load of sins and sorrows, of disappointments and mishaps: an ever-recurring, nameless labor, never ending, always renewing itself, bringing with it no consciousness of noble talents grandly used, but often dissatisfaction illy concealed, misjudgment, even open abuse from those he has tried most to benefit.

To all this, the usual routine of a missionary's life, in Father Gallitzin's case there was added the entire charge of the temporal interests of his congregations, which had grown in a few years to be an immense weight. In his anxiety to provide homes for those who had no prospect of any elsewhere, to sustain those who were falling away from religion, as well as to encourage and fortify those whom he had already selected as the nucleus for the great hope of his life: an educated, pious, unworldly Catholic community, large enough and strong enough to leaven the whole surrounding country, — he had continued to buy land in large quantities, thus obtaining it much cheaper, which he sold again at a low price, to be paid in instalments as the buyer found himself able; becoming the creditor of a great number of persons whom no one else would have trusted for a dollar, and held it in his heart, in every little thing, to add to the independence, the self-respect, and to encourage to unwearying industry, those who had never, perhaps, been considered by others or by themselves to have a right or claim of any kind, which should be accorded them openly, fairly, without evasion or struggle.

The work and the worker had grown together; his mind was of that order that it would go on developing and enlarging as long as he lived. It is not at all likely, that when he first stood in that narrow pass, and held the present garden spot of the American Church against the world, the flesh, the devil and the Protestant religion, he had any idea of the endurance of the battle he had to fight, to the size of the army he was yet to lead. No great work can be performed except in detail, in thorough self-abnegation and self-sacrifice, and such is the weakness and incompleteness of our nature, that it is doubtful if a man could look abroad upon the magnitude of the work entrusted to him and the immensity of those branching from it, and keep his head. So, mercifully, the vision is limited; the laborer does not raise his head to look at the far mountain he is to make straight, but keeps his eyes fixed upon the furrows he is at the moment sowing. It is easy for us to look back now at this slight figure in the blue homespun, shading his eyes with a hat a sunburnt beggar would have disdained, and then abroad over that rich and beautiful country with its numerous priests, from that weather-stained, never-painted chapel past the gilt crosses of its beautiful churches, to the many steepled cathedral. But he and his saw but the wide waste of trees, the unploughed land, the slow-growing corn of their still stubborn farms, the log church, and the undecorated grave-yard the end of all. That not one of his charge should lay a guilty head, or an unclean conscience under that hard earth, had been the first thought of the pastor's life.

But while that thought never left him, work of all kinds multiplied upon his hands. He had to keep his penitents, the hardened old sinners he had coaxed and warned out of the way of temptation, from longing after the flesh-pots of Egypt, and at every inconvenience to which they were subjected, they were not slow to murmur at him, who had *brought them into the desert to perish*. It was, also, a great annoyance to him that he could place no reliance upon the time of receiving his allowance from Germany, and could form no idea of what it would be when it came. Bonaparte's movements were a serious perplexity to the mountain missionary, for the rates of exchange were continually fluctuating, banks were failing, letters unsafe. ocean travelling excessively dangerous, as the great "world conqueror," pursued his way to the terror of Europe, even of this country.

The Russian law-suits were most expensive, and his mother's property in Germany was more and more endangered as European affairs became more gloomy and threatening. As soon as he received anything every one knew it, and he found a thousand uses for it, not only for charity to families and individuals, to whom he gave without counting and without question, it was a case of "first come first served" as they knew very well,—but for his land business now grown to great importance.

Upon the church land given by Captain McGuire, had been built in the first place the church and a little log hut for the pastoral residence; Father Gallitzin spent a great deal of money in clearing and improving this land, and built himself, after some years, a larger cabin of hewn logs, retaining the other for his kitchen and housekeeper and orphan's house; where his own property met the church-land he put up (1804) a grist mill, worked by two horses, for the use of the farmers, who had previously been obliged to carry their grain to be ground fifteen or twenty miles, sometimes on pack horses or mules, generally on their own backs to where Altoona now stands. A large part of his own land he laid out for a town and named it Loretto, the remainder he cleared and cultivated for the use of the church, the priests who should succeed him, and such institutions as should in time arise.

In the meantime a number of Welsh had emigrated to Pennsylvania, and keeping together, avoiding all mixture with other nationalities, all change in their own manner and habits, as their custom is, had formed a village by themselves on the Black Lick Creek not very far from Loretto, where they were under the guidance of a Baptist clergyman, Rev. Morgan J. Rhees, who had laid out their town and named it Berelah. The Welsh are very frugal and industrious and in a short time Berelah showed all the signs of material prosperity, continuing until, two miles east of it, some seven or eight miles from Loretto, another of Mr. Rhees' villages, called Ebensburg also started by Welsh emigrants, flourished still more visibly.

In 1804 it was proposed to form a new county out of Huntingdon and Somerset and these three towns, Berelah, Ebensburg, and Loretto contended for the honor of being its seat of justice. Father Gallitzin used all his influence, and it was already very great, to obtain the coveted prize for Loretto, but as Ebensburg was really more central than the others it was chosen; but though this was unquestionably a loss to Loretto of much temporal advantage, it may, perhaps, have been a spiritual gain, for to have obtained it might have robbed the Catholic village of the very simplicity and steadiness which were its most precious virtues. Ebensburg rose rapidly after this and Berelah sank as quickly, until it entirely disappeared, as Loretto might have done, had it been built on no other foundation than that of material prosperity.

The new county, named Cambria by the Welsh, in remembrance of the mountainous part of their own country, when permanently organized in 1807, laid, as now, between the main Alleghany chain, and a parallel range coming up from Virginia and reaching to Ebensburg, known as Laurel Hill, forming its eastern and western boundaries; it contains, at the village called Summit, five miles from Loretto, the highest point of the Alleghanies, from which rise two little streams, which flow on, one towards the east, becoming in time the bountiful Susquehanna, the other taking a northwesterly direction, monopolizing all the creeks and streams within its reach, cuts away through Laurel Hill and the Chestnut Ridge, and becomes the picturesque Conemaugh, with the loveliest scenery in the world, divides Westmoreland from Indiana County, increases in importance, until at Saltzburg, Indiana County, it loses its individuality in the Loyalhanna and is afterwards known as the Kiskeminetas*.

* The history and geography of this beautiful river, which the Pennsylvania Central Railroad follows from Wilmore to Blairsville Intersection, some forty miles, have been made extremely interesting in a little book entitled: *The Valley of the Conemaugh*, by Thomas J. Chapman, published at Altoona, an indispensable handbook for one desirous of obtaining a clear view of this section of country. The Conemaugh

The formation of the new county threw increased business into Father Gallitzin's hands, he was agent for several firms in Philadelphia, and other large cities, for the sale of lands in Western Pennsylvania, and there was an endless amount of papers to be drawn up, registered and attended to, in regard to it, even of that kind known as ejectments, leading some times to lawsuits, for there were not lacking swindlers and imposters to take advantage of his well known charity, obtain land from him for a trifle and on credit, and sell it over again at a good profit, or occupying it, to the annoyance of their peaceable and orderly neighbors, without any intention of ever paying for it, and he was not one to be imposed upon with impunity at any time, least of all, when he no longer regarded himself as his own property, but as the servant of the poor, the agent of the Lord in a noble work. He was as swift and keen in justice as in charity, and the more so that he knew the full danger of establishing precedents, or giving dishonesty of any kind the slightest foothold in the new country. The temporal interests of his settlement required him to attend the courts in other counties, and made long journeys to Greensburg, in Westmoreland, and even to Lancaster, frequently necessary, which in addition to the increasing missions he had to attend in discharge of his spiritual duties, kept him constantly moving.

At the same time his heart and soul were in Loretto, the centre of all his hopes, where he never for a moment abated his vigilance. He had his rules for all spiritual exercises as clear, distinct, and unalterable as the famous laws of the Medes and Persians. Everything with him was exact, precise to the minute, and this not only from habit, from long training, but of every necessity for his own time, as well as for their discipline and order. When it drew near the time for Mass on Sunday, he would come from his house to the church, the long train of his cassock thrown over his arm, passing with his peculiar rapid step from group to group of

---

Valley comprises Cambria County, and parts of Somerset, Indiana, and Westmoreland; a portion of Pennsylvania which seems to have run wild in beauty, only surpassed by the inexhaustible and varied riches beneath.

the men gathered on the church grounds, talking together
before Mass, while the women were devoutly saying their
prayers inside the church; for every one he had a word of
some kind, always friendly, often amusing, even then, for
ever reverential, ever dignified in every word and act, he
had no need to be unnaturally serious upon occasions, and
this was his greeting to his children, whom he saw but seldom
at other times, numbers of whom had come that very morning, as he knew, many a weary mile to hear Mass, fasting,
too, perhaps, and his cordial salutation, his smiling inquiry
for every member of their numerous family, whatever he
chose to say, flushed the bronzed faces with pleasure, and
lightened their hearts for days to remember. Only once was
he known to pass an expectant face without a word of kindly
greeting. It was during the war of 1812; a company had
been formed and sent from Loretto, when the approach of
the English to Baltimore and Washington sent terror through
the country; two of its members returned without permission to Loretto, and on the following Sunday morning, held
forth to the usual gathering, of their marvellous adventures
by field and flood, heroes of the hour, in spite of the shadow
of uncertainty concerning the propriety of their unexpected
reappearance. They enjoyed the wonder, the attention of
their audience, until Father Gallitzin appearing at the door
of his cabin, the usual hush of respect and expectancy took
place, as the people lowered their voices, speaking only a
few sentences among themselves, while they watched him
coming brightly, cheerily, and stately as ever, along the
path to the church. Then it was that one of the travellers,
flushed by previous success, perhaps, went forward, concealing all embarassment under an appearance of heartiness, as
befitting one who had seen the world, "Ah, Doctor, good
morning!" he said holding out his hand, "Glad to see you
again, Doctor," but the doctor's slender hand kept its place,
clasped behind his back, and the dark eyes raised to the face
before him, expressed surprise, but no welcome. "I never
shake hands with him who deserts his post," he answered
quietly, and passed on. "I pitied the fellow," commented a

looker on, "I'd a rather ha' been shot than got that there word from the doctor, but I'd a knowed I'd a got it, 'fore ever I'd shewed myself; for, see you, that there was just the doctor's way."

In the church there were no pews nor benches, the utmost ease ever allowed in it consisted of two or three stools, for the use of several very aged persons who came there; the children knelt in front, by the altar rails; the women were placed on one side, the men on the other, with a narrow passage way between, which neither ever ventured to decrease; all superfluous dress had to be left behind, and at the church door every woman, young or old, was required to take off her bonnet, and put a kind of handkerchief over her head; the slightest impropriety in dress, and the fashion of the day admitted plenty of it, was so well known to be hateful to him, that if brought there it would be sure to be considered as a defiance of his admonitions, an insult to the House of God, and bring upon its wearer a scathing rebuke. As much as Father Gallitzin hated meanness in a man, he despired coquetry in a woman, not that pleasant sparkle which comes with good health and a clear conscience, for he liked that within reasonable limits, but whatever showed itself in the lowering of the immortal to give precedence to that which perishes, was to him a crime and a folly, for which no denunciation could be too severe. He knew, also, the poverty of the generality of the people, and was careful that there should be no extravagance, no rivalry, no room for envy, by permitting even those whose circumstances would perhaps have admitted some display, to make any beyond the means of the simplest and poorest, and so clearly did he make all feel that they were alike children of God, so well did he know to say the right word in confession, that to a stanger looking over the congregation they would have appeared as children of one father, dressed with different tastes, it is true, but with equal plainness. Father Gallitzin dreaded the advent of finery into the settlements as he would the small pox, or cholera, especially as there is no known remedy for the diseases it brings.

When the greetings outside the church door were all made, or whenever the moment arrived for the people to enter, he left them, and, when, later, there was a gallery for a choir, went up stairs, other times remained at the back of the church, while they went in; when all was quiet, and that had to be very soon, he would sing the Litany, and that ended, go twice round the outside of the church, lest any one might be lingering there, instead of preparing for Mass inside; then in the stillness which he insisted upon, every ear would be strained to hear behind them that never-to-be-mistaken step, quick, but never hurried, that marked his progress up the narrow passage, through the church to the sanctuary, while everyone, however demurely kneeling with clasped hands, and downcast eyes, knew well that his keen glances were piercing to their inmost heart, for then it was that the least irregularity of dress, or posture was made note of.

When he came back again it was to sing the Asperges, and sprinkle them with holy water before Mass; the holy water brush was a marshall's *baton* in his hands; he knew how the devil hates it, and every irregularity just noticed, brought upon the wearer, or doer, a special quantity. At one time a Protestant, from some distant settlement, went up to Loretto, on purpose to have some fun over the Catholic worship, and "Priest Gallitzin's" doings, and got wedged in with the crowd by the door, when Father Gallitzin came down the aisle sprinkling and singing the Asperges, which appeared so amusing, that the young man laughed heartily, undismayed by the evident indignation of all around him; as the priest came nearer he stared boldly at him, his mouth open for another laugh, when in a moment he clasped his hands before his face, and was glad to push his way out into the open air, choking and gasping, while the chanting of the psalm continued, without the wavering of a note.

Father Gallitzin always preached two sermons at Mass, one in English, and one in German, neither of which was his mother tongue, for French was the language most natural to him; he spoke English with perfect ease, German not so well;

his sermons were plain, and suited to the times, the circumstances, and the needs of his people, with which he was as familiar as with his own. He knew just the snares likely to be laid for them, just the temptations they had to avoid, just the virtues they most required, and his words to them from the altar were dictated accordingly. He was especially anxious they should be thoroughly grounded in their religion, not merely in its letter, or in so much of it as might seem to apply to their daily life, but in its spirit and immensity. He had a horror of superstitions, of religious sentimentality, of all spiritual morbidness, and he knew that ignorance is the fruitful source of all these; he wished also that his people should live like kings in the regions of the soul, no feast too grand for them, no robes too costly for them to wear; he poured out upon them the luxuries of spiritual intelligence, preparing them for it by every possible effort of training, explanation, and constant care; he assured them there was nothing in their religion too nice or fine for their daily life, if they made that daily life what it should be, and when he demanded simplicity in their dress and manners, forbade every thought of luxury in their way of living, he threw them the keys of the Church treasury, and urged them to hoard up wealth for their souls. And some of them were so good! They never suspected it themselves, but it was to him a joy, an edification, a foretaste of the society of the saints in heaven, to mark the gentleness, the patience, the sweet regularity, and the bright courage, ready for any emergency, fearless in the peace of their conscience, and confidence in God's protection in doing whatever He willed them to do, of the women, the honesty, straightforwardness, the forbearance, the real, practical piety of the men, and when, at night, as he urged upon all, in every cottage, not only in Loretto, but those buried in the darkness of the surrounding forests, the axe and the spade laid aside, the spinning wheel silent, the fire low on the hearth, and the baby asleep in the corner, in the small dimly lighted room that did for kitchen and parlor, parents and children knelt together saying the rosary, before the tired limbs sought rest on the rude bunches of straw, so often their only beds, only God can tell how many a savage beast tramped aside, his hungry jaws aching for their prey, at sound of the last AMEN, as the worshippers, blessed of God, laid down in their unsafe homes, unconscious, and unfearing, as the saints of old in the horrors of the Roman arena.

Sunday was the day of happy meetings, for family gatherings, when married children, living miles away, came back to the old home, for a few hours with their parents; a day of leisure, of peaceful conscience, of domestic reunion, and happiness, as God meant it to be, on which each one was to gather new heart and hope, new love of God, new softening of the heart, new strengthening of olden ties for the week to come, and though no loved ones came to share with Father Gallitzin his solitary meal, on that day, it did not sadden him, for he knew the happiness of the rest, and rejoiced in it; it was a busy day for him, too, for all manner of spiritual necessities were brought to him then to be attended to, and if any one was especially happy in some unexpected meeting, or some unusual good news, "the doctor" would be called upon to hear it. Towards evening, when those living in the distance were obliged to turn home, no one passed his door, without a thought of him, or a long look at his little cabin. In his private rules and regulations for each individual life, he was even more exact and searching; even the little children, as they stood between his knees, twisting the buttons of his cassock, going through the process they called confession, felt that nothing was unknown to him, and that he would neither misunderstand one, nor be deceived by evasion or coloring. Nothing was of indifference to him which was serious to his penitent; even the child who confessed with frank eyes, and much stammering, that he had stolen a wheelbarrow, found nothing strange in the quiet question of the priest as to what he did with it, for a wheelbarrow is rather a large thing for a little boy to steal or to conceal. "I rode my sister three times around the yard, and then I put it back," said the child, and when, afterwards, the little penitent told of it, and of the serious advice given to ask the owner's consent next time, one could see that it was from the very earliest moment, he took care that they should neither exaggerate, nor lessen the faults they committed. As he grew older, and advanced more, himself, in perfection, it might be said that all that he accomplished, by other means, was as nothing in comparison with the work effected by him as a confessor. His penitents did not feel as if they were speaking to him, naming over a catalogue of sins; in so far as it can be explained at all, and it is one of those things which never can be explained, it was like an earnest and searching interview with an injured parent, whom one has reluctantly consented, in coldness and pettishness to meet, before whose love and tender reproach all the barriers of time, of hardness, and neglect, break down, and with tears of relief all the past is reviewed, its wrongs, seen now for the first time as they really are, sobbed out, a comfort to tell them, and be forgiven for each.

Thus Father Gallitzin's spiritual and temporal duties flowed together, so that any attempt to separate them under different heads must always fail. They grew together, they crowded upon him, hand in hand, he could not evade one without neglecting the other, and they had come to such magnitude that they strained every nerve, and even then he felt he could not meet them; not only was his health giving way, but even his brave and energetic spirit quailed before the calls upon it; he began to dread the future, and longed to have some one to take a little, though but the smallest part of his responsibility from him, one who, perhaps, would be enough conversant with his duties not to let them drop at once, if he should be called away in the midst of his labors. Mr. Heilbron, still in Westmoreland, was, as in the beginning, the only priest within a week's journey, and he was old, no longer strong, able to speak but very little English, and, like all the rest, overburdened with work; he, however, made it a point to come every summer, and spend a few weeks with Father Gallitzin, recruiting his own strength and courage and giving his host a little of the priestly society no man ever craved more; for his was no solitary nature, he loved life, movement, social intercourse, and was full of wit, of the kindliest nature, with that peculiar, sparkling gift of conversation which never dazzles, or bewilders, or comes out in abrupt brilliancy, like sudden flashes of lightning on a dark night, but a bright, fresh readiness of speech, which made him delightful and never exacting company. He was also tormented by fits of depression, which were partly hereditary, — his mother at times suffering so greatly from despondency, without any cause, that it amounted to a disease, and the gloom it engendered was regarded by her as the strongest temptation of the devil,—which was increased in his case by the real mental isolation in which he lived, for there actually was no one who merited to be called a friend, in the full sense of the word, and partly from his frequent illhealth, occasioned by irregular meals, poor food, and rigorous fasting. So bravely did he fight himself, at these times, that few would believe he ever lost heart or hope; but no one, not afflicted in the same way, can form any idea of the suffering endured, when, all at once, gloom and fear take full possession of the mind, and the least trouble, or care, looms up like the grotesque, yet terrifying shadows of some dimly lighted, lonely street; when all one's acts and words, all that has been done, or is to do, keeps before the eyes distorted, and frightfully caricatured. The evil one knows as well as possible that this is his time to work, and how easy then to confuse the conscience, and disarm the will! It was then he would represent to the poor priest, how unwisely he had acted, how little good he had accomplished here, persisting in taking a work upon himself no one approved of, repeating to him, with a new meaning, all the objections which had ever been urged to it, all the lack of sympathy he had met in the good and pious men whose judgment he should have taken, and, as reason does not have everything clear before it at such times, and no consistent line of argument is necessary to break it down, no reasoning, no facts that Father Gallitzin could urge would silence the voice of despair speaking to him; it was then when he most needed not to be alone. This was a bitter persecution, permitted by God, in which, as in a furnace seven times heated, was tested, hammered and shaped, the iron of his intention.

Except during Mr. Heilbron's yearly visits, he had no priest with him for any time, until he had been on the mountains some five or six years, and then the bishop permitted Rev. Mr. Fitzsimmons to remain with him for a little while, although it is not very clear that he was of much assistance in Loretto, but may have attended some of the other settlements. Previous to Mr. de Barth's being stationed at Lancaster, Rev. Mr. Fitzsimmons who had previously been in Canada, came to this country, and, probably at the time the bishop thought of placing Father Gallitzin there, was put in charge of the slightly turbulent congregation at St. Mary's Church; he is first mentioned in Father Gallitzin's letters of 1804, in which is also found, quite unconsciously on the part of the writer, intimations of the great charity towards his brother clergymen, for which the Pastor of Loretto afterwards became so conspicious:—

REV. D. A. GALLITZIN TO RIGHT REV. BISHOP CARROLL.

Lancaster, Febr. 21 1804.

My Lord,

Coming hither on business relating to our new county and countytown, (in which I have now great reason to flatter myself of success), I found an unhappy misunderstanding, and division had taken place in the congregation. As I am sensible of the uneasiness it must create in your Lordship's mind, to receive accounts so very unfavorable to the character of Rev. Mr. Fitzsimmons, and especially from a person of such respectability as Mr. Risdel, I thought it my duty to communicate to your Lordship what I found out (by impartial investigation) to be the real facts, leaving it to your Lordship's prudence and wisdom to form a judgment thereon.... With regard to Mr. Fitzsimmon's sermon, on Candlemas day, it appears, evidently, that the utmost necessity compelled him to make *Money* part of his subject, tho' I own if he had been acquainted with the spirit of the people here, prudence would have suggested some other means; — he was in America, not in Ireland. At the same time it must be owned by any person, not altogether blinded by prejudice, that if Mr. Fitzsimmons gave offence, he certainly repaired the scandal more than sufficiently by his wonderful humility.

* * *

In short it appears plainly that there was a scheme laid to insult Rev. Mr. Fitzsimmons and to have him removed by your Lordship. The good Catholics are unanimous in believing him to be a pious, holy, and very zealous clergyman, which coincides with my humble opinion. However it appears plainly to me that he will never be happy here, as the Dutch party, headed by Risdel (which is the richest) is absolutely against him, and you know, my Lord, how difficult it is to remove their prejudices. A great many of those that remain faithful to their pastor, and some of the ablest amongst them, are preparing to move to Clearfield Settlement very soon. Would your Lordship please to gratify their, his, and my desire by allowing the Rev. Mr. Fitzsimmons to move to that settlement in order to assist me there in the discharge of my duties, that are become too heavy for my shoulders alone.

Granting this request will be sincerely acknowledged by,

My Lord,

Your most humble obedient servant,

Demetrius Aug. Pr. of Gallitzin,
Secular Priest.

P. S. An answer to Rev. Mr. Fitzsimmons will be sufficient, as I shall not be here to receive your answer to mine.

SAME TO THE SAME.

Near Loretto, June 4th, 1804.

My Lord,

I embrace the opportunity of Mr. James Gallagher's [visit to Baltimore.] to let your Lordship know that I am at present in a very good state of health, and very much pleased at the surprising, rapid increase of this settlement, but at the same time very desirous of assistance as the task begins to be too heavy for my shoulders. I expect your Lordship did receive the letter which I directed to you from Lancaster, in which I perhaps made too free, in requesting from your Lordship the favor of Mr. Fitzsimmons' assistance here. What induced me to it, and now induces me to renew my humble request, was my intimate conviction of his not being fit for Lancaster, of which I suppose your Lordship likewise convinced. I believe him to be a virtuous, zealous clergyman, but at the same time, somewhat imprudent, and not endowed with a sufficient share of the so necessary knowledge of the world, of mankind in general, nor sufficiently provided with the no less necessary gift of discerning the differences between nations, countries and other peculiarities. From the knowledge, however, which I have of my congregations, it appears to me that he might do exceedingly well here. As for a maintenance I engage to find it for him, or for any clergyman your Lordship shall think proper to send. I do not know of any at present that has a desire of coming hither except Mr. Fitzsimmons, who seems very much confirmed in this notion by his best friends, the best Catholics in Lancaster, removing from that place and coming to this settlement. I shall with the greatest submission resign myself to your decision.

* * *

I remain with the greatest respect,
My Lord,
Your most humble obedient Servant,
Demetrius Aug. Pr. of Gallitzin,
Parish Priest of Loretto.

Unfortunately Father Gallitzin did not know his congregations quite as well as he thought, and an imprudent priest among them would soon find himself without the influence and control which a priest should always have over his congregation, and lacking which neither pastor nor people can be contented or attend to their best good. If now they were orderly, regular in all their duties, with their heart in all they did, it was because Father Gallitzin kept them to the mark he had set for them, his zeal animated even those who would least acknowledge it, his resolute ways of acting and speaking, his thorough self command, and appreciation of his place and theirs made ready response natural and easy to them; but when, at times, an easy going man, accustomed to let things take their own course when there appeared nothing reprehensible on the surface, received the care of missions upheld, like these, by the fervor and strength of one man, it was wonderful, humiliating, how soon they fell apart, and slipped away from the earnestness and regularity which had so long appeared as a second nature to them; this, at first, in the merest trifles, exciting no uneasiness, perhaps indeed, no more than a careless thought that Dr. Gallitzin was too punctilious, too much of a clerical martinet, and that such strictness as he used was quite unnecessary; but trifles led so quickly to more momentous failures, and these to serious results which were harder for Father Gallitzin, when called upon in haste and fear, to repair than it had ever been to build up. When will the world learn that it must not trifle with the regulations of the physician, the general, and the priest!

As yet, there were but few indications of such possibilities, and these, looked upon in amazement and indignation, were at once repudiated by all the people, and appeared to him merely as a passing annoyance, soon to wither and die, leaving no trace. Temporally and spiritually he had reason to feel confident that all was going on well, and that he needed only a little help in both, to keep all that he had gained which meant to carry it on as he had commenced, for in work like this to stand still is to be pushed aside and driven back, only after superhuman exertions, if even then, ever to regain a firm foothold on the ground lost. This assistance which he so ardently desired, and asked so quietly, was rarely given him, and many times for the want of a small sum, ready at the moment, he had to lose great advantages, toiled for through many trials, but he never urged, nor complained; he did the best he could with the means he could procure, and attended to the smallest good of those he had in charge, as if he had no greater aim on hand, as appears illustrated by a note to Bishop Carroll in the early part of 1805.

REV. D. A. GALLITZIN TO RIGHT REV. BISHOP CARROLL.

February 4th, 1805.

My Lord,

It was only the 1st Inst. I received your kind favour including the Pope's Indult and the letters from my mother*. In reply to these I can assure your Lordship that I am perfectly resigned to the will of God, and do not feel in the least concerned about the loss of my property, if it is the will of Providence that I should lose it. I had long ago consecrated it, in my own mind, to the service of God and His sanctuary. I am now in Aughwick Settlement, about seventy miles from home, travelling on a sleigh, or rather, sled, from one valley into another, until I go through all the different congregations under my jurisdiction, which will keep me from home until the 12th, or 13th. I hope your Lordship will not object to my postponing the publishing of the Jubilee to a later period than the one mentioned in your circular letter; the winter is so very severe, the snow so deep, that a great portion of the congregation, particularly poor people not sufficiently provided with clothing, could not attend. Out of several hundred communicants, that never miss their Easter or Christmas communion, I had only about sixty these last holidays. I beg leave, therefore, to postpone that business until some time in the Spring, to which your Lordship will undoubtedly agree, if you have any idea of the roughness of the climate and country, at this unpleasant season of the year....

I hope, if your Lordship will assist me, that the church property here shall, in a few years, exceed any other church property in this state.

With sincere respect,
My Lord,
Your most humble obedient servant,
Demetrius Augustine Smith.

---

* Given in the preceding chapter.

CHAPTER XIII.

THE FIRST PERSECUTION.

(1804.)

In perils from my own nation, in perils from the gentiles, in perils in the wilderness, in perils from false brethren. (II. Cor. xi. 26.)

The false brother.—Confusion of Gallitzin and Smith.—His mistakes, faults, and peculiarities of temper.—A boy's quarrel.—An injured friend.—Gallitzin as a physician.—Adopts a family of orphans.—Hopes of a religious order of teachers.—Consequent opposition and calumniation.

Not very long after Mr. Fitzsimmons' visit, another clergyman, less virtuous and zealous than he is described, wandered into the wilds of Pennsylvania, unauthorized by the bishop, and investigated its resources. He was rather disgusted with the aspect of affairs in Westmoreland county, on account of the poverty of the church, but looking towards Cambria and Huntingdon counties, which were under Father Gallitzin's care, discovered some gleams of hope in the far future, under proper management, even for Loretto. He became acquainted with some members of these congregations, found out, in homely phrase, "how the land lay", and was very much liked by those with whom he affably conversed, or graciously shared the usual hospitalities. His decided opinion was that they were all entirely too much under the control of their pastor, and that they were competent to manage their own affairs, unassisted by any clergyman, for priests are appointed to attend to spiritual requirements, not to regulate the way we should live, what we should eat and drink, and what clothes to wear, which, if we mistake not, was very much the view, held a number of years ago, by an uninvited guest in the Garden of Eden. Of course the reverend gentleman was too thoroughly charitable ever to give open expression to this opinion, but there certainly were people who did not doubt he held it, and when they themselves came to think about it, they could not say it was wholly unfounded. Besides, it is always pleasant to meet a priest of one's own nation, and whether or not their present pastor was a German foreigner, as generally supposed, it could not be questioned that this off hand, easy, and free spoken gentleman, who did not feel above a cheering glass even with an humble backwoodsman, was of their own tongue and nation, and it would be a fine day for Loretto if he would sometime come there to live, or, at least, to visit and assist the present pastor at Easter and Christmas, perhaps.

It will be noticed that notwithstanding his naturalization, Father Gallitzin had twice signed himself in letters to Bishop Carroll, Prince of Gallitzin, his father's rightful heir, as his lawyers in Russia were endeavoring to have him practically acknowledged. He had never meant at any time in his life to renounce his family name, not even, as has been supposed, in his most humble mood, for it is not likely it ever occured to him that anything pertaining to him was of such brilliant importance that it needed to be concealed; he had always, even by nature, great simplicity of character, and never in his life attained to any complications of virtue, or any affectation of sanctity. It is true that had he remained in Europe, or returned to it desiring to live a retired and holy life, he would too soon have learned the value placed by the world upon his birth and fortune, and would have been compelled either to renounce them, become entirely dead to the knowledge of the children of men, or live among them a sort of prince-priest receiving, in spite of himself, the honor due to his worldly position, instead of the higher veneration due to his spiritual rank, but of this in a republican country he could fear nothing, of course. He simply neglected to resume his family name when deciding to remain here, and when he became aroused to the necessity for doing so, his pastoral and business sphere had so enlarged that he found himself encompassed by embarrassments, whether he spoke or remained silent. In one way and another his true name was becoming known to many, and when used in the hearing of those who knew him only as Mr., Father, or more truly in country parlance as *Priest* Smith, gave rise to misunderstandings, and finally to real annoyances. To those who understood the position of a nobleman setting out to see the world with the desire of quiet, and the conventional requirements of a title in Europe, not a word of explanation was necessary, but these were very few, and he himself, of course, could not enter into the details of such a position necessary to the enlightenment of those around him. He did the best he could in asking a priest who was visiting him, Mr. Heilbron most likely, to mention the matter in church, and set the people right concerning it. But this only made matters worse, for either the speaker himself did not understand it, or did not know how to express it, for his English, which was of the most limited, was incomprehensible, and his German confusion; nothing was gained except the authorized fact that their pastor had two names; the wildest fancies, the silliest stories were set afloat at once; even to this day there are those who heard that announcement, who believe in their hearts and freely say that he was the eldest, or only son, report varies, of a great king, in some far country, not clearly mapped out in their geography, and the excitement about his going to Europe, of which something was known, was occasioned by the demand of his subjects that he should come to them, now that his father was dead, and occupy the waiting throne, but he, persisting in his refusal declared he wanted no throne but one beyond the skies! Others, too sensible for such mistakes, admitted themselves unable to reconcile all points of the subject, certainly it could not be denied that it was rather singular that a man of such rank, as he was *said* to have, should care to live in the woods like the poorest of the poor, unless——. The wise men pondered over it, and having read history as they thought, in their school-books, regarded it as mysterious to say the least, and the rest was left to the imagination.

It is not to be denied that Father Gallitzin sometimes made mistakes; no one ever yet learned to do a thing well without making many failures in the process, else why are there schools, apprenticeships, and novitiates? One does not need to enter a mechanic's shop, an artist's studio, to discover that it takes years of practice, of sad experience, and many errors, to make a master hand. When he went to the mountains he was still a young prince, whose life, as far as it had progressed, had been passed only with those who loved and esteemed him, and made his welfare and happiness their great study, from his earliest childhood he had been addressed only with deference from his inferiors, affection and respect from his equals and superiors; he had known no society but that of the learned, the polished and the high-minded, in great part that of sincere and courteous religious. When he settled in the backwoods, as it could well be called, he had to learn to deal with a very different class of men; men who believed no man honest until he had been proved so, and even then with reserve; who looked upon all other men as imposters and swindlers, against whom it was well to be ever on guard, and with whom to get the upper hand in the game, if cunning could do it; men who were less depraved than these, but still with little faith in him or any one, and very uncertain principles of their own; others, besides, who were honest and sincere, but impressible, weak, suspicious, and not to be relied upon in an emergency, and if, sometimes, he was deceived, overreached by thorough duplicity, or even if, now and again, he confounded with these one who was not of them, it was hardly surprising, all things considered.

He had also, in himself, certain traits and habits of thought, certain peculiarities of temperament, and effects of association to overcome, from which he received many a smarting wound before he could discover their hiding place. Like most men of active, stirring character he looked to results, formed decided opinions, which he was not unwilling to press upon others; it is true, that even when convinced the good aimed at was not to be doubted, he would cheerfully demonstrate to others why it should be so; he did not always duly consider that the most lucid illustration of the double rule of three, is rather lost upon a man who cannot put five and six together without counting it on his fingers; persons thus put aside, unable to give him counter-demonstrations, might be silenced but they were not always mute. He was hasty, quick to form judgments and as quick to express them; there was no bitterness, no malice in his nature; the angry word would no sooner be spoken than keenly regretted and pardon begged for it; more than that it was not so ready the next time; but, unhappily, what [is said, is said, and more than once a word spoken in the heat of the moment, rankled in the very heart upon which he daily laid benefits and fondest atonements. It was even true, as began to be whispered, that he was arbitrary, and capable of terrible anger, with a look of fire, a voice of thunder, and a will of iron, like that grand old Sixtus Quintus who declared: "While I live the criminal shall die", and made the watchword of Rome, SIXTUS REIGNS. There are no words fitly to describe his mastering spirit that never was broken, and could not be bent. The men, strangers to him and his religion, who strode up to see a funeral pass, baptism administered, or hear a sermon preached, who had never bowed to any command, at his word: "Kneel down, Sir. Take off your hat", obeyed, powerless to resist, while the rapid words were yet on his lips. At other times his voice rang out until the very rafters thrilled and trembled; the fast coming words, the cutting sarcasms, the broad, trenchant blows of his doctrinal sermons once heard could never be forgotten. Magnificent in his wrath he seemed born to hurl the thunders of the Church at the heads of sacrilegious kings, and announce the scourging of God to cowering nations, and it was felt instinctively there was a power there not well to arouse. He was careful to honor the selfrespect and family reserve which he knew to be a safeguard against the petty gossip and scandals which are the bane of all small communities, but at the same time in his eyes they were all members of one family and he their father, and he would sometimes speak to all of the errors of one, not indeed, personally, but too plainly, intending only to use it as an illustration, and a warning to others. This of course, never in any serious case of misfortune to those innocent of evil intention, or part in the disgrace which one unworthy member will often bring upon an entire family; for these he was full of tenderness, sharing their sorrow as if it were his own. It was generally in trifles, but they were sometimes painful ones, when they brought disapprobation from him.

He was also, in small matters, extremely credulous, and apt to believe the first story told him, he who would weigh the statements of a world renowned author with all care and prudence, who would take no assertion of moment from the most reliable source without keen investigation, would yet make the not uncommon mistake of confounding rudeness of speech with honesty of meaning; no child's story was too small, or clumsily constructed for him to notice, no petty quarrel, if brought to him, too mean for him to pronounce upon, generally with mild and just reflection, leading to full reconciliation, other times with severe and, perhaps, unexpected rebuke; undoubtedly he had always his own reasons for such a course, but they were not always apparent, and the last thing ordinary people will forgive in those in superior position, is that which looks like caprice or inconsistency.

To illustrate his credulity, his hasty judgments, and his tenderness of heart two anecdotes may be repeated, although occuring some years later, when he was known as "Dr. Gallitzin." One Sunday morning one of the most upright and respected of his parishioners, known as "the squire", who was also a firm friend upon whom Dr. Gallitzin knew he could rely in any emergency, a man who strove in every relation of life as husband, father, citizen, and neighbor to fulfil all his duties, as the priest, speaking in God's name, had set the standard, listened attentively, and with much personal interest to the doctor's English sermon, which was on the duties of parents to their children. "Children" he said, "are commanded to honor their parents, and obey them in all that is not sin, but the duties are not all on the children's side, parents are bound to exact and to merit honor and obedience no less than the children to give it," a just and truthful statement which the "squire" had no thought of questioning, even had it come from less sacred lips than those that now uttered it; "Any parent", the preacher went on to say, "who let his children run about as they pleased, quarrelling, inciting others to anger, or luring them to idleness, to disobedience to parents and superiors, and the various sins of vagabond boyhood, need not look for salvation though he wore his own knees off praying and reduced himself to a skeleton by fasting and mortification, even gave half of his substance to the poor, for God at the Last Day, at the very hour of death, would demand an account of the souls entrusted to him." From this he proceeded to sketch a man, honored and esteemed by all, obedient to every command of the Church, every advice of his pastor, charitable, generous, just in all his dealings with others, who nevertheless, was cancelling all his good works by his carelessness in regard to his children, his over indulgence, permitting them to grow up in pride and stubbornness; making the description so personal that it could not be doubted he had a living original of the portrait in his own mind, and that original the squire, who, himself, soon saw that something had happened. Many a time "the doctor's" keen satire and crushing rebukes had been heard by him before, but they had generally fallen on the heads of those who could have been reached in no other way, and never until now upon one who loved him, as tough old veterans their bright young captain, whose very severity of discipline increases his fascination, whose concise command is more potent than all the raging of their higher officers, whose imperiousness is their pride, his despotism their delight, but whose least neglect, whose least personal anger cuts deeper than the sword of an enemy. "If he had only sent for me, made any complaint, asked anything of me, I would have said it was all right," groaned the squire, returning to his home, with his weeping family, "anything but this." Questioning his children, he found there had been a boys' quarrel between them and a person, who was working for Dr. Gallitzin, in an adjoining field, the day before, over the merits of their respective teams, in which there had been considerable boasting on each side, as there always will be when horses are under discussion, it is human nature, but not more than the boys felt aggravated to make by the superior facility of language employed by the other; though it had to be admitted that when they found themselves outdone in speech, they jumped the fence and decided the case in a more emphatic, and less judicial manner. According to the report made Father Gallitzin the provocation, the aggravation, the boasting and the depreciation (they were the priest's own horses, in which he took a reasonable pride himself), had all been on one side of the fence, and that the boys' side. Father Gallitzin did not stop to consider that there are almost invariably two parties to a quarrel, especially to a fight, and other stories following this, in illustration of the wicked ways of the victorious youths, naturally worked upon his mind, as the narrator, perhaps, was not unwilling it should.

In the afternoon of that unhappy Sunday, the father was induced to walk over, and see "the doctor". Father Gallitzin had then a fence around his yard, and and a gate at a little distance, at which it was his custom to meet his visitors; whom he could always see from the window of his room, long before they reached his house, and now, as usual, came down the narrow path in his own stately way, with a smiling welcome, to which the man who felt himself wronged, could not so easily respond, and frankly, but with due respect, said so, giving his reasons why, to which Father Gallitzin listened in all humility, and at once sent for his informant. But telling a story in the heat of the moment to a sympathizing listener, was found to be different from repeating it, in cold blood, before an audience disposed to be critical, and this informant was obliged by his own words, to show plainly that this other parties were not quite the reprobates they had been represented. The instant this became apparent Father Gallitzin's eyes filled with tears, and walking up to the others, took the squire's hand in his own, and said, calling him by his first name, "I was wrong, what can I do to repair my mystake? Anything and everything that I can do, I wish to do."

"All I care for, doctor," replied the other warmly," is that *you* should know the truth, and not think me so bad as you represented me this morning, so now it's all right," and it was, and both could smile at it afterwards. Later when times had so changed that a plate collection was taken up there as in other churches, an offence of a far more serious character, was related to him, just before church, as having been committed by one of his collectors, a pillar of the church, who stood, without flinching, through a denunciation more severe even than the other had received. After Mass he set the plate down in the sacristy before Dr. Gallitzin, saying, "There! that's the last collection I will ever take up in this church."

"And why," demanded the priest.

"Because I suppose you meant me this time?"

"I did."

"Then, doctor, I can tell you you have made another mistake," and as before the story was investigated and the accused honorably acquitted.

"It was the same thing before," said the collector," when you gave Squire M—— that backset, and I said then if it had been me, I would never go round that church again, and I will not."

"Yes, Johnnie," Father Gallitzin replied, laying his hand on his shoulder, and looking up to him, in his own winning way, "you will, won't you? I spoke too soon, I am very sorry, but you will not stay angry with me for that, will you?" and in this case it was all over at once.

But it was not often so, especially in the beginning before he had grown with his congregation, so that they knew him, in such things, better than he knew himself; and with those whose consciences told them that they deserved still more than they received, straws like these were carefully laid away, ready, if a storm should ever arise, to be made use of, if only to show which way the wind blew. They were the utmost that could be established against him in all the years of his life as their priest, a life that had no secrets or disguises, and was under continual observation from beginning to end, open to the interpretation of all manner of minds, some of them too coarse, too foul, too low for an angel to pass them by unsoiled.

All that Father Gallitzin made himself to his people in their daily life culminated, reached its perfection in the hour of their death. When the message came to him that any one was ill, it reached him as the call to a father in the field to hurry home for one of the children has been hurt; he was the physician as well as the priest, learning his profession by the bedside of the sick, who had only him to look to, and healing came from his hands, from his simple prescriptions, so often and so unexpectedly, that a whole college of physicians could not have inspired a tithe of the confidence with which it would be said: "Such a one is sick, run, quick and tell the priest." It was thus he became known as "the doctor", and was very soon regarded as an experienced physician, who, they never doubted, had had a thorough medical education. As soon as he had acted in this capacity, to the best of his judgment, he appeared as friend and father, on whom all mental cares were laid, all responsibilities and perplexities confided. He had scarcely arrived among them before he was called to see a sick man, who was broken hearted at leaving a large family of children, nearly all girls, for whom he had not been able to make the least provision; as soon as this was made known, Father Gallitzin assured him he might make his mind easy for he would adopt the whole family and bring them up himself, a promise he faithfully fulfilled. It was no small household that fell upon his hands in this way, especially as he repeated the proceeding at different times, so that always as long as he lived he had at least one family growing up around him. He took the greatest pains to observe the manner in which the better class of farmers provided for their children, in order to do the same by those he had adopted, that when they grew up and were settled in life, they should find themselves suited to their surroundings, neither isolated through superior and unnecessary accomplishments, nor contemned for ignorance or poverty. He undoubtedly regarded the position of an intelligent family living in the country, with security against need, with all the duties and independence of life on a farm, which was, also, the highest position to which they could possibly have aspired had their parents lived and prospered, the one most conducive of happiness and content.

He would, therefore, have them taught all household duties, and given education enough to be able to go on of themselves if other paths should open to them, or unexpected talents be developed; if any romantic dreams of being cared for as the children of a great noble, ever entered their young heads, it was through no fault of his, for it was a thought which could not possibly occur to him. But womanly modesty, womanly reserve and dignity, like manly honesty and sobriety, belonged in his estimation, to no rank of life, but were the rightful property of all God's children, and he who would neglect to secure them for those entrusted to his care, an unjust guardian; he who would withhold them, a swindler and a robber, thus all the restraints of the highest conventionality, all the divinity which hedges in a true gentlewoman, which were familiar to him in his mother and sister, and all the ladies of their circle, appeared to him equally necessary in the poorest and lowliest of his flock. It was needful, then, for him to find some one who would be able to carry out this plan of education for the family thrown so suddenly upon his hands, and, indeed, not only for them, but for the children growing up around him. As yet there was no thought of sisters, or nuns to assist in such a work, for even if there had been any religious order of women established in the United States, years and years must pass before they could be spared for the world beyond the mountains. The only ones here at that time were the Carmelites, closely cloistered nuns, who had come in 1790, and the *Poor Clares*, driven from France in 1792, who were few in number, and very poor, trying to support themselves in Georgetown by teaching, Miss Lalor and our dear Mother Seton had not yet found "the path just fitted to their foot." For help in this direction, as indeed, in all others, Father Gallitzin had nothing to look for outside his own congregations; here the women were overburdened with the labor belonging to a new settlement, and absorbed in the daily household cares which no true woman can leave, until they first leave her, but Providence seemed to point to him, as the most suitable person for the care of his large household, a lady, young but past her early girlhood, who had been educated in Baltimore, had a free heart's love for all good works, some tendencies to a religious life, and no special duties to claim her elsewhere, as she lived with her widowed mother in, or near Loretto. At first it is not likely he had any other thought or plan than that she being womanly, pious, intelligent and educated, was well fitted to be an instructor for the children, in whose care she would have an aim and occupation in life, without which no woman, worth the name, can ever be contented. He gave her charge of them, and exacted of her the most precise concurrence in his views in their regard, in the minutest particular; he was very strict, as it seemed, in comparison with the freer ways of bringing up children then in vogue, and demanded the most implicit obedience to his rules, requiring of her to obtain it. He had been brought up with severity himself, and was undoubtedly urged by the sense of responsibility, arising from his promise to the dying father, and by the fears always more to be felt for the after life of those who have had no parents' intuition to guide them, to equal strictness, and so conscientiously did she respond to his demands, that the children soon found they had no evasive, all concealing advocate in her.

As time advanced his hopes grew, and fairly blossomed into expectations that if she was not designed to be the founder of a community of religious, specially adapted to the soil from which they sprang, at least to be another Dr. Overberg, who would devote her life to the service of God, His church and His children, no less sincerely than though she took the vows and wore the habit of a nun, becoming in time, as the good doctor was, the teacher of teachers, devotedly attached to a single life, and the duties devolving upon them as instructors, not only in secular matters, but in religious education. Whether carried away by the fervor of Father Gallitzin's devotedness, inspired by his glowing zeal, or whether, as he believed, sincerely and earnestly determined to carry out an undoubted call to a religious life, it was certain that she did her utmost to fit herself for it, as so many women, now venerated as saints, had striven while waiting the moment in which to act. She dressed with the utmost plainness, attended faithfully to the duties placed upon her, was obedient to the pastor in all things, and endeavored to inspire others with the desire for a similar life. But when her relatives saw how things were going, they were alarmed, and indignant at the idea of her becoming a nun, especially as they would not believe she had any vocation, and that her seclusion was unnatural, the effect of undue influence upon the part of the priest, from which they earnestly sought to take her as quickly as possible, before she should have bound herself by any vows or even promises to a religious life; in this they were joined by others, for the young lady had many admirers who, like other men, could never be made to believe they were refused simply because they were not desired, and were fully convinced, each of them, if the notions put in her head by the pastor were once abolished, there would be plenty of room for thoughts more favorable to their suit; even her own mother was of those who were confident she had no vocation, and violently opposed her new way of living. But Father Gallitzin, who could never let go one coin out of the Church's treasury, who had not forgotten the suffering he had endured from the opposition to his own choice of a state in life, doubted by all those who most of all should have had faith in him, was only aroused by this to render her all possible assistance in keeping firm to her purpose, which he believed God-given. He gave her a home in his house, when she was persecuted in her own, and assured her, that, if she persevered, she should be provided for, and hastened to have a house built where she could live independently, and which he no doubt hoped might lead to greater things, when she should demonstrate by her piety, and perseverance, the truth of her vocation. But even before this little home could be made ready for her, many arrows had met in one mark, every shadow of ill feeling which had ever been excited against him in any way was revived and got ready for use. Some persons visiting Baltimore mentioned the circumstance to the bishop, of course from their own point of view, and the kindly prelate, knowing nothing of the manner of men he had to deal with, expressed some suprise, and one of those conventional phrases of regret, which mean nothing to those who are accustomed to them, but to others everything. We all know and deplore the evil effects upon the imagination of theatres and novels, of sensation plays and romantic reading, but only start an idea with a thread of mystery or scandal in it, in the minds of half a dozen country people, and it will take fire like dry stubble in a high wind. The bishop's words, forgotten almost as soon as spoken, were carried back to the mountains in exultation as an acknowledgment of his sympathy and turned and enlarged until they were made to contain an intimation of episcopal interference.

The bishop knowing nothing further than what had been told him in Baltimore, kindly mentioned the circumstance to Father Gallitzin, and, as of old, advised him to prudence, to moderate his zeal, and recommended, as a means of silencing all disaffection, that some other place should be found for her schoolroom, than the one she at present occupied. To this he replied that the winter had been so severe that it had been impossible for the men to get her house in a fit condition for any one to seek shelter in it, or he should have taken this measure sooner, but now it was nearly ready, and she would move in a day or two, and commence teaching, having among other pupils the daughter of one of the most prominent Catholics in Lancaster, Mr. J——, who had lately come up to Clearfield, in consequence of the difficulties in the congregation there, and taken some of Father Gallitzin's land, intending to make his permanent home in the Loretto parish. With respect to a person who had been foremost in opposing his plans, "I have to observe," he wrote, "that she is now making ready to pay your Lordship a second visit, intending, as she says, to apply to you for her Easter duty. I told your Lordship, I believe, with what impudence she treated me when I walked twenty two miles across Alleghany mountain, in order to assist her in what everybody expected to be her last sickness; how she told me then, (and alleged your authority for it) that she would never confess to me again, sick or well. She was a second time in the same situation when I was in Baltimore, refused to have Mr. Heilbron sent for, [*probably because of his having sustained Father Gallitzin in his course*] but sent to Virginia for Mr. Cahill, who did not choose to come. She did recover, however, but has never been at Mass from the time she left your Lordship, though I treated her in as friendly a manner as possible, and sent her word several times to come to church without fear of being disturbed, and even promised her friends to do all I could for her again, if she would only humble herself and submit to her Church. I hope your Lordship will be pleased not to forget what lying and scandalous accusations they have brought before you against me, and I trust likewise to your prudence and goodness.....What little you did say before them, and that very innocently, has been very much handled and perverted by them, to the great detriment of my character."

Few things in Father Gallitzin's life, are more touching than this his gentle and only remonstrance, when the bishop, for whose good name he would have freely given his life, had, as it were, though unconsciously, failed him at the moment when one indignant, spirited word, such as his intimate knowledge of Father Gallitzin's singularly innocent character perfectly enabled him to speak, would have put a stop to accusations, to slanders which now came thick and fast upon him, who surely had troubles enough already. But he had just resigned the last hope of seeing his mother and sister, had left his fortune to take care of itself, and the devil, who hated him, could not do otherwise than take active part in the persecution to which he was now subjected, and it may have been permitted by God, that no human hand should be extended to assist him, the better to test and prove his virtue and draw him nearer and nearer to Him, his only Friend.

But though this removal took away the most plausible pretext for complaints it did not end them. The young lady remained several years in her new home, devoting herself to the life she had chosen, in which she was imitated by several others, anxious to consecrate their lives in an especial manner, to God's service, but it did not appear, finally, that she was called to this state of life, for she married a Maryland gentleman of excellent position and for the rest of her life, as wife and mother, had, undoubtedly, opportunity for the practice of the virtues which had marked her early youth, and secured her the esteem of her noble pastor. But though Father Gallitzin's hopes were, by this means, and the falling off of others, entirely disappointed, the seed sown was not lost, and the inclination to a religious life awakened in the community, though it bore no fruit in his life time, did not die out when thus dropping away; for children of several of the pioneer families of Loretto, relatives and descendents of this very lady, as well as of those converted by him to the faith, are now in different orders, active, fervent religious.

Having gained an advantage as it might be considered, by an apparent concession, the spirit of opposition increased and multiplied; the rough element that to this day hangs about every new settlement, was already looking towards Loretto, watching and biding its time. Money had ceased to come from Germany, in consequence of the great expenses of the law-suits, the bishop was pressed and could not afford any help, and expecting day after day that the next would surely bring his regular allowance, Father Gallitzin held to his land, not being willing to part with it, until the last moment, creditors began to be impatient, he himself became more and more uneasy, more frugal, more careful, and finally really alarmed and in great need, facts which did not escape the notice of others, who were quick enough to take advantage of his difficulties, waxing bolder as the enemy's lines appeared to waver; the wind must have whispered the first suspicions, for no one could tell whence they came, but there were plenty to take them up, and expand them into the loudest assertions. Some vague idea in connection with his name, it being half suspected that he had been called by some other than the one they knew him by; the extensive land purchases in which he had engaged; the inducements he had held out to them to come to the mountains; his rigid rules; the stern moral law demanded in Loretto; the sudden stoppage of money from abroad, added to the trouble just passed, and immediately revived, all took a new and portentous meaning, and while it was gathering and muttering like the far off storm soon to sweep the mountains in a raging tempest, the slender young priest walked among them as stately, as kind, and as severe as ever, just as circumstances required, unbroken by the severest blow he could receive: the lessening confidence of his people, unbroken though with Moses he could well have cried: *Lord, what shall I do with this people, a little more and they will stone me.* Unbroken but cut to the heart, grieved beyond expression, afraid lest all that he had attempted to do, all that he had accomplished should be undone.

CHAPTER XIV.

THE SECOND PERSECUTION.

(1804—1806.)

Peculiar trials.—Hatred of evil.—The restraints of Loretto.—Munster.—Appeals to the bishop.—Continued opposition.—His life in danger.—Charges of interference in private affairs.—Rebellion in the church.

The weapons used by the backwoodsman are as different from the polished shafts with which more cultivated people undermine a character, as a battering ram from a needle gun. The men who now believed, or pretended to believe, that the priest whose word had been their law, was not all he seemed, was an adventurer, was a false priest, was no priest at all, did not conceal their meaning in fine phrases, and the very sound of their coarse language was in itself a bitter and disgusting persecution for a nature so refined, so high-bred, and made still more delicate, fine and pure by the life of continual recollection, of intimate union with all things high and sacred, to which Father Gallitzin was raised by his priesthood, and in which he lived and moved by prayer and the graces belonging to it. He had already that hatred and horror of sin, of everything in the least displeasing to God, which goes with the ardent love of goodness, increasing as perfection draws nearer; he wished sin might never be known, even as existing elsewhere, to his little community, if such a thing could only be, and when he was obliged to warn his congregations against it, his detestation of it was so great that no words could describe the fire, the force, the loathing which he expressed for it; his voice so round and full, so exquisitely modulated, like the richest music, when he spoke of virtue, and the joys of heaven won by it, deepened as he denounced the sinner's ways, grew shrill and sharp as he warned from every vestige of evil; his eyes flashed fire, his whole figure changed, and he appeared so terrible in the wrath and contempt aroused by the very thought of sin, that the people, even the most innocent, shuddered and trembled as he spoke, and the children looking at him, not understanding, clung to each other, sometimes even burst into frightened sobs and loud crying in church. Now all kinds of evil, all manner of sins and wickedness, seemed stirred up to fill the minds of his congregation, seething in the whispered conversation of the more timid and self-respecting, boldly leading the talk of the less shamefaced, and he the cause, he the centre of all the malice and rancor which gave life to the growing slanders. His consecrated hands were denounced as the hands of an extortioner, his consecrated lips as of a hypocrite and deceiver, the very life he had laid under the feet of the poor and the outcast to serve them as stepping stones to comfort, shelter, and return to grace, was branded as a lie; every act dictated by the lowliest self-sacrifice, and the best good of those under his charge, was pronounced a deed of ambition, of self-aggrandizement; every step he had taken, in pain and self-abnegation, over that mountain wilderness, was pointed out as the track of a fugitive, as the snares of a despot.

The first pretext had deceived a few, and gathered to itself all the vague and floating thoughts, fancies, imaginings, and suspicions of those fretting under the stern rule imposed upon his congregations, and once that rule had been defied, there were not lacking more to come forward rebelling against it, denouncing him who enforced it as imperious, a tyrant, an oppressor of the people. A meaner or a weaker man could well have been such, yet carried through no aim held in view, but Gallitzin's nature was mighty as the broad river sweeping to the ocean, all its currents, swift and strong, set to God; his tyranny was the tyranny of truth, the inexorable iron hand of the law of God, the softest hand when laid in benediction upon those who obey it, the most terrible in justice. There is no peace on earth like the freedom of the true Christian; he who lives in the eyes of God cannot go so far wrong as to feel his chains; no thief in the night can disquiet him whose conscience is at rest, whose debts are paid, whose treasures are in heaven; but terrible is the chain of the law to him who strives against it, more galling than the bonds of a Nero, the restraints of religion to him who knows no liberty but that of sin. Not for this did Father Gallitzin's hand ever unloose the chain, and let the impenitent sinner go free to mock his Saviour, and do His enemy's work, and well they knew it! Inflexible, incorruptible as the sentry by the gates of a beleaguered city, he guarded the walls of his citadel from foes without, as from traitors within. Well did he place his beloved people under the special patronage of the gentlest of women, the queen of peace, of angels, and of heaven, that their homes might ever be lighted by the love and lowliness of the Holy House of Loretto, but well he knew, besides, that the Church on earth is the Church militant, and wisely put his own under the charge of the iron willed leader of the heavenly hosts, the inflexible St. Micheal, who set his imperious foot upon the neck of the prince of rebels, and with wrath that flashed scornful lightnings through all times to come, hurled the traitor over the heavenly ramparts, into the burning lake below.

To those who lived as they ought, the restraints of Loretto, the high moral law reigning there, were loved and cherished as walls of defence, so sure and safe that they could live without dread, or fear; to others they grew every day more insupportable; the desire for wealth, for display, for living what is called a free and easy life, yet is the least free and the most confused of any, which had been so long under restraint, grew bolder at the sound of its own loud boasting and imprecations, but it saw no way to act until virtuous indignation should again fire the heart of the people, "'of a set of ragged vagabonds," as the Rev. Mr. Lemcke says, "who had reason to thank God if they could raise enough corn and potatoes to keep body and soul together during the winter, making an uproar, setting themselves up for judges, as if the salvation of the whole world depended upon them," (p. 228) who should be leaders in a second crusade against their pastor.

Although Father Gallitzin lived in great poverty, and the greatest economy on the church land, his position was not an unenviable one in the eyes of some other clergymen, especially of the one already mentioned as having won the affections of several of the people; this not, as might be supposed, because of the superior inducements to an austere and saintly life which it offered over any others in the country, but because a man who chose to live there according to the dictates of common sense, making the most of the farm, taking reasonable tithes from the congregations, and leaving the people to look out for their own temporal affairs, not coming to buy land from him for one dollar an acre when he had paid four dollars cash for it, could make a very good living there, especially if he let somebody else adopt the orphans of the parish, and put his own thrifty relatives in charge of the house and farms. Besides, as this same reverend gentleman was obliged to admit, when now and then, he met with some farmer of the congregation, nothing in the world could keep a town from growing, land from rising, and money from increasing like the attempt to govern it as if it were a cloister. There was no law of the Church forbidding a man to provide liberally for his family if he could, and making the best of a good bargain when he had the opportunity. He was very sorry for the good people, naturally anxious to turn an honest penny and get along in the world, but he could do nothing for them, for although their pastor was continually begging for an assistant priest, he did not really seem to want one, for all his, the speaker's, offers to assist, had been evaded, he could not tell why; perhaps because the priest wished to have things all his own way, and no one about who could address him as an equal. If at any time a new congregation was formed, and the people wished it, why, then, indeed he might come to them.

The thought was an inspiring one, and the very man whom Father Gallitzin had most assisted to find a home in

Loretto, who had prospered there, and having got on so well in the world wished to do better, became, in his own mind, the founder of a rival colony. He was joined by several others, who forgot whose charity had given them the first start, and animated by the double motive of escaping his vigilance, and of building up speedy fortunes, made use of all possible arts to inflame the people's minds against their pastor, that they might follow into the new town. This was intended to be some three miles from Loretto, between it and Ebensburg, and to rival them both. It was laid out on what proved to be the poorest land in the county, and called Munster, after the city in Ireland of that name, and not, as has been supposed, in honor of the home of Father Gallitzin's youth. Rev. Mr. Lemcke suggests that it should have been called Carthage, for the Punic wars raged there for thirty years, and ended in its destruction. It gave rise to as beautiful a series of faction fights as the most enthusiastic historian could desire to record.

At the first intimation of this new settlement, Father Gallitzin took fire, seeing well what it would lead to, and opposed it with all his might. He had fled from settlements formed on the same principle of mere material prosperity, without any reference to spiritual needs, and now after having, at such cost, cut a way through the woods, and founded a community upon the broad and lasting foundation of the true religion, having ever before it the cross of Christ, for one planned in pride and worldliness to set its flaunting standard at his very doors, as a refuge for all who fretted under the restraints of the Church, opening temptations to those who had never thought of discontent before, luring from the right way many who had only the most honest intentions in seeking a livelihood in the new village, was the greatest outrage that cou'd be conceived. Father Gallitzin never played with fire, nor trifled with danger; if there was a strong smell of burning, a heavy smoke seen, indicating that the house was on fire, it was never his way to lay a feather bed over the burning place, close the windows, draw the curtains, lock the doors, and go about with the air of there being nothing the matter. He lost not a moment; he spared no exertions to make the projectors of the new scheme see that it was begun in anger, and would end in wrath, he assured them, when they continued stubborn, that if he could prevent a plan so opposed to the good of the people from succeeding, he certainly would. They knew, all his congregations knew, that he had come to the mountains to build up a Catholic Community, to make a homestead for the Church to come to in days of trouble, in which she could educate her young soldiers, and find rest for her veterans, her wounded and disabled, and that never should another spirit obtain there, with his consent. True, others had followed him and raised up other towns and villages, he could not help that, but out from his own people for such to go forth, was to him insupportable. In a lower sense he opposed it no less, the land was poor, in a bad position, people would give up the homes they were just beginning to find comfortable hoping to gain something better, would lose what they already had, and obtain nothing to replace it, and then it was that all the opprobrium possible to be thought of, was heaped upon him, as only such men possessed by the desire for wealth, blinded by passion, could do. If he would not regard them as members of his congregation they freely declared they knew where to find a pastor more complaisant, more like themselves, who would take all care of their souls.

But as many who, they thought, would like to join the new settlement, were deterred by the priest's disapproval, these men hastened to the bishop with all manner of accusations, hoping to have him taken away, and the other priest mentioned, put in his place. Thinking to disarm them by mildness, and calm investigation, the bishop appointed Rev. Mr. Heilbron his agent to go to Loretto, or Clearfield, as it continued to be called, all the people not being as yet accustomed to the new name, and make full inquiries concerning the whole subject of complaint. The venerable priest, to whom Father Gallitzin had ever been most tenderly attentive, waiting upon him as a light-hearted youth upon his aged parent, humoring all his little peculiarities, taking lively part in all his fancies when they were together, even when his own heart was the heaviest, came to him now as a judge, as a superior, to whom was brought every little story malice or stupidity could invent, or cunning could extract from the simple minded and unsuspecting, even from the children he had adopted, who, as children will, had decided opinions about the strictness of his late housekeeper and their teacher, and all the accounts which could be gathered up of his opposition to the new village of Munster. But Mr. Heilbron, though at an age when men are sometimes more easily influenced than they would have been in their younger days, though hardly likely to feel the fiery indignation at the ingratitude of those who, after all that had been done for them, should seek to raise an antagonism to his treasured work, which Father Gallitzin felt so keenly, nor fully appreciating the danger of such a refuge for all rebellious or disaffected children of the Loretto church, saw nothing to justify a single complaint, and so reported to the bishop, who, besides kindly letters to the pastor, reprimanded those who had made charges against him, and sent an open letter, expressing his confidence in their pastor, which was nailed up at the church door, where all could read it:

RIGHT REV. BISHOP CARROLL TO THE CONGREGATION OF CLEARFIELD.*

It seems to me necessary to acquaint my dear children in Christ, the faithful composing the congregation of Clearfield, who are under the pastoral care of the Rev. Mr. Smith, that I am not unacquainted with the uneasinesses which prevailed for some time between the Rev'd gentleman and some individuals of his congregation. Every inquiry that could be made at so great a distance, has convinced me that Mr. Smith, throughout the whole business, was influenced by the best motives of Christian charity, and zeal for the welfare of those, who were given to him in charge; that he insists on

---

* From the original, preserved at the pastoral residence in Loretto.

nothing at present, which ought to be an objection to an entire reconciliation; that he is willing to act towards all persons of his flock with fatherly tenderness; and that they ought to give him assurances, and proofs of their confidence, and willingness to profit by his services. They should, moreever, be thankful to him for undergoing so many hardships on their account, and depriving himself, for God's and their sake, of the many temporal advantages he might elsewhere have enjoyed.

J. Bishop of Baltimore,

Nov. 30. 1804.

This letter calmed the fears of the timid and undecided who had stood aghast at the beginning of the troubles, and who, later, had been frightened, doubtful, not knowing what to think, while those who had openly taken part against the pastor were beaten back for a time, and driven to the rear by the hosts of friends who had never doubted, and encouraged by the bishop's so politely, though rather feebly expressed confidence, rallied boldly to his defence. But it was only a lull in the storm, a momentary defeat. The new village did not fill up as rapidly as its originators expected; one or two persons who had bought land there in good faith, got sick of their bargain, and longed to get back to Loretto; as usual in every difficulty, they applied to Father Gallitzin for advice how to get out of the trouble; he lent them his own wagon to do their moving back, and encouraged their return, which naturally was resented by those whose interests were all in Munster, and exaggerated into his having forced the people to leave, his pastoral position was still coveted, and again all sorts of reports and threats were set flying; some of the Loretto people began to feel keenly in the mattter, and sides were fast being taken in earnest by those who had previously simply deplored any separation of interests. A division among his people was the crowning distress of all for Father Gallitzin, and he could not forbear opening his heart to his only friend, the bishop, as evident from the reply:

RIGHT REV. BISHOP CARROLL TO REV. D. A. GALLITZIN.
Baltimore, Dec. 12, 1805.

Reverend Dear Sir,

.... I am sorry to learn that your tranquility is disturbed by the complaints and dissatisfaction of some of your congregation; some of which have been laid before me. I have given no answer nor can give any, to charges so vague as are contained in the letter to me. The principal one though generally expressed, is your interfering with the private concerns of your flock, taking a part in their disagreements, deciding on the character of those concerned, without hearing, or speaking to the party against whom you decide. This, perhaps, may be a sufficient clue to find out to what particular fact this complaint refers. I expect from the style in which the complaint is made, that it is to be followed by a formal appeal to my episcopal authority, and, therefore, hope that you will furnish me with such information as you may deem necessary. I am with great affection,

Dear and Rev. Sir,
† J. Bishop of Baltimore.

It was hardly possible that Father Gallitzin's tranquility could be otherwise than seriously disturbed, for not only were his ears filled with accounts of the illwill borne him, — accounts which every one rushed to repeat to him, with the evident idea that the more uncomfortable the news the more important the bearer, — but he had good reason to know his life was threatened in wicked earnest; it seems incredible but it is known to be true that there were men sworn in their hatred to prevent his remaining among them. His missions extended at least sixty or seventy miles in different directions, and he had, besides, calls from what might be considered the near neighborhood, which required him to ride day and night through the unbroken country, and nothing could be easier than for it to appear that he had lost his way in the woods, been eaten up by the beasts of the forests, or carried no one could tell where by the Indians who still lurked by the very doors of the Loretto settlement. He himself told as an illustration of the circle of danger surrounding the village, how one evening returning from a sick call in a direction with which he considered himself well acquainted, he rode and rode, sure that he was near home, yet finding himself ever in the depths of the forest, until, at last, confused and exhausted he was obliged to dismount, tie his horse to a tree, wrap himself in his cloak, commend his soul to God, and wait for light. He was by nature excessively nervous, though fearless as a lion in real danger, and after he had been sometime at Loretto, under annoyances and trials which would have worn the toughest and stoutest nerves, he became an intense sufferer from them, he would see lights and hear unearthly noises where all was dark and still to other people's senses, so that it has been thought that, like others aspiring after the highest perfection, it was permitted that he should be especially persecuted by the devil, who had made a profound impression upon him at Livingston's, but now as so often, he was obliged to remain all night alone in the woods, with the horrors of darkness about him, uncertain of ever seeing a human habitation again, should he even find his way out of the thick forest. When morning came he saw that he was indeed in a dense inclosure, but yet only a few yards from his own door. Such being the state of the country and some of its inhabitants outdoing its wild and savage character, he considered it his duty to provide himself with some means of defence not only against the wild animals whose fiery eyes so often glared about the sheepfolds of Loretto, but against the lawless crew who prowled about his humble home, threatening him even in the very house of God, but mentioning this intention to the bishop he was advised to forego the only measures which would have been at all effectual.

Rev. D. A. Gallitzin to Right Rev. Bishop Carroll.

Baltimore, Febr. 23, 1806.

Rev'd and Dear Sir,

After assuring you of my heart felt pleasure in hearing of your health, I must proceed to express my apprehension that my answer will not be so full as your letters required. Mr. Little came hither on Saturday afternoon (yesterday), and was exceedingly anxious to set out to day on his return; it is, as you know, the first Sunday of Lent, and consequently both days were fully employed in the functions belonging to them. It was impossible to dismiss him to day and it is now past six in the evening before I was able to give that consideration to yours which is requisite, or to take a pen in hand to make to it any kind of reply.

I begin with No. 1. I saw Mr. C——. on his return as was mentioned in my last; but nothing was said by him of his transactions with J—— [Originator of Munster.] to the best of my memory. There remains no doubt on my mind of your giving him such advice as in your judgment the confidence placed in your deserves; tho' perhaps, as you knew J—'s disposition towards you, had you referred C—— to some other person of competent knowledge in business it would have saved you from some part of obliquy with which you are loaded, and it would be a good general rule for you, when you have such characters to deal with, never to entangle yourself in their temporal concerns, or furnish them with a pretence for accusing you of meddling with matters not immediately relevant [to] your ministry. It was very painful to me to read that threats denounced against you induced you to be always armed. I dare not give any positive directions on such a subject, without investing myself with your feelings, and seeing the dangers surrounding me as nearly as you do. But my general idea is that a pastor is best protected by the respect, love, and esteem of his parishioners, and possessing these as you do of almost all under your fatherly care, it ought not to be expected that any would be so desperate as to use violence towards you. Tho' St. Paul enumerates his incessant dangers in *periculis latronum, periculis in via, periculis in solitudine* and *in falsis fratribus*, yet we read not of his arming himself against them, but he adds that the Lord delivered him from them all. Possibly other times and places may demand other precautions, and what is written above is no more than a recommendation to you to consider whether you cannot substitute some other defence more consonant with your character of minister of peace. If you should unfortunately be rudely attacked, and under the influence of a sudden movement of passion make an unfortunate use of your arms, as it is so uncommon for clergymen to carry them, the same malice which now persecutes you would be redoubled, and allege it as a presumption of premeditated assault.

Your fortitude and sacrifices under so many trials excite my admiration; I cannot think without veneration on a person of your education, habits, and former prospects for life, devoting himself to the painful services which employ you so entirely, and expose you to the ingratitude with which your services are sometimes requited. After acting as you say towards N. M. and W. W., you can do no more but recommend them to Almighty God. She insults me when she has the effrontery to say that she has my directions for abstaining from hearing Mass.

....No. 2. E. N. J. alone has come forward with charges against you; but his charges are almost a volume; besides his first letter, which I have not looked at since mine to you, and which, as far as I have any rememberance of it, dealt only in generals, another came to hand about three days before Mr. Little's, containing three sheets of very close writing. To read yours, and his, and form some general estimate of them, engaged me until eleven o'clock last night. For tho' his had been received before, as I have said, my other pressing occupations prevented me from going through it sooner.

....This, my dear Sir, is an imperfect sketch of what I would write to you if more time were allowed me. I ought likewise to acknowledge the certificate of your congregation generally, and the special letter signed by George Boaser, John Lilly, and others; but you will apologise to them for me, and assure them that I do not now entertain, and hope never to have cause to entertain a design of removing you from them. Depend not upon Mr. Fitzsimmons, who is, I fear, too fickle. I know not whose heroism must to admire, yours or your most venerable mother's.

Believe me most affectionately, Dear and Rev. Sir,

Your most devoted servant
† J. Bishop of Baltimore.

Living in the orderly and quiet city of Baltimore, the good bishop could not place himself at all in Father Gallitzin's position; it is evident that all his attempts to do so were complete failures. The very reasons and motives which caused the formation of Loretto, were the very ones which made an interference in the people's affairs, temporal as well as spiritual, imperative and a matter of course. For the greater number of the people that he did so was the greatest inducement held out to them to settle in Loretto, and its vicinity. To them it was no interference, but the guidance of a strong hand which sustained them, upheld them in all their troubles, cares, and perplexities, blessed their joys, and crowned their happiness. The bishop could hardly realize, not seeing it, that in a settlement of the kind, even in one self-constructed, or made up by accident, the priest is often the only man of education within reach, the only one who knows anything of "familiar science", who is looked to in every emergency, without whom every thing would go wrong; he it is who knows best the different talents, dispositions, capabilities and temper of each member of each family, and is consulted with as much faith in questions concerning the choice of employment, of marriage, all perplexing and disputed points of ordinary life, as in matters of religion, about which, indeed, there could be no doubt or question, and if a rebellious child received little sympathy from the pastor of Loretto, or an over exacting parent found the decision going against him; if where brothers disputed and came to him, one was pronounced right and the other in fault, he was not to blame; it was in the nature of things. Nothing could be more touching and more safe in its way, than the confidence thus begun, continuing from parents to children, so that the little ones who came sobbing to him, in disgrace at home, and were led back to be reconciled and made happy again, felt no hesitation in later years in opening to him thoughts and feelings, intimated to no other, which if kept in silence and concealment, would have become sickly, and injurious to the whole system, but brought into the clear and radiant atmosphere surrounding him, bloomed into fresh and vigorous life, to to bear abundant fruit in days to come. He knew them all so well, just how they were suited to each other, that a courtship or an engagement approved by him, was sure to be blessed, and the marriage happy in true and constant affection; if sorrows came, if the cares of life pressed hard, no man, no woman, however stricken, sorrowed alone, while he lived. No skeletons were hidden in closets, no poverty thrust out of sight when his foot was on their step, and many and many the ugly gap, the breaking plank bridged over, and the sliding feet upheld by him in the darkest hour of temptation, passed in safety, that no one knew of, and many a gray head went on in merited honor to its final rest, saved by just such interference in its youth, from a reckless life of sin, of every disgrace, unsuspected of any.

Had Father Gallitzin shut himself into those things which strictly belonged to his ministry, he would have done but half his work; it must be remembered he was not simply a priest sent to a certain parish to perform the regular spiritual duties, he was far more, he had formed the parish of which he was pastor, he had chosen the people who composed it, he had bought the land on which they dwelt and given it to them for a merely nominal price, enough to save their independence; there was a tacit understanding, as clear to both as the most imposing parchment contract, between him and the people, that they were to live a life with higher aims than those they had left, that they were to strive for the highest perfection possible in the world, that their Sunday piety was not to be contradicted by their week day indifference; to see them once a week at Mass, to hear their sins in confession, to visit them in an emergency, and the rest of the time to let their lives run on as they might, was by no means the idea upon which he had planned and founded Loretto. Only those who were in every way unworthy of this, disputed it, but those who disputed, disputed vehemently, madly, and nothing could turn them from their course; no law ecclesiastical or civil could restrain them.

In the very beginning of trouble, when the first intimation of calumny came to his ears, Father Gallitzin rose up and traced it to its originators, he knew that his good name was the good name of the Church, and not for a moment would he let it be trifled with, if any means within his reach could stop it, a slur upon it was a shadow upon religion, and filled him with double indignation. He demanded an instant retraction, it was not given, and he then sued the chief speaker for slander; a court of inquiry was held composed entirely of Protestants of the highest standing in Huntingdon County, nearly all of Scotch Irish parentage, not disposed by religion or nationality to be over partial to a Catholic and a German, as he was generally supposed to be; they decided entirely in his favor, awarding him three hundred and fifty dollars damages, a large sum in those days. The money was never collected, and the defendant made a full and explicit denial of his belief in a single one of the charges, as well as of having made them. This certificate of denial is now on the records of the county, the calumny and the calumniators forgotten*. For a short time this resolute measure awed his enemies into silence and caution; afterwards, as we have seen, they revived.

It was during this time of real persecution that his enemies, their ranks recruited by two or three worse even than themselves, wild "border ruffians" who attracted by the mischief gathering there, had drifted to the frontiers of his parish, to be on hand, ready for any wickedness that could be devised, forced their way, armed with congenial clubs and sticks, into the church, to tear him as they had threatened, from the altar, if he made the first attempt to say Mass. It was a terrible day, and a really awful hush that fell upon the people, as his ringing step bore him with head erect, and keen, searching gaze past the little altar, to the stand on which his vestments awaited him. All knew what was intended, all more than half expected to see him murdered before their very eyes, while they looked on as if in a spell; for although his friends were many and strong, they were cowed,

---

* From Mr. McCabe's unpublished notes.

as the orderly and quiet majority too often is by the swearing, swaggering few. *But Elias, the prophet, stood up as a fire, and his words burnt like a torch.*

When he was ready for the *Asperges*, he turned and faced the people, for one moment under his stern and steady look there was utter stillness, the next, and there was a muttering and surging towards that slender figure, standing there defenceless, in his long white robe, which rose, and swelled and swept forward as the mad ocean waves, black and tumultuous, against some fair white sail riding for an instant upon their breast. He took one step to meet it, something rising into his eyes and bearing more powerful than their rage, and quietly said:

"I now proceed to offer up the Holy Sacrifice of the Mass. Let no one dare to profane this church, or insult the Christ here present, by one word or movement. And I tell you this," advancing one step more, and speaking in a voice of concentrated power, "and I tell you this, if any man raises hand or foot to take me from this altar, or to interrupt my words this day, another day shall come when he will call for me, and I shall not be there." As he spoke the uplifted arms fell as if paralyzed, he alone was calm and firm, as he walked through the aisle, singing the *Asperges* and sprinking the holy water. Mass went on without interruption, and never again did any one dare repeat the attempt to prevent it.

His words were never forgotten, and of those who at this time, or later, publicly defied him, not one, since dead, received the last consolations of religion, although in one case, at least, that of a man suddenly injured, almost superhuman efforts were made by the priest sent for, to reach him while life remained, but it was not to be; no human effort of religious zeal or Christian charity was permitted to over-ride the decree of the Almighty. *Tossed with tempest, without all comfort, behold I will lay thy stones in order, and will lay thy foundations with sapphires!*

CHAPTER XV.

DEATH OF THE PRINCESS.

(1806.)

> *I have fought a good fight, I have finished my course, I have kept the faith.*
>
> (TIMOTHY IV, 7.)

How the news was received.—Consolations.—The princess' last illness and death.—Some traits of her character.—Effect of his sorrow upon Father Gallitzin.

In Father Gallitzin's life at this time, blow followed blow so thick and fast that often several struck together. In the midst of the coldness of those whose reverent affection should have been the warmest, the apparent aversion of others, the multiplied insults of his enemies, it pleased the God who rules us all, to deprive him of the only strong hand that had ever been reached out to him, the only heart that had ever beat firm and fearless response to his own.

He was standing one morning in the late Autumn of 1806, by the door of his cabin, whither he had hastened to meet a returning messenger from Baltimore, — there were no post-offices as yet any where near Loretto, — when a letter was handed him from the bishop. He opened it quickly and found enclosed another, heavily sealed with black, that for an instant made his heart stand still. He read but a few minutes before the crowd of children composing his household, who had been half unconsciously watching him, saw that something dreadful had happened, and were so terrified at the sight of his face convulsed with grief and tears, that they burst into frightened sobs and suppressed wails, without in the least understanding why. After a while with

that instinctive blind reaching out for human sympathy
which belonged to his loving nature, he said to them, "It is
my mother; she is dead." She was no stranger to them; it
was his delight to tell of her, and all who had ever heard
him allude to her, however slightly, felt a fascination in the
least word concerning that brave, generous, beautiful lady,
around whom even the rudest of them wreathed their scraps
of young romance. What it was to him no one can say,
when the youngest child there was stunned with wonder at
the incomprehensible sorrow. No one could know the bitterness of that hour, the agony of that loss. May it be that for
the sake of the motherless little ones whom he had cared for,
some comfort came from God through them that sustained
him then!

When he had become more collected his love, as it always
did, found expression in action, he prepared to pay her memory the last honors, and to procure for her soul all the comforts and blessings of the Church, though hoping she was
past all need of help; to have had nothing left to do for her
would have been to sink exhausted and beyond rescue into
the depths of sorrow and despondency. He sent the children for the two men who composed his choir to receive his
orders, and as they went on their errand, crying all the way,
so that they could scarcely deliver their message in the end,
every one learned at once of their pastor's affliction, in
which even the coldest hearted of his parishioners could
hardly fail to bear part.

In the package of letters was one from the bishop, as an
accompaniment to the packet enclosed to his care, the others
were written on one large sheet, by five different persons,
Princess Mimi, Count and Countess von Stolberg, and the
two brothers von Droste*.

 Right Rev. Bishop Carroll to Rev. D. A. Gallitzin.

  Rev. and very dear Sir,
The enclosed contains an account which will be very pain-

---

* Rev. H. Lemcke, p. 238. Unfortunately Rev. Mr. Lemcke gives only
the letters of the princess and the count, and all efforts to obtain the
original letter or even an authentic copy, have proved unavailing.

ful to your feelings, but full of comfort to your more deliberate and Christian reflections. It was enclosed to me in a letter from Count Stolberg who requests me to prepare you gradually for the intelligence conveyed by your sister's letter. Not being able, considering our distance from each other, to comply with this request, and knowing that after leaving your father, mother and kindred, you will find the best motives present to your mind, I have determined to send you the letter without any other preparation than this cover to it. Since I received it, I have often recommended her myself, and prayed our other brethren to recommend her to the mercy of God, tho' I entertain no doubt of her éternal felicity. It is not only on account of her relationship to you that I interest myself and desire others to interest themselves for her, but because she was the active, useful, and earnest friend of religion in this diocese, and earnestly sought to promote it. On this occasion I will only add my sincere condolence with you at being deprived, in this world, of the blessing of possessing a mother so truly estimable, and who has the merit of being, under God, the chief instrument of those precious graces which have been showered on you.

I am with the greatest attachment
    Rev. Dear Sir,

                        Your most obdt st,
                        † J. Bishop of Baltimore.

PRINCESS MARIANNA GALLITZIN TO HER BROTHER.

                        Muenster, April 28, 1806.

Dearest, best brother,

The paper which I must now use in writing you, will announce to you at once that which it is so hard for me to put into words. Yesterday morning at half past two o'clock, the dearest, the best, and the most precious of mothers, now our guardian angel before God, fell gently asleep in the Lord. My mind, as well as my heart, is so stunned by this hard blow, that you must forgive me if, for the present, I can say no more. As soon as I shall have recovered myself and become somewhat collected, I will more fully detail to you her sufferings, her splendid patience in her trials, her happy death in Christ, — a death at which I had the intensely painful, but never-to-be forgotten satisfaction of assisting, holding her in my arms at the last moment. Best of brothers, forgive me, indeed, I can write no more. I am weaker to bear this grief than I can express. May God strengthen you, and enable you to find our dear mother in Him when this life is ended.

Your faithful sister,
M. Gallitzin.

COUNT VON STOLBERG TO REV. D. A. GALLITZIN.

Praise be to Christ Jesus!*

She praises him now better than we, dearest Mitri!—I cannot call the dear son of my dearest friend by any name but the one she used, and which you will surely allow to me. —She praises him now better than we, but we still praise him the best we can, and not only in a general way, for that is understood, even with every breath we draw, but in special manner now that he has so unspeakably blessed your heavenly mother. He visited her with long, painful, and indescribable sufferings, but in those sufferings he was unutterably dear to her. She resembled him in pain that she might resemble him in eternal glory. You do not need, best Mitri, that I should tell you what an angel your mother was, but in my deep sorrow I long to say to you that, since I came to know her, I could think of her only with the most profound veneration, and the most devoted love, rejoicing in the chain which God in his mercy linked between her and myself. My soul is deeply grieved, but at the same time my spirit rejoices for she has reached her goal, and by her powerful intercession draws me after her. Rejoice you also, dearest Mitri, that you are the beloved son of a saint, that you caused

---

* *Gelobt sei Jesus Christus*, the salutation of the Germans, especially when meeting a priest. The one saluted in this beautiful manner replies *In Ewigkeit*—For all Eternity.

her such great happiness even here; to know that with unutterable mother-love she blesses and prays for you, is indeed a great joy. I reach you my hand over the sea, beloved Mitri, and unite myself in spirit with you and our glorified one, in the salutation of the earth pilgrim, and of those whose pilgrimage is over: *Praise be to Christ Jesus in all eternity.*

F. L. Stolberg.

Sometime during that sad day Father Gallitzin made an attempt to write in reply to the bishop, but it is apparent from the circumstances mentioned in the letter that, although the date is not changed, only the first paragraph was written at that time, which is almost the only instance of inaccuracy to be found in his whole correspondence; his letters being singularly neat, precise, and carefully written.

Rev. D. A. Gallitzin to Right Rev. Bishop Carroll.

Nov. 11, 1806.

My Lord,

Your favor of Oct. 6, White Marsh, and Oct. 13, Baltimore, I only received this morning, together with the enclosed letters from my sister, etc., announcing the doleful news of that fatal stroke which deprived me of a most tender and affectionate mother, and your diocese of a most zealous friend and protector. The flood of tears it drew from my eyes, were chiefly tears of joy and exultation at the happy exchange she made after long continued sufferings of every kind. Thanks be to God, I was sufficiently prepared for the stroke by several letters previously received from several friends in Baltimore, Philadelphia, etc., early in September.

In conjunction with Rev Mr. Heilbron, I celebrated her funeral during three successive days, in as splendid a manner as the narrowness of my circumstances admitted. The church was crowded and about forty dollars collected for Masses for her departed soul*. As I wish to make a little

---

* It is customary among Catholics, when they wish Mass offered for a special intention, to make a small offering, the amount of which is

offering for the benefit of her departed (though I trust already happy) soul, I beg of your Lordship to accept of this watch, a most excellent one of its kind, and formerly belonging to my father; nobody, in fact, is more entitled to it than your Lordship who has been a father to me and more so than my real father according to the flesh.

Although the bishop perfectly understood that Gallitzin desired to apply the merit of the self-denial, slight as it was, necessary in parting with his watch, to his mother, in case she should yet be deficient in merits, he scrupled accepting so valuable a present, which drew from Father Gallitzin a grateful explanation.

Rev. D. A. Gallitzin to Right Rev. Bishop Carroll.

My Lord,

Your kind favor of Nov. 17, I received whilst in the courthouse of Somerset.... I am sensibly affected by the share which your Lordship takes in my affliction, and sincerely offer you my grateful thanks for remembering my departed mother at the altar, and causing your clergy to do the same. I wish your Lordship to be convinced that it was not without mature deliberation that I made this small offering for the benefit of her departed soul, not meaning at the same time (as your Lordship seems to have understood) to have as many Masses said as the value of the watch would be computed to amount to. No, my Lord, I know that my mother always had a share in your prayers, before she departed as well as since. It was this as well as the remembrance of your personal favors to my own unworthy person, and especially your protection and patronage at the time when the opposition of all my friends in Europe seemed to frustrate

---

fixed by the laws of each diocese, to the priest of whom they request it, not in payment for the Sacrifice, for that can never be paid for, being infinitely valuable, but in order that by the deprivation, mortification or self-denial caused by the offering they may have closer part in the Holy Sacrifice, as in the Old Law the faithful were required to bring the lambs, etc., which the priests were to sacrifice.

my intention of embracing the clerical state, it was this, I say, made me consider it one of the sacred duties incumbent on me to make an offering of the only thing I possess worthy of notice, to your person, and in your person (as the highest representative of Almighty God in this country) to God Himself, for the benefit of my departed mother. I beg of your Lordship to accept of the watch, and keep it as an offering from your most sincere friend, for the above intention.

In reply to a letter of condolence written her by the bishop at about the time the sad news reached her brother, Princess Marianna wrote:

PRINCESS MARIANNA GALLITZIN TO RIGHT REV. BISHOP CARROLL.*

Monseigneur,
The letter with which your Lordship so kindly honored me, dated Nov. 6, 1806, excited the liveliest gratitude in my heart, while giving me also the first news I have had of my brother since my mother's death. Alas!'Monseigneur, you have too high an opinion of me, and that which you had the goodness to say of me to Count de Stolberg very much humiliated me, by causing me to recollect that, having had the happiness of a saint for my mother, and having still a brother who gives me such a beautiful example, God imposes upon me duties which I so poorly fulfill. I recommend myself, Monseigneur, in special manner to your charity, and hope that you will not refuse me the aid of your pious prayers.

I have since received a letter from my brother which gives me great pleasure, as it proves to me that God sustained him with his grace in the saddest moment he could pass upon earth. God be a thousand, thousand times blessed for it! I have the greatest confidence in the intercession of our dear departed, and do not doubt she is by the side of God the special patron of my brother's flock, and of all your dio-

---

* From the original in French belonging to the arch-episcopal archives of Baltimore.

cese, Monseigneur, because she had for your Lordship the most particular respect and veneration. I have written to my brother, addressing the letter to Philadelphia, as he expressed the desire I should, but profiting by your great kindness, I take the liberty, Monseigneur, of sending you a duplicate of the letter with a box for him, which I will send by Amsterdam.

* * *

Among my dear mother's papers I have found a letter addressed to you, Monseigneur, which I will take the liberty of sending you, with a copy of this*, and the packet for my brother, by Amsterdam, as also the two letters Mr. Gouppy begs me to send you.

They write me from Brabant that this spring you will have two excellent missionaries; I pray God to bless their undertaking.

Accept, Monseigneur, the assurance of the profound respect and lively gratitude with which I have the honor to be,

Your Lordship's most humble and obedient servant,

Marianna Gallitzin.

Muenster, 8 April 1807.

It was no mere conventional form which prompted the assurances of the eternal welfare of the dear princess contained in all these letters. So far as human eyes could see she had always lived the best life she could find, and had conscientiously and anxiously sought to find the best; after her conversion she had indeed lived as those to whom the eternal reward is promised. In early days, as one of her biographers expresses it,† "she had earnestly sought to satisfy, by means of philosophy, the cravings of her soul after knowledge and virtue, with the sacrifice of all the advantages which the world had bestowed upon her in rich abundance.

---

* On account of the uncertainty of the mails, letters were generally sent in duplicates, each copy by a different vessel.

† *Life of Bernard Overberg*, translated from the German by the Hon. and Rev. George Spencer. Derby 1844.

She had striven in this way, with persevering courage, after a more elevated ennobling of herself; she had searched, she had practised, she had fought, she had suffered; but she could find no rest for her soul, till she came to Him, who calls to himself all who are laden with toil and trouble, who invites them to learn of Him meekness and humility, and promises peace to their soul. She captivated her understanding to the obedience of faith in Him who was crucified, who to the Jews indeed was a stumbling block, and to the Gentiles foolishness, but to those who are called, the power of God and the wisdom of God."

Especially was this true after her son's entrance into the priesthood; her prayers had undoubtedly obtained great graces for him, to which he did not fail to respond, and he repaid them with abundance when, as a priest of God, he asked, at the altar, grace and help for her in the noble striving for the highest perfection, which she never allowed herself to abate, and which even on his account she felt incumbent upon her, as when a great king elevates one of his subjects to a position of the highest honor and trust, the family of the new favorite rise with him, and the mother, long content with the simple name of gentlewoman, strives now, in honor to the son whom the king has honored, as in gratitude to the king himself, to carry herself with all graciousness and state, as becomes the mother of him whom his sovereign ennobles.

The princess never wholly recovered from her illness of 1783, and as years advanced the seeds of disease left in her system, bore fruit in bitter sufferings, from which she seldom obtained even temporary relief. In 1805—6 she became so constantly ill that she could hardly be said to have a well day, but her immense cheerfulness in great measure concealed her sufferings and her danger. In the spring of 1806 she was so much worse as to be unable to leave her room, and arranged everything for whatever might ensue. Dr. Overberg, who continued to be her friend and confessor, remained in her house, consoling and sustaining her by exhortations which she well understood; Princess Mimi and

Countess Amalia took turns in watching by her, entreating her to permit them to do so, day and night, while one or more of the servants remained in a room near at hand within call; as the princess soon found herself unable to have more than one or two persons by her at once, and permitted only womanly hands to serve her. For her children, Mimi and Amalia, as for the persons who remained within immediate call, she was thoughtful and considerate as ever, careful that they should have refreshment during the night, be warm and comfortable, and so on. To keep her mind employed she was glad to have any one read to her, sometimes Overberg, sometimes Amalia or Mimi, and she would listen so attentively, in spite of her great pain and weakness, and with such lively interest that the one reading would be greatly pleased and instructed.

On the afternoon of the 26th of April, her physician came to see her, and after a lively interview left her without any fears of a critical accident occurring before morning. In the early part of her illness he had remained all night in her house whenever he saw any critical symptoms, but this time it did not seem to him necessary. But about midnight she was attacked by pains, and an overpowering depression, which made her apprehend that her last hour had come; she gave orders for the inmates of the house to be awakened, which she had never done before, because she did not wish to disturb any one unnecessarily and was not willing to have any more spectators of her suffering than was needful; the physician, who had been called, came after these, and found her writhing in pain, invoking the holy names: O Jesus! Mary! Joseph! imploring strength to bear her suffering with resignation, and supported in the bed by a maid, kneeling beside her. While the pains continued, she said between the pronounciation of the holy names: "I see you all, my dear children," who were present, and afterwards named: Fuerstenberg, Stolberg, Meerfeld, Droste, and others; at the entrance to eternity, to which she was now hastening, she wished to leave her friends the assurance that the love and care which she had had for them in this life she took with her into the better life. Friendship was for her a sacred spiritual bond, which bid defiance to time and space. The physician asked her if she would take something strengthening; she immediately answered in accordance with her first impulse. "No!" but a moment afterwards, recollecting that her answer was self-willed, she said "Yes, everything you wish," and took something he gave her.

There followed a moment of apparent calmness; the physician asked if she felt somewhat less pain. "No," she answered, "I suffer as before, but I am so exhausted that the pain cannot express itself." Some one asked her if she would not feel easier if she laid on the bed. "Oh, yes, "she said, "only tell me where I shall lay myself, right soon to die," "To die?" repeated Overberg, in order to sustain her in continued resignation and submission, "Would we then not suffer as long as God wills?" She replied in a tone in which the whole fulness of her interior spirit was expressed, "Oh yes, that is understood, with my whole heart willingly!" Then she turned, with such help as they could give her, to lay herself upon the bed.

In the meantime midnight had gone by, the beginning of Sunday had come, and time was precious, so Overberg, who in the first year of the princess' illness had obtained permission from the spiritual authorities to celebrate Mass by her sick bed, to sustain her with the atoning sacrifice the Son of God had made, and with the bread of life, now proposed it to her; but she wished to make preparation in this hour of death as in days of health, for this sublime act, yet felt herself unable to do so. Overberg, who knew her wish, overcame her scruples by speaking to her of the Saviour, and the strength the offering of the Lamb, slain for the sins of the world for all time, would procure her at the judgment seat of God.

The altar was arranged in the large room near at hand, the door of the smaller room in which the sick bed stood, being left open, so that the sufferer could see the altar; the physician and Princess Mimi remained with her to give her the last attentions, while the others surrounded the altar in the main room. It was an hour of sadness and solemnity beyond description.

The prayer of the Church (collect) for the day prayed that God, who shows the light of His truth to those who go astray, that they may return to righteousness, would grant that all who profess the Christian name may forsake whatever is contrary to that profession, and closely pursue that which is in conformity to it.

The Gospel repeated the words of Jesus to his disciples: *A little while, and now you shall not see me: because I go to the Father..... and you shall be made sorrowful, but your sorrow shall be turned into joy. A woman, when she is in labor, hath sorrow because her hour is come: but when she hath brought forth the child she remembereth no more her anguish for joy that a new man is born into the world.... and your joy no man shall take from you.* (JOHN xvi 16—23.) Words of significant promise to her who had so truly forsaken all that was contrary to the profession of Catholic faith, and so closely pursued that which was in conformity with it.

Overberg gave her Holy Communion with a few words of exhortation in Latin, from the Bible, which she loved best to read in that language. After Mass, she made her thanksgiving in quiet, the physician silent on one side, and Mimi, weeping bitterly, with her arms around her, on the other. That thanksgiving was never finished in this world; she died between half past two and three o'clock on the morning of the 27th April 1806, third Sunday after Easter, called JUBILATE.*

For two days after her death the remains of the beloved princess were visited by great crowds, drawn not from curiosity, but sorrowful affection, the rich and the learned were there with the poor and the ignorant who wept for the mother lost in her. On the third day she was taken to Angelmodde, as she had requested, and buried by the little village church she had so often visited, not as a guest,

---

* Katercamp's life of the princess, pages 289—295.

but as beloved child of the house. Her friends followed in crowds, with emotions too deep for words. Her monument is a large crucifix on a square pedestal, and the words which so truly describe her Christian life:

> "*I count all things to be but loss for the excellent knowledge of Jesus Christ my Lord, for whom I have suffered the loss of all things, and count them but as dung that I may gain Christ.*" (PHIL. iii, 8.)

> "So thought, so lived the Mother of the Poor and Oppressed, Princess Amalia von Gallitzin, born Countess von Schmettau, who rests at the feet of this Image (crucifix) in the hope of her glorious Resurrection."

Dr. Overberg who had daily received edification from her earnest strivings after perfection, and from her eminent Christian wisdom, intended to write her life, the better to keep her memory and her example before his vision, and among his papers were found some relating to her youth, prefaced by these words: "I thought it agreeable to the will of God, that I should bring this matter into written form, in order that I might the better be able to put before my mind's eye, and also in future keep in sight, for my edification, the deceased and her virtuous life, which I, as her confessor, was best acquainted with. If what I write should also conduce to the edification and instruction of others, to God be the praise*." But it is not always those who have known us the most intimately who can best present us to others; the artist who would take a bold, distinct, and accurate view, stands at a little distance from his subject, and for some reason, Overberg relinquished his intention. Numerous sketches have been given in different languages, but it was reserved for Dr. Katercamp, who had known her well, to write the most complete biography yet published. "External energy," he says, in commenting upon her character*, "and even great intellect are in themselves but doubtful

---

* *Life of Overberg*, p. 144.
† Page 298.

gifts. As long as it remains undecided whether they are to be used for egotistical or for higher purposes they are a soil on which vice may take root as well as virtue. Even with the highest moral standard it is not one and the same thing whether the will is determined by principles of reason, or by the sanction and unction of faith.

"The life of the princess presents this two-fold view: greatness of mind judged, first by the natural moral estimation, and then by supernatural worth, that is, the relation of the human spirit to grace.

"Clearness and strict consequence in thought and action, with rarest gifts of intuition, animated by elevated perception to spiritual aims, were in her natural gifts, which even in her early youth won her, by interior impulse, a decided conquest over sensuality. These gifts which urged her to poetry as to speculative philosophy, in consequence of her self-cultivation used for the harmony and elevation of her disposition reached, in her later years, such a wonderful height, that with the same logical consequence, and an even greater intuitive perception, she thought in sleep as when awake.

"'The strict moral standard which she prescribed herself in the philosophic period, preserved her from the ambition of displaying her talents to the world, by which the character of so many eminent persons, lacking moral principle, goes to ruin.

"This native dignity of her moral character, and her peculiar love for the beautiful hindered, for a time, her perception of the seed of evil in us all, and its gradual development. A certain passionate excitement in her mind stimulating her not only to her own perfection, but that of her children and friends, showed her wherein lay the peril of her life, that a subtile and secret pride was the motive of her aiming for perfection. After this discovery appears the great difference between her purely philosophic and her Christian efforts for it.

"True perfection, which harmonizes the interior discord, and should lay the fouundation of God's peace which is above time and space, is a gift from on high, and can be obtained only through unconditional dependence of the mind on God, through the divine institution of reconciliation, that is from Jesus Christ, the mediator between God and men, in other words, by faith and humility. When any one by aid of faith comes to this conviction he knows that he has not to climb steep heights, nor sink to deep abysses, because the end he aims at is not far from him, but near and direct, not only *near* but *in* him, in his heart (Rom. x.). This end is the highest good that can be obtained here or in eternity: Union with God, by which the human mind places itself, or rather, is placed in eternity, notwithstanding the change that occurs in time in the external demonstration, for it consists in the mutual intercourse between God and the faithful soul; God descends to her by grace, and she ascends to Him by prayer, that is, reaches up to God as with two spiritual arms: desire and confidence.

"This end of Christian life although the most sublime that men can reach is, at the same time, so simple that on account of its very simplicity it is often passed over and unnoticed in the strain of tendencies separated from faith; for usually in the agitation of search those things which operate least on the senses, are least observed. To obtain this end man must seek, turning the will from earthly inclinations, to open his mind to the influence of grace and carefully notice and quietly but attentively consider, as Mary at the Saviour's feet, every word that comes from God; first, that which is given us in external revelation, following no less with faithful love that which is caused by the internal and by other means within us, especially that which urges us onward.... This voice of God which urges onward (to virtue) speaks much lower than the voice which restrains, (from sin) and is, consequently, easily missed by the inattentive, and if neglected, unfaithfulness to it is not so severely punished; we are therefore easier satisfied in regard to it, more indifferent to it. This is the cause of the moral stand-still of numbers of really good and blameless people. It belonged to the Christian wisdom of the princess' life to listen with great attention and fidelity to the inward voice of God urging onward.... Christian life for her consisted in two exercises, in continual interchange with one another:

Going into herself by meditation and prayer,
Coming out of herself in active love, for which prayer gives the strength.

"What she effected by these exercises, partly in bringing souls back from evil ways, partly by personal deprivation in order to use her means for good to the widest extent, will only be shown at the great day when the conscience of man will be judged, for here it was for the most-part hidden. She publicly declared the principles of her life, but her good works were done in secret. One of her household often accompanied her in the evenings, after dark, to the cabins of the poor, he carrying the money she was to spend in providing for their needs, while her friends, even the other persons in the house, knew nothing of these works of love and charity.

"When she was not so ill as to be compelled to remain constantly in bed, and yet suffered at every step she took in her drawing room, in consequence of the shock the motion of walking gave her, a carpet was considered necessary that she might be able to take less painful exercise. She ordered an ordinary one from Amsterdam, but by the mistake of the person commissioned to procure it, a Turkey carpet was sent, truly more appropriate, but much more expensive. She required that it should be sold again, a cheaper one bought, and the surplus given as alms: 'It is not right,' she said, 'that I should trample under my feet that which would support a poor family for quite a while.' Fortunately, it did not come to the selling of it, for it was soon evident that an ordinary one would not be soft enough for the desired purpose.

"In returning to the Christian religion, she returned to the Catholic Church. The conviction in each respect was the result of three years of deliberation (1783—1786); she recognized in the Catholic Church, as she was in the habit of saying, the more correct result, and she was not contented when her Protestant friends spoke with praise as if in her circle there prevailed a better Catholicism than elsewhere. "

"Her adherence to the Catholic Church was unconditional and without reservation, as well in her reverence for its discipline, as for its public worship and dogma.

"She was hurt to her inmost soul when she heard that on Catholic pulpits, or from Catholic chairs in schools, the dogma of the Church was violated.

"The Church was especially venerated by her in the Sacraments. She never neglected to be present when Overberg gave instruction to the ladies at the Academy, or when first communion or confirmation was given. Her faith enabled her thus to see the Divine friend of children, who said: *'Suffer little children to come to me and forbid them not,'* pouring out the plentitude of His graces for these pure and innocent souls, whom she so willingly joined in thought and prayer.

"But especially did she venerate that great and holy Sacrament in which Christ Jesus, the Lamb slain from the beginning, the Sacrifice of all time, offers Himself with the fulness of His graces as the fountain of grace; at the same time giver and gift, sacrifice and high priest.

"In this Sacrament, as in the food of the soul she sought and found the strength by which the yoke of suffering, bitter as it was became sweet and light. Strengthened with this food she went, though under great bodily anguish, consoled and full of confidence to eternity."

All possible comfort which the knowledge of her life in this world, and the assured hope of her eternal happiness in heaven could inspire, was given to Father Gallitzin, he looked confidently forward to an eternal reunion with her, felt her presence ever about him, and that she now loved and guarded and prayed for him as she never could upon earth, and yet her death was a grief from which he could never hope to recover. But this bitterest of all earthly sorrows, running through his true heart, devoted to God, sweetened and softened his nature, and brought ever nearer the weak human hearts that looked to him for comfort, and showed him how to lead them onward to the unfailing fountain of divine compassion and eternal recompense.

CHAPTER XVI.

THE FINAL PERSECUTION.

(1806—1807.)

> *All my enemies whispered together against me; they devised evils to me.*
> *For even the man of my peace, in whom I trusted, who ate my bread, hath greatly supplanted me.* (Ps. XL.)

Renewal of trouble.—Mr. Phelan again.—The Westmoreland conspiracy.—Jacob.—E. V. J.'s retraction.—The committee visit Bishop Carroll.—John Weakland's argument.—Broken down.—End of the slander.

When Father Gallitzin at the foot of the altar turned and faced his defamers, the bitter waters of their hatred were turned backward upon themselves, but though intercepted, obstructed, divided, powerless to leap the mighty arm thus stretched across their course, they retained volume enough to gather once more, and swollen with all stormy passions to wear themselves another channel through which, by a more circuitous and less headlong descent, to sweep over him and bear him onward to the deepest gulf of shame and oblivion. Of those who quailed before him on that memorable day, many were struck with instant fear, and suddenly awoke to overwhelming consciousness of the wrong they had done him, others who had weakly doubted, or but feebly sustained him, felt sharp conviction flashed through their inmost soul, and for all their after lives bore unshaken testimony to his perfect integrity; so true it is that when truth dwells, as with Gallitzin, unshackled, master of its own abode, it scarcely needs to raise its voice to be recognized as master of all others not wholly dead to sight and sound; "crushed to earth" it can never be, save by the cowardice, the treason, or the pusillanimity of its own household.

Though few of the old enemies were left to oppose him, new ones were not lacking to keep their courage up, and to lead them in another persecution more violent and more systematic than any yet attempted. The reverend gentleman who had already caused so much mischief, far more, it is to be hoped, than he knew or intended, continued to press his services, causing great annoyance to Dr. Gallitzin, and serving to keep alive the hostile feeling now so nearly extinct. This person had faults which caused Father Gallitzin to fear his coming, lest they should break out to the scandal of his people, undermining the walls of sobriety and regularity with which he had striven to surround them on every side; at the same time, christian charity forbade him to give the reasons which alone could justify his refusal and satisfy the disaffected, who were not slow to put their own interpretations upon all his acts. The bishop also felt delicate about taking any decided step in the matter, perhaps even, in the kindness of his heart, hoped some compromise would be effected, though at the sacrifice of a little of Father Gallitzin's austerity, but he by no means approved of his residence for any length of time with the pastor of Loretto:—

"With regard to the Rev. Mr. Phelan," Gallitzin wrote Dec. 19th, 1806, "I am happy to find that I have anticipated your Lordship's desire. As soon as I heard of his being in Bedford, and desiring to reside with me until Easter, I sent him a letter in which I made mention of several reasons why I thought it very improper that he should absent himself during so long a time from his own congregation, and come to reside with me. One reason was that he was not lawfully sent. I concluded with inviting him to spend a couple of weeks with me as he had done last October, knowing or believing, at least, that this would not be contrary but rather conformable to your Lordship's desire. Knowing as I did that the greatest part of my congregation being Irish would be very much displeased at my opposing Mr. Phelan's coming, I thought it necessary to keep a copy of my letter to him, that I might be able by producing the same to you to justify myself, in case any one should attempt to misrepresent the matter to your Lordship. I should be very happy if you would mention a few words in your next letter to me testifying your approbation of my conduct on that occasion, that I may be able to satisfy those who think they have lawful reasons of complaining against me for not accepting of Mr. Phelan's services when he offered them."

Whether the invitation thus tendered was accepted, or not, or if accepted whether any open scandal occured, does not appear, it can only be inferred that additional reasons were given to increase the reluctance already felt, for when next he applied Father Gallitzin saw fit to decline his service entirely, and to give his reasons for doing so, which ended their aquaintance. The whole affair had served to estrange some of the members of the congregation, who with the proverbial devotion of the Irish people to their clergy, would have overlooked many faults in order to retain one of their own among them, but these were almost without exception new comers, to whom all their pastor's ways were unfamiliar, unlike anything they had ever seen before, and to which they believed they could never become accustomed, but in time they became so much attached to him, so thoroughly at home under his pastoral care, that the Germans, to whom they had given him up at first, became really jealous of them, so that the slightest appearance of preference on his part for either nationality made the other quite unhappy, until, as time passed on, the dividing lines growing fainter, all, of whatever birth, began to feel themselves, like their beloved pastor, Americans; at present in Loretto and its vicinity, as in great measure throughout the whole of his former charge, when one side of a family is found to be of German extraction, it is pretty safe to infer that the other is of Irish descent.

At first, though he spoke English as he wrote it, easily, fluently and with precision, Father Gallitzin was generally set down as a German; he understood the feeling with which he was regarded on this account, and would willingly have gratified the desire of his Irish parishioners, but all his attempts to do so only added to his own troubles, increasing the discontent already felt; for all who could be induced to seek a home in the wilderness with him as his assistant in early days, chanced to be of those who were unable, either by nature or grace, to understand his views or motives, or to endure at all the privations of his austere life, although he procured all possible alleviations for them, waiting on them himself, as he permitted no person to wait on him, preparing comforts for them with his own hands, such as he never accepted for himself.

The reverend gentleman mentioned was by no means the only one for whom strenuous efforts were made; in a more malignant spirit than he ever excited, three or four men, social outlaws whom their own countrymen scorned, working through others less disreputable than themselves, took advantage of this feeling, and of that other feeling of uneasiness lest if they broke away from Dr. Gallitzin they would be left without a priest altogether, to prepare the way for another, undoubtedly entirely unconscious of their schemes, of unusual talents and excellent reputation; thus by sending abroad the report that such a one would accept the other's place, these men quieted the fears while they excited the hopes of those who as yet were neutral, and succeeded in drawing a few strong allies to their aid, who would have scorned any part with them for other reasons; others on various pretexts, and by countless falsehoods were won over, and a real conspiracy was formed, in which, as usual in such cases, a few reckless men used all the rest for their own base purposes, many working for them who never suspected what they were doing. It was determined that if the bishop still refused to remove him, he should be made by fair means or foul, small matter which, to resign as of his own accord, leave them in possession of the land, the church, and all that belonged to it, after which they would see that the bishop sent them a pastor who would be more pliable in their hands.

It will be remembered that E. V. J. had alone come forward, with formal accusations to the bishop, at the time of the Munster difficulties, and that Mr. Little hastened, at the request of the better portion of the congregation, to Baltimore with an appeal to Bishop Carroll to pay no heed to any charges which might be made, and by no means to remove their pastor, in whom they had every confidence; returning, Mr. Little brought to Gallitzin his first knowledge, beyond the wild reports and rumors of the villagers, of these charges hurridly referred to in the bishop's letter of Feb. 23, 1806:

"I have received your answer by Mr. Barney Little," Gallitzin wrote in reply, April 13, 1806, "which gave me a good deal of comfort, but at the same time, it did not a little surprise me to see Mr. J—'s complaints and accusations against me. His own conscience bears testimony to the falseness of these accusations. God may forgive him. I can safely appeal to the Searcher of Hearts, before whom I am to appear at the Last Day, that nothing but a sincere wish for the welfare of my congregation in general and for the happiness and safety of Mr. J—. in particular, has directed my steps in all those matters of which he so much complains."

At the same time it began to be suspected that another person, Jacob B—. who had lived in Gallitzin's house having care of his farm, but treated more as a friend than a hired laborer, who had said, in the midst of the slanders against his generous benefactor, and this in the presence of Rev. Mr. Heilbron, Simon Ruffner and others, that having lived so many years with Doctor Gallitzin, so 'far from having observed anything irregular in his conduct, he was obliged to own that though acquainted with numbers of clergymen in Baltimore, Philadelphia and other places, he had never seen a better one; at another time declaring that he did not believe the merest child could be more innocent than he was, now, for certain ends of his own, was setting very different reports in circulation, and when they had grown enough not to be easily traced to himself, repeated them with much apparent sorrow, to the object of them all, always expressing surprise and indignation at their malignity and falsehood; together they talked over these stories, for Father Gallitzin never encased himself in the armor of self-righteousness, invulnerable to all suggestions, but when he heard any falsehood of himself keenly examined his conscience, his actions, his motives, lest there might be somewhere in himself the pebble of truth with which the pyramids of slander are so often constructed; to the eyes of his most delicate and sensitive humility many an error appeared, as under a microscope, which to other eyes, however acute, showed not so much as the merest speck; with his exquisite simplicity, it was natural, then, for him to own to faults, to distrust in himself, to review the circumstances surrounding him, and in the intimacy of friendship to show where they were the hardest to explain, to speak freely of his family affairs, his financial embarrassments, his fears for the future which he dared not show to any other, lest his creditors, becoming alarmed, should embarrass him still further. Cut off from all relations, from all society, surrounded by suspicions, by slanders of the most atrocious kind, watched continually, his lightest word weighed, twisted and wrought into a sword against him, what wonder the full heart overflowed sometimes, when with the man whom he trusted implicitly, who was bound to him by every tie of reverence, affection, and gratitude, who listened deferentially and spoke in deepest sympathy? By and bye those words thus spoken came back, poisoned weapons, to the generous heart that sent them forth.

Even yet he had not fathomed the baseness of human nature, but ascribed the treachery to a moment's anger at a passing difficulty, even refused to believe in spite of all evidence, though cut to the heart as only the treason of a false friend, long loved and trusted, has power to do. He recalled the many confidences given, the errors and shortcomings, magnified by his humility, which he had bewailed to this friend; he could not believe him lost to all honor, and as the man avoided him, wrote him in holy week 1807, the tenderest appeal he could put into words.

Rev. D. A. Gallitzin to Jacob B—.

Dear Friend,

We are now in the middle of Holy Week which loudly proclaims the obligation of forgiveness and reconciliation. I wish to take the hint and to be reconciled with everybody, and therefore beg if I ever offended you that you would forgive me, and consider me henceforward as a friend, as I make a firm resolution to be and remain in peace with you. I shall forever remember with pleasure the many happy hours you and I spent together both at home and abroad, the many hours when (with mutual confidence and friendship) we disclosed our thoughts to one another. To be sure many an imprudent thing may have been said or done at those times because friends do not guard against each other. I knew that you were my friend, and I knew that as a man of honor you would never betray my secrets, nor those of my family, no more than a priest would betray the sins and the secrets of his penitents. I knew that as a man of honor and integrity being besides engaged in my service, you would never (even if you got angry) take advantage of anything I did or said, to make me one cent the worse before other people.

I was confirmed in this opinion by what you said about three or four weeks ago to myself, viz: that you only went away because you were determined never to be at variance with me again, and you thought we could be better friends at a distance than so close together.

Dear friend, I cannot deny a great deal has been told me about what you and your wife have said. . . .

Dear friend, I leave all this to your own conscience, I know that you have a good opinion of my moral conduct, I know that if I heard forty stories . . . : alleged against you, I would despise them all, and I trust you would never believe any story that could be alledged against me. . . . . .

It is true as a confidential friend, I never guarded against you and therefore have said and done a thousand things before you which though innocently meant, and innocent in themselves yet by interpretation and malicious constructions could be completely handled against me. Yet it is certainly not my old friend Jacob, so well used at my house, that would be guilty of so base and treacherous a conduct.

Certainly it is not my old friend Jacob, entrusted with my secrets and confidence, that would betray those secrets.

Certainly it is not my old friend Jacob, witness of my upright conduct, though at the same time imprudent in many respects, that would betray me to the world, and taking advantage of what happened in the secret recess of private and confidential conversation, that would make a handle of it against myself.... Certainly, it is not our old friend Jacob that man noted for his religious principles, that would vent his tongue against the anointed of the Lord, and by such sacrilegious conduct, entail the curse of God upon himself and his family. No, from his principles, he would rather throw his cloack over them to hide their real failings than to divulge them.

See here, dear friend, the opinion which I would wish to harbor of you in spite of all I can be told, and the sentiments of friendship which I have awakened in my heart, in spite of all the devil's temptations, and which I shall try to harbor as long as I live. Any time you come you shall be made welcome here, and should I be away and the key of the cupboard out of the way, I beg you will try.... to open the lock sooner than to suffer for the want of any thing; there are no locks between friends....

O Jacob, Jacob, do not suffer the devil to lead you to destruction, but come as quick as you can to make up with
       Yr. sincere friend
         D. A. Gallitzin.

The childlike simplicity of this letter,—from which besides some unnecessary words only two paragraphs have been omitted, one enumerating under five heads the petty gossip accredited to Jacob, which though too contemptible for repitition or refutation was excessively annoying at the time, and the other relating to another person, not connected with this subject,—so far from reaching the heart to which in utmost humility and exquisite delicacy it was addressed, caused it to be paraded as testimony to the recipient's integrity and an admission of the writer's misconduct. Gallitzin spoke of secrets, meaning the matters concerning his property, his life at home, annoyances of his boyhood, perhaps childish tricks upon his grave professors, which he could hardly forbear talking over in the freedom of friendly intimacy, but which if spoken of in public would soon furnish food for the gossips, and tend to lessen his dignity if no more, as their grave and stately pastor, whom they could hardly imagine, and could not have understood, as a boy with a boy's mischief, love of freedom and out of door sports, hatred of books, and of restraint; a whisper of the most innocent boyish frolic, an intimation of difficulties now, delays and possible loss of money belonging to him, would have been as oil on fire, and blazed into the most extraordinary romances, and new accusations; thus, at that time, he was not able to unbend at all,—as in later years when all were his friends, — as Jacob well knew, but holding this letter, hardly a word or a look was required to convert the admission of secrets into a confession of things little short of crime, an acknowledgment that he was surrounded by mysteries. Father Gallitzin alluded to imprudent words and acts, in the general way in which the most saintly person might have used the words, but they conveyed no impression of holy humility to the coarse minds that now construed them; men who called the seven deadly sins lying heavy on their own conscience, "the imperfections to which we are all liable", mere peccadillos, would not be the ones to handle delicately the faint meaning of imprudent acts in one it was their policy to represent as a malefactor.

Father Gallitzin thus learned that
"When faith is lost, when honor dies,
The man is dead,"
and that it is easier to raise the dead from their graves than to resuscitate a broken friendship.

Nothing could have given his enemies greater satisfaction that this affectionate letter; possessing it they felt they could do with him, his name and his fame as they pleased; it was made to cover every slander their cunning could devise, so that even good old Father Heilbron, who never could master the simplest sentence of the English language, was staggered by it, even to the extent of not opposing the final appeal to the bishop which they now undertook with greatest confidence, for unable to accomplish anything of increased consequence in Loretto, where the majority of the people stood firm by their pastor, they had transferred their headquarters to Greensburg, the seat of Westmoreland County, where Gallitzin was not so well known, and to which a number of his opponents had taken refuge when frowned upon by the better portion of the Loretto congregation; their plan was to commence their work at that distance, and then to roll it along, like a dirty snowball, through the various parishes which he attended, in each of which they expected to find some accessions, until it should become so formidable as to alarm the Loretto people and gather them in. Some intimations of this reached his ears, and he promptly investigated it, as he wrote to the bishop whom he kept advised of all his movements.

REV. D. A. GALLITZIN TO RIGHT REV. BISHOP CARROLL.

May 11. 1807.

My Lord,

I am on the point of starting for Greensburg; whilst my horse is eating his feed, I cannot forbear giving myself the satisfaction of writing a few lines to your Lordship. I feel very curious to know what is going on at Greensburg, I doubt very foul and dirty work.... However, I shall know better to-morrow evening.... The greatest satisfaction to me is that I am completely innocent in all those cases in which I am accused, as far as I have been informed of the accusations. Another satisfaction is that not one person in the whole congregation except a handful of the vilest blackguards, believes any of the accusations. No, my very Protestant neighbors have showed as much indignation at the base, malicious, and foul steps that are taking, as some of the most zealous Catholics; they have offered their signatures to the within instrument which the trustees and congregation thought fit to send to your Lordship. I thanked them very kindly for their offers, but did not think proper to insert their names, wishing to confine myself to my own congregation.

Another satisfaction is that notwithstanding all the endeavors of Jacob B., J. C. M. etc., to set the whole congregation against me, and to represent me under the most odious and scandalous colours, their endeavors are fruitless, the number of my friends increases. N. M. himself and W. W. until lately my enemies, still pressed and solicited to join the plot, have on the contrary embraced this opportunity to get reconciled, and signalize themselves in my cause.

Another satisfaction is the increase of the Church amidst these persecutions; three of my Protestant neighbors have come forward since Easter and solemnly abjured heresy and made profession of Catholic faith, and there are more coming. Jacob B—— has spread the most infamous lies on purpose to make people talk, and afterwards with a grave and sorrowful countenance and a great many sighs, complained that he was very sorry to hear people talk so badly of me and that it had become his duty to inform the bishop!.... This is the only kind of scandal here, *Scandalum Pharisaium.*

Being in a great hurry to start I shall conclude for this time, not thinking it necessary indeed to say much more on this subject, for I really cannot think that your Lordship can feel very uneasy about any of the accusations brought against me. As for the petition, if you would think it worth while to give me a list of the petitioners, I engage to prove the said petition to be a most infamous piece of forgery, and that there is no genuine name to it only names of notorious drunkards, blasphemers, robbers, etc., men that have no more religion than horses, that never or almost never frequent the sacraments, men who publicly brag of their misdeeds....

I do not wish to dwell any longer on so disagreeable a subject, and shall only add that I have thought it necessary to subjoin and enclose a copy of a letter which I sent to Jacob B—— about six weeks ago, and which has been most infamously construed as an acknowledgment of my guilt. Your Lordship will judge what sentiments dictated it.

I recommend myself to your Lordship's prayers and sacrifices, and subscribe myself

My Lord,

Yr most hble obdt servt,
Demetrius Augustin Gallitzin.

But before he had succeeded in mounting his horse the news was brought to him that E. V. J. had returned from Baltimore, after a successful interview with the bishop, of which he was at that moment giving triumphant account to the excited villagers. If half of what was said was true then indeed was he alone, without friend or counsel, or one human arm to defend him. This, then, was to be the end of all, for this he had left father and mother, home and country, honor and wealth, ease and renown, to be tried as a petty criminal before a crowd of gaping backwoodsmen! No such thought was permitted room in his heart; he went back to his rude table, and wrote a few lines full of gentleness and dignity to the bishop, not one syllable of expostulation, but as if his only thought were of the indignity to his sacred profession. But had he been speaking for another, as after years abundantly proved, not a hundredth part as innocent as he knew himself to be, his words would have *burned like a torch*, and he would have given his life to save but the hem of the priestly garment from touching the mire through which he was now to be dragged.

Rev. D. A. Gallitzin to Right Rev. Bishop Carroll..

.May 11. 1807.

My Lord,

E. V. J. is returned from Baltimore and already the news is in circulation that Mr. de Barth and Mr. Dubois are to be up immediately to judge me. I shall be very happy to see them or any other clergymen you would choose to send, although it would be a little hurtful to my feelings that they should come under that title. I cannot but feel uneasy at the thought that Jacob B——, who has already sworn false against me and who I know has sworn vengeance and destruction against me, should be admitted as evidence against me.. Your Lordship knows it is very often impossible (for the want of evidences) to overset a false testimony, and Jacob B—— is waiting with the most eager and sanguine expectation for the happy moment when he shall be called before your Lordship or before the clergymen you shall send, in order to ruin me with his depositions.

....J. C. M. and E. V. J. and some more being partly through my fault disappointed of getting the offices of the county, are from disappointed ambition raised to the highest pitch of anger, and some of them have declared if they get no satisfaction from your Lordship, they will try the civil law, if that won't do they will try something else.

This is the only favor I shall beg of your Lordship if you think it necessary to institute an examination of my conduct; that you will not allow every person to be a witness, but that you will lay down rules by which the priests appointed may know who can be allowed to appear as a witness against a clergyman, and who not. With great respect I remain

  My Lord,
      Yr most hble obdt servt,
        D. A. Gallitzin.

P. S. I shall be back from Greensburg in about two weeks; if I find certain charges to be true I shall hardly leave Westmoreland County before I enter suits against John and Jacob B——. Such men are not afraid of spiritual punishments, and therefore ought to be handled more roughly.

If the bishop ever had any intention of sending either of these clergymen to investigate the indefinite and contradictory charges against him, which is not at all likely, the idea was undoubtedly at once abandoned, and put wholly out of mind by the consequences of the visit to Greensburg when Father Gallitzin resolutely met his enemies, tracked all their ways, unmasked their devices, and made them his own justifiers. All that he had told the bishop he was sure of was abundantly proved, there were no genuine signatures to the petition for his removal except those of the lowest of the low, and those whose names had been forged were only too glad to exonerate themselves from standing as false witnesses before the bishop, as he relates in a letter written sometime after his return to Loretto:

REV. D. A. GALLITZIN TO RIGHT REV. BISHOP CARROLL.

Loretto, June 20. 1807.

My Lord,

It is now about two weeks since I returned from Greensburg, and have been kept so busy since between the duties of my office and my duties as agent for Henry Drinker and company of Philadelphia, that little or no time was left to give your Lordship an account of my proceedings and successes at Greensburg. Indeed I was not in very great hurry as I wished you to get informations from other quarters before you would hear any more from me, and I expect you have got by this time those informations that will completely remove any uneasiness which the false accusations and forged certificates of my enemies may have occasioned. To my great surprise (though not althogether unexpectedly) I found out that a certain certificate (which must be in your hands) full of the most abominable charges, and having the signatures of John and Mary B—— was fabricated by J. C. M——, Esq., as well as those signatures, whilst neither John nor Mary even suspected that there was any such instrument in existence. Your Lordship has, no doubt, by this time received a genuine certificate, signed by John and Mary B——, wherein the facts established in the forged one are completely contradicted. I was hardly two days in Westmoreland County when I discovered by Simon Ruffner, and some more of my friends, the whole plot laid for my destruction, which was, by those certificates and oaths procured from Greensburg and circulated through this County of Cambria, to procure subscribers to a petition against me, to have clergymen appointed to inspect my conduct, and when these would arrive to bring Jacob B—— forward to swear anything that would answer the purpose, which they were certain would remove me immediately. Why so? Because that your Lordship and those clergymen, could not refuse believing what was proved on oath. After having tried (in vain) all those means which charity and a desire of bringing my enemies to repentance could suggest, finding that they wilfully and maliciously persevered, and that even coming to church on Sundays and holydays was only a cloak to propagate their poison, and trying to gain proselytes, I publicly excluded them from the benefits of the Church, debarred them from polluting the floor of the church, or the holy ground on which it stands, with their presence; I refused sprinkling the holy water upon my congregation until those ringleaders of rebellion, those forgers of libels against the anointed of the Lord would withdraw. I then commanded them by name to leave that church which under divine providence I had established with the sweat of my brow for the salvation of souls, and to which they only came for the ruin and damnation of their and their neighbors' souls, praying God to move their hearts to repentance, and to give them grace to reenter the church at the gate of submission and humility. The next day I started for Greensburg; having received informations as above, I immediately applied for two writs of scandal and had them served as quick as possible, which produced a very happy change.

John B—— though he proved himself and wife completely clear of the certificate above mentioned, candidly owned himself guilty of many lies.... but he made it appear to my satisfaction that it was Jacob B—— and M——'s craft and cunning to raise anger and spite in his heart in order to make him tell lies against me, and whatever lies he would not tell, they supplied with their forgeries. He begged pardon in the most humble manner, offered to retract what he had said in as public a manner as I would think satisfactory, and promised never to suffer himself to be led astray in such a manner again, and finally he and his wife to sign a certificate contradicting the contents of the forged one, and send the same to you; in consequence of this I have forgiven him, and sent orders to my lawyer to withdraw the suit against John B—— upon his fulfilling his promise and paying the cost and his fees.

Jacob B—— (though equally as humble as John) was not as candid, but wished me to believe him completely innocent of ever having touched my character.... I told him that I should never be willing to make peace with him upon any terms that would leave so many respectable characters under the blame of believing him, or that would put it in his power to renew his former attacks upon my character; in short that there were no other terms I would ever agree to, except pleading guilty, retracting the foul abominable lies he had told and even retracting what he had sworn. He soon agreed to every thing except the retracting of his oath, but this not being sufficient I would not listen to him any further, but mounted my horse and started. Since I came home I found my enemies here (who had entirely depended upon John and Jacob B——'s depositions) in the utmost consternation. We now enjoy perfect peace and quietness; not a loud word is to be heard; all their plots (they find) are defeated, and turned against themselves; they all wish to extricate themselves; every one tries to clear himself and blames his neighbor for leading him astray. Some have sold their places and are gone, others are in the way of selling and in a short time, thanks be to God's mercies, our settlement will get rid of one of the most corrupted set of villains that ever disgraced the Church, who were endeavoring to engross into their own hands all the most important offices of our new county, from which calamity, however, my persevering endeavors have fortunately delivered our poor country. This it was that drew the whole weight of their anger and revenge upon my head and caused one of the blackest conspiracies to be instituted against me which human malice, assisted by the powers of hell, could devise. God be praised the storm has subsided, peace is restoring fast, and all the county offices will in a short time be filled with the most respectable characters of the settlement, the ecclesiastical and civil authorities will then go hand in hand and mutually assist each other in promoting the public welfare and happiness. Amen.

I remain with great respect
    My Lord,
               Yr most hble obdt servt,
                    Demetrius Augustine Gallitzin,
                      Parish priest of Loretto.

This letter was followed by a note with which he accompanied the retraction of the most persistent of his opponents, of the longest standing and perhaps the least dishonest of any, E. V. J——, who finally laid down his arms, convinced that he had been blinded by ambition, by desire of revenge and the cunning of false friends.

REV. D. A. GALLITZIN TO RIGHT REV. BISHOP CARROLL.

                      Loretto, July 27. 1807.
    My Lord.

It is with the greatest pleasure I comply with Mr. J—s request of sending your Lordship the enclosed act of retraction, which was also at his request read in church last Sunday week. Being on the point of mounting my horse for a little excursion, I shall only add assurances of the most profound respect and sincere attachment with which I remain,
    My Lord,
               Your most hble and obdt servt,
                    Demetrius Aug. Gallitzin.

P. S. I need not add that I have not required of Mr. J—. any further satisfaction.

Please to take good care of the enclosed and send it back by the first safe opportunity.

E.—V—J—s Retraction.

18. July, 1807.

My Dear and Revd Sir.

The horror which I feel in the heinous crimes committed against your innocent character and the faults of my unsuspected heart, demands of me to humble myself before you and the congregation. First, I sincerely ask your pardon and pardon from the congregation in general, to my Lord the Bishop of Baltimore I ask pardon, and to an injured and offended God I implore forgiveness and pardon. I am sincerely sorry from my heart [for] the many scandals I have committed by keeping bad company, and suffering myself to be deluded in believing the most abominable lies against your innocence, and in joining in plots against your Reverence, and being made the messenger of so many contaminated lies to my Lord the Bishop of Baltimore.

I also feel sorry for breaking the laws of the Church by leaving you, my immediate pastor, to go to be married out of your parish. I do sincerely acknowledge the gratitude I received from Almighty God in opening my eyes and discovering the falsity of those infamous accusations alleged against your Reverence. Tho' unworthy of the least favor from you, man, or from an injured God, I do solemnly declare in the presence of the congregation, future obedience and submission, with a determination of shunning all evil company, particularly those who have so basely betrayed me, which, if required I am willing to elucidate both their wicked proceedings and their names before the congregation. As to temporal punishment I will with cheerfulness submit to your Reverence. I am willing to submit my bare back to flagellation publicly in the church by your trustees, for I consider no punishment too good to be inflicted on me the most unworthy of sinners. I ask no other favor of your Reverence but your prayers, and [of] the church, to obtain of Almighty God reconciliation and pardon &c. Any other circumstance which may be required which may have slipped my memory, I am willing to repair as far as God's grace and your Reverence may require.

I am with sincere respect and great regard,
   Your Reverence's penitent and humble servant.
   (Signed in full) E. V. J.

N. B. With permission you may publish this. I am sorry it is out of my power to come to the church. I am called upon to go to Somerset; on my return I will humbly submit to the chastisements herein mentioned.

But before the happy results to which Father Gallitzin looked forward so hopefully could be secured one effort more had to be made by his enemies to get him out of the way; the appeal to the bishop had so ignominiously failed that any satisfaction from the ecclesiastical law was put out of the question; when the last "delegates" or "committee" called upon Bishop Carroll, to state their grievances they found less courteous reception than was formerly accorded to the humblest backwoodsman who entered that dignified but fatherly presence; the bishop listened to their stories in unbroken silence, and when the full amount of their venom had been poured out, and they paused for an answer, he turned to them, it is said, with the calm inquiry: "Is that all you have to say?" They admitted it was, and then quietly rising he wished them good day, and looked after them as they awkwardly got out of the room, neither with anger nor contempt, but, if the truth must be told, with much the same absence of emotion with which one would look after some cowardly specimen of the canine species, who had ventured on forbidden ground.

The civil law was no less hopeless for they were already under its ban, there was but one thing left and to that they now resorted; it was a kind of law, a sphere in which they felt much more at home than in any other.

Father Gallitzin's house was at some little distance from the village and from any other; the McGuire homestead and the few cabins surrounding it, the real McGuire settlement, was some two miles back of him, the village commenced much nearer on his right, on the left and in front were the woods, and a little clearing, so that his house and the church really stood isolated, out of the reach of assistance. A party, therefore, thought well to call upon him in his lonely residence, and demand accession to all their wishes, with no idea of limiting themselves to mere words if he refused; after opposing them, defying them, scorning to enter into any thought of compromise with them, until he was perfectly exhausted, he succeeded in reaching the church, to die at the altar should they dare to attack him in the house of God. Vain precaution! they were too desperate to be deterred by any unseen arm, and no one knows what the end would have been had not a solitary passer by, named John Weakland, been attracted by the tumult and looked around to see what it meant. "Now John was known far and wide as the tallest and stoutest man within a hundred miles," says Rev. Mr. Lemcke*. "It was related of him that once for some hours he had maintained battle in the woods with a furious bear, his only weapon a branch hastily torn from the nearest tree; at another time he had captured a wolf, bound him and carried him home alive to amuse his children. At the same time he was known to be a man of few words, of a mild, peaceable nature who would not hurt a fly, as the saying is. He had great reverence for Father Gallitzin whom he had accompanied from Maryland to the mountains; and when he saw what was going on concluded to make an exception to his general rule, which was to mind his own business, and looked about for a branch or something of the sort; this time his eye lighted on the rail of a fence which looked practicable, with which he at once advanced upon the mob, who started back in terror expecting him to lay about with it among them, but before doing so John made them a speech, a much longer one than was customary with him, to this effect: 'I have fought with bears and wolves, it is true, but so far, thanks be to God, I have never done harm to man. Just now it might be otherwise. Go along

---

* Page 229.

home then, and keep yourselves quiet, for, after this whoever shall make a disturbance or misbehave in the House of God, or lay his hand upon the Lord's anointed may look out', and here he raised his club, 'for as sure as I am a living man I will break his head for him.'"

This being an argument quite within the range of their intelligence settled the matter; the timid good who had looked on so long in consternation praying for better times, now that they had found some one to fall back upon in case of need, rallied boldly to the pastor's side, seeking by renewed zeal in all that he asked of them to advance the cause of religion and virtue, and thus obtain pardon of God for their long inaction, while pouring balm into the sore heart of the priest, whose greatest happiness they knew lay in their fervor and piety. John Weakland's stout arm was never needed again, he walked away calm and contented, living for nearly half a century longer, a patriarch beloved by an immense posterity, leaving a name to be ever remembered with honor and affection.

But when all was over, the brave man who had struggled for so many years with foes whose contact was so loathsome, broke down completely; the long strained nerves, the constant combat with trials so mean, so petty, so vile that even to remember them, though crushed and conquered, was disgusting and distressing to the last degree, prostrated him entirely. There was no glory in such a victory, and the overpowering mortification, the countless stings of a battle infinitely more trying than to face racks and torture in a grand and heroic manner, must have caused him more misery in the recollection even than in the excitement of contest.

As soon as he was able, he wrote to his only friend, the bishop:

REV. D. A. GALLITZIN TO RIGHT REV. BISHOP CARROLL.

Loretto, Sept. 1807.

My Lord,

With a feeble and trembling hand and a sorrowful heart,

full of the deepest and blackest melancholy, I take up the pen to give myself the comfort and consolation of addressing a few lines to your Lordship. I am hardly recovered from a severe spell of sickness which attacked me at Greensburg, and which has left me so weak that I can scarcely crawl about, and have not been able to begin as yet to say Mass again. Rev. Mr. Heilbron will be here to-morrow and stay with me a few weeks until I gain strength sufficient to discharge my duty. Permit me, dear Sir, to implore your patience and to beg of your Lordship to administer all the comfort and consolation your charity shall suggest to my poor broken and sorely afflicted heart. My constitution being weak, and my heart so susceptible of deep impressions from disappointments, losses, etc., I have been wonderfully low this great while and begin seriously to apprehend that my days will not be very long. I can better feel than describe the gloomy and melancholy state of my mind especially since the death of my mother, the remembrance of former times, her tender affection to me, her last dying expressions concerning me, my own solitary situation in the wilds of Alleghany, my suffering and persecutions here, all seem to conspire to overwhelm me with sorrow and melancholy. O my dear Lord! for God's sake send me a companion, a priest to help and assist me, for my heart is ready to break. If you have one that does not even know one word of English, only for my comfort and consolation a good, virtuous clergyman, a friend to help me to bear the burden.

Your Lordship has heard how much I have had to suffer from a restless set of unprincipled ruffians. Only one favor I beg of you which will give your Lordship very little trouble, and will I believe set everything to rights again. You know that I have sued the ringleaders of the conspiracy against me. God knows my intention was not to hurt them, no, I wish to return good for evil. No, my intention was only to frighten them, to compel them to do justice to my character, and to retract those abominable charges of which they know in their conscience I am entirely clear.

They have already began to enter into negotiations with me, some have even already acknowledged their lies against me, and even in contradiction to their former lies given me a very good character. However, their acknowledgments and reparations were too private to be of any service to my character, Mr. J—. was the only one that had courage enough to make a public reparation before the whole congregation. It is my opinion that in the present state of things those unhappy people being already a good deal frightened and humbled, their spite greatly abated, only wavering as yet between pride and fear, that a few words from your Lordship would turn the scales to the right side, and cause them to make an humble submission and save them a great deal of trouble and loss. With submission, therefore, to your superior prudence and knowledge, I think that if your Lordship would (after some little observations on the heinousness of the sin of slander and calumny especially against a clergyman) require of them to give me in writing by way of reparation and retraction that testimony to my character which you think and which they know my conduct entitles me to, I think they would submit to it. If they do so, and pay the trifling cost of the suits, I am willing to forgive them, and give them no further trouble, for in my present weak situation, I wish seriously to prepare for a better life, and to live in peace.....

......I beg for a few words of a speedy answer to be sent (via Greensburg) to the postoffice at Beula, near Loretto, Cambria County,

And remain with great respect,
My Lord,
Your most hble obdt Servt
Demetrius Augustine Gallitzin.

But the slander which, like a rank and poisonous weed shoots up in a night, dies as suddenly. The consolation he pleaded for so touchingly came to him from a higher source; with the cool bracing autumn weather, he recovered health and spirits, and the serenity of his soul came back to him as clear and fleckless as the lovely skies that smiled upon his mountain home; all that had been said against him appeared to be forgotten, and never again, in dark hours or bright, did the faintest breath of calumny arise to stain his shining name; the foul miasma which had so long hung over him vanished all at once like the morning mists before the sun, and left the air pure and sweet.

It is with unspeakable relief that this darkest chapter in his life is closed. For though the contumely and bitter persecution which tracked his footsteps for so many years, noted all his incomings and outgoings, caught every word that fell from his lips, keeping him day and night under the most intolerable surveillance, that of ravenous, wolfish hatred, only served, by lifting the veil of his manly reserve and pious humility, forcing his character into the full light of day, to prove him, in radiant scorn of every slander, modest, generous, good and great in every word and thought, astonishing even those who had most believed in him; though no virtue is secure until it is tried, no sanctity acceptable until it has been defamed, gladly would we have spared ourselves suffering the shame and pain which can never reach him more.

Gladly, too, for the sake of those who kindled the fire in which his virtue was to be tested, would it have been passed by, were it possible to bury with them the evil men do. It is terrible to think that though one's sins are as scarlet and can be made as white as snow, the consequences of them may be stalking the earth, spreading new seeds of misery and wickedness, living and working for ruin long after the sinner having repented in sackcloth and ashes is at rest; the memory of their wrong must remain long after they are forgotten.

For those who at the time knew not what they did, and afterwards learning sincerely repented, it is the last reparation they can make that through them he is shown more strong and fair; the last tribute their children can give them patiently for their sakes and in further expiation, to bear the pain the recollection must ever cause; for those who never repented, if there were such, let them stand as a warning that "the evil men do lives after them," that God is no less just than merciful, that not only must men themselves suffer for their sins, but their names shall be in reproach long after their bodies are dust, and that an evil work deliberately pursued in the fancied security of solitude or obscurity, against the unknown and defenceless, shall be made known in the light, reprobated with horror, again to be blazoned before all the world at the day of final reckoning.

And now should any say of Father Gallitzin and his true friends that he was beloved, respected, honored to the utmost, revered in life and held sacred in death because of his name, his wealth, any accidents of his birth or secluded life, it will be seen that it pleased God that he should prove himself, unaided by any of these things, and fight his battle single handed and alone. It was no playful warfare nor doubtful victory; so thoroughly did he vindicate himself that afterwards it seemed impossible for him to be misunderstood, even under the most trying circumstances; the most cordial sympathy was established between him and his people, he needed no longer to be on guard with any one, whatever he said or did being taken as meant, in honest, truthful spirit, and when, years afterwards, a stranger coming among his parishioners seeing them acting as one man according to his least word, ventured the astonished remark that no other priest in the United States would dare assert a tithe of his authority, he owed it to the very influence he affected to despise, that he escaped safe and unharmed from the indignant flock, every one of whom had become a John Weakland in defence of their pastor.

CHAPTER XVII.
FINANCIAL AND DOMESTIC MATTERS.
(1807—1808.)

Settlement of the Russian law suit,—Computation of the estates.—His sister's regard and solicitude.—Building in Loretto.—Effect of Gallitzin's persecutions upon the Protestants of the neighborhood.—His severe rule of life.—Appointment of new bishops.

For sometime previous to his mother's death Gallitzin had failed to receive the usual remittances from Europe; this, as he learned afterwards, on account of the great expenses of the Russian law suit, which very much embarrassed her own resources, no income being received by her from the contested property. However, as she knew the money was only detained, not lost, she encouraged him in patience, and wished him to rest secure that such delays would not often recur. Shortly after her death he received a small sum, with promises of more right away, but in the autumn of that year the frightful disasters to Prussia in consequence of the war with France, disarranged everything, depressed business and property, so that Princess Mimi found it unsafe to remain in her mother's house at Muenster; sea travelling had become more dangerous then ever on account of French interference so that letters arrived but seldom, and after long and perilous passage, oftener did not come at all. The affairs of the original church property in Loretto, that donated by Captain McGuire, were of course kept separate from his own, under the care of the trustees of the church, but it, like the farms he held for the same purpose, was only kept up at great expense to him, and at best could do no more than offer ground for future buildings. As he had in the beginning contracted in his own name for great quantities of land for the use of the church, and as homes for the congregations, which returned him nothing, these delays kept him in a state of ever increasing anxiety and most painful suspense, and the efforts he found himself continually obliged to make to keep his embarrassments under control, finally filled him with real alarm, rendered the more vexatious by renewed assurances of speedy relief from home, which, for the reasons given, were seldom fulfilled, and when they were the money almost always lost on the way. He neglected no means in his power to increase the independence of his American possessions, but he was obliged to lose a great deal of the property he held, give up many of his most cherished plans for lack of means at the proper moment, and often compelled to entreat the forbearance of those with whom he had made the contracts, and others to whom he was otherwise in debt, for knowing the great wealth of his family and not knowing the depression caused by war all over Europe, he could not believe that remittances, hardly missed at home, could long be withheld; coming they would abundantly cover all that he owed, and leave a handsome amount for future operations; it was his great comfort in these trying days to plan agreeable surprises for those who had assisted him in times of emergency.

"I am happy to see that your Lordship," he wrote Bishop Carroll, April 13, 1806, "is not forgetful of my perilous situation in money matters. I have a great deal of money coming to me yet, but no prospect of getting any soon enough to prevent great losses.

"Mr. Diggs who owes me about seven hundred (but is not able to make that money just now, as it is all standing out) promised me to write to your Lordship, in order to encourage you in assisting me, by showing that your Lordship is perfectly safe in doing so.

"I beg of your Lordship for God's sake, and for the sake, of my dear congregation, to help me immediately."

Again in Sept. 1807: "There is another favor I must beg of your Lordship which if granted would relieve my mind greatly. I have formerly informed you of the state of my debts, and applied for the loan of money. Thank God my debts are greatly reduced, there is only one that makes me uneasy, though but a trifling one of about four hundred dollars, due in Philadelphia mostly to Lorent & Lang who were so kind as to advance the same to me, expecting to be reimbursed by Mr. Caspar Vogt of Hamburg, who had received the amount from my mother, and had committed the payment of said money to F. L. Steinbach of New York; however, Steinbach refusing to pay me, Lorent & Lang very kindly offered to advance me the money, and took my draft upon Caspar Vogt for it; Caspar Vogt protested the bill as having already discharged the payment to F. L. Steinbach, in consequence of which I must lose that money with cost and interest. This is the second disappointment of the kind I have met since I came to this country. Lorent & Lang have threatened to sue me immediately if I do not refund the money. Where to get it I do not know unless your Lordship could borrow the same for me for about six months, when it shall be punctually returned with interest.... My sister laments very much that the present situation of affairs, the French army cutting off all communication between Germany and Russia, puts it out of her power for the present (her letter is dated April 10.) to get any relief or to send me any. I beg your Lordship would pray for the happy recovery of my estate; you know it is not intended for my aggrandizement, but for the good of your diocese."

Sometimes by parting with a portion of his land, sometimes by the patience of his creditors, Father Gallitzin generally succeeded in meeting these immediate and pressing demands, but their constant recurrence preceeded by such torturing anxiety, and followed by such exhaustion, coming, too, at the very time of his persecutions, threatening his own present, and the dearer future of his beloved congregations, for they depended upon him, and in many cases if he had fallen would have lost all they held as their own from him, and endangering the loss of all that he had accomplished for the church, were almost more than he could bear, and his bravery in standing against them is the more wonderful, because at any moment he had chosen to do so, he could have abandoned his whole undertaking without loss of personal credit, collected the money owing him, sold off land enough to pay all his debts, retaining sufficient to yield him a comfortable support, and either in some of the larger cities of the United States, where his talents would have made him famous, or by returning to Europe, fulfill his priestly duties in a more cultivated sphere, with honor and regard. So far from being censured for abandoning an apparently impracticable scheme, he would have been universally commended for the clearest exhibition of sound common sense he had yet made to the world.

But he never had the least idea of giving up, and it was, therefore, with unbounded gratitude that in the midst of his troubles, he received word that the Russian law suit was settled, and in his favor, or what was the same thing, his sister's; for as the princess, his mother, had often said in corroboration of his father's remark to the same effect, it made no difference which of her children, if only one, received the property, for both were loyal, and either would faithfully share with the other, as Mimi herself declared: "I need not repeat to you," she wrote him in April 1807*, "that you may be perfectly easy. If we only receive the property whether under your name or mine makes no odds amongst [between] us. I shall divide faithfully with you, dear brother, as I am certain you would with me, if all fell into your hands. Such was the wish and the will of our dear father, of our dearest mother, and such will always be the desire of my affectionate love and devotedness towards you, my dearest brother."

The news of this settlement was sent him by his agents in a report signed by them all:

REPORT OF THE RUSSIAN DECISION.

Dear Prince,

The question concerning your and the princess, your

---

* Gallitzin's own translation.

sister's claims to your father's property in Russia, is so determined by the Senate of Petersburg, that you, dearest prince, in consequence of your having embraced the Catholic faith, and the clerical profession, etc., cannot be admitted to the possession of your deceased father's property, and that, therefore, the princess, your sister, is to be considered as sole heiress to the said estate, and is to be put in possession of the same. The Council of State has given the same decision, and the Emperor has by his sanction given the sentence the force of law.

The princess, your sister, has now by the laws of Russia, perfect control over the income, but cannot give the property away, or dispose of it by will; however, she is at liberty to sell it, and to dispose of the moneys arising from the sale.

You see, then, dearest prince, that you are only nominally excluded. Your dear and respectable [respected] mother often thought it possible and even probable, that the decision would fall out the way it did, and was wont to say: "*It is immaterial whether the sentence in Russia be pronounced in favor of both my children, or only of my daughter, my son can lose nothing by it.*"

Even in Russia the business is considered in the same light. We can, therefore, congratulate you on the happy issue of that business, without minding the killing letter of the law, whereas in this case the spirit of justice and charity makes up the loss to you.

With sincere respect and friendship we remain, dearest prince,

Your devoted friends and servants

FRANCIS, Baron de Fuerstenberg,
FR. L., Count de Stolberg,
C. AUG., Count de Merveldt*,

Muenster, 1st of Febr. 1808.

---

* This report is in Gallitzin's own translation, certified as correct by Baron Francis de Mallitz, Charge d'affaires of the Emperor of all the Russias.

The Princess Mimi also wrote, though somewhat later, Aug. 6th and 18th 1808, and again on Sept. 12th and 24th of the same year, in the most affectionate manner. After speaking of the decision of the court she says: "This sentence, which I know is perfectly in accordance with your feelings, and I can say also with your interest, leaves some uneasiness on my mind, for fear that I should be called out of this world before I can have sold the property and thus saved it for you, as the law does not give me the liberty, either to give the property away, or to dispose of it by will.... The wish, then, to take the necessary measures to secure you in all contingencies, and the repeated assurances that this could not be done without my personal appearance here [in St. Petersburg] prevailed with me to undertake this long journey of six hundred leagues (eighteen hundred miles) notwithstanding the weakness of my health.... I repeat it, you may be quite easy. You are too good a brother to doubt of my good will, and of the sincerity of my affection for you, and I am sure, were the case reversed, that you would do all in your power for me. But, perhaps, you may doubt and with good reason, of my capacity in transacting business matters; here, also, you may be perfectly easy as I do not take a step without the advice of some eminent characters, who are well acquainted with this country, its laws and customs, etc., so that I can flatter myself more and more with the hope that I shall die easy and contented, when reflecting that God has spared my days, in order to save for you a property which you certainly intend to spend for his glory, and which you wish to have only for this purpose."

This property was computed by the distinguished gentlemen who acted as his agents to consist:

1st. Of seventy thousand roubles (about twenty three thousand dollars) in money.

2nd. Of real property: of the village of Lankoff in the Government of Waladmir, and the villages of Fabanzin and Nikulskin in the Government of Kostrom, with all the lands, mills and other property thereto belonging, with one thous. and two hundred and sixty male subjects (serfs).

He was therefore the assured owner of immense wealth, of large and productive estates, and, dividing the ready money with his sister, something over twelve thousand dollars was awaiting an opportunity to reach him, was very likely already on its way to him, while he was happy in the assurance that large sums from the income of the property would follow regularly, until it should be sold, and the capital placed in his hands. Those who had trusted him, were called upon to share his good fortune, to hear the glad tidings which secured them the full payment of all he owed them, paltry sums indeed they appeared by the side of his colossal wealth. Still he was prudent and cautious about building, not wishing to draw upon his property in advance of its actual possession, and only went on with such work as he felt to be extremely necessary.

In 1806 he found the grist mill which he had built in the beginning was really an expense, it costing more to feed the horses than it was worth, and replaced it by one worked by water, built at the foot of the eminence upon which the church stands, and put up in such fine style that it was the admiration of the surrounding country, "the pride of the county". Indeed everything done at his order had to be of the best materials and of the most thorough workmanship, for which he was always charged at least twice as much as any other would have been.

This famous mill, long in ruins and for years the object of sad and curious reflections to many who have come from afar to visit the scene of his labors, has now fallen, and hardly a stone is left upon a stone, but the spot on which it stood in its triumphant youth, will long be pointed out as the beginning of the group of landmarks, ending with his monument, which sanctify the entrance to Loretto, witnessing to his boundless charity, his indomitable courage, and splendid perseverance.

Two years later (1808) after receiving the news concerning the Russian property, the log church in which he had said the famous Midnight Mass, was doubled in size and renewed in strength, of course entirely at his own expense, with many a pleasant meeting under his enlivening influence of the men and boys of the congregation, who were its builders. When the addition was completed, and the church reopened, the whole appeared so large that the wise men shook their heads, as wise men will, and groaned in spirit at the folly of it, for they knew very well it could never be comfortably filled, and if it should be, how would it be possible for any speaker ever to make his voice reach from the altar to the vestibule? The latter fear, however, was dissipated upon the first intonations of the *Asperges*, or if any doubts lingered, as soon as Father Gallitzin commenced his sermons, for when his voice was raised it appeared as if the surrounding mountains might well have heard. Yet it was not so much that his voice was so powerful, as that it was clear, rather high, and exceedingly distinct, perfectly under his own command; in conversation it was low and gentle, capable of every imaginable modulation.

The wise men were also mistaken otherwise; people kept coming and coming to the mountains, up from Virginia and Maryland, across from Southern and Eastern Pennsylvania, rejoicing at the prospect of procuring a comfortable home with small means, and of security in spiritual matters, for it was well known that Father Gallitzin was not a mere sojourner in the wilderness, but one who meant to stay as long as he lived with a congregation whom he dearly loved, and in an incredibly short time there was hardly room in the spacious edifice, at it was considered, for the late comers into their father's house, the many converts whom he received into the Church.

One good and direct effect of the persecutions so violently assailing the pastor of Loretto was the attention thus drawn to his character and conduct. Men who regarded whatever belonged to his belief and profession as something entirely out of the sphere of their thoughts or interests, hearing the whole neighborhood ringing with the account of his alleged misdeeds, and obliged to listen to hot arguments about him, became curious in spite of themselves, wished to know more, and to a mind of any candor it soon appeared that he was, to say the least, a man of unusual force or there would not be all this tumult about him, a man who evidently had got some fixed idea in his head and knew very well what he was about. From further knowledge of his life and character they could hardly avoid speculating on his singular views, wondering what there could be of harmony between such a man and such a religion; some went further, and as all the Church asks is to be investigated, they found to their amazement that the man and the religion were one, that the mainspring of his acts was love of the faith he professed, the one true faith, complete in all its parts, consistent, perpetual, thorough, containing all that the mind, the heart, the soul of man can desire. Unhappily to know is not always to do, and many stopped there, not daring to look, to think, to advance one step beyond, persisting in being blind, deaf dumb, motionless before the radiant truth, but some seeing believed and gladly enrolled themselves under the banner of the Cross.

These troubles forced Gallitzin himself into a wider acquaintance with the lawyers, the magistrates, and the leading men, most of whom were Protestants, of the western counties; many of these had never met a Catholic priest in conversation before, and with the readiness, even eagerness of the American people to make religion the subject of discussion, his peculiar views, as they were considered, were almost invariably brought up for elucidation; the great dignity of his bearing, the rare charms of his conversation, his delicate humor, which made hours in his company pass away as one, gave grace to his clear, concise explanations; the terse logic of his arguments was not only unanswerable, for that counts for little, after all, but opened new trains of thought, lighted up dark chambers of the brain, and made the listener feel not that his retreat was cut off, but that there was a royal road opening before him which rendered it unnecessary to retrace his steps through the dark defile, or wander longer by the obscure and tortuous path of doubt and uncertainty.

When the good Bishop Flaget was being received as a saint throughout France, and some one ventured to ask him if the honors lavished upon him did not make him fear for his humility, he replied that with great trials God gives proportionate graces, and, speaking of what he might be called upon to endure, he added : "It would be the greatest happiness for me to be imprisoned; I may be deceived, but it seems to me I should glory in it. *That which I fear, is an attack upon my character;* for instance, were my reputation blackened by an atrocious calumny, I should be sorely tried."*
That trial had come to Father Gallitzin, and the very sensitiveness with which he repelled the petty gossip, the atrocious calumny, which others might have treated with cool indifference or silent contempt, drew admiration and interest from the more refined and manly spectators, however little versed in the science of the saints. It was instinctively felt that the man whose cheeks glowed, whose heart was pierced, spirits depressed and health destroyed by the imputation of wrongs which, judged by the world's standard, were hardly wrongs at all, must have within himself a moral code of his own of the most elevated and the most rigid character, for the resentment, the anguish so evidently endured were as different as possible from the ebullitions of wounded pride, or of artificial, conventional ideas of honor. Much as his stately appearance, his attractive manners had previously impressed the Protestants with whom he came in contact, the inner qualities thus brought to light surpassed all, and gave authority to his words, a new inducement to learn more of the religion which shone through all his words and deeds, smiled from his eyes and rested ever on his lips.

His converts were thorough ones who came to the Church fully understanding what they were about, knowing their only hope was in her, their only heaven through her, and often shamed the older Catholics by their fresh vigorous faith, the courage with which they avowed their belief in all

---

* *Life of the Right Rev. B. J. Flaget*, by M. J. Spalding, D. D. p. 332.

the doctrines of the Church, as well as by their pious and exemplary lives.

But for every sign of prejudices giving way, of grace not rejected, there came to him the longing for help which was the hourly cry of others far less isolated than himself. No longer for his own peace and comfort, but for the harvest so abundant and none to gather it in, he begged and prayed for one to labor with him. Well, too well, did Bishop Carroll know the burning desire underlying the apparent calmness of his request; it came to him from all quarters of the vineyard he held as his stewardship; but he was no better able to respond to it now than he had been in the beginning; the good priests were bound to their own congregations; new priests were not yet to be had, and a hundred places were ready for every one that should come; the only ones at liberty were the two or three or more who will be found to the end of time, weak, unprofitable servants. One of these, desirous of leading a better life, the bishop, after reading the pathetic letter of Sept. 1807, offered to send to Loretto, hoping that there he might be able with the assistance of its pastor's influence, to overcome his temptations, an offer Father Gallitzin accepted not without misgivings, for though there would be many exterior aids to a sober life, there were, he knew, the trials of loneliness, of great physical exertions and consequent exhaustion incident to a missionary's life, to be met and conquered.

REV. D. A. GALLITZIN TO RIGHT REV. BISHOP CARROLL.

Loretto Dec. 3. 1807.

My Lord,

Your favor of Nov. 20 was handed to me by Mr. Gills last Sunday after Mass, and gave me a great deal of comfort. I am so exceedingly fatigued after walking since last Monday about fifty miles through rocks and mire after sick people (having lost my riding horse,) that I am obliged to confine myself to a very few words. I am (thanks be to God) a good deal better in health than when I wrote last. In answer to your Lordship's proposal of sending a certain ... priest to live with me, I shall only observe that I think myself in duty bound (and that for several reasons) to accept your proposal, provided your Lordship thinks it probable that the said clergyman is not likely to give any more scandal in the way you mention. From what little experience I have it appears to me that total abstinence from spirituous liquors is the only sure way of breaking a habit of that kind, and as I never keep any kind of liquor, nor drink anything but water or milk, I think if he seriously means to leave off the practice of drinking, he will have a fine chance of curing himself effectually by living with me. It is too late to expect that he could be here in time to afford me any assistance during the Christmas holidays. If he could be here, therefore, sometime before the beginning of Lent this is all I could expect, as it appears from your Lordship's letter that he lives in some distant country place.

* * *

I beg your Lordship to excuse my scrawl owing to excessive fatigue,

And believe me most respectfully,

My Lord,

Yr most hble & obdt servt,

Demetrius Aug. Gallitzin.

But the experiment like others of the same kind already attempted, appears to have been successful only for a short time, for the same entreaty is found in subsequent letters.

Although no calm and experienced judgment will deny that Gallitzin's abstemious life was the best of all models for those with stronger inclination for the material good things of this world than he ever knew, or that one overpowered by temptation could not feel secure under any less austere regimen,—for it is the restive horse that needs the curb,—it may be admitted that the manner of living which his noble nature, strong will, and religious culture made comparatively easy to him, would naturally appear rigid beyond endurance to another whose evil inclinations scorned bit or bridle. Austere and overexacting in comparison with many others

Father Gallitzin certainly was, his rules of life for himself and all under his guidance were taken, not from custom or the average conduct of other people, but from the lives of the saints and the teachings of the Church; if he knew they were thought severe he knew also, no man better, that it is an evil day for the cause of religion when the rein is loosened and the law stretched to its utmost "liberality". No man can serve two masters; the master he had come out into the desert to serve was not the delight of mere material existence; he never abated his austerity nor relaxed the severity of his discipline either for himself or others, but he made due allowance for the weakness of human nature, and with all the flowers and gems, the music and poetry, the wit and grace of spiritual things he strove to make beautiful the galling chain of restraint, knowing well that patiently borne the iron links become as silken cords. Few who came to him in their hour of trial long resisted the tenderness with which he received them, the courage with which he cauterized their wounds, the spirit, the real lively enjoyment with which he lightened the heavy days of depression and remorse, which followed the breaking of old habits, and the weary bending to the new. But there were some whom he could never reach, who never regarded his rigor as well timed or necessary, but of these none have, as yet, been proposed for canonization.

Rev. D. A. Gallitzin to Right Rev. Bishop Carroll.

Loretto, Sept. 23, 1808.

My Lord,

Your last favor of Aug. 11th I received at Greensburg two days after it had been delivered by Major Noble of Brownsville*. The news contained in my sister's letter and

---

* The name here mentioned will recall one of the most remarkable of the early Pennsylvania conversions. Major Noble was a Protestant of means, position, and unusual thought and culture, who had long been unsettled in regard to religion, and had arrived so far as to be convinced that of so many conflicting doctrines only one could be true, when Rev. Stephen Badin, in 1807, stopped at the little village of Brownsville, *en route* from Kentucky to Baltimore, and preached in the

in that of my attorneys Baron de Fuerstenberg and Counts of Stolberg and of Merveldt, are of the most pleasing nature. Our whole property is recovered by a judgment of the Senate of St. Petersburg, confirmed by the Council of State, and sanctioned by the Emperor, and although according to the said judgment I am declared (on account of my religion and clerical profession) unable to inherit, yet according to the declarations of my attorneys in Germany and of Baron de Rosenkamp our common attorney in Petersburg, I am only nominally excluded, as according to the marriage contract of our dear parents of blessed memory, and according to their will, in every case the whole property was to be equally divided between my sister and me. These are the words of my attorneys*.

* * *

I have great reason then to thank Almighty God for protecting us so visibly, and granting us so complete a success in an affair in which, according to human probability, a far different issue was to be expected.

My sister, whose letter is dated February last, promises me speedy assistance after leaving me two years without a cent, which after contracting to a very great amount for land, has left me in a very critical situation. I cannot too much acknowledge my gratitude to Almighty God, for protecting my little property here during this time of general distress, and not permitting any of my creditors to enter suit against me.

I am now in daily expectation of a considerable sum of money which will probably come to your hands....

I find myself obliged to importune your Lordship again for the assistance of another clergyman. The enclosed from

---

Methodist chapel there, after which Major Noble, who had been much impressed by the sermon invited him to his house, which visit resulted in the baptism and reception into the Church of the entire family. Other circumstances of a supernatural character combined to this end. See *Sketches in Kentucky*, p. 180.

* As on page 258.

our trustees will be probably sufficient to prove the necessity of another one here. I should be very glad if your Lordship could send one about Christmas if no sooner convenient. I am informed that Rev. Mr. Shaeffer is ordained; although I am very far from wishing to choose, yet from the acquaintance I have with said Rev. gentleman I cannot refrain from testifying my opinion that we would very well agree together. I should be very happy to have him with me, if he is not already disposed of.

It is my wish to confine myself within the limits of Cambria County, which alone would be more than sufficient to occupy two clergymen. My best time is past, I am upon the brink of thirty nine: and besides its being contrary to the weakness of my constitution.... to ride about much, and live upon every kind of diet, I find I could render more essential services to the mission by being more at home, and carrying on a more regular correspondence with some able friends in Europe, of which I have received several very broad hints.

I beg of your Lordship to tell the clergyman whom you shall pitch upon, that he may depend upon a handsome maintenance without being beholden to the congregation for one cent. I wish him to be convinced of the necessity of harmonizing with me in all matters: two clergymen well united, perfectly disinterested, and guided by the sole motive of promoting the glory of God and salvation of souls, may do a great deal, in this part of the country. I have now on hand several Protestants and Presbyterians, who show a great desire to embrace the Catholic faith.

Besides the above reasons for staying at home I could mention another very material one, viz: that the management of my property here (which is, in fact, the property of the church), requires my constant attention and presence; an experience of several years teaches me that faithful domestics are very seldom to be found; after changing several times, I got one whom (on account of her skill, age, and experience, and especially her assiduity in frequenting the sacraments of the Church), I thought I might safely depend upon. After keeping her almost five years I had to turn her off, finding her guilty of dissipating my substance to the benefit of her friends and relations.... Overpowered by the strongest evidences, with whom I confronted her, I was compelled to believe, and turned her away. I have enlarged the church property so considerably that with care and prudent management it will be sufficient to maintain four clergymen, but I should be very sorry to depend again upon strangers, who through carelessness or knavery might during a few days' absence defeat the fruits of a whole year's industry.

Your Lordship's circular* I read in the church on a Sunday and made it the theme of that Sunday's sermon. God knows whether it will be attended to, to answer your expectations. As soon as I am in possession of my property I shall not forget what I owe to your Lordship, and to the Church which has opened to me her sanctuary, although very unworthy of it.

I am very much afraid of the issue of next election†. Our Irishmen are ready to go mad for Snyder, and Charles Kenny, Esq., of West Chester, by his artful and virulent publications in the *Aurora*, and in Dickson's Lancaster paper, keeps them up in a state of enthusiasm for Snyder, and against sound, genuine principles. Under the signature of Tyrconnell, he made an attack upon my political character and principles, in order to prevent his countrymen of Cambria and Huntington Counties from listening to me. I yesterday sent my reply to be published in Hamilton's Federal Gazette of Lancaster.

Recommending myself to your sacrifices and prayers, I remain with great respect,

    My Lord,
      Yr very hble & obdt servt,
        Demetrius Augustine Gallitzin,
          Parish priest of Loretto.

---

*Asking contributions towards the building of a cathedral in Baltimore, it is believed.

† Gallitzin, like Bishop Carroll, was a strong Federalist in his political views.

At this time the diocese of Baltimore comprising the whole United States, could boast of eighty churches and sixty eight priests,* and Bishop Carroll earnestly entreated the Holy Sea to divide it into several bishoprics. At this very time Rome was occupied by French troops under General Miollis, who were endeavoring by every aggravation, annoyance, and even open insult to force a pretext for accomplishing the ruin of the Holy Father, Pius VII, but although his officers were taken from him under one pretence or another, even the members of his cabinet and his secretaries long subjected to humiliating espionage, being arrested or removed as rapidly as possible, his Holiness was able to attend to the request of the American bishop and by a Brief of April 8. 1808 constituted Baltimore an Archbishopric, with four suffragan bishoprics: New York, Philadelphia, Boston, and Bardstown, with Rev. Luke Concannen, of the order of St. Dominic, Rev. Micheal Egan, order of St. Francis, both natives of Ireland, Rev. John L. Cheverus, and Rev. Benedict Flaget, Society of St. Sulpice, both of France, for their bishops. Rev. Luke Concannen, being in Rome at the time, was appointed bearer of all the necessary papers and rich presents for the new bishops, and was himself consecrated by Cardinal Antonelli, prefect of the propaganda, April 24. 1808, after which he started for the United States, but at Naples he was detained by the French as a British subject, where he died a prisoner, two years later. The news of the appointment, therefore, reached America long before the arrival of the official documents, and after the Holy Father had been hurried out of Rome in the dead of night by General Raget's gend'armes, and like his predecessor, made Bonaparte's prisoner.

The new Bishop of Philadelphia, Micheal Egan, had been for many years a hard working priest at Lancaster, and was known to be a man of great piety, earnest and selfdenying, still, the ties between Father Gallitzin and the bishop who had received him as a youth, had been his fatherly friend

---

* *Shea's History*, p. 89.

through his student life, had ordained him, and been his only confident through years of bitter trials, could not be broken without a pang.

Rev. D. A. Gallitzin to Bishop Carroll.

Loretto, Nov. 22d 1808.

My Lord,

Whilst I thank Almighty God for your Lordship's promotion, which adds so much to the lustre and dignity of the American Church, I sincerely regret and lament my own fate in being no longer under the immediate jurisdiction of your Lordship, whose paternal affection, prudence, and authority have so often afforded me most powerful protection against the poisonous shafts of slander and persecution, surrounded as I am by a set of the most corrupted class of Irish, who are as void of religion as they are of honor, or any kind of feeling that distinguishes man from the brute creation, and know of no kind of happiness but that of intemperance.... I have reason to fear that my constant endeavours in trying to reclaim those unhappy men, condemning their abominable pratices...will cause many of them to embrace the chance of a new bishop (especially knowing that he is their countryman), in order to renew their persecution. It is a very unhappy circumstance that the triumph of democracy in this state has raised their impudence, their ambition beyond all bounds. Their intrigues have already put them in possession of the most important offices of the county, which adds a great deal to their influence, and, no doubt they will be more successful under the next governor. I do not know whether I ever mentioned to your Lordship the attempt made last winter by two of those unhappy men, assisting a Presbyterian from Mifflin County in taking forcible possesion of some of my land, whilst I was performing my official duty in some distant settlements..... I have still reason to thank God for the increase and propagation of religion in this part of the world, the greater part of my congregation, and even a good many of the Irish, frequent the sacraments, and are of edifying principles and conduct. Some Protestants open their eyes; last month I took a whole numerous family of them into the Church; and I dare venture to assert that numbers would follow their example were it not for the bad and scandalous example of our own members.

The Confraternity of the Scapular has made very great progress here, and contains already a good many more members than I am able to hear on days of indulgence.

I hope your Lordship received my last letter by John McLain from Sinking Valley, in which I humbly begged for the assistance of another priest. I now renew my prayer, the granting of which is, under present circumstances, of the highest importance for the benefit of religion. Besides many reasons I mentioned in my last, I cannot help adding that my absence from here (although sometimes unavoidably necessary whilst I am alone), has proved highly detrimental to my temporal affairs, which, whilst entirely deprived of any help from Europe, require a great deal of care and attention. After spending enormous sums in converting a most frightful forest into a fine plantation, I have met with serious losses by being obliged to depend in my absence upon unfaithful domestics. Besides that, I find that the absence of the pastor, even for one Sunday, from the flock, gives a great chance to the wolf to tear the sheep; instances of the kind have been so frequent here that I never absent myself from here, without the greatest uneasiness and anxiety of mind; being almost certain to hear bad news on my return. Rev. Mr. Heilbron, having lost the greatest part of his burden by the appointment of Rev. Mr. O'Brien, writes to me that he expects to be with me pretty often for the time to come, and that he probably will be with me soon, I expect after Christmas duties at Greensburg. Your Lordship need not be uneasy, therefore, if you cannot provide the desired assistance for Christmas next....

I once more venture to represent to your Lordship my present embarrassments in consequence of being for better than two years deprived of any help whatsoever from Europe.... I have the greatest reason to thank God that I have been spared, during that time, by my creditors, otherwise I should have been ruined. The case, however, is a little altered of late, some of my creditors begin to get out of patience, and insist upon my entering judgment; this I would do without hesitation were it not that it would open the secret of my circumstances to those very persons in office, of whom I made mention above, and put me in their power; my situation would soon be made public and all the rest of my creditors would fall upon me. From the present state of my affairs in Europe it is morally certain that relief will be in my hands before the expiration of six months.... It would be a great relief to my mind to hear that my prayer will be granted....

Receive the assurances of the most profound respect with which I remain,
My Lord,
Yr most hble obdt servt,
Demetrius Augustine Gallitzin,
Parish priest of Loretto.

CHAPTER XVIII.
FINANCIAL EMBARRASSMENTS.
(1808—1809.)

Poverty of the church.—Gallitzin's appeals fruitless.—Continual disappointments and losses.—Visits Philadelphia.—Bitter trials.—A last offering.—"Entertaining angels unawares."—His buildings and farms.—Views on temperance.—An Act of the Pennsylvania Legislature.

As the speedy assistance so solemnly assured him by his sister, in her letter of Feb. 1808, did not arrive, Father Gallitzin wrote her in the early autumn fully explaining his position. The mails were so insecure that it was customary to send three or four copies of a letter, each by a different vessel, in hopes that at least one would succeed in reaching its destination, still, as demands were pressing upon him, he did not venture to await their uncertain course, but once more presented his case to the bishop, hoping that, at the prelate's request, some of the wealthy Catholics of Baltimore would advance him, at good interest, a sum sufficient to meet such debts as must be paid before an answer could be expected from Europe. But no words can describe the poverty of the church at that time, the bishop himself was in debt for church expenses, the newly appointed bishops could scarcely raise money enough to enable them to reach their dioceses, property which would to-day be worth millions had to be refused when offered in various places, as a gift to the church, for lack of means to keep it, and although Father Galltzin had, not only in Europe, but in this country, property which offered excellent security, his letter was not even answered. It is true the debts which tormented him were church debts such as now-a-days belong to the congregation to pay, but which he assumed as his own, weighed down by them as a man of the keenest sense of honor might be by an unexpected failure, and consequent inability to discharge debts contracted for his own personal enjoyment, rendered in this case the more distressing and exasperating by the knowledge that there was belonging to him thousands of dollars for every hundred he owed, kept from him for no earthly reason that he could understand.

The first letter on this subject to the bishop bringing no answer, not even an acknowledgment of its receipt, he found himself forced to renew his appeals, making every offer his situation permitted, and which would seem to be all that could be required for the most prudent creditor. The second letter, that of January 1809, was perhaps not received, those which followed in March and April though they reached their destination, do not appear to have brought him any reply until sometime in August.

Rev. D. A. Gallitzin to Right Rev. Bishop Carroll.

Loretto, March 7, 1809.

My Lord,

Not having received an answer to a long letter which I sent to your Lordship about two months ago, I conclude that it never reached your hands, and find myself compelled by the most urgent necessity to renew the application made in said letter.

It will soon be three years since I received the last remittance from Europe.... Having shortly after my father's decease contracted for land to a large amount, and that at a time when it was morally impossible to foresee the vexatious steps and attempts of some of our relations to wrest from our hands the estate lawfully derived from our ancestors, I found myself suddenly involved, without any possibility of fulfilling my contracts, unless by exposing for sale the very lands I had purchased. This method I tried as soon as the hopes had vanished of getting cash from Europe; but the general depression of business and scarcity of money rendered my endeavors nearly fruitless; my debts increased from year to year (owing to unavoidable expenses and accruing interest), yet the astonishing indulgence of my creditors, and the happy news of the recovery of our estate, kept up my spirits, and caused me to entertain no small hopes of a speedy and favorable change. No doubt such a change will take place soon now, but it will in all probability be too late to prevent the greatest distress with regard to myself as well as to some of my creditors.... I have already three letters ready to my sister, containing a detailed account of my present situation, which will certainly produce upon her mind the desired effect.

I shall with the greatest anxiety of mind expect your Lordship's answer.... I am very sorry that the throng of business daily increasing upon my hands, besides the want of money, deprives me of the satisfaction of waiting personally on your Lordship.

Receive the assurances of the high respect with which I remain,

    My Lord,

                      Yr most hble obdt servt,
                      Demetrius Augustine Gallitzin.

Same to the same.

                      Loretto, April 23, 1809.

My Lord,

I gave myself the pleasure of writing two letters to your Lordship, one sometime in January, I believe, and the other in March, neither of which came to your hands, I fear. I therefore take the liberty of repeating what I have presumed to represent in those letters, viz: that my situation has become truly alarming, this being the third year that I am left destitute of any help whatever from Europe.

            *   *   *

Mr. Haiden (Heyden), merchant in Bedford, is to be with your Lordship in a few days; as a particular friend of mine, who feels very much for me, he will be apt to confer with your Lordship on that subject, and I shall consider it a very great favor to receive by him a few lines of information from your Lordship on a subject so interesting to me, and more so to the welfare of religion in this county.

The three enclosed are to my correspondents in London enclosing letters to my sister, in order to procure in the speediest manner what will repay your Lordship. These I would wish, therefore, to be sent by three different vessels.

In hopes that my distress will be considered a sufficient apology for my boldness and presumption in intruding upon your Lordship, I subscribe myself with the greatest respect,

My Lord,

Your most hble and obdt servt,
Demetrius Augustine Gallitzin.

A period of the most intense and overpowering anxiety and suspense was now silently endured, for whatever answer, if any, Mr. Heyden brought back from Baltimore, it certainly was not one to relieve in the least the pressure of affairs. Had Gallitzin's embarrassments endangered all that he owned for himself alone, they would have occasioned him but slight uneasiness, for he cared nothing about wealth for his own comfort, but the property he was braving these storms and floods to keep, was the church property, the lands which were to add to the support of the church erected there and its future pastors, without any tax upon the congregation who were for the most part, though prospering, sufficiently burdened with the care of their families; lands that were to yield a rich revenue for colleges, convents, asylums, and all works of religious education and Christian charity. To let them go for the need of a few hundred dollars, which might arrive an hour after all was lost, was to throw away what could never be regained, for even at this time, had he but just arrived, instead of ten years earlier, it would have been impossible at five times the outlay, to secure as profitable beginning as had been made. It is said that the land on which Ebensburg stands, was cleared at the expense of a hundred dollars an acre, and that which Father Gallitzin owned must have cost fully as much; to throw away these rich farms just as their harvests became sure and abundant, to abandon the work of his life just as its labor was at the end and its reward beginning, above all to leave his dear congregations, as he well called them, to struggle on unassisted by word or deed was very hard. Any work an earnest man undertakes is relinquished only with a terrible wrench, how much more so the work undertaken for God!

During all this time, whatever were his mental anxieties, he was occupied with spiritual labor enough to keep four or five clergymen constantly employed, and never for a moment permitted temporal affairs to interfere with his smallest spiritual duties. In September he had the relief of receiving a note from the bishop, enclosing two letters from his sister, one of which had been nearly a year on its way, sent as usual, under cover to Bishop Carroll. In these she informed him that she had deposited five thousand roubles with the Russian Consul for him; the news came not an hour too soon, but he thanked God, not too late; his creditors had not yet seized his property though on the very point of doing so; the rest is better told by himself.

REV D. A. GALLITZIN TO RIGHT REV. BISHOP CARROLL.

Loretto, Oct. 30. 1809.

My Lord,

I embrace the present safe opportunity to let your Lordship know my present distressful situation. Immediately after receiving the last from my sister, accompanied by your favor of August 29, I wrote a letter to Mr. Daschkoff to which I received the answer enclosed, the contents of which are so contradictory to that of my sister's, that it very much perplexes my mind. Her last to me of March 28, written about six months after her return from Petersburg, has the following lines literally translated from the German:

"I have (whilst in Petersburg) borrowed five thousand roubles for you, and paid the same to the Russian Consul, Mr. de Daschkoff, who is to go this spring as consul to Philadelphia, and he will likewise give you some letters which I entrusted to his care, whilst at Petersburg."

In another letter, of Sept. 12. 1808, written at Petersburg, are the following lines:

"Now in order to help you out of your present distress which you describe to me in so lively colors, I have borrowed five thousand roubles, and have paid the same to Mr. de Daschkoff," &c. &c.

According to my sister's account Mr. de Daschkoff has more than fourteen months ago received five thousand roubles for me, according to his own account he has not one cent for me. Unfortunately I, immediately after receiving my sister's letters, was compelled to divulge the good news of having five thousand roubles ready in Philadelphia, as my creditors at that very time began to urge immediate payments, having previously exacted judgment bonds from me. Your Lordship may guess what I felt when I received Mr. Daschkoff's letter...

I am preparing to start for Philadelphia in order to try my fortune there. Mr. Daschkoft's letter came too late to hands to enable me to meet him in Philadelphia; where to find him I do not know, nor am I able, for want of cash, to travel very far after him. If I do not get speedy relief I cannot see any other method of extricating myself, except by giving up the little property gathered with a good deal of toil and labor, and applying for the benefit of the act of insolvency, which would be truly painful to my feelings......

....Mr. Daschkoff seems willing to certify the present good situation of my affairs in Russia, so as to convince any one disposed to help me, that this may be done with perfect safety.

So much on this truly disagreable subject.

Mr. Byrne will be able to give your Lordship some circumstantial account of my state of health....I was very much pleased with Rev. Mr. Byrne, he promises fair to be a zealous laborer in the Lord's vineyard......

To meet a few lines from your Lordship in Philadelphia
would be highly gratifying to
My Lord,
Your most hble obdt servt,
Demetrius Augustine Gallitzin.
Care of Mr. John Carrell,
No. 32 High Street.

The Rev. Mr. Byrne here mentioned was the first of Father Gallitzin's congregation to enter the priesthood; he was not young when admitted to the seminary, and had little previous education; he was, however, gifted with the liveliest faith and the most edifying piety, which with his exemplary conduct, his remarkable perseverance and humble consciousness of his early disadvantages, won him the esteem and veneration of all who knew him. He only went to Loretto at this time to visit his parents and relatives, the bishop thinking he would be better placed among strangers, but in the short time spent with Father Gallitzin he gave evidences of a piety which could never be forgotten by those who witnessed it.

It may be stated in explanation of the foregoing letter that the trip which the Princess Mimi made to St. Petersburg in order personally to attend to all necessary formalities, and to make arrangements to sell the estates whenever a favorable opportunity occurred, cost her no less than eight thousand dollars, and this taken in connection with the fact that the ready money due her could not be immediately collected from those who had been in temporary posession of the property, rendered it really difficult if not actually impossible for her to send her brother any of his portion sooner. The money which she borrowed for him, and believed sent him by Mr. de Daschkoff, is supposed to have been detained by some of her agents, as it never reached that gentleman's hands, to his sincere regret, for he greatly sympathized with Father Gallitzin's distress, as soon as he heard of it, strange as it must have appeared in view of the great wealth he knew him to possess in Russia.

It was with the courage of desperation only, or more truly, with faith in God leading him on in spite of all human probabilities, which caused Father Gallitzin to make one last effort to save his property.

Rev. D. A. Gallitzin to Right Rev. Bishop Carroll.

Philadelphia, Nov. 29. 1809.

Most Rev'd Sir.

I feel very grateful [for] the interest which your Lordship seems to take in my truly distressful situation. I arrived in the city on the eleventh day of this month very much fatigued and very much distressed in mind, not knowing how to extricate myself, or where to apply for assistance, as I was sensible that I had not that kind of security to offer which would induce even the wealthiest to lend money.... I applied to many, all pitied me, and lamented my case, but nobody thought himself safe in assisting me. Mr. A. promised help, and (without assigning any reason) recalled his promise. Left with only a couple of dollars in my pocket, the remainder of what I borrowed for travelling expenses, I was thrown into a state of despondency; the shock was so great, the anguish of my mind such, that I fainted upon Mr. Carrell's floor.

Such was my situation for several days after I came hither, and such it would be yet, if Divine Providence had not interfered: having gathered up all my little store of faith, I made a little offering to Almighty God out of the remnant of my fortune, and in a short time I found myself in possession of what will be sufficient to discharge my most pressing debts. John and Edward Carrell, Chief Justice Tilghman, Mr. Benjamin R. Morgan, a lawyer and a quaker, and Mr. Springer of our congregation, have agreed to lend me as much as will disengage me from those pressing demands for most of which there were judgment bonds against me, about two thousand dollars.

Having received notice from a lawyer in Huntingdon that the judgments are due about the beginning of December, and not being able to spare any money, I am obliged to start immediately for Huntingdon, which deprives me of the very great satisfaction of seeing your Lordship. I am very uneasy for fear that unfavorable reports with regard to my circumstances, being, perhaps, occasioned by my long absence, would cause my creditors to fall upon my property. I shall, therefore, leave the city next Saturday, December the second, and expect to reach home about the Saturday following.

I recommend myself to your Lordship's prayers, and remain with the greatest respect, my Lord,

Yr most hble & obdt servt
Demetrius Aug. Gallitzin.

Mr. Daschkoff who probably will be in Baltimore in a few days on his way to Washington, presents his respects and compliments to your Lordship.

This was not the only case in which Divine Providence had come to his relief when human hope had failed; there was one other to which he never alluded without tears, though he related it not as having happened to himself, but as of one whom he had known; but his emotion in speaking of it, as well as other circumstances easily put together, betrayed him, and left no doubt of the real truth upon the minds of the persons to whom he mentioned it.

Previous to his visit to Philadelphia he had received word, by Rev. Mr. Byrne, from a Baltimore firm, that a debt of something over four hundred and fifty dollars, which had been owing them for full two years, must be immediately paid or he would be sued for it; one lawsuit would have been the signal for all his creditors to fall upon him, and besides his fear of publicity, it was, of course, bitter misery for his natural high spirit, and religious principle to be in any one's debt, or to fear that others were suffering from his non-payment as he from the dilatoriness of his sister, to whom, instead of his agents, he looked for his portion. It was just at this time that Mr. Daschkoff's letter plunged him into cruellest disappointment, his health had long been very poor, broken by the fatigues and privations to which he was necessarily subjected, the irregular meals, the constant anxiety for the spiritual welfare of his flock, the pressure of business matters, the nerve-shattering suspense and distress endured by not knowing what to depend upon in regard to European affairs, and by the apparently inevitable failure of all that he had sacrificed his life to accomplish for the good of religion. Living in greatest poverty, misunderstood, misrepresented on every side, the very efforts he had made to raise up a happy community, free from want and the temptations of worldly care, appearing to result only in dragging them and all who had trusted him into deepest distress, without friends to comfort him, or to believe in his plans, however much they might credit his motives, the prospect before him became too dark for him to face. His nature was open, free, and simple, concealment was foreign and antagonistic to him at all times, but he was now like one passing over ice cracking beneath his feet, to go back was death, to stop to speak, to call a friend to his side, to pause for breath certain ruin, his only safety was in rushing lightly but steadily onward, a hurried movement or stumbling step would surely plunge him into the black waters surging beneath.

His depression and distress, increased by lack of sleep and loss of appetite occasioned by his anxieties, culminated one bitter day in intolerable anguish; as the twilight came on with its saddening influences, his forebodings and gloom grew overpowering, and when he closed the door of his room for the companionless evening, the long, silent night, it was to look over the precipice of despair, and feel the uncontrollable longing to throw himself into the dark abyss, which is said to possess many healthy and even happy people when looking dizzily downwards from some dangerous point; as one thus sinking might grasp at a blade of grass or tuft of moss to break the fall, he mechanically looked about for one gleam of hope, one human hand which he might seize on his downward course, when mind and sense, heart and faith seemed to have slipped over the brink of reason and of grace; there was nothing to cling to, not a sight or sound to arrest him, and he made no conscious resistance to the despair, the growing thought of self destruction which pressed upon him.

Just then a light knock at his door, which he always opened himself, somewhat aroused him, its repetition fairly so, and if only by force of habit, he arose and went rapidly to it, for he never kept any one waiting his humor or convenience; he met on the threshold a young man whose face he did not remember to have seen before, who, indeed, acknowledged himself at once a stranger, by asking if this was the priest's house. Hospitality was a virtue which Father Gallitzin never failed to exercise in its fullest sense, even when, later, voice and motion lost to him, he could only slowly and painfully raise his weary eyelids to turn a welcoming look to his deathbed visitors, so he at once invited the stranger in, put his deep dejection aside as far as human weakness permitted, and prepared to comfort, advise or console his visitor as might appear needful. But instead of commencing with his own affairs, as the custom was, the young man spoke of Loretto, which appeared to have great importance in his eyes, seeming to be sincerely desirous of learning more; a conversation interesting to both began at once, for almost immediately Father Gallitzin found in his guest a ready, intelligent reponse and appreciation of the few brief remarks he made concerning the little village's past and intended future, entirely new to him; he had been so accustomed, whenever the subject of his life's work was mentioned, to be obliged to explain, to arouse the listener's mind, to dwell upon the higher and better motives which should shape all our enterprises, and to feel that his most sympathetic listener was more than half mazed and skeptical, that, with all his depression, he could not help remarking to himself, with pleased surprise, that all these things were taken for granted now, and that he and his visitor were conversing on the even ground of a perfect understanding; he was even drawn into acknowledging that good and desirable as it had all seemed, at first, he was losing faith in his work himself, half doubting if it were God's will it should be continued, fearful of the end; but here with a steady cheerfulness the young man disagreed with him, pointed out phases of it which were new even to the worker, made practical suggestions, and perhaps spoke freely, without effort, and with the joyous enthusiasm which seldom if ever greeted Father Gallitzin's ears in those trying times, of the secure ways of the Almighty, and the impossibility of destruction when we leave ourselves in the hands of God. At all events, in a short time Father Gallitzin had freed his heart of its long accumulated load of sorrow and care, confided everything fully and without reserve to his visitor, or rather had seen that, by marvellous intuition and soul sympathy, all was known and understood, and now was more than ever his light-hearted, bouyant self again. When about half an hour, as he judged it, had passed, he suddenly recollected a host's first duty, reproaching himself for having been so absorbed in conversation as not to have considered that his guest, though it was not yet late, might be both hungry and tired. Apologising he arose at once, hastening to repair his inconsiderateness by providing something for him, but the young man, also rising, detained him, and pointing to the window, smilingly said: "It is not necessary, for, see, it is morning, and I must go." In amazement Father Gallitzin looked and saw that it was so, the East was already bright and glowing. No apologies, no entreaties could induce his guest to remain, and all he could do was to accompany him to the door and look lovingly after him as he crossed its threshhold, but after taking two or three steps the visitor disappeared, leaving his host brave and sustained as one might be who had opened his whole soul to an Angel of the Lord, in whose presence hours had flown as minutes.

Although there is reason to believe this visit took place previous to the journey to Philadelphia when his distress was the greatest, it is not impossible that it occurred afterwards, when the same debt still pressed heavily upon him, and though temporarily relieved of the others, he had abundant cause for overpowering anxiety, borne down as he was by the troubles of the past, the terrible mental strain so long kept up, and by the nervous and physical exhaustion which followed the heartbreaking trials and mortifications endured at Philadelphia. In his letter to the bishop, Nov. 22, written just previous to his return, the debt is mentioned as one impossible for him to pay until he should hear from his sister. The next he heard it was paid, it is generally supposed by an unknown person, and the receipt sent him. Soon after reaching home he received, most unexpectedly, five thousand roubles (fifteen hundred and ninety six dollars) from his sister, whether an additional five thousand, or the same she supposed sent by Mr. Daschkoff, miraculously restored, cannot now be ascertained. The fact of the debt, the visit, the sudden payment, the unhoped for receipt of the remittance are thoroughly authenticated and incontestibly proved.

After this he continued the cultivation of his land, although greatly annoyed and hampered in attempts to improve it, by continued delay in receiving the money expected, which would enable him to meet all his contracts, relieve him from the payment of interest which seriously diminished the amount received from the farms, and prevented the accomplishment of the improvements, the buildings and the additions which he was most impatient to commence, for he was now nearly forty years of age and felt anxious to see greater practical results than yet appeared.

When extra labor was required at seed and harvest times, he was in the habit of speaking a word or two about it when all met outside the church on Sundays, asking who would be willing to lend a hand during the week, and the response was almost universal, for such workdays were full of enjoyment for all. On the days appointed he remained for the greater part of the time in the field, walking along back and forth among the "hands", full of humor, making comical comments upon the work, telling amusing little anecdotes, and now and then good naturedly turning a joke upon some man or boy, who evidently enjoyed being the cause of wit in others, quite as much as they in laughing at him, for well they knew they were safe with Doctor Gallitzin; if he had anything against a man he had no need to cut with a jest, or wound with a joke, if angry he was quite able to speak his mind in plainest fashion, without any disguise. He did not pay these voluntary laborers who willingly gave their work, but he provided an excellent dinner for them, kept them lively and merry all the day, and towards evening would bring out his violin and play all the airs he knew while they finished off their work. Whatever cares were on his own mind, he never let any shadow rest from his on theirs, and he heartily delighted in amusing them and preparing pleasant surprises for them; it is still remembered how he brought his reapers home at sunset in great wagons drawn by stout mountain horses, the harness ornamented with vines and wreaths, the head of the village choir playing the clarinet, and he himself walking beside them. Days like these were like a rural idyll in the midst of the rude realities of everyday life, and, undoubtedly, attached pastor and people to each other beyond what either knew or suspected; only one thing ever marred their festivity; there was a distillery not a thousand miles away, and, although he was by choice in favor of abstinence Father Gallitzin did not object to a moderate stimulus for hard working, sober men, but as he walked up and down the lines, after dinner, if his keen eyes noticed the least sign of one having gone too far, however slight the appearance, his face would change, the light vanish from his eyes, he would stop in the middle of a sentence, and without another word or look, walk briskly away, and no one need expect to see anything more of him that day; he was like a child whose play has been suddenly spoiled, a girl who has seen an asp in her bouquet, as well as a man vexed, a pastor grieved and disappointed.

In the proper place he preached and labored against every thing likely to lead to intemperance, it was a vice for which he had a most violent repugnance, and he would not allow any notorious and unreclaimed drunkard to rest in the same church yard with the sober ones of his flock. In proportion to his contempt and hatred for the vice, was his pity for its victims, his unbounded sympathy for those families rendered wretched by one intemperate member; and many a hard contest was held between his rigorous principles and his loving heart, in such cases, and very transparent the artifices by which he attempted compromises between the two. Fortunately, the glorious mountain air is stimulus enough of itself, a stranger going to Loretto from any of the cities, feels the very atmosphere to be as exhilarating, almost as intoxicating as champagne until he becomes somewhat accustomed to it, and Doctor Gallitzin, as the people love to call him, had in his congregation for the most part, honest, hearty farmers, who brought healthy appetites to the meals won by honorable labor, whose blood coursed warm and red through the vigorous limbs, who had nothing to be ashamed of, no sins or cares they were afraid to face with due hope and trust in God's mercy, nor morbid cravings for unnatural stimulus.

If one fell away from the right path it grieved the doctor more than almost any calamity that could have occurred, and he especially forbade any such to be discussed or talked about, so far as he could forbid it. At one time a sad death occcured suddenly under most painful circumstances; a man full of life at night was found in the morning past all human blame or pity. The good and pious mourners stricken with a grief beyond all others, because it feared for the soul more than it wailed for the body, did not dare to call upon Dr. Gallitzin to share their sorrow, as was the first impulse always of every one in trouble, knowing as they did the life the lost one had led, and the circumstances of his death. In Loretto there were no secrets, with the first dawn of light every one knew what had happened, and rushed to the priest's house each eager to be the first to tell him of it, some of the "unco' gude", perhaps, not unwilling to gain esteem by their loud condemnation of the poor soul already before its judge. "Not a word," said he at the first sentence, in a stern voice that made sudden silence, "don't one of you dare to tell me one word about it. Not one single word more, do you hear?" and taking his hat and cane went straight to the house of death, before they had recovered breath.

"Why would he not hear about it," one asked when the incident was related.

"Oh," answered the informant naively, "if he had known it he couldn't have went to the house, him being the priest, you know."

Besides the relief obtained by the visit to Philadelphia, the close of the year 1809 brought to Father Gallitzin another satisfaction: the final settlement of all difficulties occasioned by the assumed name under which he had first become known in this country. Fearing serious difficulties in the future he was advised to apply to the legislature to legalize the acts and purchases made under that name, which he did in a petition read by Mr. McSherry of Adams County, Dec. 16, 1809.

Petition

To the Honorable the Senate and House of Representatives of the Commonwealth of Pennsylvania in General Assembly met.

The Petition of your very humble servant respectfully sheweth:—

That your humble petitioner Demetrius Augustine, Prince of Gallitzin, having come to the United States about seventeen years sgo, solely with the intention of improving himself by travelling, and having in obedience to the dictates of his parents adopted the name of Augustine Smith, as they conceived that his name or title would or might expose him, when travelling through this and other parts of the world, to very considerable and useless expense:— Your humble petitioner having afterwards abandoned the idea of returning to his own country, and having under his adopted name, Augustine Smith, by naturalization, become a citizen of the United States: finding, moreover, that his real name is known to a great many, which obliges him to make use of it on many occasions, and fearing that inconveniences, or, at least, trouble and uneasiness might arise to himself or others after him, with regard to the holding of real property or conveying of the same, etc., he, therefore, prays that your honorable body may enact a law to establish his name, Demetrius Augustine Gallitzin, so that he may under that name enjoy the same benefits and privileges to which he became entitled by naturalization, under the name of Augustine Smith, and your humble petitioner, as in duty bound, will ever pray, etc.

Demetrius Augustine (Smith) Gallitzin.

December 5, 1809.

This was referred on the 16th to a committee composed of Mr. McSherry, Mr. Bethel, and Mr. Weiss, and an Act was passed in compliance with the requests contained in it.

This authoritatively settled the matter for which custom had already prepared the way, the name Smith having been gradually and imperceptibly dropped, the more easily that he was generally spoken of in his congregations as "the priest", and "the doctor". No occasion had as yet arisen for a more public use of his name; if such should come no one who knew him need doubt the spirit and firmness with which it would be sent forth.

CHAPTER XIX.
STILL AGAINST WIND AND TIDE.
(1810—1814.)

Princess Mimi's explanations.— Troubles in Europe.—Pius VII at Fontainebleau.—On the way to Italy.—His reception at Rome.—Rejoicing throughout the Christian world.—Loss by the invasion of Russia and Prussia.—A famous speculation.—F. Gallitzin's care of the altar.—His love of books.

The letters which Gallitzin had sent to his sister on business matters caused her great distress, both on account of that which he was suffering, and the doubts they implied of her readiness to fulfill her promises. "However," she wrote him, after some complaints of his harshness, "however we will say no more about it, I know that a very great distress will sometimes overcome us, and cause us to become very bad humored, and full of suspicion. Only remain friendly and good to me and believe firmly in my sincere friendship." Better still, she gave him a partial explanation of the cause by allusions to the events transpiring in Europe, of which she took it too much for granted he was thoroughly informed, on which the archbishop, as we must now call him, the long delayed pontifical papers having at last arrived in this country, still further dwelt when forwarding the letters so anxiously awaited.

ARCHBISHOP CARROLL TO REV. D. A. GALLITZIN.

Baltimore, Oct. 17, 1810.

Rev. and very dear Sir,

The enclosed letter from the Princess, your sister, though brought by the worthy Bishop Flaget, was not delivered to me for more than a month afterwards, with another for myself; and since I received them and knew of the importance of hers to you, I did not choose to send them before I had a safe and undoubted opportunity. Your sister desired me to read hers to you, and therefore did not seal it, and she desired me to efface such expressions, if any appeared in her writing, which might be thought disrespectful to you. However, I did not use this privilege for she exhibits evident marks of being most deeply and painfully affected by your displeasure, yet she never forgets that deference which she owes to you. Her heart is grievously wounded, but she retains all the warmth of sisterly affection. If she has been tardy in meeting and relieving your embarrassments, make allowance for her own, her health and necessary journeys, and the difficulties produced by the convulsive state of all public concerns in Europe. In a word, she deserves words of comfort from you, and you, in obedience to the dictates of natural affection, as well as of Christian justice ought to give them to her. Do not alienate her heart from you.... Show in your answer the feelings of a brother for the mortification you have caused her to suffer.

I write this but a few days before the consecration of Bishops Egan and Cheverus, and should be happy indeed if you could be here on that occasion. Whatever satisfaction I experience from the erection of new dioceses (and indeed the satisfaction is very great); yet it is accompanied with the painful consideration, that I am no longer so closely connected as heretofore with many clergymen who merit and enjoy my highest esteem and friendship; nor with many congregations and individuals to whom my heart clings with the warmest affection. Amongst those clergymen be assured that you hold a distinguished part, and that I am, dear and Reverend Prince,

Your most obd't serv't.
† J. Bp. Baltre.

The advice thus enforced upon Father Gallitzin's already contrite heart, made him resolve never again under any circumstances in thought or word to doubt his sister's good faith or feeling, and whatever happened, always to believe that she would in due time explain or right it; a resolution he kept only too faithfully.

The near approach of the consecration of the new bishops, consequently of his passing under a new superior, awoke in his heart the old regrets at sundering the ties which had so long united him to Baltimore, and roused the fears of new troubles when he should be subject to one unaware of his former trials, and real character; he especially trembled lest Bishop Egan should be influenced to remove him, as he had the power to do at any moment at his own discretion, from his beloved Loretto. But, happily, Father Gallitzin was better known than he feared, and deeper rooted in the affections of his congregation than he could have believed.

ARCHBISHOP CARROLL TO REV. D. A. GALLITZIN.

April 8th 1811, Balt're.

Rev. and dear Sir.

Mr. Wille arrived to day with your favour, of various dates* which I was indeed rejoiced to receive after so long interruption of our correspondence, but its contents respecting the deplorable state of your health abated much of the pleasure of hearing from you. Be assured that my endeavours shall not be wanting to urge Bishop Egan on the subject recommended by you of sending a priest to your assistance: he may be more fortunate than I was in being able to do so. His countrymen may offer their services to him with a better assurance and reliance on his attachment, than to me. It has been lately rumored here that your friend, Mr. Brosius, was endeavoring to dispose of his school, and adjoining lots of ground, and after settling his affairs to remove and unite himself with you. His solicitous and too timorous conscience disqualifies him for such duties, unless his mind has recovered from those perplexities, which disturbed him before he went to Philadelphia.

---

* These letters are missing.

I am glad to hear of your having written to your respected sister a consolatory letter. Her inexperience exposed her probably to place undeserved confidence in her agents, and as I often hear (merchants) say, the furious enmity of Bonaparte to commerce, and the shackles multiplied every day by him on its transactions, produce incredible difficulties, sacrifices, and losses in the remittance of money from one country to another. Impute, therefore, your disappointments not to her negligence or a diminution of her affection but to the real and irremovable difficulties she has to encounter. *Dabit Deus*, as we may hope, *his quo que finem*. It is certainly a hard task to keep your mind in peace, whilst you are so harrassed, but use your best efforts to compose it, on many other accounts, but especially because it will help to restore your health. Our latest accounts from His Holiness are that he is still (28th Dec.) a prisoner at Savona in the Territory of Genoa; not indeed a close, but always a guarded one. No communication is allowed between him and any of his flock, except the persons around him. Though a great dinner is prepared every day for him nominally, yet in truth for the Emperor's minions and spies around him, yet he never partakes of and asks or accepts of no more than the common portion of common prisoners.

The Rev. Mr. Enoch Fenwick now lives with me; he is a pupil of Georgetown, but lived one year at the seminary where perhaps you knew him. His brother, Benedict, is at New York with Mr. Kohlman. Mr. Dubourg, after suffering much from the rheumatism, went to Martinico in the winter, proposing to return in May or June. The Right Rev. Bishop of Kentucky [Flaget] and Mr. David leave Baltimore for their destination the last of this month, passing by and taking boat at Pittsburg. Mr. Heilbron's sickness gave me much uneasiness for that honest good man, a truly respectable German character. Mr. Elling died last week but one at Philadelphia, leaving, as I hear, his property to a nephew in Germany.

I am with the utmost affection dear and beloved Sir,
    Your most obd st.   † J. Abp. of Bre.

There were stirring events going on in Europe at this time, of the greatest interest to all men, and of special interest to Gallitzin as a Catholic, and as a Russian by birth and fortune.

The glamour of enchantment which Bonaparte appeared to have thrown over the young Emperor Alexander after the defeat of Prussia in 1806, which resulted in the treaty of Tilsit and the great personal friendship of the two emperors, who planned to rule the destinies of Europe together, had worn away, and Alexander, more and more inclined to the policy of his own nobles, who were all opposed to Bonaparte, refused him his sister's hand preferring to marry her to a comparatively obscure German prince; animosity followed coldness and reached a declaration of war in 1812. England and Sweden alone retained strength and boldness enough to openly side with Alexander. Napoleon marched so rapidly to Russia that the Emperor was taken by surprise and only saved himself by the retreat of which every one knows the terrors, the suffering, the heroism of the Russians who burnt their own cities and destroyed all supplies as they went, stationing starvation and bitter cold all along their route to receive the pursuing army, which after incredible sufferings and losses, escaped, as best it could, to France. But all the world knew that a defeat to Bonaparte was like a wound to a wild animal, it but made him attack again with redoubled fury, and, refusing all compromise which would but serve as a cloak for his enemy until he could recruit his strength, Alexander, urged on by England and reviving Prussia, appealed, in 1813, to Europe as its redeemer, inaugurating a real crusade against the common foe, which brought the allied armies through the gates of Paris, in triumph, finally, by proving he fought against Bonaparte not against France, won high favor even with the French, and became the hero of the Congress of Vienna in 1814. After Napoleon's escape from Elba, Alexander signed the proclamation, which made his former friend an outlaw among the nations; Waterloo followed, the allies again entered Paris, and Bonaparte's power was forever at an end.

In the autumn of 1813 it became known at Fontainebleau, where Pius VII. was a prisoner, that an armistice had been agreed upon between the French and the allied armies, and that a Congress would be held at Prague to decide upon something which would secure peace to Europe. The Pope was advised to reclaim in the face of Europe his rights and those of the Holy See, and with his own hands expressed his rightful demand in a letter to the Emperor of Austria, Francis I., carried to the papal nuncio at Vienna, in spite of the vigilance of the French police, by young Count Benetti, afterwards Cardinal Secretary of State under Gregory XVI.

Bonaparte, however, had already begun to feel misgivings in regard to his conduct towards the Holy Father, even as a matter of policy, and various ambassadors, more or less formally accredited, were sent to negotiate with the Pope, one of these was what the witty Cardinal Pacca designated as veritably an ambassador *extraordinaire*, the Marquise de Brignole, but the lady of the court, bishops, and government officers received alike the same reply: "The restitution of the States of the Church was an act of justice, and could not be made the subject of a treaty." In January 1814, as matters grew desperately dark for Bonaparte, he offered the Holy Father the restitution of Rome and the provinces as far as Perugia, but Pius refused to make any compromise or enter into any treaty whatever, and in a less formal conversation which followed this resolute decision, said that he demanded freedom to return to Rome; he had need of no assistance, Providence would conduct him there.

Matters grew worse and worse for the man who had so long mastered fate; his enemies were fast approaching the capital, and the next they knew at Fontainebleau was the arrival of a string of empty carriages, followed by the information of the officer in charge of the prisoners that he was to conduct the Pope to Rome, starting on the morrow. When this news was formally announced to the Holy Father he earnestly entreated that his cardinals might be allowed to accompany him, and when this was refused that even one might go with him, but in vain, Monsignore Bertozzoli alone was permitted in the same carriage with him; in a second carriage were the Pope's own physician and one appointed by the emperor, and with this simple retinue, surrounded by *gend'armes*, the successor of St. Peter made a march through France to Rome, more thrilling and wonderful than that of any Cesar from victorious battle. It was hardly possible for the soldiers to keep open a space wide enough for the carriages to pass, through the crowds of men, women and children who, indifferent to the sabres of the guards, threw themselves upon their knees, under the horses' feet, or climbed the carriage wheels, begging the papal benediction.

In April (1814) the Provisional Government of Paris issued orders to the civil and military authorities to remove all obstacles, such as Bonaparte had placed in the Holy Father's path, and to the uncontrollable demonstrations of the people was now added the official honors due to a sovereign. The firing of cannons, the peal of the joybells, salutes from all the ramparts, illuminations, announced his passing from city to city, while young men in uniform, meeting him outside the towns, took the horses from his carriage, attached ropes of red and yellow silk to it, and drew him onward under triumphal arches, amidst showers of bouquets and wreaths, and acclamations from a kneeling populace, who did not cheer, as in other cases, with crape about their hearts.

The cardinals who had not been permitted to depart for some days, and then only in parties of two and three, were able by rapid journeying to overtake the Pontiff at Sinigaglia, in the beginning of May, and to take part in his grand and magnificent entrance into Rome, on the twenty fourth of that month. They were joined, a few miles from Rome, by the King and Queen of Spain, Charles IV. and Maria Louisa, and their daughter and son in law, King and Queen of Etruria, and other noble personages; at one of the gates of the city the Commission of State, that is to say, the prelates and laymen charged with the Provisional Government of Rome, awaited His Holiness, with a vast concourse of people, and formally received him, twenty four young Roman gentlemen insisted upon drawing his carriage, while a crowd of little boys and girls, dressed in white, carrying palm branches, supplied by the family of Bresca,—to which, in recompense for services in the days of Sixtus V. was given the privilege of providing the palms used in the Roman churches,—flocked about the carriage, looking to the people like angels of peace, accompanying the Pope to the Quirinale palace, to which he was welcomed with indescribable acclamations, although, as Cardinal Pacca, who was in the same carriage with him, candidly admits, there were many who did not join in these demonstrations, but were silent in the midst of the tumult of happiness: their sobs and tears of relief and joy prevented any livelier welcome, tears streamed from the eyes of Pius himself, and even the grave and stately cardinals were in danger of losing their self possession on that memorable day.*

There were no Atlantic cables in those days, not even mail steamers or regular sailing packets, but is was understood in this country that the Pope was free, and the Roman welcome was echoed, clear and sweet, from the depths of the American forests, the wooded heights of the Alleghanies:

Rev. D. A. Gallitzin to Most Rev. Archbishop Carroll.

Loretto July 4. 1814.

My Lord,

The events which your Lordship anticipated have taken place, the Iron Scepter is broken, and all Europe at peace *Ecce mutatio dextera Excelsi*. In thanksgiving for so great a blessing, and especially for the restoration of our holy father, the Pope, *I sung Te Deum Laudamus* on the day of St. Peter and St. Paul* and a solemn Mass. If I did not wait until the happy news was officially announced, it was

---

* See *Histoire du Pape Pie VII, par M. le Chevalier Artaud*, tome troisième, chapitre V., and *Memoirs of Cardinal Pacca*, translated by Sir George Head. Volume second, chapter xvi and xviii.

* June 29.

because I could not restrain the sentiments of gratitude and joy that filled my heart on receiving those tidings. Long live Alexander! To call him *The Great* would be to defame his character. May our once happy country obtain a share of those blessings granted to Europe after a scourge of twenty four years.

But when the first emotions of joy at the restoration of the Supreme Pontiff had subsided into deep and quiet gratitude, and the full accounts of the disasters to so many of his friends, and to his own property arrived, Father Gallitzin found he in his distant home had shared the misfortunes of his native land in no small degree. "I feel very uneasy at not hearing a word of my sister these two years past," he wrote in the letter just quoted, "Muenster, her residence, must have suffered considerably from Davoust's army, situated as it is in a straight direction from the Lower Rhine to Hamburg. God grant that she may have effected her escape to Vienna in time, for I think it probable she would choose that city above all others as a place of refuge."

There was indeed reason for these fears, for he afterwards learned that the French had been quartered upon his mother's house, to the injury of the property, and great loss to his sister, while in Russia the burning of Moscow, near which were his estates, rendered them unproductive for some years; he had not received any remittances since 1811, and then by the difference in currency he lost nearly three hundred out of every four hundred dollars. He was, however cheerful and kept up good courage, as the same letter shows:

Under continual disappointments, and with severe losses, I cannot be too thankful to Divine Providence for having so often protected me and my property, when I saw myself repeatedly on the brink of ruin. I am greatly indebted to the exertions of the Honorable Judge Tilghman and other gentlemen of Philadelphia. I have finally applied to and obtained from several banks considerable sums of money which will be left in my hands until sufficient remittances from Europe enable me to refund those sums. We are literaly surrounded with banking institutions, thanks be to the wisdom &c. of our legislators.

I should be happy if my circumstances, and my business spiritual and temporal, would afford me money and time to visit Baltimore, and to pay my respects to your Lordship. After many years struggle I begin to reap the benefit of my labor, and find myself able by means of my farm, stock, mills &c. to discharge gradually many debts, but my circumstances are critical and require the utmost economy and attention to my business. Times are particularly favorable for our part of the country, and produce of every kind is very high and ready sale....

If I should receive in the course of this summer a letter from my sister, or any information from Baron Rall [Russian agent] relating to remittances, it is more than probable that I shall then immediately repair to Philadelphia, and on my way home to Baltimore, which will afford me an opportunity of testifying personally to your Lordship the great respect with which I remain,

My Lord,
Yr most hble & obdt servt,
Demetrius Aug. Gallitzin.

It was always a great grief to Dr. Gallitzin that the failure of his European supplies compelled him to divert the profits of his American farm and mills from their original purpose, the cause of religion and charity, but it was a source of great comfort to him that there was no failure about them; all that his most sanguine hopes had promised him of their productiveness, was verified, and though he made mistakes sometimes, which the old farmers would have avoided, he made many discoveries and applied theories successfully which they would never have dreamed of; no farmer far or wide could equal the richnes and abundance of his harvests, the excellence of everything raised by him. His barns and granaries were filled to overflowing, and what he did not and could not need for his own use, was never wasted nor given carelessly away; when his cattle were killed, he had an abundance put by for himself, that is, for the household which consisted always of one, generally of two or more families of orphans, several widows to look after them, the men in charge of the farm, and the stranger within his gates; then this old woman, that sick or helpless old man, the family lately arrived and hardly yet settled, and another which had not been successful this season, all received a portion; after which the store houses were shut up, and the barns closed; but when the storms came and the scanty supply of smaller or less careful farmers came to an end, it was not hard to find who owned their contents; and the good pastor took his frugal meals just as contentedly, if not more so, when his abundant supplies were exhausted, as when there had been plenty and to spare. In time of scarcity, it is said, he opened the doors and gates, and all who wished to come did so, helping themselves without a word; sometimes even that permission was not waited for, though against this he took the greatest precautions, for he would not leave a loophole for temptation to enter, and could be as vexed as any other careful farmer at any poaching on his domains. He had the ears of a lynx for such, and they tell how one evening in particular he started to hear the stealthy step of an intruder, evidently desirous of secrecy, passing his window on the way to the barn where his hay was kept, and as quietly and more lightly he followed in pursuit. It was, however, no ordinary thief who was fumbling at the doors, but a poor man driven out of his sober reason by hard necessity and long contemplation of the last wisp of hay which had made the scanty supper of his only cow, the faithful animal upon which all his dependence was placed; it was not a mind, this poor man's, of very broad or complicated dimensions, there was only room in it for a very simple course of reasoning; if the cow had no food she would give no milk, and if the children had no milk, they would starve, for there certainly was nothing else for them; when this thought was sufficiently considered it went out of sight, while the narrow stage of his mind gave room for the next one; Dr. Gallitzin had plenty, he always did have plenty, he never refused anybody anything, and he had a mint of money across the sea, that would make all right as soon as he got it, and what was a handful of hay, more or less, to a man of such expectations? Putting these two thoughts together they took him to Gallitzin's barn and inside the doors; while there a third idea, founded on the seventh commandement, tried to push itself forward, but there was hardly room for it; he was one of those who sometimes, in unaccustomed mental excitement, mutter their thoughts aloud, as Dr. Gallitzin reached the outer side of the barndoors he heard a voice repeating slowly, like a half forgotten lesson: "Honesty is the best policy," after which a pause, a rustling as of an armful of hay being pressed into a bundle, and again the words, spoken this time with more assurance: "Honesty is the best policy," followed by a sound, light indeed, as of a bundle dropped and falling apart, and a muttering as of one in deepest thought: "If the cow has no hay, the children will have no milk," and so on, over and over again, until, at last, Dr. Gallitzin drew hastily aside as a man passed, empty handed, with drooping head but resolute step, without a glance at the temptation thrown behind; he knew the voice and guessed at the face vaguely seen in the starlight, but he neither spoke nor moved until the man was well out of reach, then he carefully closed and secured the too easily opened doors, and going lightly by another path, roused his deeply sleeping serving man.

"Come! Come! wake up; I want you."

"Ah! ah!" groaned and ejaculated that astonished individual, "Is it me, your Reverence?"

"Yes, you, get up quickly, and put up the sled—"

"Put up the sled!" repeated the man in amazement," why, your Reverence, it's the middle of the night!"

"So the quicker the better. Put up the sled and carry a load of hay to——right away."

This was a most astounding order, and it was some little time before Dr. Gallitzin could make the good man comprehend that he was in earnest.

"Faith, and they'd think me crazy to wake them up at this hour," he repeated, puzzled, and none too good humored, reluctantly and with much grumbling preparing to obey, as there seemed no help for it.

"Well," he asked gruffly, coming around to Father Gallitzin's room, at last, when his hay was loaded, "what will I say for rousing up——like this?"

"Oh," answered the priest, glancing up from his book, with a very demure look about the corners of his mouth, "just leave the hay and tell him: *Honesty is the best policy.*"

Not much enlightened, the other went his way, carrying out the unaccountable freak of his master; it is likely, however, that the receiver of the hay was not so slow of comprehension.

Once the doctor undertook a small speculation; the results are historical. It was quite at the beginning of his career in the mountains that the idea struck him and some of the farmers that they paid a very high price for the few luxuries which were brought around at times from the cities, and sold to them for several times their cost, and that it would be an admirable plan to go into the exchange business on their own account; accordingly they combined together to load up a wagon with different kinds of farm-produce which they proposed to send to Baltimore, to receive in return tea, coffee, and other domestic articles not easily obtained in the country. This grand coöperative scheme met with the most thorough approbation from all who were able to invest in it; the famous wagon was loaded, drawn by five splendid horses got up in the best possible style, at Father Gallitzin's expense, and "deep freighted with human hopes" was driven gaily out of Loretto, by a young man in whom the priest had every confidence, amidst the cheers of the whole village.

In course of time the women began to look uneasily down the road for its return, rich laden with tea and calico, while the less patient sex knocked out the ashes of the last bit of tobacco, fuming considerably at the slowness of the five horse team, and as people wait and look and watch and question of some fair ship long since, if they but knew it, at the bottom of the ocean, the good people sought of every traveller news of their venture. At last, the driver returned to Loretto to recount wonderful escapes and marvellous adventures, by wood and field, from which he did not return empty handed, for he still retained possession, it is believed, of the whip which he had cracked and flourished in triumph when setting out upon his travels. For the rest, their ship had gone down forever, but the sea that engulfed it was never that of *clear cold water*. It may be considered a striking evidence of the hard heartedness of human nature, that there was a plain lack of appreciation of the boldness and adroitness with which (when his money was at an end), this "sole surviver", had effected his escape from the snares and pitfalls of the city, and brought his own precious self back to Loretto. Father Gallitzin alone appeared touched by this result, and in response to the man's entreaties for forgiveness took him into favor again, appointing him overseer of a saw-mill, which he had put up at great expense, and lost by fire in one night through the carelessness of this very person, who seemed born into the world for the express purpose of injuring his benefactor.*

After this he sent his own wagon down, under the charge of more reliable persons it is to be presumed, in the autumn of each year, until better means of transportation became available, with the surplus of his farm produce, when his winter purchases would be made for himself, his farm and the church. He was even in his deepest poverty extremely fastidious about everything used for the service of the altar, all the linen was of the finest, and not an atom of dust ever permitted to rest about the sanctuary, inside the rails of which he never permitted layman or woman; his sacristy for a long time was a wardrobe or bureau in the sanctuary, and every vestment was folded without wrinkle or crease and with the utmost precision. Fortunately for his slender means,

---

* See Lemcke, p. 183, and Dr. Heyden's *Life of the Rev. Prince D. A. Gallitzin*, p. 98.

the greater portion of the articles required for the altar had been sent him by his mother, sister, and European friends; they were of the finest material and workmanship, such as few city churches could aspire to at the time. He also received from home some excellent religious paintings of German masters, one of which, *The Adoration of the Magi*, still hangs over the chapel altar at Loretto, half lost, however, in the dimness of age; some small engravings for his own room, and abundance of little pictures for the children. He conscientiously contributed his mite towards the foundation of Catholic literature in this country, by purchases of books in Baltimore, which with those he had brought with him when he came to America, and those sent him in profusion by his mother, made up a choice and excellent library.* The severe training of his youth which impressed upon his mind the works of the greatest writers, even before he could understand or care for the subjects of which they treated, served him admirably in later life, by placing at his command authorities and notes which a life long student might have envied. Many and many a time in law, history, most of all in religious discussions, it was attempted to trip him up with some high sounding quotation, or some crushing fact of which the quiet mountain pastor, clad in homespun, overwhelmed with business and the care of honest but uneducated congregations, was supposed to be as a matter of course entirely ignorant; nothing could be more amusing than his opponents' consternation at the easy way in which he would then turn their own guns against them.

The time was at hand when the store house of his mind would be called upon to show forth its treasures.

---

* The remains of this library are said to be carefully preserved at the pastoral residence in Loretto, but the writer was not permitted to see them. Prince Augustine Gallitzin remarks in *Un Missionaire russe en Amerique*, p. 29: "He loved books, he could not pass them by; he had collected a large number, seeking to do good in taking them, and committing no error in inscribing on the dear companions of his solitude this formula of dedication: *Gallitzini et amicorum.*

CHAPTER XX.

DEFENDER OF THE FAITH.

(1814—1825.)

"I never see a Seventy-four without rendering a more lively and appreciative homage to the canoe of the first navigator."

Madame Swetchine.

The war of 1812.—Captain Richard McGuire.—The Loretto recruits.—A national fast.—A war sermon.—DEFENCE OF CATHOLIC PRINCIPLES, Mr. Hayden Smith.—Mr. Douglas.—The minister's vindication.—LETTER ON THE HOLY SCRIPTURES.—Personal influence.—A spirited woman.—Mixed marriages.—A public announcement.

While the Old World was racked with wars and rumors of wars, the New World was not allowed to remain in peace. The long war between England and France had thrown the business of ocean commerce into the hands of the neutral nations, especially of the United States, and as the Americans were accused of making money under the shield of neutrality, England and France proclaimed the most extensive blockades, disregarding the rights and interest of commerce.

Our government had been so very economical that we had no navy of any account to protect our trading vessels, which were seized on the slightest pretext, and the sailors impressed into the British service; this led, after great injury to business and bitter humiliations to the young republic, to that which is known as the war of 1812, in which the despised little navy gloriously resented Brittania's rule of the waves.

In the late summer of 1814 word reached the remote districts of Pennsylvania telling that the British troops were advancing on Washington; the President [Madison] appointed a day of fasting and prayer; enlistments were made in haste, and the citizen soldiers hurried to the defence of the national capital, arriving rather late in the day, however, for the English had already leisurely entered Washington, burnt, pillaged, and as leisurely left it. Captain Richard, son of the old chief McGuire, already in the army, came to raise a company of volunteers, in which he was ably assisted by Dr. Gallitzin, whose soldier-nature had long outstripped his Federal politics. While Captain McGuire drilled his recruits in the open space near the pastoral residence, Gallitzin would often stand at his door or window, looking on; they were not quite such fencing lessons as he had received in the military academies of Europe, but the captain was very proud of his men as of his own skill in handling a sword, and when, one day, the pastor was seen coming quietly from the village towards the parade ground, his hands behind him, as usual, crossed on the slender sword cane he always carried, the officer took the liberty of meeting him, and taking the proper attitude, made a show of fencing with him. The challenge was accepted without any ceremony, and with hardly a perceptible change of position, while the men looked on in breathless interest, to see the captain's sword meeting the doctor's cane; after two or three movements, enough to put the officer on his mettle in earnest, the spectators were amazed to see a sword whirling in the air, and almost at the same instant the doctor, absorbed in his own thoughts, his hands behind him, crossed upon his cane, quietly pursuing his way, as if there had been no interruption. Captain McGuire picked up his sword and went on with his drill, rather proud than otherwise at defeat from such skilful and honored hands.

Nothing could be more touching than the departure of this little band from Loretto. After Mass, at which each member received communion, they were drawn up in front of the church, their banner blessed with the greatest solemnity, a parting blessing given with an exhortation to courage, to faithful devotion to God and their country, fresh from the heart of the soldier priest who bade farewell to each as to a beloved son. When, later, one proved recreant to his duty, and slipped away from his post, as we have seen, his welcome was as stern as the parting had been tender.

The day appointed by the President for fasting and prayer was observed at Loretto with rigorous exactness, with the offering of the Holy Sacrifice, alms and mortification, in the Catholic manner of humiliation. Elsewhere the occasion was seized for political sermons by the ministers of the various denominations, who not unlike their brethren of the present day, having exhausted the Bible, were driven to take their texts and inspiration from the newspapers and to hold forth on the last sensation. For these the public penance was a special blessing; they prepared for it by most elaborate sermons, knowing that they could seldom look for fuller houses and better opportunity for the display of their too often unappreciated eloquence. By a happy unity of sentiment, delightful to notice in the disseminators of so many opposite doctrines and ever clashing creeds, these sermons all displayed more or less animosity to Catholics, Papists and Romanists, as these high bred gentlemen nicknamed them, and had for their general text the disloyalty of the Catholics in the United States, and the crying necessity of their extermination. Some of these sermons were so well liked that the amiable hearers obtained that they should be printed in the newspapers, even in pamphlet form; one preached by a Rev. Mr. Johnson of Huntingdon county, though mainly a re-hash of one got up by Dr. Smith of Philadelphia, attracted considerable attention as it was particularly happy in its allusions to the pope, the priests, the Church in general. In this elegant discourse the Succesor of St. Peter was gracefully introduced as an old cow; the famous paintings at which the whole world has gazed in rapturous admiration for centuries, were defamed as the monstrous idols before which the heathen papists bent the servile knee; in a word, it contained all, or nearly all, the slanders which successive generations of heretics and infidels have been able to concoct against the Church of Christ. The Protestants were jubilant; if their minister had not, by prayer and fasting, driven the British out of Washington, it was plain he had dealt the Catholics some staggering blows.

So much was said of this master piece of pulpit eloquence that Dr. Gallitzin, judging that silence under all such attacks might be misunderstood, addressed the minister, through the Huntingdon Gazette, demanding an apology and retraction of his slanders. This receiving no answer, he published several *Letters* explaining the true doctrine of the Church and answering such of the minister's objections as a gentleman could notice.

These Letters created a great exitement, were soon published in one pamphlet, and went through many editions in a few years. Later they were enlarged "by permission of the author," somewhat toned down, diluted, changed in arrangement, and published in Baltimore as : "*A Defence of Catholic Principles in a letter to a Protestant Clergyman, by Rev. Demetrius A. Gallitzin*.[*] Originally the signature was in full with his favorite addition *Catholic Priest of Loretto*, and was the first public use of his name beyond the columns of the newspapers of the vicinity. When he thus came out of the obscurity of his mountain parish, and boldly advanced to take up the gauntlet for the Church, it was like the coming forth from their desert caves of Anthony and the old hermits into the streets of Alexandria and Rome, when persecution was at hand; their long silent lips pouring forth the hoarded eloquence of their prolific solitude, confounding the scholars, the great, and wise, hurling the thunderbolts of unalterable truth in the face of despots; going about exhorting the timid, sustaining the weak, laying holy hands upon the heads so soon to wear the martyr's crown, gathering up sacred relics for generations to come, and when persecution dropped exhausted, returning to silence and the desert as before.

By means of these letters Gallitzin, if we mistake not, was the first in this country to enter the controversial lists in behalf of the Church. His success was from the beginning

---

[*] Now published by the Catholic Publication Society, New York.

most remarkable; this and a second little book written some years later, have been translated into German and French, and widely circulated in England, Ireland, France and Germany, as well as all over the United States; it is said by American and Irish bishops and priests, who have ample opportunities for judging, that they know of no books of their kind in the English language which have made so many converts. Hardly was the *Defence* published than he was applied to for instruction and reception into the Church, by whole families of his own neighborhood, among them persons who had been notoriously bitter against Catholics, while others came great distances for the same purpose, most of whom had never heard or read a word in explanation of the Church's doctrines beyond that contained in his letters to Mr. Johnson; after the publication of his second pamphlet, the *Letter on the Holy Scriptures*, as many as seventeen stood up at one time in the little church at Loretto and made their profesion of faith. The incidents related in connection with these conversions are innumerable; one of the best known is, perhaps, that of Hayden Smith, the architect, son of Irish Protestants, brought up in such hatred of the Church that his father when dying, enjoined upon him never to associate with Catholics, or touch their books or anything belonging to them, of course never to enter a Catholic church, if possible to avoid living in the same town with Catholics. So solemn and earnest, we should say so horrible, was this death-bed injunction that it made the deepest impression and the youth determined to carry it out to the very letter; he journeyed from city to city in England, Ireland, Canada and the United States, but everywhere the cross was before him, the Catholics about him; finally, he found himself in one of the bitterest towns of Pennsylvania, where the most violent animosity to the Catholics was freely displayed. In that very stronghold of ignorance and prejudice, Mr. Smith met with a copy of the *Defence of Catholic Principles*, he was about to throw it down in disgust, when it occurred to him that nothing could afford him better arguments against the despised Catholics than one of their own absurd books; he read, and he believed; he could not doubt, was received into the Church, and spent the greater portion of his long life in planning Catholic churches; he was the architect of the brick church in Loretto, of St. Mary's in Lancaster, and many others, and at the time of his death was occupied in beautifying the famous Central Park in New York.

.An Irish Protestant is a hard man to soften, but he is more than matched by an old fashioned Scotch Presbyterian. The first Protestant family to settle in the present Cambria county is believed to be that of John Douglas, a rigid Presbyterian in whose mind the wars of the Stuarts was fresh and intensely clear. His descendants were not less bitterly anti-papist,—never could they bring themselves to call Catholics by their right name,—and in the midst of the Catholics constantly increasing about them, preserved all the bitterness and hatred of their creed and country, and being stalwart, athletic men worthy of their famous name, gifted with "unco" power in argument, discussions with them were not very eagerly sought; one in particular seemed endowed with an especial gift for "rigging the papishers," as his neighbors expressed it; ridicule, contradiction, contempt, the most venomous abuse was always ready for the least allusion to anything Catholic, while in argument he had the true Presbyterian long-windedness, only growing more powerful as his adversary's lungs and brains showed signs of weakness and confusion; he not only had the Bible at his finger's end, but he could expound on any text, "as good as any preacher," and interpret the knottiest point, the most confused metaphor, the most mystical expression with perfect ease. It is true, he was not afraid of his enemy, and would listen very willingly to hear what his opponents might wish to say for themselves, but it sometimes appeared that the canny Scot only listened for a purpose, for he would forge weapons out of their own words to fight them anew.

It happened that this gentleman one morning called upon a Catholic family, whom he found at breakfast; as he had already breakfasted, he declined their invitation to join them, and took up a book with which to entertain himself while waiting; it proved to be a controversial work, such as Gallitzin approved of and was glad to see in the houses of his parishioners. When about leaving Mr. Douglas asked permission to take it with him, but a young lady of the house said: "Oh, it is a religious book and I am sure you won't like it," but he insisted and carried it away with him, and it perhaps made a deeper impression upon him than he knew or would have owned to himself. He read the Huntingdon war sermon with triumphant delight, and looked for Gallitzin's letters with great eagerness, but their effect was very opposite to his expectations; he saw to his dismay that the arguments were unanswerable, and too brave a character to fail acting in accordance with his convictions, he gave in his allegiance to the truth. Gallitzin welcomed him right warmly (an honest foe turned to a friend is far more to be loved and trusted than one who is a little of each), and with a certain kindly humor peculiarly his own, very winning to a rugged, earnest nature. Dr. Gallitzin did not think it necessary in this conversation to make any elaborate attack on Protestantism, for, like a house of cards, that uncertain structure does not require to be fought in detail, the very breath of truth passing by, makes it shake and totter to its fall, and, perhaps, he shrewdly surmised that the affair would long ago have tumbled for Mr. Douglas, had not its crumbling sides been held together by the iron bands of hatred of the Church. In the end Mr. Douglas became a devout Catholic, an ardent champion of the religion he had so long abused, so much so that it was said there was not a layman far or near, who could so well explain and expound the Catholic doctrine as he; but this not without many trials, for his relatives were almost heartbroken at the change, and felt it as a disgrace to the family. It required the greatest effort of Christian charity on his part to forgive the Catholics of his early acquaintance for not knowing their religion better, and for letting him so often silence or confuse them in argument; he himself brought a number of others to Gallitzin for final instruction and reception into the Church. It was remarkable that Dr. Gallitzin's converts though not always of high standing or wide influence, almost invariably brought him more, as if they could never rest until they had proved their gratitude to God for the grace bestowed upon them, by being his instrument in conveying the same glorious gift to others, which is, indeed, the feeling of all true converts, the world over.

In those days the spirit which warred against the Church, though no more malicious than now, was less subtle and insidious; it was bold, vituperative, ill bred, very loud and vulgar; Gallitzin met it with manly courtesy and true Christian charity.

The Protestant minister had represented the Catholic religion as the grossest superstition, and went over the huge catalogue of slanders with which we are as familiar as with the nursery story of the HOUSE THAT JACK BUILT, which is one much more logically founded and put together than the edifice of falsehood which is ever falling down, and ever being built up again by the votaries of error, who, as the world goes on, pick up the dropping stones, laying them on again, anywhere where they can be made to stay, until the whole affair has come to present such an incongruous and unsafe appearance that its defenders are growing ashamed of it themselves, and would willingly destroy it and build it anew, could they find any but the same old crumbling stones, thrown up in heretical eruptions, years ago, to do it with.

Dr. Gallitzin took up the general charge of superstition, defined the word's meaning, and reviewed the doctrines of the Church to see if among them could be found one to agree with the definition and support the minister's accusation. This summary of the Catholic doctrine is brief, clear, and concise, every point supported by passages from Scripture. This done he takes up "those tenets which distinguish the Catholic Church from all others", these are: Confession, the Holy Eucharist, the Sacrifice of the Mass, Communion under one kind or form, Purgatory and prayers for the dead, Honoring the Saints and applying for their intercession, Veneration of images, pictures and relics, and the Pope. In explanation of each he gives the real Catholic doctrine, the scriptural texts which support it, brief testimony of the Fathers of the Church, references to the Councils which have defined it, even the approval and belief of Protestant leaders, especially of the reformers, for it appears that each of these clung to some one doctrine of the Church, while rejecting the rest, so that among them all pretty much the whole truth may be found, broken, mutilated disfigured, buried in the rubbish of error, of no use to the owners, until they join hands, put what they have together and find completion in the Catholic Church. He then passes on to consider and refute the principal objections urged against these doctrines, and all this with such force and clearness, such unexpected and subtle charm of chosen words, with now and then a gleam of quiet humor, of keenest sarcasm, that the attention is riveted to the least detail, and even the dryest explanation has its own fascination. When, by consideration of the doctrines peculiar to the Church, he has shown the charge of superstition to be entirely groundless, Gallitzin answers admirably the charge of intolerance, so often-brought against the Church by those whose limited understanding can see no reason why truth should object to fraternize with error, and in conclusion adresses the minister directly, with true priestly dignity and soul stirring eloquence.

The ministers had so long had it all their own way that a reply from the Catholic side had never entered their calculations; such an answer as this in language suited to the simplest intelligence, and yet taxing the profoundest intellect, by an evident masterhand, could not be passed over. The members of Mr. Johnson's congregation freely admitted their inability to confute it, controversy was not their business, but it *was* their minister's, it was one of the things they had engaged him for, and they looked to him to demolish his antagonist. Mr. Johnson spent nearly two years in preparing a reply which he entitled: *A Vindication of the Reformation*, in which he made a show of answering the arguments put forward in the DEFENCE, taking up certain minor points to which Gallitzin had alluded, and misquoting his words with that lovely disregard for the sacredness of quotation marks which is the instinctive refuge of hunted error, all the world over; the rest of his pamphlet being made up of the old slanders, so fully met by the DEFENCE, and such other loud assertions of things he must have known to be false as his ingenuity could devise or reading furnish, Gallitzin did not deem him worthy of reply, but addressed an APPEAL TO THE PROTESTANT PUBLIC in which the weakness of the *Vindication* was thoroughly exposed, with an entreaty to right minded people to seek the truth above all things.

Mr. Johnson's congregation were so vexed at his failure to sustain his part in the controversy that they turned him off as an incompetent workman. This was manifest injustice, for although the minister had not shown himself foeman worthy of Gallitzin's steel, he had by no means fallen below his brethren in logic or in style; his *Vindication* as an argument for Protestantism was much superior to many more pretentious books published before and since in the same interest; but, unfortunately for his credit, his lot was cast among a set of people who did not understand the difficulty of his position, and when they saw their cause getting the worst of it believed it to be all the fault of their champion. It is consoling to learn that, later, a number of Protestants who had taken part against him after his discomfiture, becoming better acquainted with the subject of discussion, openly acknowledged their injustice, for he had really gallantly defended a very weak cause. Gallitzin himself, a few years afterwards, publicly thanked him for his *Vindication* which had considerably enlarged the congregation of St. Michael's, and "if I had any favor," he said*, "to ask of the Protestant minister, it would be that he would please continue to write against the Catholic Church, and to vindicate the doctrines of the reformation. I promise to make a good use of his writings, and to draw from them a great deal of useful information, for the conversion of all sorts of Protestants to the Catholic faith."

---

* Preface to *Letter on the Holy Scriptures.*

The DEFENCE was not only carefully read by many Protestants, and eagerly welcomed by all the Catholics of Pennsylvania who had long borne the sneers and gibes of their Protestant neighbors, without any authority to show for their replies beyond their own word, but it was of the greatest service to the priests all over the country, who were, for the most part, the hard-working pastors of poor, despised and illiterate flocks, set in the midst of sharp Yankee wits and shrewd American Protestants not very well read, but with the Bible at their finger ends, as familiar to them as the Multiplication Table, men with keen, investigating minds, however narrow their mental vision, who could discuss religion day in and day out, with Jew, Christian and Mahomedan, in season and out of season, with cheerful and serene disregard of all logical rules. Many of the priests had difficulty in speaking English fluently, and though of necessity patient and admirable controversialists once they set about it, had seldom half an hour to spare for an "argument"; the DEFENCE was short, cheap, suited to the most ordinary intelligence, if those who sought discussion were sincere they would find in the little pamphlet all explanation and instruction that could be desired, if they were not sincere the less of our clergymen's precious time they took up in useless discourse the better. "I am on my way to my native country (Orleans)," Rev. Stephen Badin wrote in May 1819," where I have family concerns to settle. I take with me your *Apology for the Catholic Religion*" (Mr. Badin means DEFENCE, Gallitzin was the last man in the world to make an apology for that which never could require one) "which will be a memorandum ever dear to me. I am informed that you are about to reply to an answer of the minister; it would be equally agreeable to me to take that additional token of your faith to Europe.... I have made remittances to the Rev. Mr. O'Brien for the one hundred copies of your work...."

The *Defence* was written in the winter of 1814-15 and the *Appeal to the Protestant Public,* in consequence of the length of time required for the minister's rejoinder, full two years later; but though the controversy ended there as far as discussion between the original combatants was concerned, Dr. Gallitzin was not allowed to lay down his pen as easily as it had been taken up. He received letters from all parts of the country in relation to the subjects treated in his little book, and was drawn into correspondence with many Protestants, strangers to him, who wished to discuss further some points of difference between Catholics and Protestants, to whom he had not always time to reply; he was strongly urged to appear once more in print and in a letter to one answer the questions and solve the doubts of many, who were not ready to acknowledge themselves convinced by what he had already written, to which he finally consented, and in 1819 published the LETTER TO A PROTESTANT FRIEND ON THE HOLY SCRIPTURES, *being a continuation of the Defence of Catholic Principles** already mentioned. This is a complete and elaborate refutation of the charge that the Catholic Church rejects the Bible, which was a famous accusation in those days, when nearly all the sects professed the most extraordinary reverence and affection for the Holy Scriptures, from which they drew the religion or creed which best suited themselves. It is written in a more polished and leisurely manner than the *Defence*, which was necessarily more of a summary, full of unction, and ardent charity, and lighted by his own peculiar humor, keen, delicate, lightly veiled, the gleam of summer sunshine through the fast falling rain of grave and earnest thoughts. After answering the absurd charge that the Church concealed the Scriptures, when it is to her alone we owe their preservation, proving the necessity of an infallible guide to make us sure that the Bible is really the word of God, devoting three chapters to the *canon, the faithful translation* and the *true sense of Scripture*, he explains some matters of Church discipline which distorted, like her doctrines, by those who hate her, had reached and troubled the mind of his "Protestant friend;" they have a whole repertory of these which they go through year after year, generation after generation, just as comfortably as though

---

* New York; Catholic Publication Society.

the calumnies had never been told or refuted before. In this *Letter* Gallitzin took up and explained the true meaning, history, or reason of adoption of the celibacy of the clergy, the Inquisition, works of superogation, persecution of Protestants, miracles wrought by priests and monks, and the celebration of Mass in an unknown tongue, and concludes:

My dear Protestant brethren:

"Do not be deceived; there is only ONE LORD, ONE FAITH, AND ONE BAPTISM. (Eph. iv.) Only ONE church, raised by the hands of Jesus Christ, against which all the powers of hell shall never prevail. (Mat. xvi. 18.) Only ONE church in which the Spirit of Truth abides for ever. (John, xiv. 16.) Only ONE ark of salvation, of which Jesus Christ is the pilot, until the consummation of the world. (Mat. xxviii. 20.) Whoever is not in that one only vessel shall suffer shipwreck; whoever will not hear that church will meet the fate of heathens and publicans. (Mat. xviii. 17.)

............"To know all these things, my brethren, is so essentially necessary for salvation, and to know them is so completely impossible, without a divine infallible or unerring authority, that, to deny this infallible authority, so clearly and pointedly established by Christ, is to subvert the religion of Jesus Christ, and to establish in its place the fluctuating opinions of men.

"Pray then, my friends, pray sincerely, that your eyes may be opened; pray for humility to submit your understanding in all matters of religion to the dictates of the ancient church of Jesus Christ, which alone is guided by the Spirit of Truth for ever, which alone is Catholic or universal, spread among all nations and embracing about three-fourths of Christendom, which alone is the immaculate spouse of Christ, without spot or wrinkle."

With these two volumes in their hands, there was little, if they dared to read them, left for Protestants to doubt or misunderstand. Gallitzin never went out of his way to make converts, but as he said well:* "Protestants, as

---

* Preface to *Letter on the Holy Scriptures.*

long as I live I shall consider it my duty to undeceive you; to remove the prejudices in which you have been raised; to counteract the schemes by which the ministers of the pretended reformation have ever tried to render the Catholic Church odious and ridiculous. I shall never cease calling upon you in the name of your and my Saviour, to forsake the criminal schism in which you live, and to return to the pale of the Catholic Church from which your ancestors departed." He never permitted them to pass over the plain words of the Bible: *who believeth not shall be condemned.* Once they saw the necessity of a consistent religion their path to the Church lay plain enough before them, but he was well aware that to know is not always to do; he did not expect intellectual conviction to make men Catholics, it is not every one who has looked at the truth who is found worthy to receive it, and of all miseries what can be more poignant, more crushing, than to stand outside the barred gates of the Church, knowing heaven can be reached only through them, and lack the loving will to throw one's sins or worldly belongings behind and enter in! So to his instructions Gallitzin added the sweet example of a most beautiful life, fasted, prayed, and endured many mortifications for others' sake, obtaining grace for many a wavering one to walk firmly over the pitfalls of doubt and temptation into the safety of the Church; he seemed given a special wonderful power to melt their hearts as the rock of old under Aaron's rod; his voice, his eyes, his least touch was magnetic, ever more so as years passed on, and he grew thinner and more saintly in his appearance, as if the soul, for which his body was but the slight, transparent shell, was every day increasing its dominion, shining out fairer and stronger, and mastering the base material in all others. Great, hearty, blustering men, full of their own conceits, would come to out-argue the frail and low-voiced priest, and when they had been a few minutes in his presence forgot every argument so carefully impressed on their memory before coming, or felt what they would say answered before spoken, dissolving into puerility as they were about to sound it forth; even strangers passing him in the street, having no idea who he was, and merely glancing indifferently at him have mentioned the singular impression made upon them, as in the instant of passing, the bright, gleaming eyes with one glance startled and aroused them as from sleep, puzzling and piercing them through with a passing look, and in more than one case the most unexpected results followed words and actions of his, apparently certain of producing the very opposite effect.

The story is told of a stranger going, as the Protestants of the whole neighborhood often did, to the church at Loretto to hear "Priest Gallitzin" preach, -- his sermons were much like his writings, animated, always dignified, and pointed, — who found it so crowded that he could only get about half way up the stairs to the choir, where he stood wedged in with others pressed out like himself, who, being Catholics, were all devoutly kneeling, which he scorned to do. He was gazing intently at the "popish" altar, with due disgust for the prostrate crowd, standing more upright and rigid as he marked their lowliness, when the priest, in his cassock, came to the stairs above him; suddenly a hand just touched his shoulder, as Gallitzin said, gently: "Every one kneels here," and he told afterwards, that the instant the priest touched him, he felt as if he had been struck by lightning, his knees trembled and gave way before the last word was spoken, so that he could not have stood again during the service had he tried.

Usually a look to a stranger, however obdurate and determined, was enough, but once a look did not suffice. One of his most trusted parishioners had married a Protestant lady residing some distance from Loretto, whom he brought home with him, to the no small distraction of his neighbors, for she was plentifully supplied with all the fine fashions which had been so rigidly excluded from Father Gallitzin's congregation. She was very much "down" on the Catholics, although she had so far conquered her distaste as to marry one, probably expecting him to keep his religion entirely in the background. She listened rather contemptuously to the conversations in which the pastor of Loretto was mentioned, and understood that he was law and gospel for the poor, benighted people surrounding her, which, likely, heightened her antagonism and strengthened her opposition to him, his Church, and all connected with his religion or influence; but of this she said little, and consented, to her husband's delighted surprise, to accompany him to church on the Sunday following her removal to Loretto. Naturally her appearance was an event; she was large and fine looking, handsomely dressed, thorough mistress of herself, and stood conspicuously on the women's side, near the boundary line, calmly but intently watching every movement of the priest, too well bred to affect indifference, vulgar curiosity or to show fatigue. The least irregularity, the slightest movement, not in order, of any of his congregation, never failed to attract Dr. Gallitzin's attention, drawing upon the offender a rebuke as straight and swift as a flash of lightning; no one ventured to watch the new comer lest they should be suddenly in disgrace, but those whose hearts were not as absorbed in their prayers as they should have been, though they knelt like marble statues, motionless, expected every second to hear the very rafters tremble at his voice commanding her to kneel. But Mass went on quietly, and whenever they dared steal a look from under demure eyelashes at the stranger, they saw her standing unflinchingly, steadily, quietly watching all that was passing at the altar; whatever distress the irreverence caused Father Gallitzin he made no sign, until his very silence became more oppressive to the others than the most ringing command, perhaps he saw what no one else did, that in her defiance there was no boldness, nor thought of what she was doing, but a simple determination never to bend her knee to the idols of the heathen. Finally, he turned to give communion, facing the congregation, the chalice in his hands; before giving the absolution, he looked at her signing to her with that look to kneel; but she confronted him with perfect calmness, gazed straight at him, and remained standing as a sentry at his post; then his eyes flashed with the eagle look that terrified the children, and before which an army might well go down as one man, but she did not waver even when he motioned to her to kneel; then he said in a low voice, never disobeyed before, "Kneel down, woman, kneel down!" but she changed neither her attitude nor expression, though around her the women and girls nearly fainted in terror, half expecting some visible judgment from heaven to fall upon them all, in revenge for the disobedience to God's minister, the irreverence to the Blessed Sacrament; an instant after, as the thunder breaks through the dark, intolerable calm before the storm, it came again, crashing through the church, far beyond the church, terrible in wrath: "WOMAN, KNEEL DOWN"; and she knelt; not the stoutest oak of the forest but would crouch before the tornado of those three words thus spoken.

He went on with the remainder of the Mass, unagitated, stately, gentle, reverential as ever. But he had not forgotten what had occurred. After Mass he always read the Gospel of the day in English and in German, and gave his sermon; for his English sermon of this day he made some remarks telling why he could not give communion while any head was unbowed or knee unbent, because it is the body and blood of Christ, actually present.

"You who are Catholics," he said, "know well that the Sacrifice of the Mass at which you have just assisted, is the greatest of all Sacrifices, of which the offerings of the Old Law, the most holy and the most sacred which the world knew of for thousands of years, were but figures and types. You know what terrible punishments were inflicted by God upon the Israelites for the least transgression of the ceremonies prescribed for their sacrifices, the least irreverence in holy places; if then, so much, under such dreadful penalties, was required for the type what must be the demand for the reality, and the punishment of transgression?" He then spoke of the awfulness of the Sacrament for which the Mass was a preparation and a thanksgiving, and of the grief caused to every Catholic heart by any irreverence to it, so much so that for ages people have devoted their lives to prayers and mortification and adoration in reparation for the coldness and disrespect of the world, while others have gladly laid down their lives to preserve it from insult. Why this belief should be held he explained at length, giving the history of the institution of this most holy Sacrament, and a most clear and thorough account of the doctrine concerning which even the disciples exclaimed: *This is a hard saying; who can believe it.*

All this was spoken in a kindly manner, but full of authority, as of a father explaining to his children, and like all his sermons was given in language so concise, so free from verbiage of ornament or repitition, that no one could fail to understand and remember it; many old persons whose memory was never cultivated, could repeat in their old age instructions he had given from the altar when they were but children, and this when they could hardly remember anything else. Generally he spoke quietly, but, at times, as on this occasion, his deep emotion would burst the bonds of self imposed restraint, his eyes would light up, his voice round to wondrous power and flexibillity, and words of burning eloquence come forth as from lips verily touched with sacred fire, until recollecting himself, he would force it back, and resume his calm, explanatory manner.

It was impossible to tell from the attitude of the lady who had given occasion for this incident, if she were stung to indignant resentment, ready to break forth at any moment, of if she were deeply and seriously offended beyond all future forgiveness; as she made no allusion to what had occurred, but refused to go again to church, to mention the subject of religion, or to read a Catholic book, her husband and family felt convinced it was an anger which would never pass away, and they deeply regretted that she had gone to church at all, since Dr. Gallitzin was so uncompromising, and devoid of tact.

"It is all up with her becoming a Catholic now," her husband said to his friends, "Dr. Gallitzin has settled that question," forgetting there was no question to settle, for she had never given the least hope of any change. "There was no occasion for such severity; my wife has been accustomed to kindness and respect, all her life, and now she is dead set against everything Catholic."

"Now, John," some one replied, "You have been so much among Protestants that you think too much of them. You know very well that a priest could not give communion with a person standing up in that way. I only wondered he didn't come out with it sooner, I never knew him wait so long before."

In a short time the young couple moved away from Loretto, the husband still feeling sore against its pastor, for his lack of conciliation, none the less so, that no one quite sympathized with him. About six months afterwards a lady accompanied by a young relative came to the village, and sending her escort in another direction went alone to the priest's house. Dr. Gallitzin received her, as he did every one, with a cordial smile and a hospitable welcome, but without responding to his courtesy, she said: "I do not suppose you know me, Sir; I am Mrs. So and So, the woman you told to kneel down in church about six months ago," as if that announcement would surely chill his reception of her, but he continued smiling, rather amused by her stiffness and expectation of severity from him. When she was seated, he looked up brightly to hear what she had to say, and when she reminded him that she was the Protestant wife of a Catholic husband, he answered frankly:

"I know it, I was very sorry indeed that one of my best parishioners should have married outside the Church."

"You do not approve of the marriage of Catholics and Protestants?"

"By no means," with emphasis, "the Church disapproves of it most decidedly, and I never permit it in my congregations."

"But what could you expect John to do," she asked, "if we loved each other and were otherwise suited?"

"Did he not instruct you in the Catholic religion?"

"I would not listen to one word about it."

"Did he not give you any books to read?"

"I would not have touched them."

"He did very wrong," replied the priest gravely, "I would not have thought it possible one of my own boys that I have instructed from his cradle, would have done such a thing; he should have explained his religion to you."

The lady smiled a little; the priest unconsciously assumed that had she known she would, of course, have believed. "I have come to you now to know if you will receive me," she answered. He brightened up with almost childlike joy, and answered warmly: "Ah, I ought to know John would attend to his duty! So he has explained to you?"

"John has nothing to do with it," she replied, "I have never said one word about it, but I have believed the Catholic religion to be the true one from the moment you told me to kneel down that day in church. I never had an idea that Catholics really believed as they said in the Real Presence and other things, but I knew you did or you would not have spoken to me, and as I knelt I believed myself."

"Why did you not come sooner?"

"I wanted to be calm about it, and, besides, all my husband's relations wanted to convert me, and force me into the Church to please him."

Gallitzin understood perfectly, and did not too severely rebuke the natural pride which had endeavored to show she had become a Catholic from conviction, not from compliance, or the influence of affection. Great was the surprise and joy of all when, having been duly prepared, she came out and bravely announced herself a Catholic. Afterwards she removed with her husband to Baltimore where he acquired a large fortune, and high social standing, establishing a character for uprightness and charity which was more precious still, and which his wife fully sustained.

Thus by his writings, his personal influence, the light of his own faith, his saintly life, assisted by the piety and virtue of his once obdurate congregation, now thoroughly devoted to their religion in practice as in theory, Father Gallitzin enlivened the faith in many cold and indifferent hearts, and brought into the fold of the Church many and many of those stray sheep for whom the Good Shepherd searches so anxiously. So many were prepared by reading and by his indirect influence, whom he could not personally address, that he needed to call them together by a public announcement, one of the most curious of advertisements, which appeared in the Cambria County Gazette in 1825:

Notice.

"A certain number of Protestants having manifested a great desire of becoming members of the Roman Catholic Church, I hereby acquaint the said Protestants, and the public in general, that I have appointed the Second Sunday after Easter (17. April), for admitting them into the Church, according to the Rites and Ceremonies of the Roman Ritual.

"Demetrius A. Gallitzin,
Parish Priest.

"Loretto, March 22, 1825."

This was responded to by calls for the necessary preparation, and a large group was received into the Church at the time specified, and many more during the summer.

CHAPTER XXI.

AT HOME AND ABROAD.

(1815—1823.)

Death of Archbishop Carroll. —Of Mr. Nagot —Withdrawal from the Society of Saint Sulpice. —Bishop Egan. —Philadelphia difficulties.— Bishop Conwell. —Father Gallitzin's plan for a diocese in Western Pennsylvania. —Bishoprics refused by him. —Death of Rev. Mr. Heilbron.—Appointment of Rev. F. X. O'Brien. —Irish laborers. —Rev. C. B. Maguire. —Rev. T. McGirr. —European affairs and marriage of the princess.

In the meantime many changes more or less directly affecting the pastor and people of Loretto, were taking place in the outside world. On the 3rd of December 1815 Archbishop Carroll breathed his last, at the age of eighty, after quarter of a century's service in the episcopal chair; a loss which caused Father Gallitzin double sorrow, for he mourned in the venerable prelate not only the deeply lamented father of the Church in the United States, but a friend and spiritual guide, who had been the first to receive him when he came in his youth to this country, a haughty young prince, full of ambition and affections long repressed, and yet a lonely boy in the crisis days of his life, had opened for him the gates of his ministry, and for twenty years had received his unlimited confidence, his unvarying reverence and affection. He could never enough admire the calm and prudent judgment, the cool, collected bearing, which distinguished the archbishop, and were so far beyond the reach of his own fiery and impetuous temperament; under the most trying circumstances their mutual esteem and affection seemed only to brighten and increase, continuing unabated even when the priest and his charge had passed to the jurisdiction of another bishop.

Archbishop Carroll was succeeded by Rev. Leonard Neale who had been his venerable coadjutor; at this time there were in the whole United States but eighty-five priests, of whom forty-six belonged to the diocese of Baltimore.* Archbishop Neale was already seventy years old, and laden with infirmities; he died in June 1817, and was succeeded by Rev. Ambrose Maréchal.

Only a few months after the death of Archbishop Carroll Father Gallitzin in common with the whole Church in America, was called upon to mourn the loss of his early director and superior, Rev. Francis Nagot. Although Father Gallitzin had joined the Society of Saint Sulpice while yet a deacon, and to the end of his life looked upon the seminary, where he was greatly beloved, as his home whenever he went to Baltimore, the great financial difficulties in which he had of late years been involved by the failure of his European remittances, caused him, with characteristic delicacy, to gradually avoid appearing as a Sulpitian, lest his temporal troubles might indirectly reflect discredit upon the Society, or possibly convey the idea that the seminary was in some way responsible for his debts, in which his superiors tacitly concurred, but this by no means diminished the affection existing between him and the venerable president, who had spoken so bravely and firmly for him in the days when all his friends united to oppose his entrance into the priesthood. He revered the president as he did the archbishop, as fathers of his clerical state; their loss left him the more desolate because they alone on this side of the ocean had known his mother's character and devotion, and by their correspondence with her up to the time of her death, had linked themselves with her in his thoughts, so that their death seemed to renew hers.

---

* *Shea's History*, p. 93.

When his charge passed from the Baltimore diocese to the new diocese of Philadelphia, Bishop Egan made no changes in his regard, but left him to go on in his own way with his work. Only one thing had he desired of the bishop but this without avail: that he would visit the interior of the state, and administer confirmation to all his congregations. Bishop Carroll had attempted to do so, but when he got so far as Chambersburg the accounts given him of the terrible state of the country, its wild forests, its impassable roads, its entire lack of accommodation, so alarmed him that he turned back, and those who desired to receive the strengthening sacrament and could afford the journey were obliged to go to Baltimore for it. Bishop Egan did reach Pittsburg, which was a fast-growing town, where the Catholics were just beginning to rise from a most deplorable condition of spiritual poverty and ignorance, having been until late years entirely without a priest, save when Father Heilbron, at long intervals, was able to visit them and say Mass in an old house hardly better than a stable, and also Brownsville where he celebrated Mass and administered confirmation in Major Noble's log cabin, but avoided as much as he could the rough interior, much as his heart must have yearned to leave the ninety-nine and seek the one lost in its wildernesses, this probably on account of the hard travelling and the great expense, the only mode of travelling practicable being on horseback; the congregations however desirous to see a bishop among them were unable to provide for him, and he himself felt too poor to undertake the long and toilsome journey on his own account. This was a bitter disappointment to the pastor, who burned to obtain this blessing for his people, set in the midst of temptations of all kinds, and greatly in need of the strong, sustaining and steadfast gifts of the Holy Ghost to enable them to battle manfully against all outer and inner foes, to persevere in virtue and preserve their faith through all things; there is no doubt that he was fully resolved the moment he received his patrimony to cheerfully bear the whole burden of expense, the whole labor of providing endurable means of travelling, smoothing by every effort of self-sacrifice and unlimited devotion the rugged mountain ways, if by so doing he could enable a bishop to reach his congregations.

Bishop Egan was a man of the most edifying piety and exemplary virtue, but it has been thought he lacked spirit and firmness in the matter of the Philadelphia church troubles, which rapidly grew beyond his control and undoubtedly shortened the years of his life; he died in 1814, and the greatest difficulty was experienced in finding a willing successor to his thorny mitre. It was first offered to Rev. Mr. Maréchal, on his refusal to Rev. Mr. David, who hastily declined it, then to Rev. Louis de Barth who had administered the affairs of the diocese since the death of the bishop with signal ability, but, perhaps because he knew better than any one else the difficulties of the position, he more positively and determinedly refused to hear of it, and it was finally bestowed upon Rev. Henry Conwell, Vicar-general of the diocese of Armagh, Ireland, a venerable clergyman, past seventy years of age, who ignorant of the state of affairs, accepted, was consecrated in London, immediately embarked for the United States, and entered into possession in 1820, perhaps as little fitted by age, temperament, and association to put down a fierce rebellion as any man who could have been chosen.

There was one person, much nearer the scene of action, who alone appears to have had the necessary force and firmness, the indomitable courage and the all-mastering will to face and to thoroughly conquer the storm the others dared not meet; it was the place for Father Gallitzin's immense faith and magnificent spirit; he alone appears endowed with that lion like nature, fortified by long trials and experienced in the wickedness of rebellious man, inspired and strengthened beyond all human force by the battle cry forever in his ears : *God wills it*, which fears not, single handed, to meet a legion of enemies. But a superior wisdom so ordered it that the evil thing should have its day and run its course.

Father Gallitzin had already been many times proposed for new bishoprics, and had steadily refused, finally stating his reasons in a letter to Bishop Flaget,* when becoming acquainted with the proposal to nominate him Bishop of Cincinnati, and afterwards to Archbishop Maréchal when nominated for Detroit, in such clear and decided manner, dwelling upon the position in which he stood towards his present charge, that it was plainly understood he was in earnest in his refusal, and would never voluntarily accept any position, however desirable, which should separate him from those who had become dependent upon him as upon a temporal and spiritual father, and for some years his peace was not disturbed by such proposals. For a time they had made him very unhappy, the fear that his objections would be overruled hung over him for many weeks, and when, at one time, all appearances indicated that he would be forced to accept a distant bishopric he was so depressed at the idea of going among strangers, of being placed in such an exalted position, from which his humility revolted all the more that he had the very highest idea of its dignity and responsibilities that his trouble communicated itself to his parishioners, and many of them came to feel almost as grieved for the distress it would be to him, as for the loss to themselves, and a great number were prepared to go with him, if he were forced to accept, that they might not be deprived of his care and he not be left alone among new scenes and new people. But in regard to the Philadelphia diocese it is possible, in view of the bitter troubles there, and its comparative nearness to Loretto which would still be in his charge, he might have been induced to accept had it been offered, but in that case it is hardly likely that the schism would have had full opportunity to manifest its malignity, or the tares been permitted to grow with the wheat until harvest time.

But though Father Gallitzin escaped the well known Philadelphia rebellion, he was not wholly relieved from the necessity of facing other troubles which rent his heart to see, and roused his very soul to meet. One of Bishop Conwell's first acts had been to appoint the pastor of Loretto vicar-

---

* *Life of Bishop Flaget*, by Archbishop Spaulding, pp. 166, 216, 250.

general of Western Pennsylvania, as he had been in reality for many years, all the congregations and the priests who from time to time officiated there looking up to him for advice for the settlement of difficulties of all kinds, but as the bishop did not define the limits of his jurisdiction he did not for some time exercise it in any formal manner.

In Westmoreland county, or that part of it which was in Mr. Heilbron's charge, the Catholics were very badly off indeed; the land left by Mr. Brauers, for lack of means to cultivate and keep it up failed to supply even the simple wants of good old Father Heilbron, while the congregations he was still able to attend having every reason to believe that were he a better farmer it would be fully sufficient, and feeling their purses well emptied by the expense of putting up a shed-church next his unfinished log-house, for which even the nails were an important item procured only with the greatest difficulty and at great price, paid him no salary, so that towards the end of his life, when his health and strength failed him his poverty was very great, until the congregations under his immediate care made him up a sum which secured him from actual need; he grew very feeble and was besides painfully afflicted by a tumor in the neck, for which he was induced to make a journey to Philadelphia, where the physicians advised him not to attempt having it removed; on his return he was obliged to rest at Carlisle, and his health not improving was overpersuaded to have the tumor taken out, after which he sank rapidly, and died there in 1815 or 16, at about seventy years of age; he was buried near the sacristy of St. Patrick's church. He was a most estimable priest, a courteous whole-souled gentleman, cheerful, affable, kind to all, excellent company and most thorough and exact in his spiritual duties, with a soldier like discipline and careful regard to details very rare to meet; his life in Westmoreland county was a most laborious one, and as he was past fifty when appointed to share with Father Gallitzin the immense district, now forming the dioceses of Pittsburg and Erie, his endurance appears almost miraculous. For the greater part of the first year of his missionary duties he attended mainly to the Catholics within comparatively easy reach of "Sportsman's Hall," as they had been so long without a priest, and required constant attention, instruction, and all the efforts of a zealous pastor to secure them in the practices of their religion; as soon as this was done he sought out Catholics everywhere, riding as Father Gallitzin in his district, thirty and forty miles to say Mass for two or three families in some lonely forest, with the same interest and willingness with which he visited the larger settlements, the principal of which were: Brownsville on the banks of the Monongahela River at the boundary of Fayette and Washington counties; the "Settlement," near Jacob's Creek, between Mount Pleasant, Westmoreland and Connellsville, Fayette County; Pittsburg, Redbank, Clarion County; Slippery Rock, Butler County; and Buffalo Creek, Armstrong County. After his death some of his parishioners moved to different parts of the state, and others unable to preserve their faith through the trials and spiritual neglect which ensued, fell away from their religion altogether; these were principally Irish families; but the generality retained the impress of his priestly care and imparted it to their descendants, missionaries who have since attended congregations once under his charge, most of whom were baptized by him, have joyfully observed the quiet and regularity with which they attended to their spiritual duties, without any of the extravagances and eccentricities of superficial piety, and the order and harmony of their sober, industrious lives.*

Shortly before the division of the original Baltimore diocese, Bishop Carroll appointed Rev. G. F. X. O'Brien, one of the earliest priests ordained by him, pastor of

---

* The greatest gratitude is due to Very Rev. James A. Stillinger for these reminiscences of Rev. Mr. Heilbron, whose apostolic labors for sixteen long years under the most trying circumstances, have been entirely overlooked by our historians. Very Rev. Mr. Stillinger has made it a labor of love to collect and preserve the memory of his venerable predecessor in the Westmoreland mission, and to keep alive the recollection of his edifying virtues and inestimable services to the Church in the United States.

Pittsburg, where there were not more than twenty Catholics, thus relieving Mr. Heilbron of the stations in its vicinity and farthest from "Sportsman's Hall". Father Gallitzin had earnestly entreated that Mr. O'Brien might be permitted to reside with him as assistant in his burdensome mission, for he knew him to be just such a priest as he would desire to have associated with him in his labors, but the bishop thought best to place him at Pittsburg within reach of the older missionary. He visited Mr. Heilbron, probably for the first time, on the feast of All Saints, Nov. 1. 1808, shortly after his ordination, and then set about building St. Patrick's church in Pittsburg, riding on horseback from there to Baltimore and back to obtain contributions from priests and laity; Bishop Carroll also subscribed liberally for it.

Besides attending this church, the Catholics in Brownsville and vicinity, he made occasional visits to Erie, where Mr. Heilbron had established a station, and at times, during Mr. Heilbron's sickness visited Greensburg, Sportsman's Hall, and Butler county, that these congregations might not be too long deprived of the sacraments and of the Holy Sacrifice. But though there were now three missionaries laboring in the field where there had so long been but two, Father Gallitzin obtained no relief from his burden, on the contrary, as time passed and the country filled up more rapidly, he found his own portion heavily increasing, while Mr. Heilbron's failing health obliged him to have an anxious care for those nearest his own district and beyond their pastor's ever shortening reach. After Mr. Heilbron's death, he and Mr. O'Brien had all upon their shoulders while awaiting the appointment of another pastor; Mr. O'Brien felt the strain greatly and his health very soon showed signs of breaking under the accumulation of hardships and solicitude, which had so long weighed upon his co-laborer. But as if their situation were not already hard enough it was decreed that a national turnpike should be made through Uniontown, Fayette County, and Brownsville, a state road from Chambersburg to Bedford, thence over the Alleghany mountains to Greensburg and Pittsburg, and still another from Harrisburg to Huntingdon, thence to Holidaysburg, by way of Ebensburg to Pittsburg; to be built by Irish laborers; Catholics, who rapidly emigrated to this country and lined the sides of the projected roads,* all clamorous for the attendance of a priest, and only these two missionaries, already pressed beyond endurance, to find time to visit them in their rough unfurnished shanties, put up for the moment's shelter, to say Mass on such a temporary altar as could be made from a few boards placed over barrels, when such props could be obtained which was only in the more luxurious quarters, eating, sleeping among them, and, it may be truly said, edified by them, for never does our religion appear more sublime, more catholic, than under such circumstances. Finally, in 1817, a new priest, Rev. Charles B. Maguire, arriving in this country, the administrator of the diocese, Very Rev. Louis de Barth, hastened to request him to take Mr. Heilbron's place at Sportsman's Hall, as it continued to be styled. Mr. Maguire accepted the charge, and having relatives in Cambria county, visited Father Gallitzin on the way, preaching a German sermon in the Loretto church, while the pastor, who was always regarded as a German, gave an English exhortation, somewhat to the surprise of the faithful who said: "Here an Irishman preaches in German and a German in English!"

Mr. Maguire was born in the County of Tyrone, Ireland, Dec. 16, 1770, just six days previous to Father Gallitzin's birth, in Holland; was educated at the propaganda, where he was ordained, and sent to Germany. His adventures there and afterwards in France during the stormiest days of the Revolution, his narrow escapes would fill a volume. At the time of his arrival in this country he was in the full vigor of his manhood, tall and portly, of a commanding presence, with a good humored, highly colored countenance, a rich, sonorous voice, ready command of language;—a popular preacher with no apparent predilections for the caves

---

* Again thanks to Very Rev. Mr. Stillinger. Much confusion has hitherto existed in regard to Mr. O'Brien, on account of different ways of spelling his name. He himself wrote it as here given.

of Egypt or the rocks of Subiaco, but one who thoroughly appreciated an easy chair, a dinner well served, a good story well told; jovial, witty, equal to any emergency, and overpowering in argument He was heartily welcomed by the Catholics of his new charge, and as "Sportsman's Hall" wore a very poverty-stricken appearance, it was thought by some of the flock to be entirely unworthy of so fine a personage, and an effort was made to have an exchange effected between it and Loretto, at which it is needless to say Father Gallitzin's long silenced enemies took heart and hope, but only for a moment, for the plan failed ignominiously.

The aspect of the farm at Sportsman's Hall was desolate indeed. Nothing could better illustrate the wisdom of Father Gallitzin's course in personally assuming all the debts of the church in his mission, retaining the land bought for it out of his own money, in his own name, to the endurance of the odium and distress occasioned by the necessary expense of keeping it up which he was so often unable to meet, than the troubles occasioned by the opposite way of necessity pursued in Westmoreland. There a few hundred acres of land given to the church some ten years previous to his purchase, had proved for already over twenty-five years a source of continual expense, of long litigation, of quarrels innumerable, unproductive, worse than useless, for lack of means or credit on the part of pastor or people to keep it in order, even to give it the first necessary cultivation. When it was clearly settled by the famous trial, that it should remain the property of the church as it was known Mr. Brauers intended, subject to the reverend occupant duly appointed, it was found necessary to let out portions of it, as the only means of getting it cleared and cultivated, but the tenants generally failed to make a living from it, no one having money enough to start it, as Father Gallitzin had his.

By the advice of Mr. O'Brien the congregation prepared for Mr. Heilbron's successor by finishing the log house he had left, adding a new room to it. There had been a barn on the premises for many years but as it was now nearly in ruins, Mr. Maguire, who, like his predecessors intended to "farm" the land, promised the congregation if they would put him up a new one, he would go to Europe and collect money enough to build them a brick church on the site designated by Father Brauers, but he was not able to do so, although the congregation at once generously acceeded to his request, taking upon themselves the whole labor and expense which, for those times and their means, was very great indeed. Mr. Maguire, who had his brother and sister with him, found himself unable to bear the temporal difficulties and spiritual burdens his position imposed upon him, and in 1820 retired to Pittsburg, to the great dissatisfaction of the people who had done their best to keep him, and were distressed at the prospect of being again without a resident pastor.

Mr. O'Brien's health had become so much impaired by his laborious life, that he was obliged at this time to yield up his charge, and retire to Maryland, where he died on the feast of All Saints 1832, just twenty-four years from the day he first visited Mr. Heilbron at Sportsman's Hall.

"I became acquainted with Rev. Father O'Brien," writes Rev. Mr. Stillinger, "at Conewago whilst I was a student at Mt. St. Mary's.... He related to me some of his hardships on the mission in Western Pennsylvania. I did not think at that time that I should be going over the same ground. His health was delicate and his constitution so much impaired that he had no hopes of recruiting it again. He was, however, pleasant and cheerful, and his conversation very edifying and agreeable."

By Mr. O'Brien's retirement Mr. Maguire became pastor of St. Patrick's, the Westmoreland Catholics were again without a shepherd, and once more Western Pennsylvania was shared by two priests. Mr. Maguire, however, made one or two visits to his former charge, where his brother still retained possession of the farm, and Bishop Conwell being now settled in Philadelphia, appointed Rev. Terrence McGirr resident pastor, who arrived in 1821, but was not able to move at once to Sportsman's Hall, as Mr. Maguire's brother was yet ther

Mr. McGirr was just such an Irish priest as we sometimes read about, but now rarely meet; he was good at heart, devoted to his religion, equal to any hardship it might require of him, humble, simple minded, sound and ripe within undoubtedly, but with the roughest and most prickly outer shell, entirely undisturbed by the usual conventionalities of life, and, unfortunately, as careless of the decorum and dignity his sacred profession required; his manner of speaking from the altar was the same he used in ordinary life, and in ordinary life it was rough, unreserved, often harsh and in the last degree overbearing. Father Gallitzin had only time to thank God for a third missionary, before his heart was rent by rumors of disagreements between the new comer and his parishioners, between those in possession of the farm upon his arrival and those who expected to have charge of it under him.

No one could have a higher conception of the dignity of the character of a clergyman than Father Gallitzin, in his own person he never departed from it, and in whatever circumstances he was placed, whether in his own church, by the sick-bed of his people, in the laborer's shanty, among the children, in the offices of business men, or in the courts, his sacred calling could never be mistaken, the Catholic priest breathed in every word he spoke, was engraven in every line of his countenance. He burned with indignation at the account of any indignity to a clergyman, and the misconduct of one filled his eyes with tears, while it aroused his fiercest wrath. Not only in life and in manner but even in the smallest details of dress and bearing he desired to see only the priest. It is related that he was one day called upon by a gentleman of unusually elegant appearance, wearing a high standing collar and the elaborate ruffles then in fashion. As he saw the visitor coming up the path to his door, he met him with the kindly smile, the softly searching gaze, the cordial welcome which never failed friend or stranger, rich or poor, the known or unknown, who crossed his threshold; he drew him gently in, and not until the guest was as comfortably placed as the simply furnished room permitted did he leave opportunity for the self introduction he appeared eager to make; when all hospitable duties were complied with, for

"The good house, though ruined, O my son,
Endures not that her guest should serve himself,"

he listened attentively to his explanation, from which it appeared that the visitor was a Catholic clergyman, at which Father Gallitzin expressed some surprise: "I had no idea of it," he said; "from your dress and general appearance I supposed you a man of the world. No man should disdain his uniform. We should always bear our sacred calling with us wherever we may go," he added kindly, rising as he spoke, and gravely but with irresistible gentleness, with light and rapid touch turning down the high collar, and buttoning the coat over the ruffles which had so misled him, and then surveying the change, continued: "Whenever you do me the honor to call upon me in the dress suited to your rank, I shall be most happy to receive you."

Inhospitality to a priest was a crime in his eyes, as one instance never to be forgotten in Cambria County attests. A poor priest, homeless and ill, found his way to Loretto, and appealed to the pastor for aid. Father Gallitzin saw that on account of his own limited quarters he could not give him the comfort, the space, and attention his health required, and made arrangements with a well-to-do couple living in a commodious house near at hand, to receive the sick man and take all care of him. Soon afterwards he himself was obliged to go to Philadelphia, and the first news he heard on his return was that, during his absence, the sick priest had been sent away by the people with whom he had been placed, had dragged himself to a stump of a tree in a neighboring field, where he was found half sitting, half lying down, and nearly dying, by some passers by who carried him to the nearest shelter, where he died. Nothing could exceed Father Gallitzin's indignation and anguish at the news, he turned about and went at once to those who had done the inhuman deed, and for once in his life threatened vengeance, God's vengeance upon an evil doer: "You could not even leave him a bed to die in," he said, "and neither of you shall die in your bed." Not long after the woman died a wretched death, frozen at night in the open field not far from her own door, and the man was eaten up by wild animals in the woods.

With such veneration for the priesthood it can be imagined with what grief he heard, first that Mr. Maguire had left his charge, and next that Mr. McGirr was meeting with opposition on all hands. It also revived the memory of all that he himself had suffered, and crediting Mr. McGirr with a sensitiveness others failed to discover, he treated him with the utmost kindness, and was repaid by discovering under the rude and despotic exterior a warmth of attachment to himself, a submission to his advice which gave him great hopes that he would soon win his way to the affection of his congregations. But still foreseeing difficulties in the future, he felt anxious and troubled, distressed to see such a large portion of the beautiful vineyard of the Lord permitted to run to waste, the places already promising fruitful harvest becoming oversowed with tares, and the bishop whose strong hands should guard the land, too far away, and harrassed by more immediate cares to attend to it. It was at this time he began to press his idea of forming a new diocese out of the western portion of the state, with the episcopal see in its centre, from which the whole could be easily overlooked.*

His own private affairs continued to give him much uneasiness and to exercise all his prudence and skill. In 1817 he received a letter from his sister in which it was written: "In order to save the property for you I have sold it." This was indeed joyful news, for it was sold to a person worth millions, and he considered himself perfectly safe, master of a handsome property and as he said himself, his only uneasiness in that year proceeded from his temporary inability

---

* Archbishop Spaulding considers this idea to have been first mentioned in 1825, by whom not stated (*Life of Bishop Flaget*, p. 250), but as will be seen by the letter about to be given of Father Gallitzin to Archbishop Maréchal, the plan was proposed by him at least as early as 1823.

to satisfy his creditors who began to complain seriously of long protracted payments; people were now as anxious to lend him money as they had formerly been reluctant to do so, for no one could doubt that a magnificent sum would soon reach him. With these loans he paid off a large portion of his debts, built and invested in several mills, tanneries, etc., in order to start such industries, no one else having any capital to put into them, and then built the famous frame church which in size, style, and thorough workmanship surpassed anything even contemplated in that whole section of country. Catholics and Protestants came great distances just to see it, and when they went home described it to their neighbors as something really fine. It was built on an elevation near his own house, in the simplest form, but in the most durable manner, the altar at the east end, a gallery for the choir opposite, and from the door from early spring to late autumn as lovely a view as the eye may often meet, and in midsummer, when fields on fields of many colored grain, with here and there the dark foliage of the innumerable hills to guard them, glance in the brilliant sunlight, there is seen a luxuriant feast of color never to be forgotten. Standing on the church steps it is as if nature laid all her wealth and beauty at its feet, and within all that could be done to make the house of the Lord fair and edifying had been thoroughly secured; it is true, that was but little, but the very absence of profuse ornament, the quiet-colored walls, the simple altar free from all glaring, discordant hues, would prove a rest and solace to the eyes of the devout worshipper even in our day. An exquisite neatness, a general air of devotion pervaded it, and only God can tell what beautiful souls went straight to heaven through the narrow doors of that now neglected and discarded temple.

The murmurs which had arisen when the log church was enlarged were, of course, renewed when a far larger and handsomer church was planned, but as Father Gallitzin paid all the expenses no murmurs prevented its completion, and though for a short time the congregation seemed lost in it, as before children grew up, new people moved into the neighborhood, converts came and brought their families, so that soon they were kneeling close together even in that roomy temple, then the gallery stairs and outside steps became so crowded the door could not be closed, and, at last, even the windows had to be left open that those who could not get inside might still hear Mass, and see the altar.

But while he was building this church with gratitude to God for his final success, a new and most unexpected blow was being prepared for him; in that very year his sister, then forty-eight years old, became a bride; and two weeks afterwards wrote to her brother as the Princess of Salm Reifferscheid-Krantham, saying: "However, dearest brother, my new state of life will not cause the least alteration in the relation which exists between you and me. My husband is too noble minded to have sought anything else by forming this new connection than a helpmate and a friend.... and would have it that I should keep the full possession and control over my property, and declared before our marriage that you should lose nothing by it."

But although he did not in the least doubt his sister's word, knowing her embarrassments being now ended by the possession of so much ready money at her command, paid and due her and him for the Russian property, that she could no longer have any difficulty in transmitting hundreds of thousands belonging to him, he was extremely impatient to have it in his hands, and as month after month passed away without any fulfillment of her promises, wrote the most earnest letters, not only to his sister as formerly, but to his mother's old friends also, insisting that something should be done, for he had not even yet received his share of his mother's property left to him in the most explicit manner by her will. These letters occasioned the greatest amazement among his friends abroad, who had hundreds of times heard his sister express the most anxious care for his interests, and understood from her that she was constantly dividing the income of her mother's and her father's property with him.

Instead of the promised payment he received about two years after the marriage, a letter without signature, but from a source he could easily divine, in which the writer, having heard of his situation by means of these informations, "considered himself bound in conscience," to inform him of the manner in which large sums paid into certain hands for him had been "applied for their own benefit, expenses incurred by their marriage, removing from Muenster to Duesseldorf, payment of some of their own debts" — and also that they received regular remittances from Russia. This letter would have aroused him to the truth, and have led him to different measures than any yet employed, had it not been immediately followed by various sums, amounting in all to something over eleven thousand dollars, accompanied by the most solemn assurances that the rest was on its way, which restored his confidence.

Sixteen years had now passed since his mother's death and not a penny of her legacy had ever reached him; her executor Count Von Stolberg, who was also one of his own agents, died in 1819, and Baron von Fuerstenberg nine years earlier, both, as it afterwards appeared, undreaming of any wrong to him, supposing, with Count de Merveldt, that after the decision of the Russian law-suit their appointment was a mere matter of form, and that he was like his sister in regular receipt of his property, and so though still far from suspecting the truth, Father Gallitzin decided at last to attempt through the Russian ambassador to obtain less dilatory justice, and for this purpose wrote to Archbishop Maréchal to obtain an introduction to him; it is in this same letter that he unfolds with greatest earnestness, his desires for the spiritual welfare of his flock.

Rev. D. A. Gallitzin to Archbishop Maréchal.*

Loretto, Cambria County, Oct. 28, 1823.

Monseigneur,

I take the liberty of addressing your Grace, to learn if the Russian ambassador who left France with you has arrived

---

* From the original in French belonging to the Archespiscopal archives at Baltimore.

in this country, and where he now resides. My letters, although much diminished in number, are still sufficiently considerable to cause me uneasiness, and I have taken the resolution to seek our ambassador directly, to see if I cannot obtain from my sister, by his intervention, that which belongs to me. Four letters which I have written to my sister since my last journey to Baltimore still remain unanswered.

I beg your Grace, therefore, to send me without delay a letter of introduction to the ambassador, with which I will visit the place you may indicate to me as his residence. It is likely he is acquainted with the Princes Gallitzin, my uncles and cousins, of whom several live at St. Petersburg, occupying various offices: Captains of the Guards, *Grand Veneur*, Chamberlain, &c.

It seems to me you have been heard to say that the ambassador is a Catholic. Will you have the kindness to give me the necessary information on these different points as soon as your leisure permits.... Permit me to add that I am, with the most profound respect, Monseigneur,

Your most humble and obedient servant,

D. A. de Gallitzin.

P. S. I hope that you have received the letter which I had the honor to write you in the spring, in which I detailed my reasons for refusing the bishopric of Detroit. As your Grace did not reply to it, I took your silence as proof of your approbation. Indeed if you knew the mission of Lorettol you would agree with me that it is one of the most important in the United States, and that it would ruin it, and ruin me to remove me from this mission. When I established myself here in 1800 the entire County of Cambria was but an immense forest and almost inpenetrable; by force of labor and expense (expenses which already reach to more than forty thousand dollars), I have succeeded, with the help of God, in forming an establishment wholly Catholic, extending over an immense extent of country, which is rapidly augmented by the annual accession of families who come here from Germany, Switzerland, Ireland, and from different parts of America. Now, to form my establishment, I have been to great expense in establishing the various trades which are the most necessary, so that I have part of my funds in tanneries, &c. &c. and it is impossible to draw them suddenly without ruining many families.

...... Several years ago I formed a plan for the good of religion, for the success of which I desire to employ all the means at my disposal, when the remainder of my debts are paid. It is to form a diocese for the western part of Pennsylvania. What a consolation for me if I might before I die see this plan carried out, and Loretto made an episcopal see, where the bishop by means of the lands attached to the bishopric, which are very fertile, would be independent, and where with very little expense could be erected college, seminary, and all that is required for an episcopal establishment! We have now a bishop without having one, the great distance of Philadelphia, the dependence of the bishop, [*on the contributions of his flock.*] his small means, the poverty of so many thousands of Catholics who are unable to reimburse him as they ought for visiting them, will remain for many years insurmountable obstacles, which would no longer exist if there was a diocese west of the mountains.. It could be commenced by establishing a bishop here who would be merely *Vicarius in Pontificalibus* to the Bishop of Philadelphia, who would give great comfort by administering confirmation in all parts of Western Pennsylvania; at the death of the Bishop of Philadelphia two dioceses could be formed. If your Grace would take the trouble to look over the map of Pennsylvania and take notice of the chains of mountains which traverse the State, the great distance from Philadelphia to the western extremity of the State, on the other side of the mountains, your Grace would be of my opinion. If time permitted I should have other remarks to add to these, but the mail is about leaving and I have still several letters to write, and therefore, have the honor &c. &c.

Permit me to add that no bishop has ever penetrated to the distant missions of Western Pennsylvania. Archbishop Carroll was on the way in 1802, but frightened by the horrible description they gave him at Chambersburg of the mountains, the roads &c. he retraced his steps. Bishop Egan penetrated as far as Pittsburg and the neighboring congregations, but went no further. Bishop Conwell has not done so much. There are, then, many missions which have never seen a bishop, and never will, at least not until a bishop is established on the mountains, and one willing to fulfill the duties of his charge, even at his own expense, without waiting for other recompense than that which comes from above. I hope that my experience of more than twenty years on these missions will be a guarantee to you that I speak with knowledge of the subject, and that I am animated with the sincere desire of advancing God's work.

CHAPTER XXII.

FINAL SETTLEMENT OF THE EUROPEAN PROPERTY.

(1817—1828.)

The Prince of Orange.—King of the Netherlands.—His affection for Gallitzin.—Dr. Overberg comes to the rescue.—The collection of antique stones.—Count de Merveldt's intervention.—Death of Princess Mimi.—Her Will.—Death of Overberg.—Father Gallitzin's position.—His statement of business matters.—Visits Blairsville and the Irish laborers on the canal.—The Russian minister.

It will be remembered that almost the earliest playmate of little Prince Mitri Gallitzin was Prince Frederick William, son of William V, reigning sovereign of the country, whom his mother used to take with her to *Nithuys*, to amuse himself with Mimi and Mitri while she and the princess conversed on philosophy. The friendship thus formed continued through childhood and youth, and when Mitri was about starting for America, the two princes parted from each other with all the fervency of youthful friendship,[*] with mutual promises of assistance if the vicissitudes of life should ever place either in the position to need it, Mitri leaving in the other's charge a watch and chain, some rings and a snuff box, which of little value in themselves were probably made sacred by some special association, too great for them to be risked in the American journey.

Since then many changes had indeed come to both, hardly more to Prince Mitri than to the Prince of Orange. About

---

[*] *Reminiscences of Dr. Gallitzin* by R. B. McCabe, Esq. Blairsville Record, July 14, 1858.

the time that one entered the seminary, the other, who, in 1792, had married his cousin, Princess Frederica of Prussia, was called upon to defend his country, throne, and family against the French, by taking command of the army of the Netherlands, which he retained with varying success until Jan. 1795 when the French entering Holland, the stadtholder was compelled to abdicate, and accompained by the prince retired to England, after which Holland was made a kingdom by Bonaparte with his brother Louis (who married Hortense Beauharnais and was the father of Napoleon III) for its king. After the downfall of Bonaparte the Congress of Vienna annexed Belgium to Holland making it one kingdom, and the Prince of Orange was proclaimed its sovereign with the title of William I, King of the Netherlands and Duke of Luxembourg, residing alternately at the Hague and at Brussels.

He is represented as having had a wonderful memory which retained the knowledge acquired in his youth under the severe training of his mother, with a clear head, prompt judgment, strict attention to his duties as sovereign, an obstinate temper, little love for art or literature, and economical in the smallest details, even to parsimony. "He could make or sanction large expenditures, but he had neither natural generosity nor delicacy in his way of giving; if he opened his purse it was more from calculation, the demands of religion or the interests of his position, than from inclination or the charm attached to the thought of making others happy."* However that may have been, he gave orders as soon as he came to the throne, to his minister in this country to search out his old friend, of whom little was known abroad beyond the bare fact of his residence in America. Mr. McCabe recollects letters passing between the Dutch minister and prominent gentlemen of Pennsylvania in regard to this matter, which led to the discovery of the rich and handsome Russian prince in the poor and harassed, but ever benign and stately priest of the Alleghany forests. Though

---

* *Revue des Deux Mondes*, vol. III, p. 64.

the king assuredly had no temporal advantage to gain by a renewal of olden ties, he caused every offer of assistance to be made in his name to the missionary, all of which, however, were persistently declined, until he himself finally succeeded in inducing him to accept of two thousand dollars in exchange for the articles entrusted to his friendly care so many years before, and which it was not likely there would soon, if ever, be an opportunity to return: "'I knew well enough,' said Dr. Galiitzin, relating the circumstance,* 'that this was done through friendship for me, for it was ten times the worth of the articles. He thought I was poor, and his delicacy found this mode of approaching me; I could not refuse to receive it, for our boyish vows of friendship, and every consideration that could move me was invoked, and I felt to repulse it would be rude and ungrateful, for I believe its acceptance gratified him even more than it benefitted me.'"†

When by the letters written to his mother's friends Dr. Overberg, became aware of Father Gallitzin's embarrassed situation consequent upon the non-arrival of the money belonging to him in Europe, his grief was excessive. It could not well be otherwise when the good priest remembered, as

---

* *Reminiscences of Dr. Gallitzin*, by R. B. McCabe, Esq.

† By the Revolution of 1830 the king lost his control over Belgium, and was finally obliged to acknowledge its independence; other troubles disturbed his reign and his attachment to Countess Henriette d'Outremont, a Belgian and a Catholic, gave great dissatisfaction to his Protestant subjects, so that he abdicated in 1840, married the countess and resided in Berlin as Count of Nassau until his death in 1843. He left a private fortune of forty million dollars. He was succeeded by his son, William II, who had been with him in England, and just previous to the downfall of Napoleon I, expected to be married to the English Princess Charlotte, but before it was entirely settled she refused him and accepted Prince Leopold of Saxe Cobourg, who was just than visiting England with the allied sovereigns. When Belgium became independent the prince hoped to be its accepted king, but he was rejected, and the same rival preferred before him; he married the sister of Alexander I of Russia.—King Leopold of Belgium married for his second wife a daughter of Louis Philippe, by whom he had several children, one of them the unhappy Carlotta, wife of Maximilian.

he ever did, the munificent generosity which had loaded him with favors and placed the princess' house and all possible comforts at his command, wherein the very lowest menial was better clothed, fed, sheltered and cared for in sickness and in health, than the only son of that house. What explanation the Princess Mimi may have made him is not known, but he appears to have been satisfied she could not do more than she had done, so he set about to devise some means of assistance. The princess on her death-bed had given him a most valuable collection of Greek and Roman antiquities with the injunction to apply it for some pious purpose, according to his own discretion. It was a collection such as only a royal personage could be expected to purchase, and had once been offered by the princess to Catharine of Russia, who, however, was obliged to decline it as at that moment she was somewhat embarrassed by difficulties with the Turks, which put it out of her power to make any addition to her scientific treasures at that time. Up to 1817 Overberg had been unable to find a purchaser for the collection, on account of its great value, but in his anxiety to relieve Father Gallitzin he induced Princess Mimi to offer it to William I, who more out of regard for his early friend, it is likely, than from desire for the collection, valuable though it was, agreed to take it for fifty thousand Holland guilders (twenty two thousand five hundred dollars), which he paid over to the princess, shortly after her marriage, for her brother, while Dr. Overberg was careful to take a receipt from the princess and her husband which was dated June 25, 1819, and later a written promise to send Father Gallitzin the money, for the good doctor wisely considered the design of the princess could not be better carried out than by relieving the necessities of her beloved son, assisting a devout priest in his work for the good of religion, and in promoting the success of the pious foundation of Loretto. Father Gallitzin's liabilities at this time were about twenty thousand dollars, the king's Holland guilders were, therefore, enough to pay all he owed and to relieve him from anxiety, without regard to the hundreds of thousands coming to him from the sale of his father's property, and from his mother's legacy, which he every day expected. What joy to the frail and sensitive priest when the burden borne for fifteen long years, should be cast off, and he could stand once more erect and free!

Besides this the Duke de Serent, who had now returned to France with Louis XVIII, and was in good circumstances, paid the princess twenty thousand francs, being half of a debt owing to her mother, of which, according to the will of Princess Gallitzin which commanded an even division of her property between her children, one half belonged to Father Gallitzin, and was actually sent him; it brought him about eighteen hundred dollars, which he paid over at once to his principal creditors.

Letters still arriving in Germany urging expedition, Overberg discovered to his intense amazement, that the money obtained by the sale of the collection had not been sent, and, though little used to business or any severity, he demanded an explanation from Prince de Salms, who answered in July 1821:

"On the 20th of July 1821 I sent Prince Demetrius, my brother in law, a document signed and sealed by myself and my wife, promising him the quickest possible payment of twenty two thousand five hundred ($22.500) Berlin dollars. The measures already taken by me give me a certain prospect of making remittances over Holland &c. &c. and in six months at furthest the money will be in his hands."

Dr. Overberg sent this letter to Father Gallitzin, who, towards the end of the year receiving nothing further, drew upon his brother in law for the amount named; his bills were returned protested. The anonymous letter before mentioned as arriving about this time, solemnly assured him that the money received from the king was being spent by Prince de Salms and his wife for their own benefit. Count de Merveldt at last heard of these transactions, and roused to the highest indignation, though old and ill, drove seventy-five miles to Duesseldorf to see the prince and insist upon immediate payment, which resulted in something over half of this money being sent to Father Gallitzin, but of that received for the Russian property, the sale of his mother's house in Muenster, the income from other sources, nothing could be obtained, and just as he had decided to see the Russian ambassador and force payment, his sister died; the news soon after reached him, with the announcement that all her property was left to her husband, though there was a show of something to him. "In her trouble," wrote the good and charitable Dr. Overberg*, "she could not do otherwise; she desired to help both you and her husband, for it is stipulated in her will that after all the debts [that is, the debts of Prince de Salms, which are supposed to have been legion, mainly the most dishonorable debts in the world, those called "of honor,"] are paid, the third of what remains over and above expenses, should be sent her brother. It is a satisfaction to me that you say in your last letter that you can get along now if Prince Salms, as you do not doubt, will keep his word. His word he will keep undoubtedly, because he is a very religious gentleman; but whether he can do it, if he has not yet done it, is another thing. [rather an obscure passage.] He is deeply in debt. The word you refer to must be that which he wrote me in 1821, when he and his wife signed the document promising to pay you twenty-two thousand, five hundred dollars, the price of the stones- Thanks be to God you have already received part of it."

Others informed him with full particulars of the substitution of a false will for the one the princess supposed she was signing, a strong hand guided hers, certain menials of her house-hold attested it,† and her brother was cut off from his inheritance beyond hope. She was not permitted in death to do that justice which for some reason, whether entirely her own fault or not, she had failed to secure him in life. He was strongly urged to return to Europe and have the will set aside, which it was thought could easily be effected, but he shrank from the exposure of other's sins or weaknesses,

---

* Rev. H. Lemcke, p. 253.
† R. B. McCabe's *Reminiscenses.*

and could never raise himself to that point of severe justice which would nerve him to save himself at the expense of another, however guilty.

Dr. Overberg once again endeavored to assist him by trying to dispose of the princess' library left to him in her will, and which he could not feel comfortable in retaining while her only son was in need; but as nothing more was said about it after the announcement of the intention, it is probable that he was unable to find a purchaser in the short time yet remaining to him. He died in 1826, a death worthy of his lovely and saintly life, and with him departed the last of that circle of fatherly friends, of which the princess had been the golden clasp, to whom her son could look for sympathy, if for nothing more.

And thus, as he said himself, the farce was ended; his sister's death and the terms of her will deprived him of the last hope of justice; after being deluded for fifteen years by promises he would have considered it criminal to doubt, he was left penniless and forsaken at the very time when he had every reason to believe an immense fortune was at his door; past fifty years of age, with no resources, with hundreds depending upon him in one way and another, he was obliged to pay a crushing debt, which by interest and various extortions to which he would have to submit in order to obtain breathing space, would, he feared, not only not diminish but keep always on the increase, always ahead of him, threattening and reviling him, crossing his path at every step he would take for good, and crushing every effort he might make for the cause of religion. He had never before doubted that the day would come when he would gloriously redeem his word and lift every breath of misty doubt from his business fame, when he would not only pay to the last farthing all that he owed, but all that gratitude could suggest; a day when all would be explained and understood, and the world seeing his abundant means would wonder, not that he had been so lavish and extravagant, but that he had been so prudent and cautious. Now he knew that day would never come, and in all human probability he would descend to the grave under the cloud of distrust which even the most charitable of his friends had no means of dispelling.

But the silver lining of the cloud was more widely visible than he could believe, and it was very beautiful. Though placed in a position inexplicable to others, almost to himself, a position which could not rebuke the darkest suspicions and the loudest reproaches of his creditors, and those aware of their claims, people knew not how to doubt his honesty or sincerity; he was believed in when every appearance was against him, and those who held faith in him could not lessen it even on the evidence of their own senses. How much more tender the good God seems to us than to his own Son, whom he permits us to take as our model, likening our trials to his! The sneers and gibes of the rabble followed the Lord to the last, but now the mob was dispersed, their mockeries and calumnies unheard, and kindly faces, pitying eyes, and hopeful words met the weary priest as once again he took up his cross and dragged it along his dreary *via dolorosa*.

But for a time his great sensitiveness made him doubtful and fearful; he knew how it could well appear to others, and that if the cruel voice of slander should again be raised to denounce him, he would have small evidence to produce against it. In justice to his creditors as well as to his good name and his sacred calling, he drew up a full statement of his expectations, their solid foundation, and their bitter disappointment, that those who should lose through him might at least have the solace of knowing they had not been imposed upon by a deceiver, or that they had been over-credulous in their transactions with him. It is from this paper the greater portion of the foregoing details of his business affairs has been gathered. Next to the most rigid economy and unflagging efforts to do his utmost to pay what he owed, this was all he could see that he could do, although at times he had thoughts of making a voyage to Europe where he would be able, very likely, to obtain without any publicity, some small remnant of his fortune, which would suffice to ransom him. But unless certain of procuring this, and whose word could he any longer trust? he perhaps considered to undertake so expensive a journey was too great a risk, as it was possible for it to fail, and involve him in new difficulties from which he could never be able to free himself. He, therefore, finally abandoned the idea altogether, and set to work to do what he could with his farms and American investments; he hardly permitted himself sufficient food, and what he did take was of the cheapest and simplest kind; his clothes were so old and poor that they were pitiful to see, but with it all he could not save himself from his creditors; in 1828 his little cabin was advertised for Sheriff's sale, and the hour was at hand when the princely heir to grand old castles and lordly palaces, should find himself without a roof above his head. Only a few hundred dollars was needed to rescue it, but he might as well have looked for millions.

In this emergency it was proposed to the man whom kings could not induce to accept presents, that he should visit the Irish laborers at work on the canal in Westmoreland and Indiana counties, for it is written that *they who serve the altar should live by the altar*, and perhaps obtain some little help from them. The men were always overjoyed when a priest came among them and were very liberal to Mr. McGirr who made them occasional calls, though like the people in the stations around, they thought it pretty hard to be forced to put up with that gentleman's peculiarites; it was therefore a double joy for them to learn that Father Gallitzin would visit them.

He arrived in Blairsville one Saturday and was entertained at the village hotel, where Mr. McCabe met him, as related in his *Reminiscenses* :

"We had a very free conversation, for with all his acknowledged intellectual ability and superior education, in social intercourse he appeared as frank, sincere and simple as a child.

"In this conversation the doctrinal characteristics of various sects in religion were discussed. He knew I was not of his communion, for he had learned from myself that I had been raised a Presbyterian. The fact was adverted to by him that the leading doctrines of those who separated from the Roman Church, or the Catholic Church as he preferred to call it, as Protestants, had been taught by various distinguished men before the separation...... Having given a good deal of attention in previous years to theological readings, Church history and biography, I was not altogether unprepared to consider and understand his remarks upon the various topics of our discourse, and I observed next day that his sermon, which I heard, noticed incidentally most of the doctrinal points we had conversed about.

* * *

"At the very time of this conversation his homestead at Loretto was advertised for sale by the Sheriff of Cambria county, and I could not suppress all emotion in view of the hardships which appeared to menace his old age. And indeed I ventured to say something to this effect. But he replied smiling, 'My son, the Lord has provided for me hitherto, and will hereafter. I have no doubt of that!'"

In this same sermon Father Gallitzin spoke with great force of the duty of respect to pastors duly appointed for us, and very severely rebuked his listeners for their opposition to Mr. McGirr, who was a good and virtuous priest, whom they should obediently accept as such, whatever might be their feeling towards him otherwise. After the services were over Mr. Campbell, a Catholic gentleman present, obtained the honor and pleasure of Father Gallitzin's company to a quiet dinner, and the next day, Mr. John Brown, another resident of Blairsville, drove him to a station some miles away, where the laborers on the canal were collected to meet him as if it were Sunday; after Mass was over Mr. Brown went around and spoke to the people, and brought back quite a handsome subscription, which was probably the first collection Father Gallitzin ever received; it affected him deeply, and he never after spoke of it without emotion. At another station he arrived before the day appointed for services, and for the first time saw the men at their work; Ireland has never sent us anything to surpass those first emigrants, and as the priest watched their strong arms, and noticed that none of them seemed much past their early youth, the hope of aged parents, perhaps, far away, he turned away and said to Mr. Fenlon, whose guest he was: "I cannot do it; when I saw how hard the poor fellows were working, I felt I never could have the heart to take anything from their hard earnings." But his friend combatted this view of the case with easy spirit, and being highly gifted with the persuasive eloquence of his countrymen, proved conclusively that there was nothing the Irish would like better than to assist him. "I assure you," he said brightly, "there's not a man among them who would not cheerfully contribute his dollar for this purpose."

The result is readily imagined; Father Gallitzin said Mass, preached, administered the sacraments as required, and Mr. Fenlon having influence and position, attended with a light heart to the rest; in a short time he collected some five or six hundred dollars, and the pastor of Loretto's home was saved. "The noble Irish" he said to Mr. McCabe, "relieved me at once, they raised the money and the debt is paid."

Among the loans which Father Gallitzin had sought or which were offered to him at the time his prospects were the brightest, was that of five thousand dollars pressed upon him by the Russian minister at Washington, who knew his urgent need; when his hopes failed Father Gallitzin was so distressed at his inability to repay this debt that he went to Washington to have a personal interview with the ambassador, who invited Henry Clay, of whom the good priest was quite an admirer, the minister from Holland and others to meet him at dinner. "After dinner," Father Gallitzin related,[*] "some smoked cigars, and for their accommodation a lighted candle was placed on the table. I chanced to sit near the candle and noticed the Russian ambassador rolling up a paper very carefully to make a light. My eye involuntarily followed his hand till the paper was put to the candle. Then I discovered my name on the paper. It was my

---

[*] Mr. McCabe's *Reminiscences*.

bond for five thousand dollars he was burning. When I spoke to him on the subject, which I did at the first opportunity, he declared it settled. Nor would he hear anything more from me about it." The same ambassador showed him the greatest deference and kindness, partly, as Gallitzin liked to believe, at the desire of the legal Prince Gallitzin who now occupied the place in the world for which he had been destined, and of whom, though he had never seen him, Father Gallitzin spoke with the most affectionate regard

From time to time small sums arrived from Europe, not large enough to be of any assistance in diminishing his debts, but of some help in his charities. He spent of his own money about one hundred and fifty thousand dollars for the foundation of Loretto, erecting of churches, improving the surrounding farms, and buildings of various kinds; from the income derived from these he hoped by prudent and careful management, with God's help, to free all from debt before he died. The greatest patience and kindness was manifested towards him by all his creditors, while his own faith and fortitude will ever make his example an edification, and it is to be hoped, a bright encouragement to those who for one reason or another, may be tempted to feel that ruined hopes, plans destroyed, expectations come to naught, life's whole purpose crushed out, make a sea of troubles too wide and deep for manly honor or even religious principle to venture to cross.

CHAPTER XXIII.
AS VICAR GENERAL.
(1827—1830.)

F. Gallitzin and Bishop Conwell.—F. Gallitzin as a mediator.—Extent of his jurisdiction.—Rev. Mr. Heyden.—Rev. Mr. O'Rielly.—Mr. McGirr and Mr. Maguire.—F. Gallitzin uses his authority.—Mr. McGirr's idiosyncrasies.—F. Gallitzin's patience.

The continued obstinacy of the rebellion in Philadelphia, rendered more complicated and painful by the unfortunate result of outside interference, bore heavily upon Bishop Conwell, and cast gloom and sadness over the faithful throughout the country, the more distressing that the prelate's counsellors were of many minds, and were not always personally attached to him, beyond the veneration due to their spiritual superior. The greatest affection sprang up between the worn, harrassed, and constantly insulted bishop, and the good pastor of Loretto, who stood by him in his hour of trial with the devotion of a woman, and the fearlessness of a giant. There was no room in Father Gallitzin's nature for any compromise with wilful resistance to the authority of the Church, and his advice was to the most vigorous and decided measures; he was frequently called to Philadelphia for consultation, and always left the bishop strengthened and fortified by the influence of his counsels, so that it was earnestly desired that he might be always at hand, but Father Gallitzin was fast becoming a little bishop in his own field, to which new priests were now coming to take charge of congregations he had formed, and in 1827 the bishop formally defined the limits of his vicar-generalship, which very soon gave him ample occupation of a new kind. With all his stern and uncompromising nature, Father Gallitzin was a born mediator; his extreme tenderness of heart, his delicacy of feeling and inexhaustible charity, acting with his noble will and determined spirit, resulted in an influence which was irresistible; he denounced without estranging, warned without hardening, and pleaded with the sinner without in the least veiling the sin, while with singular penetration he seemed to know the rocky soil from the good, when all appearances were against his judgment; thus he would be seen to uphold one in whom no sign for hope appeared to others, and would treat with crushing severity another in whom there was apparently little to blame. He was consulted and appealed to on matters of conscience, and his mediation sought in difficulties from all parts of the country, and in the most remote dioceses, and under the most eminent prelates, his judgment and influence saved many a bruised reed that seemed beyond hope, and drove more than one wolf in sheep's clothing from the fold, unsuspected of the world. Though often his decisions appeared against all reason, his charity to some entirely thrown away, and his severity to others unmerited, time invariably justified his actions; the priests on the point of irremedial disgrace, whom he quietly rescued, begging with tears that they might be given one chance more, proved to the astonishment of all who knew them, worthy of his boundless charity, lived penitent lives, performed their duties with noble results, and went to their graves honored and esteemed, full of hope in the mercy of the God who had sent them such a messenger in their hour of temptation and trial. His own persecutions, the sworn testimony of his enemies bearing false witness against him, gave him an insight into the malice of evil which he never lost; no evidence against a priest could startle him, knowing what he knew of his own life, and the accounts given of it by those who maligned him; against all proof he would believe that which he himself read in one accused, with firm faith in the guiding light of the Holy Spirit to which he trust его decisions. Once learning that a quarrel had taken place* between a congregation and its pastor, which would undoubtedly lead to a law suit and angry scenes, he started immediately on a long and toilsome journey to the place, arrived unexpectedly, took the priest and those who were engaged in the difficulty into the church, threw himself upon his knees, and declared with tears that he would not rise until they had all promised reconciliation and friendship; an appeal that could not be resisted.

At the time Bishop Conwell formally appointed him vicar general, there were four priests under his charge in what had formerly been his own and Mr. Heilbron's district; these were Mr. McGirr at "Sportsman's Hall", Mr. Heyden at Bedford, Mr. O'Rielly at Newry, and Mr. O'Neill who attended some of the other missions.

Rev. Thomas Heyden, the son of Father Gallitzin's early friend, the merchant of Bedford, was ordained in Philadelphia by Bishop Conwell, May 1, 1820, and soon after was placed at Bedford, attending Newry, Sinking Valley, Phillipsburg, Huntingdon and so many other stations which Dr. Gallitzin yielded up to him, that it took him four or five weeks to go the rounds of all, allowing one or two days to each: He was repeatedly called to Philadelphia, and for a time was the reluctant pastor of St. Mary's, the church so long the scene of rebellion, from which he returned to reside permanently at Bedford, where he was of the greatest comfort to Dr. Gallitzin, to whom he was as a dear son.

Rev. John O'Rielly who with Rev. Mr. Kerns of Chambersburg, attended Mr. Heyden's district during his absence in Philadelphia, at other times residing either at Newry or Huntingdon, was a native of Ireland, educated at Emmetsburg, ordained in 1826 and immediately appointed to assist Dr. Gallitzin in the Pennsylvania mission. Besides the numerous congregations passed over to him by the pastor of Loretto, Mr. O'Rielly attended to the spiritual wants of great numbers of the Irish laborers employed upon the canal, with whose assistance he built a brick church in Hunting-

---

* Rev. H. Lemcke, p. 302.

don, and in Bellefonte, contracting for another in Newry, where he was residing when appointed, in 1831, to the assistance of Mr. Maguire at St. Patrick's church in Pittsburg. Mr. O'Neill was an Irish priest ministering to the faithful in Butler. Other priests than these occasionally attended to different stations, among them Rev. Mr. Duffy who was for sometime at Ebensburg, and very kindly regarded by Dr. Gallitzin, who protected him from injustice upon several occasions. The burden was, however, still heavy upon the veteran missionary, the increase of population keeping his mission always great notwithstanding the zealous assistance of so many young and active priests, the more so that the difficulties between Mr. McGirr and his flock continually required his mediation, which appeared to be effectual only for the moment, and so far from receiving advice or comfort from the bishop he was obliged to keep his troubles somewhat in the back-ground, and do his utmost to uphold the bishop in his accumulated trials.

In the hope of putting an end to the scandals in Philadelphia, word was sent from Rome appointing Rev. William Matthews of Washington administrator of the diocese inviting the bishop to Rome, and removing the priests, who had caused the trouble, to Ohio. It was at this time that Dr. Gallitzin was thinking of going to Europe to endeavor to obtain some portion of his inheritance, and was urged to accompany the bishop, as seen from a letter to Mr. Heyden:

VERY REV. D. A. GALLITZIN TO REV. MR. HEYDEN.

† Loretto, Dec. 3. 1827.

Rev'd Dear Sir.

I returned from Washington and Baltimore via Harrisburgh, and got safely home Monday Nov. 26th. My journey was premature, which obliges me to go down again after Christmas, when I shall take Bedford in my way. I reached Baltimore Friday night, Nov. 9th and on the following Tuesday whilst I was amusing myself on Madame Pochon's piano, who should stand behind me but the Right Rev'd Bishop of Philadelphia. I had hardly time to look around, when both his arms were around my neck and myself overwhelmed with kisses. Pray, who are you? Why; don't you know Henry Conwell, B'p of Philadelphia? I really did not know him, he was [so] close to me. After getting his blessing he took me away to the Archbishop's, and told me on the road that he had nominated me his coadjutor and had written or was going to write to Rome on the subject. I told him I hoped not. The Archbishop and the Bishop seem to be united in their desire to see me appointed. I don't know what to say about it there [are] so many obstacles in the way, so many difficulties to overcome.... my voyage to Europe which I shall (almost certainly) have to undertake next spring. When I mentioned my voyage to Europe the Bishop replied that he was glad to hear it and would go with me, as they wanted to see him at Rome.

I left the Rev. Enoch Fenwick almost dying at Georgetown College, with poor hopes of his recovery. The Archbishop of Baltimore is also in a very bad way, Dr. Chatard and other attending physicians are of opinion that his heart is affected; the former told me that he would not be surprised to hear of his sudden exit. Nothing positive has transpired in regard to his successor, some think that Rev'd Dr. Deluol is in nomination, others Rev'd William Matthews. From a conversation I had with the Archbishop I do not think he has nominated any one yet, but he thinks seriously about it. Excuse my hurry and believe me,

Rev'd dear Sir,

Yr very hble servt and friend
Demetrius A. Gallitzin V. G.

Dr. Gallitzin very soon found himself obliged to exercise the authority, given him at the time of this meeting, in the cause of Mr. McGirr whose variance with his congregations had ripened to open quarrels, by no means subdued by the part which Mr. Maguire, who still kept an interest in Sportsman's Hall, thought proper to take in regard to the matters in dispute. Immediately upon the appointment of Mr. Matthews, and in the absence of the bishop who had refused to interfere, great efforts were made to have Mr. McGirr removed, and Mr. Maguire left free to visit the congregation from Pittsburg, retaining the honors and emoluments, such as they were, arising from Father Brauer's will, without the trials and privations of life upon his farm; a course Dr. Gallitzin resented with indignation. "My feelings are overpowered," he wrote Mr. Heyden, Dec. 13, 1828 "Oh, the abominable doings in Westmoreland! The impious K——. after going from door to door, and getting (*Deus sait* by what means) some persons to swear scandalous things against Mr. McGirr, gets a petition with a number of subscribers, Mr. Maguire is prevailed upon to sign it. .... K——. goes down to Washington, is received by the Vicar Apostolic with distinction, obtains all he wants, and returns the bearer of Mr. Matthews' dispatches, one letter appointing Mr. Maguire judge of the charges against Mr. McGirr, and another letter enjoining upon Mr. McGirr to abide by Mr. Maguire, his enemy's, decisions."

"From all mendicant friars" he says again; "O Lord deliver us! I have always revered the holy institutions of St. Francis whether Capuchins or Franciscans, but an observation of many years has convinced me, that if you take a member of these sacred institutions out of his monastery, and put him on a mission, you take the fish out of the water and put him on dry land to perish. This I believe admits of very few exceptions. Freed from their vow of poverty they become most raving mad for money."

Before the news of Mr. Mathews' action, in which the vicar general of the district was not so much as consulted, as common courtesy required, reached Loretto, Dr. Gallitzin having exhausted all arguments and entreaties, often visiting the disaffected, and exhorting them to obedience, without permanent effect, Mr. McGirr being in great trouble and distress, he considered it incumbent upon him to address Mr. Maguire, whose influence constantly defeated his own, directly upon the subject. The postcript, which has a characteristic ring, was added immediately upon hearing of Mr. Matthews' dispatches:

VERY REV. D. A. GALLITZIN TO REV. C. B. MAGUIRE.

† Loretto, Nov. 23. 1828.

Very Rev'd Sir.

With heartfelt sorrow I find myself compelled to address your Reverence as a continuance of silence on my part would be criminal.

Some years ago the Right Rev. Bishop saw fit to appoint me Vicar General, but having neglected to designate the limits of my jurisdiction, I considered the appointment as nugatory, and did not act under it. However, happening to meet the Bishop in Baltimore, and the subject of my appointment being mentioned at the late Archbishop's, I requested him to state the limit of my jurisdiction; whereupon, in the presence of the Archbishop and of his clergy, viz: the Rev. Messrs. Whitfield (now Archbishop) Smith and Peese, he replied that my jurisdiction embraced the districts of the Rev. Messrs. McGirr, O'Neill, Heyden, and Rielly. Such being the case I now address your Reverence in my capacity of Vicar General of the above districts.

I have learnt from a respectable character in Ebensburg, that your Reverence has been prevailed upon to take an active part in the persecutions carried on by an impious set against the Rev'd Mr. McGirr. It does not belong to me to investigate your motives, which I hope are not revenge and self-interest (as is supposed by some persons) but this much I know, that a terrible woe must fall upon him who will seek or promote the downfall of a brother clergyman. More than thirty-three years spent on the mission have taught me that Catholics will go any length when animated by a spirit of hatred against their pastors, and had your Reverence been in this country in 1807, it would have raised the hair on your head to have read the horrid Depositions and Certificates fabricated against me, and sent to the Bishop by certain persons well known to you, and among the rest by some of the very same whom I now find arrayed against Rev'd T. McGirr. Thanks be to Divine Providence, and to Bishop Carroll's wisdom and penetration, all their hellish plots proved harmless to me, but I am afraid not so to themselves; and I now declare unto your Reverence that with the help of Divine Providence I shall exert all lawful means in my power to render abortive and harmless *to Mr. McGirr* the machinations of the impious Catholics of Westmoreland, together with your interference, and as a preliminary and precautionary measure I, as Vicar General of the Westmoreland district, now positively release your Reverence from the trouble of interfering directly or indirectly with the Catholics of said district, or from officiating in that district except in *articulo mortis* viz, in the case of a dying person who could not confess in the English language. If your Reverence had confined yourself to your own district, and not been so willing to admit the Westmoreland rebels (which I always refused to do) and if you had not been so willing even to officiate for them in Mr. McGirr's district, (which caused your Reverence to meet with an unpleasant refusal and to be insulted) the rebellion never would have ripened to maturity or assumed so horrid a shape.

I remain respectfully,

Yr hble servt,

Demetrius A. Gallitzin,

Parish priest of Loretto and V. G.

Dec. 13, 1828.

P. S. I am just informed that you are appointed by Rev. Mr. Matthews to investigate Rev. Mr. McGirr's conduct. I cannot for a moment suppose that you, his professed adversary, would be so ungenerous, so mean, so void of all sense of propriety as to accept of such a commission. However, as the must unlikely things sometimes turn out to be matter of fact, I, as Vicar General of the Westmoreland district, do solemnly protest against your appointment as judge over Rev. T. McGirr, and I do again enjoin on your Reverence not to interfere with Rev. Mr. McGirr's district, or with any part of my district as Vicar General, unless superior orders (after receiving Mr. McGirr's protest) should finally compel you to it. The laws of both church and state authorize such a protest, and during its pendency before the superior, you are in duty bound not to begin proceedings, or to suspend them if already begun.

Demetrius A. Gallitzin,
Vicar General.

Not content with this protest, for the cause of the priests under his charge was dearer to him even than though his own, Dr. Gallitzin wrote immediately to Rev. Mr. Heyden informing him of the steps taken, and urging him to lose no time in adding his own testimony in favor of Mr. McGirr, lest it once becoming known that the poor priest was under censure, he might lose the few friends and the confidence he still retained. He comforted and consoled the one in trouble and at once wrote to Mr. Matthews a letter full of spirit and sorrowful indignation which it seems impossible could have failed of its object, the complete removal of all suspicion. These prompt and loving efforts, though falling far short of their design, were not wholly unavailing; Mr. McGirr was not tried or removed, still less was he willingly accepted by all the members of his congregations, though many were able to overcome personal dislike and submit to his harshness, in reverence for his sacred position.

VERY REV. D. A. GALLITZIN TO VERY REV. WM. MATTHEWS.*

†

Very Rev. Sir,

I just now read a letter which your Reverence wrote to Rev. Mr. McGirr, in which you state that you have appointed Very Rev. Mr. Maguire to take cognizance of and to pronounce upon the subject of certain accusations against the said Rev. Mr. McGirr. This is tantamount to a suspension....

If Bishop Carroll (that almost perfect man) had proceeded in the same manner in my case in 1807 there can be no doubt that I should have been suspended; the accusations

---

* This letter is copied from one found among Dr. Gallitzin's papers, which appears to be merely the rough draft of the one sent.

against me were more grievous than those against Mr. McGirr, and also supported by an old clergyman; the messenger selected was E. J——, Esq. protonotary of our county. Bishop Carroll having read the deposition and certificate turned about and said: "Sir, I am very sorry for one thing."—"What is that, my Lord?"—"Why to find your name on this infamous paper, and now, Sir, clear yourself immediately from my presence, go home and give satisfaction to your pastor."

This I have from Mr. J—— himself whose testimony in such a case cannot be suspected, and who, accordingly, came on the following Sunday to the church and at the foot of the altar, before the whole congregation, acknowledged and deplored his guilt in calumniating me; which example was followed by several more of them. Thus ended my business, and thus I contend, ought Rev. Mr. McGirr's business to end.

It is shocking to both Catholics and Protestants (and you must know, Very Rev. Sir, that Rev. Mr. McGirr, a gray-haired gentleman, is much respected by all the respectable characters of both parties) it is shocking, then, I say, to hear that impious free-mason, Mr. K—— who is no Catholic (no matter how many signs of Catholicity he may have exhibited at Washington), to hear him relate with how much respect he was received by you, to see him made by your Reverence the bearer of your letter to Mr. McGirr, and to hear him exult in his victory.

Did you know, Very Rev. Sir, that this detestable man travelled about from door to door, even to a distance of many miles *sicut Corugiens* on purpose to make persons swear against Mr. McGirr, which besides being most infamous in itself was a notorious breach of the law which he is sworn to support?

..... Would you be willing after the lapse of so many years, even to listen to such stuff or to permit the character and livelihood of a clergyman to have to depend on such untimely testimonies?..... When our worthy bishop appointed me vicar general over the districts of the Rev. Messrs. McGirr,

O'Neill, Heyden and O'Rielly, he particularly recommended me to be like a father to them; it became my religious duty, of course, (whenever I heard of the accusation against one of them by an impious set, before your Reverence) to prevent you from being taken by surprise and to put you upon your guard....

I had reason to suppose that my age, my thirty-three years' residence on this mountain and thorough acquaintance with persons and circumstances, would give my recommendation some weight. Alas! I find myself mistaken, and whilst on the one hand an impious man breathing spite and revenge brags of your respectful attention, I have to acknowledge that no attention whatever is paid to my letter....

Two or three years later Mr. McGirr was removed from Father Brauers' farm, and at the request of the bishop (Kenrick) confined himself to such duties as Dr. Gallitzin should think proper to place upon him, and to say Mass only at Loretto or in his own house, near Ebensburg. He lived for a time with Dr. Gallitzin, or made him long and frequent visits, and was always treated with the utmost kindness and regard, although it was a wonder to all how one so fastidious as the delicate doctor, could put up with the blustering peculiarities of the less cultured priest. The country abounds with recollections of McGirr's idiosyncrasies; he was especially particular about his food, not requiring dainties or luxuries, for to these things he never gave a thought, but determined to have substantial and abundant meals, and so many times had he been deluded in regard to such, and for want of what he considered due precaution, been half starved on his missions, that in later years he left nothing undone with which to reproach himself afterwards. In this respect, as in so many others, Dr. Gallitzin was at the other extreme; people wondered that he could live on so little; he provided abundant meals for his guest, but under the plea of delicate health, poor appetite, or sudden calls, avoided as often as possible participating in the good things so keenly relished by the strong and hearty visitor, and would take his frugal meal, consisting of a single light and simple dish, by himself, in his own room, reading or standing, or sitting on the door step, as Rev. Mr. Lemcke relates*, after the daily Mass, which, on account of the day's work was said very early, taking a breakfast of soup from the plate on his knees, while the children, who also had to make themselves useful during the day, played around him, eating the bread and butter they had brought from home, preparatory to the lesson in the Catechism he would give them before they went to their work. When he was on his missions, he passed by the more pretentious houses of those well pleased at getting up in the world, and made his home with some pious family in humbler circumstances, where he would sit surrounded by the delighted children, for whom he had always some little picture or keepsake, satisfied with the milk porridge or potatoes placed before him. If he arrived too late for the regular meals, he would not allow anything to be cooked for him, taking nothing but a piece of bread and a glass of water until the usual time. When Mr. McGirr accompanied him on his missions the case was different; before dismounting, Mr. McGirr would closely question the landlord, or house father, who had hastened out to hold the horses and receive the distinguished guests with due hospitality, as to the resources of the house they were about to honor, and if the essentials were found lacking, he would persist in riding on to some better filled larder. "Mr. McGirr," said the doctor to him with great politeness, after listening, with a peculiar smile, to one of these long colloquies between host and guest, to which he had now become accustomed, "Mr. McGirr, don't you think the next time you had better bring the potatoes (for these were the absolutely essential) with you in your saddle bags, and then, you know, you would always be sure of them?"

An advice which was probably not taken, for some time afterwards, the two gentlemen went out about three miles

---

* Page 314.

from Loretto, to look at one of Dr. Gallitzin's mills, he having sent word in advance to a bountiful provider in the neighborhood, that he and Mr. McGirr would take dinner at his house. The good woman of the house at once made all possible provision to show her delight at the favor, but in those days, in such places, cookery was hardly one of the fine arts, there was only a fire-place to work by, and not much variety was admitted. When the mill had been properly investigated Dr. Gallitzin brought his visitor to the house where a bountiful dinner awaited them; Mr. McGirr looked intently at the table, with the eye of a general reviewing his troops before the battle, the house-mother stood by in conscious virtue, having surpassed herself, the children hung about in respectful shade, and perhaps mentally calculated probable remainders, Dr. Gallitzin sat at a distance apparently unconscious of any unusual pause; all at once Mr. McGirr broke the solemn silence, and his words were not of commendation; the famous potatoes were not *au naturel* as he always desired, and the good woman, with tears of vexation and wounded pride in her eyes, had no choice but to prepare them according to his orders, as quickly as possible; what made her humiliation almost intolerable was, that her own pastor, Dr. Gallitzin, for whom she would have died a hundred deaths, witnessed her undeserved condemnation, without a word or look of excuse or regret. All was finally satisfactory, and Mr. McGirr did justice to the amended meal. When all was over, and they were about leaving, Dr. Gallitzin lingered a moment, quietly asked for some wrapping paper, which was brought him with a little silent wonder; he spread it upon the table, apparently too absorbed in his work to be conscious of any one's presence, much less that all were watching him, puzzled beyond measure; as daintily as a French *confectionière* picking out candied fruit for a favorite customer, he delicately lifted the brown skinned potatoes left upon the table, until not one remained, then making them into an even package with elaborate care, he folded them up, and for the first time raising his eyes, turning with an expression of childlike innocence to his companion he handed him the bundle saying, softly: "They will be all ready for the next time," then made his adieux and rode away, leaving his good parishioner perfectly satisfied with the reparation, and Mr. McGirr himself could not help a hearty laugh at the quiet rebuke.

But though he might, in his own way, take notice of Mr. McGirr's little unconventionalities, Dr. Gallitzin would not permit others to speak of them, and everywhere insisted upon due reverence being paid him, and people were sometimes at a loss how to show their decided preference for the doctor, without offending him by any apparent depreciation of his guest, who was also his assistant; the pastor's own tact and delicacy alone helped them out of their difficulty, sometimes when they least expected it. For instance, somewhat later, when he was much past sixty, and suffering from an attack of severe illness, a little girl of twelve or thirteen, living with her parents at Munster, was in danger of death, and Mr. McGirr was requested, as the doctor could not leave his room, to come and hear her confession; but when he came to the sick child, and she saw who it was, she burst into violent crying, and no commands or entreaties no fear of death, or terror of unforgiven sins, could induce her, though an unusually pious girl, to go to confession to any one but Dr. Gallitzin; they told her the doctor was sick in bed, it was impossible to ask him, and that he would be very angry if he knew of her resistance, she only cried the more and refused Mr. McGirr's assistance the more decidedly. The family were very much frightened and distressed, a priest was a priest, and if she died in that spirit they knew not what would become of her; finally one of them, a young woman who, perhaps, fully sympathized with the child's feeling, on account of her own veneration for their pastor, proposed that she should go to Loretto, and if Dr. Gallitzin would see her for a few minutes, tell him of the matter, and obtain some message which would cause the sick girl to submit.

When he learned that her errand was of importance, the doctor admitted her, he was sitting in an arm-chair (wooden, uncushioned, and straight-backed) looking pale and very feeble; she told her story: "Poor child!" he said, calling the girl by name, showing no vexation, and paying no attention to the messenger's excuses, " of course, she could not go to confession to him. Will it be soon enough if I go to-morrow morning?"

"You, doctor, you do not think of such a thing?"

"Yes, please God, I will go up in the morning."

She begged to be permitted to accompany him, she could remain with her relatives all night, and it was unsafe for him, so ill as he was, to go out alone, especially such a distance.

"By no means," he said, "it is best you should try to go back this evening, and tell them that I will come in the morning, then they will not be uneasy, and to-morrow I will take my dog and my stick, that is all I need, and walk over."

The messenger was, therefore, obliged to return that she might relieve the anxiety of the family, whose joy at his coming could not but be shadowed by the thought of the pain and danger to him. Early the next day the children of the house went of their own accord down the road to watch for him, when they saw him coming, ran to meet him, and one on each side of him, holding an end of his coat, accompanied him through the village street, to their sister's door. The sick child cried softly with joy and relief when he came to her, made her confession with fervor, received the last sacraments, and died like a little saint, who feels that her soul's father stands beside her, to lift her firmly over the dark passage from life to death, and place her securely in the strong arms of the waiting angels.

Mr. McGirr occasionally celebrated High Mass at Loretto, upon which occasions Dr. Gallitzin would go into the choir and sing the responses. As soon as he left the altar, it was Mr. McGirr's way to go up to the little stand on which the vestments were kept, and drag those he was wearing over his head, often turning the sleeves of the alb inside out, as the quickest way of getting it off; the moment he turned away, having unvested himself, and thrown the garments, all in a confused heap upon the stand, Dr. Gallitzin would be seen in his place, with rapid and reverent touch smoothing out every wrinkle, folding every article with tenderest care, Mr. McGirr serenely unconscious of anything out of the way, saying his prayers undisturbed, while the pastor laid all away, and closed the drawers.

CHAPTER XXIV.
UNDER BISHOP KENRICK.
(1830—1831.)

Rev. Mr. Matthews resigns.—Rev. Mr. Kenrick appointed coadjutor.— F. Gallitzin's anxieties in regard to Rev. Mr. McGirr.—His counsels to Bishop Kenrick.—Pleads for his reverend brethren.—Confirmation at Loretto.—The missing mitre.—Mr. Heyden's disappointments.

Rev. Mr. Matthews retained the position of administrator of the diocese of Philadelphia until 1830, when he insisted upon resigning the burdensome charge, which he had long felt heavy upon his shoulders. The bishop having returned from Rome and consenting to the suggestion of the council of Baltimore to receive Rev. Francis Patrick Kenrick, of the diocese of Bardstown, as his coadjutor, Mr. Matthews' resignation was accepted, and Mr. Kenrick being appointed by the Holy See, was consecrated at Bardstown, Kentucky, in June 1830, taking the place which had been so much urged upon Dr. Gallitzin, and which it was generally supposed he would be induced to accept.

Rev. Mr. Kenrick was a much younger man, to whom the Bishop of Bardstown, the venerable B. J. Flaget, was so devotedly attached that it almost broke his heart to part with him, he had not even the courage at first to announce to the bishop elect the great honor awaiting him.

Immediately upon receiving the news of his appointment Rev. Mr. Kenrick wrote to Dr. Gallitzin:

REV. F. P. KENRICK TO VERY REV. D. A. GALLITZIN.

Bardstown, May 3, 1830.

Rev. and very dear Sir,

The intelligence of my appointment to the coadjutorship

and full administration of the diocese of Philadelphia, has, of course, ere this reached you. To me it is a matter of serious regret that you or some of the veteran missionaries of the diocese have been left in the humbler and more tranquil spheres of your ministry, whilst I am called from this peaceful recess to so perilous an elevation. Opposition, however, I have deemed fruitless, and have, therefore, preferred a ready acceptance to any exercise or display of humility. I am consoled by the reflection that the diocese offers me several learned and zealous co-operators, amongst whom the *Defender of the Faith* holds a conspicuous place. I flatter myself, then, that those talents which have been so successfully employed from the pulpit and the press in defence of our holy religion, will continue devoted to the same great ends in the same diocese which has already derived from them such advantage, and that your counsels, and prayers, and exertions, will considerably aid me in the discharge of the arduous duties of my station. On my part, as no ambition has prompted my acceptance, no spirit of domination shall characterize my exercise of authority, but I shall regard myself as a brother of all my clergymen, above whom, though far inferior in merits and services to several, I am raised by the inscrutable councils of Providence. For you, Reverend Sir, I shall cherish an affection blended with veneration, and grounded on the solid basis of your universally acknowledged merits.

I beg of you to continue to exercise the faculties which you already possess, in all their amplitude, and I further empower you to grant all such matrimonial dispensations and exercise all such other powers as may not already be contained in your faculties, and which I could impart were I personally consulted. These extraordinary powers you will at discretion exercise until such time as I shall be within the limits of the diocese.

The consecration is intended to take place in the cathedral of Bardstown on Whit-Sunday, if it suits the convenience of Dr. England whom I have invited to preach on the occasion, otherwise shortly after, perhaps on *Corpus*

Christi. I should have chosen Philadelphia for the place of consecration, but I was anxious to give this mark of my attachment to the apostolic prelate of this diocese, who parts from me with all the impassioned sorrow of a parent. The precise day I shall endeavor to have notified in the public prints. If you could conveniently attend, you will confer on me a high favor, and I am confident you will feel no small gratification in witnessing the splendid edifices which religion has raised in this country.

In conclusion I request the participation of your prayers and sacrifices for me personally, and for the diocese to whose administration Divine Providence has called me.

With sentiments of profound respect and warm attachment
Your affectionate friend and brother in Christ,
Francis P. Kenrick,
Bishop el Aratha and Coadjutor Phila.

But not even these flattering expressions of the esteem and veneration of the expectant bishop could conciliate the lion-hearted missionary, who saw in the appointment of one so ready to exercise his full authority, a slight to the venerable prelate whose cruel sufferings he had taken grievously to heart. With his usual sensitiveness Dr. Gallitzin, after the sense of relief at his own escape was over, thought only of the feeling Bishop Conwell would naturally experience by being, in reality, superseded by a young priest from a distant diocese, who had never felt with him the stings of insult and bitterest opposition in the discharge of his rightful authority; he feared that no stranger would render to the aged bishop the deference due to his position, and his sorely wounded heart, in which spirit he replied:

Very Rev. D. A. Gallitzin to Right Rev. F. P. Kenrick.*
†
Loretto, May 22, 1830.

Right Rev. Sir,

Your favour conveying the intelligence of your appointment to the coadjutorship and full administration etc. was

---
* From a copy found among Dr. Gallitzin's papers.

duly received. Whilst on the one hand it relieves my mind from the most serious apprehensions, it, on the other, throws me into a state of perplexity having only a few days since received a communication from the clergy of Philadelphia, conveying the pleasing intelligence of the full restoration of our worthy bishop to his episcopacy, authority and jurisdiction. It does not belong to me as an inferior to judge between my superiors, and in fact I am not in possession of any data on which to form a judgment; from the time that our Bishop took his departure from Rome until the present day, I have never received any authentic communication concerning ecclestical affairs, and all the information I have had on these important subjects, including the late synod and your appointment etc., was derived from newspaper, and from flying and often contradictory reports. In short, Right Rev. Sir, I never was in the secrets of the cabinet, and to this day have not even been favoured with a copy of the pastoral letter directed to the clergy, though report says that such a letter was published by the Synod of Baltimore. From the above you will at once agree that my line of conduct is plainly marked out for me, viz: to leave it to my superiors to settle the question of jurisdiction between them, and to await the result. Dr. Conwell was once declared to be my bishop, his jurisdiction suspended *pro tem.* is now declared to be fully restored, of course my allegiance to him still continues, until I am released by himself, or by an au thority superior to his. In this declaration you will discover nothing, I hope, but a sure pledge of my future fidelity and obedience to yourself; whenever it is made manifest to me that you are my bishop, I shall cheerfully acquiesce and sincerely thank Divine Providence which in his kindness has relieved me from all apprehension of ever becoming Bishop of Philadelphia. Both the late archbishop (a very particular friend of mine) and our own present bishop spoke to me in Baltimore, November 1827, and begged of me to suffer my name to be mentioned at Rome for the coadjutorship of Philadelphia. I at first opposed it, and if I finally concluded to remain neutral, it was merely with the view of availing myself of the chance I might derive from such a nomination, to obtain from Rome a division of this immense diocese, and to have this place, which is the centre of a large Catholic settlement, raised to the dignity of an episcopal see, for I always dreaded the idea of being Bishop of Philadelphia.

....I have stood by him [Bishop Conwell] and the most of his clergy have stood by him. We considered him as an injured and persecuted man; it was not enough that he was spit upon and dirt thrown at him in the streets of Philadelphia, which he bore with the utmost meekness.... I have spent thirty-five years in this mission, and I can safely declare that during the seven or eight years of Dr. Conwell's administration, religion has made more rapid strides than it had during the twenty-six, or twenty-seven preceeding years, and to the present moment we are left to guess what could have been the crimes, for which nearly the heaviest punishment is inflicted, which the Church can inflict upon a bishop. Permit me now, Right Rev. Sir, to give you my humble opinion as to the course you had better pursue under the above circumstances.

Instead of conferring confirmation in the various congregations on your way to Philadelphia, as you propose, I would beg of you to post on *recta via* to headquarters, in order to have the main question settled at once, that no difficulty, no scruple, or perplexity may remain in the minds of the clergy you would meet on the road. At any rate giving confirmation now would be premature. I wish to have at least the month [of June] to prepare my immense congregation for so great a blessing, of which as many as one hundred will partake, and which cannot be reiterated. For this extensive congregation, the members of which have almost exclusively to earn their living by hard labor, the very best time for confirmation would be after harvest, say at the end of September, or beginning of October. In the eastern part of the diocese, where the congregations are chiefly confined to towns, any time will do.

Moreover, I must beg of you, and this I would do on both my knees, not to interfere with the Westmoreland question* until you have first been in Philadelphia, and afterwards at Loretto, at which two places you will obtain full possession of all the facts necessary to be known, in order to enable you to form a sound judgment. As vicar-general I have been obliged to interfere, and I can safely say the difficulties are so great, that were you just now in Westmoreland, without a miraculous interposition of Providence you could never succeed in settling matters, whilst in Philadelphia and Loretto you would have time to collect your materials and digest your plan....

Bishop Kenrick was consecrated on June 6th, with great ceremony; and on the eleventh replied to Dr. Gallitzin:

RIGHT REV. FRANCIS P. KENRICK TO VERY REV. D. A. GALLITZIN.

Bardstown, June 11. 1830.

Rev'd and dear Sir

Your favor of the 22. ult. reached me on the 9th instant, three days after my consecration. This was performed by the Right Rev. Dr. Flaget, assisted by the Right Rev. Dr. Conwell, the Right Rev. Dr. David, the Right Rev. Dr. England and the Right Rev. Dr. Edward Fenwick being also in choir on the occasion. Your presence would have been grateful to many who were desirous to see the man whose writings had edified and enlightened them, and to some who longed to see once more him whom, at an early period of his ministry they had viewed with veneration. Among the latter are the families of Messrs. Elder and Moore who desire to be remembered kindly to you. To me it would have been in a high degree gratifying, but I could not claim or expect the favour.

Your letter exhibits the candid and uncompromising spirit of a veteran missionary who, through a principle of duty, adheres to a prelate dear to his heart on account of the obloquy and afflictions unjustly heaped upon him. I join fully

---

* Mr. McGirr was still there, contending with great difficulties, and the quarrels at their height.

with you in these strong and generous feelings, and I hope we shall both equally concur in the adoption of those measures which, in the judgment of the American prelates, and of the Holy See, seem necessary to terminate his afflictions. His age and his troubles demand, as they have thought, that he should be liberated from the burden of governing the diocese; and without imputing to him criminality, which the enemies of religion could alone imagine, they have provided for his future happiness. A regard for his welfare, and a still greater concern for the interests of our holy religion in his diocese, induced my acquiesence when my youth, ill-health, and other circumstances, would have required my refusal of the episcopal dignity. God is my witness that I did not ambition it; and at this moment I could without a struggle part with the high but awful honor. In accepting it I bowed only to the will of heaven, manifested by proper authority, and in exercising it, I am determined only to seek the greater glory of God, and my own salvation, with that of the flock committed to my care. Your piety and long tried zeal promised me much aid in the arduous undertaking, and though the language of your answer would appear disheartening, I feel fully persuaded that on receiving a distinct notification of my authority, you will support me most ardently in endeavoring to solace and honor the declining age of the venerable Bishop of Philadelphia, and to promote the peace and prosperity of the diocese. Should your opinion as to the expediency of the measures adopted be different from that of the American prelacy, and as to the selection of the individual should you also think differently from them, still you will no doubt yield in deference to their judgment, sustained by the solemn sanction of the Apostolic See. To dissipate every doubt arising from the rumors that have reached you, or the statements made from rumor by clergymen who had not seen the documents, I take the trouble of making an extract from the letter written by Cardinal Cappellan, prefect of the Congregation,—and to which reference was made in the Papal Bulls:

*　　*　　*

* * * The bishop is still left at liberty to exercise all public functions, to administer confirmation, and even orders, to such as with my consent shall be presented for ordination.
...... I have requested him, therefore, to administer confirmation in Pittsburg, on Sunday, the 20th inst. Rev. Mr. Maguire having solicited me to administer it; and I meant to give him in the other congregations, as we passed forward, a similiar mark of my respect, and the public this testimony of his still being recognized as a worthy prelate, though unfortunate in the difficulties which he encountered. Thus his return to Philadelphia would have been a species of triumph, and I would stand by his side to support, vindicate, and comfort him. This I am still determined to do, and if ever I recede from the kindest and most respectful course of conduct in his regard, the fault shall not be mine. · I did intend to visit Rev. Mr. McGirr's congregation with the others on my way, but I was determined not to adopt any precipitate measures. The information which you can afford me on this and other subjects will be most acceptable, and I hope to receive it by word or letter. speedily. Being sollicited to go to Huntingdon by Rev. Mr. O'Rielly to dedicate a church, and give confirmation, I may be prevented from calling at Loretto, which I greatly desire to do in order to form a personal acquaintance with its venerated pastor. If, in my power, I will gladly visit your congregation and administer confirmation at another time that may better suit.

I take this opportunity of informing you that I have directed the Jubilee Indulgence to be published by the respective pastors throughout the diocese, leaving it at their option to choose any two weeks within six months from the 13th of June. I empower all of them during that period to exercise, in favor of those who are determined to comply with the conditions of the Jubilee, all such powers as I can delegate.

I have shown, as you requested, your letter to the bishops, and believe that they lament that your not being fully informed of the extent of my powers, has led you to indicate something like dissent from measures adopted by the Holy See, at the particular suggestion of all the American prelacy in council. Your letter indeed is not in accord with those which I have received from Reverend Messrs. Maguire, Hurley, Hughes, Heyden, Kenney, O'Rielly &c.*&c.. But on a better acquaintance I hope every difficulty will vanish. Pray for me, dear and Reverend Sir, and believe in the sincerity of my respect and attachment.

Your affectionate brother in Christ,

† Francis Patrick Kenrick,

Bp Arath and Coadj. Phila.

Of course this was all sufficient, and Dr. Gallitzin at once gave in his allegiance to the lawfully appointed administrator.

He was now overpowered with anxiety lest Mr. McGirr's enemies, gaining the ear of the new bishop should succeed in effecting the long sought disgrace of a good priest, one who with all his faults, was willing and able to accomplish great good, and rough though he might be, was as a rock in his faith, and untiring in the performance of his duties. Faithfulness and good intentions were merits of inestimable value in the eyes of the vicar-general, and in his opinion atoned for multitudes of faults and shortcomings; it is known that he appealed with seemingly irresistable eloquence to the new bishop to be merciful, to accept no doubtful evidence, to consider the sacred character of a priest, the marvellous graces given, which, though long abused and resisted, must almost assuredly triumph in the end, of the terrible evil of human interference, of the hope that should never be shadowed, of the reputation which, like the uncertain glimmer of a feeble fire, might be made the last expiring spark, put out forever by a sudden breath, or the quivering gleam, gently strengthened and softly fanned until it becomes a steady flame, and brillant light, not easily extinguished. "The welfare of the accused," he said in the case of another of the priests under his protection, who certainly was innocent of the acts laid to his charge,* "perhaps his eternal happiness

---

* Rev. H. Lemcke, p. 301.

or misery is at stake, for a priest, whose name and reputation have once been shadowed, will generally be entirely ruined. Are you willing to take such a responsibility upon yourself? Remember that you will one day have to appear with him before God. I regard him as innocent, and insist that the case shall be more thoroughly examined, according to St. Paul's law: *Against a priest receive not an accusation but under two or three witnesses* (Tim. v. 19) Where are your witnesses and who are they?"

But the bishop was disposed to take a more severe view of all such cases, and to exact that his priests should be above suspicion, not knowing the circumstances and character of life and judgment in the still not over-refined districts of Pennsylvania, where the ordinary civilities and meaningless courtesies of city life, were liable to the grossest interpretation, and where a momentary indiscretion, which was perhaps atoned before God by sincere contrition and bitter penance, might easily be regarded as a crime never to be forgiven or forgotten; he desired also, with a most noble ambition, to raise the standard of exellence among priests and people, to the very highest point, and felt himself constrained to answer Gallitzin's appeals in a spirit of severe justice:

Right Rev. Dr. Kenrick to Very Rev. D. A. Gallitzin.

Aug., 4. 1830.

.... With regard to your counsels I am grateful, and assure you I am determined to respect the forms of justice as well as the substance, yet I cannot promise you that to investigate charges against a priest I shall impanel a jury, or examine and confront witnesses in the presence of the multitude, though such be the forms of administering civil justice in this country. Ecclesiastical tribunals have rules peculiar to themselves for the great ends to which they are directed, and these rules I shall assuredly observe.... There are two extremes which I mean to avoid, one that of proceeding precipitately on a mere rumor or suspicious accusation, the other that of making matters of a delicate nature the subject of a tedious investigation. I am determined always to require positive testimony, delivered in the presence of respectable clergymen.

....But do not, I pray you, hold forth the least hope, save in a temperate vindication by unsuspicious testimony. I own I am liable to be deceived, my youth may be imposed upon by designing men, but I study at least to avoid deception and bias and I pray to the God of light to direct me. Never shall I proceed in these critical matters without having first fervently implored his assistance. Age would not of itself secure me from deception, the wily may impose on the good faith of a veteran missionary, whose innocence and virtue may leave him to judge favorably of those who speak the language, and wear the appearance of piety.

Permit me to entreat you not to suppose too readily that without strong cause I would deprive myself of the services of a missionary. Let not delinquents find any hope of protection in your name, which to me is dear and venerable, but tell them to have recourse to me, and prove their innocence, and that they may be assured of my favor....

All that could be obtained for Mr. McGirr, under these circumstances, was the permission to remain in Dr. Gallitzin's immediate neighborhood, and exercise his priestly powers under his direction, an order which, as we have seen, was softened and made endurable by the delicacy, the tact, and the unvarying respect of the pastor of Loretto. In the other case in which a blameless priest was the victim of appearances, reported to the bishop by the proprietor of a hotel (called a *tavern* in those days), not far from Loretto, who undoubtedly was himself deceived, Dr. Gallitzin though perfectly certain that there was not a shadow of truth in the accusations, could not shield the accused from severe censure, unless the whole matter was investigated thoroughly, which the bishop considered undesirable, and requiring too great publicity. The unfortunate priest went to another diocese, and Dr. Gallitzin wrote indignantly, but with utmost politeness and deference to the bishop, that "since it had pleased his Lordship to make a tavern keeper vicar general of the mountains, and there was no need of two, he begged to resign his position as vicar general," and afterwards worked less directly in the cause of those who appealed to him, always encouraging and sustaining them, joining them in prayers, but preferring to have their case advocated by other clergymen as well as by himself, thinking thus to inspire the bishop with more confidence in their innocence.

In the early autumn after his consecration, Bishop Kenrick visited Sportsman's Hall, Blairsville, Loretto and the various missions of Western Pennsylvania, accompanied by Rev. John Hughes, and part of the way by Rev. Mr. Heyden, giving confirmation, listening to grievances, and carefully studying the spiritual affairs of the country through which he passed. He was received at Loretto with every demonstration of veneration and delight, and administered confirmation in the church there to no less than five hundred persons, old men of eighty and even ninety years of age, women bent nearly double with the weight of years, and boys and girls of twelve and fourteen, people of all ages and conditions, who were gathered together to receive the all sustaining sacrament, some as a treasure for their life's journey just commencing, some as a seal upon the course so near its end. Mr. Heyden assisted and counted them as they went up to be confirmed. The bishop was amazed at the evidences of piety and unexpected refinement which met him everywhere in this little mountain village, of which he had received accounts most favorable, but far below the truth. The whole party was greatly impressed by the simple but stately hospitality of the pastor from whom there radiated a peculiar gentleness and sanctity which, in spite of the simplicity and cheerfulness which accompanied it, inspired the bishop with a certain awe and a profound veneration.

"The roads and conveniences for travelling," a writer remarks concerning this visit*, "in the interior of Pennsylvania

---

* Mr. Hassard in *Life of Archbishop Hughes.*

were not much better at that time, than when Mr. Hughes went about preaching with Dr. Conwell. In journeying from Loretto to Newry, Bishop Kenrick managed to obtain a seat in some public conveyance; Mr. Hughes and Father Heyden were left to follow him with the baggage in an open wagon. Night overtook them long before they reached their destination. A few miles distant from Newry they examined their baggage to see if all was safe. Behold! the mitre and crozier were missing, they had fallen out of the wagon. 'We must turn back,' said Father Hughes, but to this Father Heyden and the driver objected; the road was dangerous; the night was very dark, and it would be impossible to find the lost articles. Father Hughes cut short the discussion by seizing the reins, and turning the horses himself. The mitre and crozier were picked up before they had gone far. A believer in omens might have thought this little incident prophetic." At all events it was characteristic; the very mitre once urged upon him now dropped at Gallitzin's door, for which Father Heyden, who also refused several bishoprics during his life would not turn back, could by no means be left behind by Dr. Hughes.

Rev. Mr. Heyden was not without his own little troubles at this time, in which Dr. Gallitzin deeply sympathized. Newry was one of Mr. Heyden's stations, and with the fervent ambition of youth, and the burning desire for God's glory of a true priest, he was anxious to make greater improvements than the bishop thought prudent or advisable. It is likely the simplicity of the mountain villages, their many inconveniences, were more noticed by the bishop as they would be by any stranger, than by Dr. Gallitzin, Mr. Heyden, and those who had seen these settlements growing up around them, and so far from considering them as indicating poverty and insignificance, looked upon each new cabin added to the place, as proof of the prosperous and flourishing condition of of the country; a view which the bishop could hardly be expected to take. Bishop Kenrick visited the district again in 1831, and made some slight changes, upon which Dr. Gallitzin wrote Mr. Heyden with his usual readiness to unite with all who were in the least troubled, or disturbed by the passing disappointments, from which no life worth living can ever be exempt:

VERY REV. D. A. GALLITZIN TO REV. THOMAS HEYDEN.
†
Loretto Aug. 27. 1831.

Rev and dear Friend,

You are no doubt apprised by this time that your letter inviting me to Newry did not reach me until Sunday about ten o'clock. Dr. Kenrick's letter of invitation also came too late. I wrote to him and sent the letter by my young man, giving him my ideas on the subject of building churches in Newry and Holidaysburgh, (as he had requested my advice.) However, I think his mind was made up....I feel much afflicted and sincerely sympathize with you, however, there is no remedy but submission. I am sorry, that your affliction prevented your coming to Loretto; on the contrary, in times of sorrow, you should visit your real friend to seek consolation. As you have more leisure in your present situation than formerly, I hope you will pay me a visit as soon as convenient. I met the bishop at Ebensburg; he arrived on the 18th at two o'clock, and left next day at seven, without being able to promise positively to return the same way. Whilst at Ebensburg he received four letters from Philadelphia, which seemed to agitate his mind considerably, from what I could learn it is not the trustees alone that give him trouble. ....Poor bishop! Had he known (whilst in Kentucky) all that was before him, he would have paused a while before he consented to accept of the mitre. O my friend! how much reason I have to thank God!

Yours forever

Demetrius A. Gallitzin.

CHAPTER XXV.

SETTLEMENT OF NEW PRIESTS.

(1830—1834.)

Changes.—Rev. James A. Stillinger.—Rev. James Bradley.—A singular call.—Ebensburg.—Rev. P. H. Lemcke.—His first impressions of Dr. Gallitzin.—The chapel at Loretto.—Carrolltown.—St. Augustine.—Summit.—Gallitzin.

The influence of the new bishop was very soon felt in the vast district of Western Pennsylvania, where Dr. Gallitzin had so long struggled single handed, only aided at times by priests who came and went, without that attachment to a permanent home in the mountains with which he so much desired to see his co-laborers animated. Mr. McGirr was removed from Sportsman's Hall, and a young priest, Rev. James A. Stillinger, just ordained, designated for his place, and another, Rev. James Bradley, the first priest ordained by Bishop Kenrick, appointed to Ebensburg, to take charge of the large mission near that growing town, and to be a comfort and solace to Dr. Gallitzin. Mr. Stillinger was born in Baltimore of American parents, April 19th 1801, educated at Mt. St. Mary's, Emmetsburg, ordained at the Sulpitian Seminary in Baltimore, by Archbishop Whitfield, Feb. 28, 1830, and attended the congregations attached to Mt. St. Mary's, until November of the same year, when Bishop Kenrick appointed him pastor of a little brick church in Blairsville, thirty by forty feet, and unfinished, which had been dedicated to St. Simon and St. Jude on their feast-day, Oct. 22, 1830, by the bishop, assisted by Rev. Mr. Hughes; his mission included Sportsman's Hall, and the entire county of Westmoreland.

Rev. James Bradley was a native of the County of Tyrone, Ireland, received his classical education at Londonderry, emigrated to this country in 1825, entered Mt. St. Mary's college in the same year, was ordained by Bishop Kenrick at the Jesuits' church in Conewago in September 1830, and almost immediately appointed to the mountains. These young priests set out in the same carriage from Emmetsburg, November 1830, travelling together until they reached Bedford, where they staid overnight with Mr. Heyden, and then parted for their respective missions, Mr. Stillinger proceeding directly to Westmoreland, and Mr. Bradley making haste to call upon the venerable pastor of Loretto, whose honored name had so often reached his ears. "He received me then and always," writes Rev. Mr. Bradley, "with true paternal kindness. I remained with him a few days, sung High Mass for him on Sunday, and he preached.... His manner was dignified, his language clear and impressive, his trumpet voice could be heard at a great distance, his articulation perfectly distinct, although he had accidentally lost all his teeth...... His discourses were generally on controversy, having been led in that direction by being obliged to defend Catholic principles, from the incessant attacks and misrepresentations of them, by the various Protestant sects. However, he forcibly inculcated all the Christian virtues, especially humility, and declaimed against the sin of pride."

Mr. Stillinger was not able to visit him until later. "In 1831," he writes, "I went to see him for the first time. On entering the hall he met me, and took my hand with both of his, so beautifully and delicately formed, looking intently into my face with his dark hazel eyes, quick and penetrating, and a countenance beaming full of benevolence and kindness, and an address so graceful, so bland, so fatherly and accomplished as at once to indicate the nobleman, the high-bred gentleman, and the self sacrificing convert and missionary.... Before I could give him my address, he said: 'Your name is Stillinger, I said Mass in your grandfather's house before you were born. You are welcome,' he continued, and said that on his first visit to Chambersburg, when he was within two or three miles of the place, he met some persons on the road and asked them if they knew where Michael Stillinger lived; they said they did, and gave him the direction by pointing to the part of the town where he lived; he thanked them kindly and rode on, but he had not gone far when he heard a person calling: 'Stranger! Stranger!' he stopped until the person came up to him, almost out of breath from running, who said: 'I come to tell you, Sir, that Stillinger is a Papist!' 'Very well, Sir, I am thankful to you for the information, I will see to that.' We enjoyed a pleasant laugh, and entertained ourselves agreeably with other matters. Next morning, though there were others that could serve Mass, he insisted upon serving my Mass, I, of course, felt honored and have ever since, for it was not deserved on my part, the reward went to him, and would add to his crown in heaven. How humble and how great! I shall ever remember the impression it made on my mind. I was the young priest but little over a year ordained, he was the nobleman, greatest among the great, the self sacrificing convert, and a Catholic in faith to the marrow; he was the devoted, humble and learned priest and venerable missionary of the Alleghany mountains."

The church at Sportsman's Hall, which was now consigned to the care of Rev. Mr. Stillinger, was a small frame building about forty by thirty feet, unnamed, and as far as was known, undedicated, no record of any such ceremony existing. Its affairs were in a most complicated and unhappy condition, and its surrounding influences of the most depressing and disheartening character, but the zealous young priest, with an admirable mixture of mildness and severity, of tact and plain-speaking, aided no little by a most commanding and attractive presence, to Dr. Gallitzin's great joy and relief, speedily adjusted many disputed matters, and placed others in a way of a peaceable termination.

Rev. Mr. Bradley after the short and edifying visit to Loretto already mentioned, established himself at Ebensburg where there was little frame church, with a small congregation. His mission included a little settlement some fifteen miles from Loretto, called Hart's Sleeping Place, in remembrance of an old Indian trader who, when all was a wilderness, occasionally rested there in his journeys, where with great energy the few families composing the village, all Catholics, whom Dr. Gallitzin had previously visited and instructed, combined to put up quite a large log church; another station about fourteen miles west of Ebensburg where there were about a dozen families, mostly emigrants from Loretto, headed by our old friend, John Weakland, who had gathered themselves about a small church which Dr. Gallitzin had very recently dedicated to St. Joseph; Indiana, about thirty miles west of Ebensburg, where there were but four or five Catholic families, Germans; Johnstown, where there was about the same number, and Jefferson or Wilmore, near Ebensburg where a negro family from Maryland had settled, been converted and received into the Church sometime previously by Dr. Gallitzin, who said Mass at their house, or in their barn, which was much more commodious, whenever he was able to visit the little hamlet where they resided. Upon these occasions the barn was duly swept and made perfectly neat, its usual inmates penned up elsewhere, not so far away but that the melancholy lowing of banished cows, the cackling of astonished hens, and the loud crowing of discomfitted roosters, could be heard from the place of their exile. during the most solemn part of divine service, but so sincere and unaffected was the devotion of the worshippers, that this was never an interruption, scarcely even a momentary distraction. After the service Dr. Gallitzin always dined with the family in whose house he had officiated, and perhaps none in the whole of his mission entertained him with more interior joy, and more charming demonstration, than this Maryland family, so ardently attached to him.

Besides taking the place of the pastor of Loretto in these stations, Rev. Mr. Bradley had in his charge about half the laborers, of which there were several hundred in all, working on the old portage railroad from Johnstown to Hollidaysburg, at the same time attending whenever he could to the distant sick calls in Father Gallitzin's remaining district, which the well-worn missionary could scarcely reach. Mr. Bradley remembers among these calls, one which illustrates the great interest and care which our guardian angels exercise for our souls. "I was roused one night from my deep slumber," he relates, "by three knocks at my door. I raised my window, but the night was so dark that I could see no one, I enquired what the matter was, and a clear, loud voice answered that there was a man at the point of death, at the viaduct about eighteen or twenty miles distant, eight miles of a turnpike and the balance of the road through a dense forest, through which a wagon road had been cut a few days before. I was anxious to have some one accompany me through that dismal path, and asked the messenger if he was riding, he answered 'No'. I requested him to go on ahead of me and I would get my horse and soon overtake him. But I saw no one until I emerged from that dreary path, by early dawn the next morning, near the place where I was informed the man was at the point of death. I met a number of laborers coming out to work, I enquired where the sick man was and no one could tell me. 'What' I thought to myself, 'what can be the meaning of all this? Could any one be so cruel as to call me out such a night, such a distance, and over such a road, without any necessity?' and whilst these thoughts were running through my mind I found myself in sight of the viaduct, I saw something falling, and presently three or four men carrying a man into a shanty. I arrived there simultaneously with them; a log had fallen upon the poor man as they were in the act of removing the centers from the viaduct. He did not seem to me to be much hurt, but he earnestly craved the last sacraments. I heard his confession, gave him absolution, etc. He cried out aloud: 'Glory be to God,' the soul left the body, the man was dead! Then I remembered and fully understood the nature of the call I had received: 'Unless you make haste you will not overtake him alive,' and, in truth, if I had been any later that poor man would have died without the benefit of sacramental absolution. Thanks be to his guardian angel! In relating this to some of my brother priests, almost all of them could relate striking instances of nearly a similar nature."

Two years later Bishop Kenrick extended Mr. Bradley's mission to the eastern slope of the Alleghany mountains, with his residence at Newry, whence he attended Sinking Valley, Huntingdon, and a great many other stations, some of which belonged to Mr. Heyden's district, from which he was at this time absent, having been again called to Philadelphia. This change placed old cares again upon Dr. Gallitzin's shoulders, which he was now scarcely able to sustain, and also deprived him of the near neighborhood of a brother priest, and that he must have felt his loneliness very much, may be gathered from his note to Mr. Heyden upon his return to Bedford:

VERY REV. D. A. GALLITZIN TO REV. THOMAS HEYDEN.
†

Loretto, April 30, 1833.

Rev'd and my very dear Friend,

I feel grieved and mortified at your long continued silence, and being so long deprived of the pleasure of your company. I do not know a brother clergyman for whom I feel a greater affection, and I am not sensible of having ever offended you.... I long to see you. Could you not (after the holidays) spare a little time, say one week, from your missionary avocations?....

Give my respects to Mr. and Mrs. Heyden, and my affectionate compliments to Mr. and Mrs. Lyon, and to Mr. and Mrs. Jameson, and believe me *usque ad ultimum spiritum,*

My dear and Rev'd friend,

tuus in Christo addictissimus,
Demetrius A. Gallitzin.

The people of Ebensburg and adjacent stations were also deeply grieved at being left without a priest near at hand, and in sympathy with them Father Gallitzin, who could only occasionally attend them, pleaded their cause before the bishop, who replied:

RIGHT REV. F. P. KENRICK TO VERY REV. D. A. GALLITZIN.

Philadelphia, Jan. 10, 1833.

Rev'd and dear Sir,

I am pleased to learn from your favour of the 3d inst. the prospects which the Ebensburg and adjacent congregations afford for the reasonable support of a pastor. You may rely upon it that I shall seize an opportunity of meeting with your and their wishes, though the necessity of providing for other places equally or more destitute, and the scarcity of missionaries leave me unable to say when. As to the good will of the people I never entertained the least doubt; though I knew not whether their number or means would enable them, after the completion of the Railroad, to support a resident priest.... If I had a German priest at my disposal, I would cherfully attend to your suggestion, but several other places need a German priest and cannot obtain him. By the aid of the Rev. F. Guth (from Alsace) I hope to succeed in obtaining some of unquestionable merit.

As I suppose that the editors of the *Catholic Herald* have forwarded the two numbers already published of this paper, I need scarcely say that the *Press* has entirely ceased, and been succeeded by the *Herald*. The Rev. Messrs. Donahoe and O'Donnell are the editors and Rev. Mr. Hughes, being engaged to repel a Presbyterian assailant, will fill the columns with interesting letters....

I wish you many years of health and happiness and abundance of those consolations which heaven usually bestows on the veteran champions of religion. Your prayers are in return asked by

Your affectionate friend in Christ,

† Francis Patrick Kenrick,

Bp. etc.

About this time, Rev. P. H. Lemcke, a Prussian and a convert, came to this country to offer his services to the American mission, and, as he himself so well relates (*Leben und Wirken*, p. 13), was in the summer of 1834, "stationed in Philadelphia, at the church of the Holy Trinity. I did not like it there.... The bishop could not let me resign until he could find another German priest to take my place. I had before this somewhere read a biography of Princess Gallitzin, and gathered from it that she had a son, a Catholic missionary in America, but no one could give any information concerning him." Mr. Lemcke at this time, did not speak English, and perhaps his inquiries were therefore somewhat limited. "At last I asked the bishop. 'He is in Loretto,' was the answer, 'in Western Pennsylvania in this diocese.' 'Is he, then, still living?' 'Certainly, but he is old and delicate, greatly in need of assistance in his widely spread congregation. As you desire to be removed from here, and I have now a German priest to take your place, you can go to him. But he is a singular old saint; many others have tired to live with him, but it seems as if no one could get along with him.' I agreed with him, and as soon as I conveniently could set out on my journey. A journey from Philadelphia to Loretto can be made now by the Pennsylvania Central Railroad in nine or ten hours, at that time it was a break-neck affair: one had then to be dragged about in miserable stages for at least three days and nights.... I arrived at last in safety at Munster, a little village laid out by Irish people on a tableland of the Alleghany mountains, only four miles from Gallitzin's residence. The stage stopped at the house of a certain Peter Collins, a genuine Irishman, who kept the post-office and hotel. From the first moment I felt at home with them, (Mr. Collins' family) as if all had grown up about me; soon it was found that I was about to visit the venerated Gallitzin and then old and young crowded around me, showing me all possible love and reverence....

"....The next morning, for it was evening when I arrived, and they would not on any account let me go on, a horse was saddled for me and Thomas, one of the numerous Collins' children, now a man of influence and reputation, stood ready.... with a stick in his hand.... to show me the way, and to bring back the horse. Thus we went off, my companion talking to me without cessation, and of what he said I understood as much as I did of the chirping of the birds, and the screech of the squirrel, and other inmates of the woods, whom the dog, coming along with us, chased up the trees. We had gone about a mile or two in the woods when I saw a sled coming along drawn by two strong horses. N. B. in September, in the most beautiful summer weather. In the sled half sat and half reclined a venerable looking man in an old, much worn overcoat, wearing a peasant's hat which no one, it is likely, would have cared to pick up in the street, and carrying a book in his hand. I thought seeing him brought along in this way, that there must have been an accident, that perhaps the old gentleman had dislocated a limb in the woods, but Thomas, who had been on ahead, came running back, and said: 'THERE COMES THE PRIEST,' pointing to the man in the sled. I rode up and asked: 'Are you really the pastor of Loretto?' 'Yes, I am he.' 'Prince Gallitzin?' 'At your service, Sir, I am that very exalted personage,' saying this he laughed heartily. 'You may, perhaps, wonder,' he continued, when I had presented him a letter from the Bishop of Philadelphia, 'at my singular retinue. But how can it be helped? We have not as yet, as you see, roads fit for wagons, we should be either fast or upset every moment. I cannot any longer ride horseback, having injured myself by a fall, and it is also coming hard to me to walk; besides I have all the requirements for Mass to take with me. I am now on my way to a place where I have had for some years a station. You can now go on quietly to Loretto, and make yourself comfortable there, I shall be at home this evening; or if you like better you can come with me, perhaps it may interest you.' I chose to accompany him, and after riding some miles through the woods we reached a genuine Pennsylvania farm house.

"Here lived Josuah Parish one of the first settlers of that country, and the ancestor of a numerous posterity. The Catholics of the neighborhood, men, women and children were already assembled in great numbers around the house, in which an altar was put up, its principal materials having been taken from the sled; Gallitzin then sat down in one corner of the house to hear confessions, and I, in another corner, attended to a few Germans. The whole affair appeared very strange to me, but it was extremely touching to see the simple peasant home, with all its house furniture, and the great fireplace, in which there was roasting and boiling going on at the same time, changed into a church, while the people with their prayer books, and their reverential manners, stood or knelt under the low projecting roof, or under the trees, going in and out, just as their turn came for confession. After Mass, at which Father Gallitzin preached, and when a few children had been baptized, the altar was taken away, and the dinner table set in its place. It was, of course, too small, but it was understood to remedy this evil for one party to sit down, after another party had dined, the children, meanwhile, standing about in the corners with their hands full, while the mother and daughters of the house went back and forth, replenishing the empty dishes from the pots in the fireplace, and pressing the food upon their guests. In a word, all was so pleasant and friendly that involuntarily, the love-feasts of the first Christians came to my mind. In the afternoon we went slowly on our way, Gallitzin in his sled and I on horseback, arriving at nightfall at Loretto....

"....In the evening we had much to talk about. Forty-two years had already passed since Gallitzin had left Germany, and in that time how much had happened! The French Revolution.... had ceased its rage. Napoleon had risen and disappeared, all Europe and especially our beloved Germany had been formed anew.... And while all this was passing, had this man destined by his birth as well as his talents, to play a grand *rôle* in the world's theatre, been announcing in the Alleghany mountains the kingdom of the Prince of Peace.... All those statesmen and warriors, who for sixty years caused so much talk, and to whom he would probably have belonged, are gone and there is no one to bless their memory; the deeds produced by their intrigues and blood-shed are almost forgotten, but what the humble, hidden man in the Alleghany mountains accomplished, has so beautifully unfolded itself, that coming generations will hold his memory in benediction.

* * *

"While we were thus deeply engaged in conversation, it grew very late, and then I saw an illustration of old time Catholic discipline, and home regularity. One of the old women of whom there were several living in the house, put her head in the doorway, asking if there would be prayers that night. 'Certainly,' said Gallitzin rising at once, and a signal being given, the household came together; the old nobleman knelt without any ceremony near the table by which he had been standing, took his rosary from his pocket and began it. After the prayers were over, he took his breviary, I did the same, the house was as quiet as a monastery. When I left my room the next morning I met the prince with his arms full of wood, intending to make a fire as it had grown quite cold during the night, afterwards when I went to the chapel to say Mass he insisted upon serving me."

This chapel had just been added to Father Gallitzin's residence so that he could reach it from his own room without going out of doors, it was arranged so that it could be warmed, as was absolutely necessary, for in the church the cold was so intense in the winters that when Mass was over, he often had the greatest difficulty in restoring animation to his nearly frozen hands; as he advanced in years he was obliged to have little braziers placed at each end of the altar, from which enough warmth was obtained to keep his fingers from becoming so numb and stiff that he could not use them. He said Mass on week days in this chapel of which he took the greatest care, and had decorated to the utmost extent of his resources: the walls were papered, the footboards smooth and painted, and the wooden altar a triumph of rustic art; in the vestibule there still hang the printed instructions which he framed and placed there, for the preservation of order and cleanliness:

Notice.

1. Scrape the dirt off your shoes on the iron scrapers provided for that purpose.
2. Do not spit on the floor of the chapel.
3. Do not put your hats and caps on the chapel windows.
4. Do not rub against the papered walls of the chapel.
5. Do not put your heels on the washboards.
6. After coming in at the passage door, shut the door after you.

Demetrius Augustine Gallitzin,
Parish Priest of Loretto.

It still remains in excellent order, almost the only material remembrance of him in Loretto that has been preserved as he left it; a few benches have been admitted since his time, for the accommodation of the faithful, who gather there in good numbers every week day morning.

"The next day," Mr. Lemcke continues, "was Sunday. The people began coming very early in the morning, from all directions, to go to confession. At ten o'clock I celebrated High Mass, at which the organ was played, and there was some pretty good singing. After the gospel, the old pastor.... stepped quickly towards me at the altar, put me one side, and commenced to preach, of course in English, of which I understood but little. As well as I could make it out it was strong against pride and vanity. Nothing in the world excited the humble man more than to perceive any luxury, love of finery, or new fashions creeping in among his children, though I must admit, there was scarcely ten dollars worth of superfluities and luxuries to be seen in the entire congregation; what special thing had aroused him just then I could not tell. Perhaps it was that at this time the first modern carriage made its appearance at the door of the Loretto church, for a man of the neighborhood who had grown rich, and now and then went to Philadelphia on business, had brought back with him a very fine carriage, in which with his family, all adorned to suit, he drove to church on Sundays, creating a great sensation. At the time the marvel was expected to make its appearance, the boys would climb the trees and fences keeping their eyes fixed in the direction from which it would probably come; in a word, it was like the Indians on the upper Missouri, when the first steamboat was seen.

"When Gallitzin had finished his English sermon, he began another in German, but to me it sounded altogether foreign; it is true he had received a German education, although at the time when the influence of the French language was at its height, but in his forty-two years in America he had had little or no practice in speaking it.... He introduced me formally to the Germans who were then pretty numerous, intimating to them that for the future I would attend to them, and that I would now preach them a German sermon, which they had not heard in a long time. He then moved aside, bowing to me with a mischievous smile, as much as to say: 'I have got through, now it is your turn.' There had been nothing of the kind intimated to me previously, he had merely requested me to celebrate High Mass, there was nothing for it, but for me to preach, more decidedly *ex tempore* than ever before in my life. When I spoke to him about it later, he laughed and said he wished to know whether I was fitted for a missionary, for he would have a treasure in one who could at a moment bring out the old and new.

"I lived in the belief that I was now at home with Gallitzin, and made my plans accordingly, how I would live with this singular old gentleman, how I would go to work to break through the crust which had formed over this noble nature, in the long battle with an ungrateful and wicked world, and how I would win myself a place in his heart. But I found I had reckoned without my host.

"On Monday morning he was ready to start out again; the horses were harnessed to the wagon, for now it was to go to Ebensburg, the county-town, to which the roads were so good that the sled was only required for them in the winter time. We stopped at the house of a Mrs. Ivory, who had grown up in Gallitzin's house, while her mother and two of her sisters still remained with him keeping house for him.

The old nobleman went about all the morning, from one house to another, and I could not imagine what he had on hand. After dinner the matter was explained. He handed me a paper saying: 'Here is a list of the Catholics of the place. Each one of them has bound himself by this paper to contribute a certain sum annually for your support. There is a little church here, but for some time there has been no priest; the congregation is small and hardly able to support one. But you will stay in this house, there are some really pretty rooms up-stairs, Mrs. Ivory is a good cook, and will treat you in the best manner possible. I will pay the board for you in advance, and in return you will come to me once a month to preach to the Germans, assist in the confessional; you will also have to attend to the stations and sick calls which I can no longer reach.' 'But,' said I, 'what are you thinking of? What am I to do here among the English, for as far as I can learn, there is not a German in the place?' 'That makes no difference, it is all the better for you, you will then learn English *nolens volens*. You have already made a good beginning, and as you have by no means appeared to fall on your head, you will soon be able to preach.' 'It may be so, but we can speak English in Loretto also, and it would in every way be better for me to live with you, and save paying for board.' 'Well, you see,' he said, rubbing his nose, as his way was when he was embarrassed, 'winter is near, as you have observed, and there is only one room in my house, beside the kitchen, in which there is a fireplace.' I could hardly keep in the laughter at this, for the bishop had told me he would not let another priest live with him, and had arranged his house in a way to have a good excuse for declining."

Mr. Lemcke therefore remained at Ebensburg, attending to a portion of Father Gallitzin's district some forty or fifty miles in extent, so that he had often to ride two days to administer the last sacraments, "but everywhere I went," he says,* "I found it light work, for Gallitzin had

---
* Page 331.

been before me and commenced it, laying the solid foundation." Once a month he visited Loretto as desired, with increased attachment to its venerable pastor. The off-shoot from Loretto, sometimes called the Weakland Settlement, which formed the congregation of St. Joseph's church, some twelve or fourteen miles distant, had long seemed to Dr. Gallitzin well fitted to serve as the nucleus of another Catholic town, upon the plan which he had himself carried through, after years of toil and bitter opposition, and with keen penetration he saw in Mr. Lemcke's immense energy and persistent nature, one well able to put the wish into practice, once he could be inspired with the desire of undertaking it. "He was continually urging me," says Mr. Lemcke*, "to do there as he had done in Loretto, promising to give me every aid and assistance." In 1836 Mr. Lemcke was able to purchase some land, and make some necessary arrangements to this end, and removed from Ebensburg to a farm near St. Joseph's, visiting Loretto and his district as before. Dr. Gallitzin would some times go over to visit him in the famous sled, and would heartily rejoice if he met with anything similar to his own beginning thirty years before. Mr. Lemcke in time laid out a village in this place, which he desired to call *Gallitzin*, but the venerable missionary learning of his intention put a stop to it at once, and suggested the name of Bishop Carroll, always so dear to him, in its place; although it must have been a great trial for Mr. Lemcke to yield the point so close to his own heart, he did so and called his village *Carrolltown*.

Many other off-shoots from Loretto took root and grew into Catholic villages about the same time, St. Augustine's, sometimes called *The Loup* from a peculiarity in the mountains just at the place, Summit at the highest point of the Alleghanies, a few miles beyond Loretto, which can be seen half hidden in the clustering foliage, as in a lovely nest among the mountain hillocks just below, and two miles further on, a little hamlet, at that time without a name, since increased,

---

* Page 334.

and resting for the most part over the longest tunnel of the Pennsylvania Central railroad, a tunnel cut through the rock, the very monarch of the mountains, and named by the railroad company in honor of the pastor of the Alleghanies. One is hurried onward through dense and unbroken darkness, and just as the first-ray of light, the very first breath of glorious mountain air breaks in, there is heard the echoing cry: GALLITZIN! the far resounding name of him who with feet *beautiful upon the mountains* opened to the entrancing sunlight of faith the gloomy caverns of heresy and sin,—a name shouted there with a startling appropriateness rendered the more striking that its deep significance was probably neither intended nor suspected. At this point the threshold of his mountain district is entirely passed, and the *great church* in which he praised the Lord, entered upon; it stretches onward, broad and far, in all directions for forty or fifty miles.

Thus after years of hoping against all hope, of heartfelt prayer, the ever present longing of the all sacrificing priest was reaching its fulfillment. He saw about him a little band of clergymen, young, active, fervent, endowed with great energy of character, and rare physical endurance, burning with zeal for the cause of Christ; high-toned, devoted, full of talents, asking only to labor how and where God willed, in obscurity, in privation, in solicitude and sufferings of all kinds if it so pleased Him. They were all devoted to the gentle, calm and saintly old priest, whose beautiful dark eyes never rested on theirs without shedding a silent benediction upon them; they were as dear to the old warrior as his dauntless young captains to the hero of a thousand battles; he looked upon them with utmost tenderness, as upon dearly loved sons into whose brave and honest hands he could freely leave his work and all his accumulated treasures; that their names were ever in his prayers the results abundantly proved.

CHAPTER XXVI.
DR. GALLITZIN AND THE PRESBYTERIAN PARSONS.
(1834.)

Tranquility of the present.—Peace in Loretto.—The outside battle.—The Presbyterian Synod.—Dr. Gallitzin's reply.

The establishment of this little band of assistants, not only relieved Dr. Gallitzin from the long journeys in all directions, which he could no longer endure, but that which was even more desirable, they lessened greatly the burden of care which for thirty-five years had weighed heavily upon him. Each in his appointed place applied his whole soul to the work at hand, with such prudence and such steady devotion, that the old missionary felt that the evening of his life was to be tranquil and freed from fear for those he should leave behind; and the children of his heart, his beloved congregations, those under his immediate care, and those who were beyond the reach of his voice, added greatly to this blessed assurance, all was orderly, regular, harmonious and as it should be, children followed in the footsteps of their parents, who, as children, had been trained by him, and if now and then evil made its appearance to grieve the heart of the pastor, it found no congenial soil upon which to take root. His debts were much decreased, no one was suffering for the little he still owed, and he lived in the firm hope that the good God, who was bringing so many of his desires to their fulfillment, would not send him to his grave with any shadow upon his name, a farthing of what was due to others left unpaid. Love and veneration met him every where he passed, and better still, love and harmony existed among his children.

But he did not forget that outside the world was rushing onward with the greatest tumult; that the devil was all alive and going about as actively as ever; that truth was struggling, hard pressed, but never overcome, against a thousand foes, and even in his tranquil retreat the noise of war stirred the old hero's spirit, and called upon him once again to take down his *Excalibur*, and send it flashing and shining with a brilliancy that dazzled as it slew, among "the godless hosts of heathens".

A Presbyterian Synod held at Columbia (Penn) drew from him six letters, published first in a newspaper, and afterwards in pamphlet-form,* under the title of:

Six Letters of Advice to the Gentlemen Presbyterian Parsons, who lately met at Columbia, Pa., for the purpose of Declaring War against the Catholic Church. By Demetrius Augustine Gallitzin.†

LETTER I.

January 14th 1834.

Gentlemen Parsons,

You have lately met in Synod, appointed a Committee to whom was referred the subject of a Presbyterian Tract and Sunday-school Society; and your committee hath made the following report, which you were pleased to adopt:

RESOLVED, That the Synod do hereby constitute a Board of Managers, to prepare, publish and circulate Presbyterian tracts and books, inculcating the distinctive doctrines of our standards, etc.

You have also appointed a committee to whom was referred the subject of *Romanism*, and that committee adopted the following wise preamble and resolutions:

WHEREAS the existence and prevalence of Romanism in

---

* As this little book is out of print, it is here given entire, with the exception of two or three local allusions, which have now lost their significance.

* Ebensburg: *Printed by Canan & Scott*, 1834, pp. 28.

this country endangers our civil and religious institutions, as shown by the nature of the system, and by the means adopted for its extension; and whereas the apathy of the Protestant Church on the subject and her general want of information in regard to the true principles and designs of Romanism, increase the danger. Therefore

Resolved 1st, That the Synod earnestly recommend to the ministry and members under our care, a more careful study of this subject, and a more intimate acquaintance with the system.

2nd, That our ministers more frequently and distinctly portray to their people the true features of *Popery*, in the way in which they judge most expedient.

3rd, Particularly, that our ministers be requested to hold up constantly to the people, the prophetic page [having] reference to the rise, the progress, the characteristics, and the fall of *Popery*.

4th, That standard books and well written tracts on the subject of Romanism be extensively and carefully circulated.

5th, That our churches be affectionately warned against the practice of patronizing Romish institutions, either by making pecuniary contributions, or by placing their children and wards under their instruction and influence.

6th, That our ministers be requested, if they think it expedient, to read the foregoing Preamble and Resolutions to their congregations.

Well done, gentlemen! Thus, you have sounded the tocsin of war. You have drawn the sword and thrown away the scabbard. Like so many heroes you stand in battle array to fight the battles of the Lord against Pope and Popery. Fame, which hath already wafted across the Atlantic the account of your heroic deeds during the ravages of the cholera, will bring your declaration of war to Rome, and fill the Pope and his cardinals with terror and dismay.

But now, gentlemen, let me tell you it is not sufficient to know how to declare war; you ought also to know how to carry it on; and as I am somewhat acquainted with military tactics (having formerly held a commission in the Russian army), charity impels me to assist you with my advice.

To secure a little respect to my advice, I wish you to observe: 1st, That I am in my sixty-fourth year; 2ndly, That I was educated in the Greek Protestant church, the members of which bear a greater hatred to the Pope than ever you did; 3rdly, That I am now, and since the year 1795 have been a minister of that religious system which you, very gentlemanly, designate by the nicknames of Romanism or Popery, and which I call the Roman Catholic Church, alias the church of Jesus Christ.

From the premises the conclusion is rational, that, knowing both sides of the question, I ought to be tolerably well qualified to advise you how to carry on a war successfully against the Pope.

Your committee to whom was referred the subject of a Presbyterian Tract and Sunday-school Society, made the following report:

RESOLVED, That the Synod do hereby constitute a Board of Managers to prepare, publish, and circulate Presbyterian Tracts and Books inculcating the distinctive doctrine of OUR standards, &c., &c.

What? Tracts and Books, the produce of the intellect of man, to inculcate the doctrine said to be plainly inculcated by the Bible? Is it possible? Your great champion has lately and repeatedly told us (in his controversy with the Rev. John Hughes) that the Bible, and the Bible alone, is the rule of faith of Protestants. Your Bible Societies everywhere proclaim their principle of sending forth the Bible among all nations of the globe, *without note or comment*. Yet you begin your warfare against the Catholic Church by entrenching yourselves within and surrounding yourselves by, Tracts and Books, the productions of mere men! Take my advice, gentlemen, knock the above Resolution in the head, and stick to YOUR BIBLE ALONE. Above all things, be consistent if you wish to succeed in your warfare; else your members may perhaps suspect the soundness of your cause.

The next and, I believe, the main subject which occupied your attention, was the subject of *Romanism.*

Your committee on that subject adopted the Preamble and six Resolutions above quoted. The Preamble consists of two parts:

1st. WHEREAS the existence and prevalence of Romanism in this country endangers our civil and religious institutions, as shown by the nature of the system, and by the means adopted for its extension; and

2nd WHEREAS the apathy of the Protestant Church on the subject, and her general want of information in regard to the true principles and designs of Romanism, increase the danger, &c.

Now, with regard to the first part of the above preamble, I have the following remarks to make.

Assertion, you know, is no proof. Give us proofs: show us how the existence and prevalence of the Catholic Church endangers our civil and religious institutions. The members of your church at least many of them, are too intelligent, to believe, upon your bare word, what the history of the United States since the Revolution, and indeed the history of many other countries, completely contradicts. And as for the second part of your preamble, I fully admit the general want of information in regard to the principles of the Catholic Church. But does not this declaration contradict your above assertion? If you acknowledge your ignorance with regard to our true principles and designs, how can you peremptorily decide on their dangerous tendency?

Take my advice, gentlemen, suppress the above preamble, and to rid you of the trouble of having anything to prove, substitute the following:

WHEREAS by our ministry we would wish to secure an ample living and respectability to ourselves, our wives and children; and

WHEREAS from the unexampled and alarming increase of Romanism it is to be dreaded that before many years, the Romans will cover the land like the locusts of Egypt; and

WHEREAS many of our neighbors are so infatuated as to

leave pure light of the Gospelthe and to embrace Romanism, which threatens to leave onr temples desolate and our purses empty; and

WHEREAS we are ashamed to beg, and not able to dig; therefore

RESOLVED, &c., &c.

Gentlemen, the last named preamble leaves you nothing to prove. I advise you to adopt it. With this advice I shall leave you for a while, subscribing myself respectfully

Your very humble servant,

Demetrius Augustin Gallitzin.

LETTER II.

January 21, 1834.

Gentlemen Parsons,

I have carefully examined your six Resolutions. I shall take them up, one by one, and give you my advice upon each of them.

No. 1, That the Synod earnestly recommend to the ministry and members under our care, a more careful study of this subject (of Romanism) and a more intimate acquaintance with the system.

Here is surely a great blunder. Ever since the pretended reformation, the reformers, and their successors to the present day, have been attacking what you call ROMANISM—the Church, at present, of one hundred and seventy millions, spread over all nations of the globe, and now, after three hundred years, you publish to the world, what amounts to an acknowledgment that you hardly know what Romanism is. So all along you have been putting the cart before the horse. You have been preaching, praying, and cursing down Romanism, with which you were but little acquainted.

I fully agree with you that it is high time you should know, thoroughly know, the system which, these three hundred years past, you have been endeavoring to pull down.

Now, gentlemen, are you in earnest? Do you wish to know what the Roman Catholic Church really is? If so, I shall send you at once to our bishops and priests. If I wished to know the principles of the Presbyterian Church, it is to you I should apply for information: to learn the principles of the Catholic Church, I must, of course, send you to our bishops, and to the priests by them appointed to teach the doctrine of the Roman Catholic Church. Apply to numbers of them,—from different parts of the globe, too; the more the better. If you could catch them in contradictions, you must be aware what a great chance it would give you in your warfare against ROMANISM.

Then, gentlemen, take the Bible: let them shew you upon what texts they bottom their doctrine. Above all things, remember your favorite principle, the Bible, the whole Bible, and nothing but the Bible. Do not suffer them to say *It means*, but let the text speak for itself.

You know, gentlemen, for you are professional characters, you know the magic power belonging to those two words, *It means*, which in your mouth transform the flesh and blood of Jesus Christ into mere bread and wine, in the mouth of the unitarian the adorable person of Jesus Christ into a mere man, and in the mouth of all reformers, a system of divine revelation into a system of human philosophy or of human folly.

But stop! what do I hear? Some friends of mine, who pretend to be much better acquainted with your views than I, laugh at my stupidity; they are very near supposing me to be a fool, for believing that you are in earnest, when you publish to the world your intention of becoming intimately acquainted with the Roman Catholic system. They tell me that the whole affair is a humbug, a farce to save appearances, and that, *per fas et nefas*, your determination is to find our religious system to be the very sink of abominations, to exhibit the same in the most odious colors before the world, and to offer the monstrosity of that system as your apology for waging war against it.

The opinion of my friends, which at first sight might appear uncharitable, rests upon strong arguments. Among all the publications (they say), that ever issued from the Protestant presses on the subject of Roman Catholic doctrine from a two-penny pamphlet to a ponderous folio, there never was one yet, that exhibited the said doctrine in its true colors. This, gentlemen, needs no proof; and let me tell you, *en passant*, that this is one of the great causes of the surprising increase of what you call Romanism.

Your hearers are not all fools willing to believe everything you assert. They have eyes to see, and ears to hear, and an intellect to judge for themselves. Thus, many of them, finding the Catholic Church far different from what you represented it to be, unwilling to be imposed upon any longer, leave your ranks to crowd the ranks of Romanism.

A careful study of the subject of *Romanism* is recommendded by your Synod to both ministers and members; and I, by way of advice, would also recommend a more careful study of that certain nondescript and indescribable thing called the Protestant Religion. If you are to pull down, it is for the purpose, (we may suppose) that (after removing the rubbish) you may build up again; and when you wish to deprive our members of their religious system, or to prevent your members from embracing it, you ought to have a very clear and distinct idea of the thing you mean to substitute in the place of what you call Romanism.

Your great champion was requested by the Rev. Mr. Hughes, to give a definition of the Protestant religion; but he, poor man, could give no satisfactory answer. However, gentlemen, the intellect has been marching since; and, besides, a dozen or two of intellects meeting together in synod can surmount difficulties, and unravel mysteries, for which one single intellect however exalted, might prove inadequate. No doubt, your collected wisdom will be able to discover the solution of the important question; what is the Protestant Religion? No doubt, you will be able to exhibit the discordant materials of the reformation and all its contradictory systems, as forming (like President Jackson's cabinet) one unit. No doubt you will be able to convince us that all the ministers of the reformation, setting up hundreds of contradictory systems, are lineal descendents of the apostles, and are all (even when preaching in contradiction to one another) under the influence of the same Spirit of Truth which Jesus Christ promised to his ministers forever.

No. 2. That our ministers more frequently and distinctly portray to their people the true features of popery in the way in which they judge most expedient. *Alias* that
"A hideous figure of their foes they draw,
Nor lines, nor looks, nor shades nor colours true;
And this grotesque design expose to public view."
(*Dryden.*)

After having spent some hours in your laboratory, in making up a monster composed of idolatry, superstition, cruelty, &c. &c. hideous enough to frighten the devil out of his kingdom, you are to mount the pulpit, and there exhibiting the monster, the work of your own creation, you are to work yourselves up into a holy rage, call that monster *Genuine Popery*, and consign it and us to the lowest pit.

Now, Gentlemen, as in doing so, you will have to exhibit yourselves before the public in the ludicrous character of Clerical Mountebanks, I advise you before you mount the pulpit, to gather a good deal of *brass*. Do not suffer a blush to suffuse your cheeks, but, stamping with a holy rage, and with now and then a hard knock of the fist upon the pulpit, go on roaring, foaming and bawling, with a voice of thunder, against the wickedness of Pope and Popery, not to forget now and then a seasonable sneer, and expressions of contempt at its absurdities. Thus you will rivet the attention of your hearers, who, almost stunned by your vociferations and frightened by your thunderings, will have no time or [opportunity] left for reflection.

Leaving you in the pulpit for a while I remain respectfully, gentlemen,
    Your very humble Servant,
      Demetrius A. Gallitzin.

Letter III.

January 28, 1834.

Gentlemen Parsons,

A very serious task is imposed upon you by your synod in their third resolution, in the following words:

3rd Particularly, that our ministers be requested to hold up constantly to the people, the prophetic page [having] reference to the rise, the progress, the characteristics, and the fall of popery.

The task is so very serious, that I must advise you, in the first place, to produce and exhibit before your people the credentials of your mission. To put confidence in your denunciations against Popery (for not all of them will be subdued by your thundering) but more especially to put confidence in your prophecies concerning the downfall of Popery, your people ought not to harbor the least suspicion that you are either self sent or sent by a self-constituted body of men, who never received any authority from Jesus Christ.

How can they preach unless they be sent? (ROM. x. 15.)
Sent as Jesus Christ himself was sent by his Heavenly Father. (JOHN xx. 21.)

Prove, then, through the long vista of ages, an uninterrupted, unbroken chain of Presbyterian ministers, beginning with the Apostles of Jesus Christ as the first links, and coming down to you.

Prove that you are among those of whom Jesus Christ says: *He that heareth you, heareth me.* (LUKE x. 16.)

Prove that you are of the number of those with whom, according to the promise of Christ, the Paraclete, the Spirit of Truth is to *remain forever.* (JOHN xiv. 16, 17.)

Prove that you are some of those whom Jesus Christ had in view when he said, *I am with you all days, even to the consummation of the world.* (MATT. xxviii. 20.)

In short, prove that you are real ministers of Christ, not imposters; prove that you really know, not the letter only but the sense of the Scriptures, at least that part of the Scripture intended for the regulation of our faith and morals, and that you are not left to the feeble light of your weak, corrupted, and fallible reason, in interpreting the sacred records of infallible wisdom. Prove that, in delivering to your people not the words only, but the meaning of Scripture, you are not guilty of sacrilegious presumption giving for the sense of the Holy Ghost your own fluctuating opinions.

Prove, in short, that [without being infallible as individuals] you derive your knowledge of the sense of Scripture from an infallible, unerring authority.

Gentlemen, I see you sneer contemptuously at the words "infallible authority," and I hear you ask: "Can any body of men pretend to infallibillity any more than individuals?" I ask you again: can you have the presumption to offer yourselves as guides in the paths of religious truth, which alone save us, unless yourselves are guided by an unerring or infallible authority? I know you will tell me, that you are guided by the infallible authority of the Bible. Ay, sure enough; and so are all your brethren of the pretended reformation,—Lutherans and Calvinists, Baptists and Brownists, Universalists, Arians, Trinitarians, Unitarians, Baxterians, Sabbatarians, Moravians, Antinomians, Sandemonians, Jumpers or Dunkers, Shakers and Quakers, Burghers, Kirkers, Independents, Covenanters, Puritans, Hutchinsons, Mugletonians, &c. &c. &c. &c.

All these say they are guided by the infallible authority of the Bible; yet from the same source they draw contradictory doctrines. Suppose, now, there are but twenty different systems of religion contradicting one another in some point of doctrine said to be divinely revealed; does not your common sense tell you that but one out of the twenty can possibly be the system established by Jesus Christ, that system which exclusively contains the truth, and nothing but the truth, that religious system which if *you believe not you shall be damned*, as your Testament expresses it? [MARK xvi. 16]

When Jesus Christ made this awful declaration, was it the uncertain, fluctuating opinions of men, or their arbitrary interpretations of Scripture he had in view? Truly, to make damnation just, as a reward for unbelief, there must have been some means left by Jesus Christ, by which we are to know *infallibly* what to believe.

I hear you exclaim: "What is the human intellect for? If the Almighty gave us the Holy Scriptures, was it not his will that man should exert his intellectual faculties in order to come to the true understanding of them? And did he not promise that *pray and you shall receive; seek and you shall find?*

True, gentlemen, very true: but tell me, were not your reformers generally men of intellect? Did not all of them pray? Luther prayed, Calvin prayed, Knox prayed, George Fox prayed; still, after all their prayers, it appears plainly that Luther's intellect pointed a different way from Calvin's, Knox's a different way from George Fox's.

The more they reasoned, and the more they prayed, the more their systems of religion increased in number.

I will give you a friendly advice, gentlemen. Take a looking glass in your hand, and hold it before your face. Now, look at that little box of yours which stands on your shoulders containing a handful or two of brains. I ask you is that little box capable of compassing the immensity of God's infinite wisdom?

Perhaps, as true heirs to the presumption of your father reformers, you will say "yes". If so I propose to you the following case in point, as lawyers would say; and I ask you by the mere light of your little intellect as applied to Scripture, to give me an infallible solution of said case.

In a little town close by, there are two meeting houses: in one of them Infant Baptism is upheld and proved from Scripture; in the other it is condemned and its condemnation also proved from Scripture. Of course, one of these contradictory doctrines must be false; now, as he who *believes not* (the truth) *shall be damned*, it is absolutely necessary to know infallibly which of the two is the doctrine of Jesus Christ.

Applying, then, your intellect to the Scripture, give us, not your opinions, but an *infallible* solution of the above case, such a one, I mean, upon which we may, without presumption, venture our salvation. In matters of revelation, but especially in practical truths of religion, nothing but perfect certainty, certainty equal to that of the existence of God, will ever satisfy us.

This, gentlemen, brings me back to the much heavier task imposed upon you by your synod (Resolve No. 3), which requires of you to hold up to the people the prophetic page having reference to the rise, progress, the characteristics, and the fall of Popery. This naturally points at the book of Revelations containing almost as many mysteries as sentences. In this labyrinth of divine mysteries, in this unfathomable abyss of divine wisdom, you are, by the light of your puny reason, to trace, step by step, the rise, progress, characteristics and (getting yourself inspired with the spirit of prophecy) even the downfall of Popery; for, you know, Popery, as you call it, is not down yet; and it is principally for the purpose of preventing any further increase, or to put an end to the whole system, that your synod was called.

À propos, I had, some time ago, a little tract, containing a collection of prophecies concerning the downfall of Popery, by a number of your brother parsons. It was printed in Carlisle (Pa.) and was very amusing. I advise you to procure it. Not two of them agreed about the period of the downfall of Popery. All these different periods, however, or most of them, have passed away; and so have the authors of those prophecies, leaving behind them Popery on the increase, and the pamphlet as a monument of their folly and presumption.

Now, gentlemen, if you wish to avoid the same fate, if you wish to shun the rock upon which your brother parsons split, either get yourselves inspired, or shelter yourselves under an ambiguous mode of prophesying, somewhat in the style of the famous oracle of Delphos:

Aio te Eacidam Romanos vincere posse.

With this advice I bid you farewell and remain, gentlemen,
your very obedient servant,
Demetrius A. Gallitzin.

LETTER IV.

February 4th, 1834.

Gentlemen Parsons,

No. 4 of your resolutions requires standard books and well written tracts on the subject of Romanism to be extensively and carefully circulated.

Gentlemen, if you apply to our Catholic booksellers in any of our cities you can procure hundreds of well written works on the subject of ROMANISM; but this would not answer your purpose. Your words have to be interpreted by the same rule by which you interpret the Bible. They say one thing but mean another. In short you are to write the tracts yourselves, to be at liberty to represent Romanism just as you please.

So you are convinced that THE BIBLE ALONE, THE BIBLE WITHOUT NOTE OR COMMENT, won't do! That Bible stands in need of your assistance, to have the desired effect: the word of God must be propped by the word of man; and although to keep up an appearance of consistency, the margin of your Bible is left blank, you are to supply the deficiency both by well written tracts and by well preached sermons!

Now, gentlemen, tell me, do you really believe all your hearers to be fools? Do you really believe that sincere inquirers after truth, sincere wishers for salvation, will hunt up the doctrines of the Catholic Church in the writings of its enemies? They will do no such thing. Catholic books are spread far and near, and those of your hearers, who are possessed of only common sense, know very well that to Catholic publications they must apply for a knowledge of Catholic doctrine, not to the productions of professed enemies, stimulated by self interest.

The very caution you would give your hearers against Catholic books, besides rendering you highly ridiculous would, in the thinking part of your community, create a suspicion against the soundness of your cause, and have an effect directly contrary to your views, for *Nitimur in vetitum semper, cupimusque negata.*

My advice, then, would be to suppress Resolve the 4th and, consistent with yourselves, to depend upon your Bible alone, as a sufficient antidote against what you call Romanism.

No. 5 comes a little nearer to the point. It has the words PECUNIARY CONTRIBUTIONS in it, and is somewhat more mellifluous than the preceding ones:

"That our churches be affectionately warned against the practice of patronizing Romish institutions, either by making pecuniary contributions, or by placing their children and wards under their instruction and influence."

Bravo, gentlemen! Don't suffer pecuniary contributions to be diverted from their proper channels. The hundreds and thousands you have laid out on Bibles and tracts have drained your pockets, not to speak of your celebrated Missionary Establishments, which, considering the immense sums they have already swallowed up, must by this time have converted half the Pagan world.

Here I would suggest the propriety of an additional affectionate address to Congress and to the Legislatures of the States, to caution them against a repitition of the crimes they have been guilty of, the former in appointing what you would call a Popish priest their chaplain, and the latter in granting charters to Catholic colleges, and raising some of them to the rank of universities.

* * *

Gentlemen Parsons, if you wish to succeed in your undertaking of pulling down what you call ROMANISM, you will have to devise new means; for all those that have been tried, since the pretended reformation, have proved vain and fruitless.

The British Government, that stronghold of Protestantism, tried its best during more than two hundred years. The whole power of that formidable empire, both spiritual and temporal, stood arrayed against ROMANISM. The most sanguinary laws were enacted and enforced against the Irish to compel them to renounce the religion of Jesus Christ, and to embrace the reformation, so called. After two hundred years [of] relentless persecution we find in Ireland about seven millions of Catholics, and hardly one tenth that number of Protestants of the Law-church.

Now, tell me, gentlemen, do you really think that if you could ever persuade the people of the United States to alter their Constitution, so as to deprive the Catholics of their citizenship, and by laws enacted for that purpose, have them reduced to beggary and subjected to the punishment of death, for hearing Mass or for going to confession, do you really think that you would then get your ends accomplished? Oh, no! the gates of hell shall never prevail against the Catholic Church!

There is only one means by which you will succeed. You have read, I suppose, how the Giants of Old tried, by piling mountain upon mountain to scale the heavens, and to wrest the thunderbolts out of the hands of Jupiter. Had they succeeded they might have ruled the universe according to their own views. This is a fable, I hear you say. Call it what you please, I tell you it is just as true as it is true that you can put down the Catholic Church or prevent its increase, without first wresting the power out of the hands of the Almighty. Do so, and then you may overthrow the Catholic Church, and upon its ruins erect your own systems.

Gentlemen, if you shudder at the impiety of my advice and feel anger rising in your breasts against me for supposing you capable of thus bidding defiance to the Powers of Heaven, I shall bid you turn your anger against yourselves and your Father Reformers. What else, indeed, have the Reformers and their successors been doing these three hundred years past?

They set out with the avowed and daring purpose of reforming the noblest of all the works of God. The same God who, about six thousand years ago, created the whole universe, this material world out of nothing (and, when created, it was perfect at once, and has continued so to the present day) the very same God created that spiritual world which we call the Church, and which, coming out of the hands of God, was perfect at once. Why so? For this simple reason; because it was the work of infinite wisdom.

Now this, the noblest, the greatest of all the works of God, your reformers, (as they impudently, impiously, and blasphemously are called) about fifteen hundred years after its establishment, undertook to reform—that is, to change for the better. Great God! to make better, to improve that which the infinite wisdom of God had made perfect from the very start! No language ever invented by man is sufficient to furnish terms to convey to our minds an adequate idea of the superlative wickedness of such an attempt. No history of this wicked world furnishes a parallel to it.

Something similiar to it is found in Isaias xiv, 14:

"I will ascend (says Lucifer) into heaven; I will exalt my throne above the stars of God.... I will ascend above the heights of the clouds: I will be like the Most High."

Gentlemen, leaving you to draw the parallel,
I remain
Your humble servant,
Demetrius A. Gallitzin.

LETTER V.

Feb. 11; 1834.

Gentlemen Parsons,

I hope you have attended to my last advice. If so, you must have found a striking resemblance between the attempt of Satan and that of the reformers, as you call them.

His attempt was to raise himself to a higher degree of power and dignity than was allotted to him by infinite wisdom, to improve in his own person the work of God, even so far as to make himself equal to his Creator.

The reformers' attempt was to improve, to make better the holy Church, the sacred spouse of Jesus Christ (Ephes. v, 25); to improve what the great and omnipotent God-man, at the expense of his sacred blood had made glorious, without spot or wrinkle, holy and without blemish (v, 27). To present the reformers' attempt in its true light, in all its enormity, and to prove that it is the most sacrilegious attempt ever made by man, I shall bring you back to the *Bible alone*, to the *Bible without note or comment*. I shall not leave it in your power to say, that I gave you my own silly interpretation for the Word of God. It shall be completely *argumentum ad hominem*, an argument entirely founded on your own principles.

By way of preliminary observation, I suppose I may take it for granted that you really believe in a Church founded by

Jesus Christ as a vessel of salvation for all nations of the globe, and as a sure guide in the ways of salvation for all men, both learned and illiterate. Starting, then, from that supposition, I ask you, upon what foundation did Christ raise the sacred edifice?

The Bible says *upon a rock*: (Matt. xvi, 18). What promise did Christ make concerning the Church?

The Bible says:

"The gates of hell shall not prevail against it." (*Ibid.*)

Did Jesus Christ appoint any persons as our guides or teachers in the ways of salvation?

The Bible says:

"Jesus coming spoke to them, saying: All power is given to me in heaven and on earth. Go, ye, therefore, and teach all nations; baptizing them in the name of the Father, and of the Son, and of the Holy Ghost, teaching them to observe all things whatsoever I have commanded you." (*Matt.* xxviii, 18, 20.)

Did Christ enable them to remember all these things?

The Bible says:

"Behold I am with you all days, even to the consummation of the world." (*Ibid.*)

The Bible says:

"I will ask the Father and he shall give you another Paraclete, that he may abide with you for ever, the Spirit of Truth." (*John* xiv, 16, 17.)

The Bible says:

"The Paraclete, the Holy Ghost, whom the Father will send in my name, he will teach you ALL THINGS, and bring ALL THINGS to your mind, whatsoever I have said to you." (*Ibid.* 26,)

The Bible says:

"When he, the Spirit of Truth, is come he will teach you ALL truth." (*John* xvi, 13.)

For what purpose did Christ appoint teachers, and send the Spirit of Truth to them for ever?

The Bible says:

"For the perfecting of the saints, for the work of ministry, for the edifying of the body of Christ: Until we all meet in the unity of faith.... That henceforth" (Mind this, gentlemen of the Reformation, with its hundreds of contradictory systems) "we be no more children, tossed to and fro, and carried about by every wind of doctrine." (*Ephes.* IV, 12, 13, 14.)

How long was the Spirit of Truth to continue with the teachers of Jesus Christ, to bring back to their minds whatever he had commanded them?

The Bible says:

"Even to the consummation of the world; (*Matt.* XXVIII.) "for ever." (*John* XIV, 16.)

Did Christ give no other power to his teachers except that of teaching?

The Bible says:

"Go ye, therefore.... baptizing all nations in the name of the Father, and of the Son, and of the Holy Ghost." (Matt. XXVIII, 19.)

The Bible says:

"As the Father hath sent me, I also send you. When he had said this, he breathed on them; and he said to them: Receive ye the Holy Ghost: Whose sins you shall forgive they are forgiven them; and whose sins you shall retain, they are retained." (*John* XX, 21, 23.)

The Bible says:

"Whatsoever you shall bind on earth shall be bound in heaven; and whatsoever you shall loose upon earth, shall be loosed in heaven." (*Matt.* XVIII, 13.)

The Bible says:

"All things are of God, who hath reconciled us to himself, by Christ; and hath given to us the ministry of Reconciliation." (II. *Cor.* V, 18.)

The Bible says:

"Except you eat the flesh of the son of man, and drink his blood, you shall not have life in you. He that eateth my flesh and drinketh my blood, hath everlasting life: and I will raise him up at the last day. For my flesh is meat indeed, and my blood is drink indeed: He that eateth my flesh, and drinketh my blood, abideth in me, and I in him. As the living Father hath sent me, and I live by the Father: so he that eateth me, the same also shall live by me." (*John* IV, 54-58.)

The Bible says:

"And taking bread, he gave thanks, and brake and gave to them, saying: This is my body, which is given for you. Do this for a commemoration of me. In like manner the chalice also, after he had supped, saying: This is the chalice the New Testament in my blood, which shall be shed for you." (*Luke* XXII, 19, 20.)

"This do ye, as often as ye shall drink it for the commemoration of me." (1. *Cor.* xi, 25.) "He that eateth and drinketh unworthily, eateth and drinketh judgment to himself, not discerning the body of the Lord." (*Ibid.* 29.)

Here, gentlemen, you have the BIBLE ALONE *without note or comment.* Now look at your reformers.

They set out with the avowed intention to reform the noblest of all the works of God, the sacred Spouse, the Church of Jesus Christ, which the infinite power and wisdom of Jesus Christ himself had built, which his infinite charity had cemented with his own sacred blood, which his unbounded mercy and love for men had provided with all those powers and those sacred and awful institutions, necessary for the sanctification and final salvation of man.

Only think of that, and say where we shall find words sufficiently expressive of the enormity of the attempt?

Satan-like they say: "I will be like the Most High. (*Isai.* xiv, 14.) For the Spirit of Truth imparted *forever* by Jesus Christ, I will substitute my own puny reason. Instead of being directed by the word of God (the sense of which is explained by the Spirit of Truth in the Church), I will direct the word of God what to say.

"The divine System of religion proceeding from the fountain of eternal wisdom, shall be moulded into a system of human philosophy. Those sublime institutions, the pledge of God's unbounded charity for man, those ordinances, so perfectly mysterious (and therefore to the reformers so perfectly absurd) shall be brought down to the level of the human intellect."

What more? "Why, pull down Jesus Christ from his seat of eternal glory: make a mere man of him," say some of the reformers. "Curtail the power of Jesus Christ," say others, "set bounds to his infinite power and charity. Convert his sacred institutions into mere human schemes; his flesh and blood into mere bread and wine; deprive Jesus Christ of the power of forgiving sins through the agency of his Ministers of Reconciliation," &c., &c.

Now, gentlemen Parsons, with looking glass in hand, take another view of that little box upon your shoulders, containing a handful or two of brains, the seat of that puny intellect (from which as from Pandora's box this abomination of desolation proceeds), which rising in its pride above Jesus Christ and all his sacred institutions, presumes to sit in judgment over the word of God, and to decide its meaning; to measure what is immeasurable, and to fathom what is unfathomable.

Farewell, gentlemen, and believe me.

Your very humble servant,
Demetrius A. Gallitzin.

LETTER VI.

February 18. 1834.

Gentlemen Parsons,

The Sixth Resolution requires of you, if you think it expedient to read the foregoing Preamble and Resolutions to your congregations.

No doubt you will think it expedient. If so, I must repeat the advice given in Letter II. viz: to gather a great deal of brass and to provide yourselves with a good many bags of dust. If you wish to succeed in your undertaking, you cannot throw too much dust in the eyes of your hearers:

1st. To hide from their view the sublimity, the beauty, the immensity, the perfect unity, the sanctity of that sacred edifice erected by the hands of Jesus Christ.

2d. To hide from their view the deformity of the pretended Reformation, exhibiting hundreds of jarring sects, contradictory systems of religion, built upon the quicksand of your puny reason; and especially to prevent their discovering your inconsistencies, and your arbitrary perversion of the Holy Scriptures.

Does it not indeed require a great deal of impudence to deny the unerring authority of the Church, when the veracity of Jesus Christ stands pledged for the continuance of the Spirit of Truth *forever* in the Church? And if your hearers were only permitted to consult their common sense, would they not, at once, come to the very rational conclusion that a Church which is not unerring, not infallible, not under the guidance of the Spirit of Truth, cannot be the Church of Christ, but must be a mere human institution, and of course, that its ministers cannot be ministers of Jesus Christ.

Does it not require a great deal of impudence, and of the most daring impiety, for poor worms of the earth, poor miserable sinners, to exhibit themselves as reformers of the noblest work of God, of that very work of God which Jesus Christ, in very unequivocal terms, declared should never require a reformation?

Does it not require a superlative degree of impudence to make your hearers believe that the pretented reformation, this prolific source of hundreds of contradictory doctrines; that this reformation, which in fact was nothing but a rebellion against Christ and the authority of his Church, and which was everywhere established by murder, robbery, sacrilege, and all manner of crime, that this reformation was the work of God?

Talk of the corruption of Rome indeed! whilst your pretended reformation is corruption from head to foot.

Corruption of the understanding, which, forgetting its place, disregarding the limits to which infinite wisdom hath confined it, hath the diabolical presumption to penetrate into the arena of Revelation and, usurping the place of the Spirit of Truth promised to the Church *forever*, substitutes its fluctuating opinions for the positive and unerring testimony of the Holy Ghost on faith and morals.

Corruption of the understanding, which proves itself by the hundreds of contradictory interpretations of the sacred text, upon which, as upon quicksand, are founded as many different contradictory systems of religion, the aggregate of which makes up the grand *unum totum*, which the pretended reformers have the impious boldness to designate with the name of the Church of Jesus Christ, whereas the true Church of Christ is essentially one in faith, morals, and general discipline.

Corruption of the heart, which, abhorring the sacred doctrine of humility, becomes the victim of the most inconceivable pride, so as to arise in judgment over the Divine Revelations, and to assume an authority paramount to that of the Holy Spirit of Truth, speaking in and through the Church.

Corruption of the heart which, being a slave to the suggestions of flesh and blood, breaks down all the barriers which infinite wisdom had erected to stem the torrent of our ungovernable passions, overthrows the sacrament of reconciliation, profanes the sanctity and indissolubillity of marriage, breaks the last will and testament of Jesus Christ, robs his children of their spiritual food and nourishment, the sacred flesh and blood of Christ, and of the great and perpetual sacrifice and pure oblation, which, according to Malachi, was to be offered up from the rising to the setting of the sun.

Now, gentlemen parsons, will you stand up in your pulpit and tell your people that all this is a reformation, or a change for the better? That all this is the work of God? Will you indeed? Then remember my advice: gather all the boldness and impudence you can, and do not forget at every sentence to throw abundance of dust in the eyes of your unfortunate hearers; stun them with your thunderings, and give them no time for reflection, for fear that, perceiving and admiring the perfect unity and beauty of the Universal Church, the Church of all ages and nations, the Church (at present) of about one hundred and seventy millions of human beings, (and you know that unity is a necessary criterion of truth), for fear, I say, that preferring the salvation of their souls to your temporal interest, they may turn their backs to your barren reformation forever, and enter the green and life giving pastures of the Church of Jesus Christ.

Many of your hearers have done so already. Lately, quite lately, I have had several of your members at confession; and now, whilst I am writing these lines, there is a letter on my table, written me by one of your Protestants, about one hundred miles from here, who laments bitterly that surrounded by so many contradictory systems of religion he had almost come to the conclusion that religion itself was a solecism when suddenly a flash of light (guess from what quarter), revived his hopes. He hath the following remarkable words: "I have never yet eat and drank the flesh and blood of the Son of God, and therefore have no life in me."

This, gentlemen, was *the Bible alone.*

* * * When standing in the pulpit, to caution your hearers against the evils of Romanism, you will remember, no doubt, to exhibit the whole of us as wicked idolators for worshipping Jesus Christ where we know him to be present viz: in the Holy Sacrament. When on that subject do not let your hearers know that Luther, the Father of the Reformation, worshipped Jesus Christ in the Holy Sacrament; do not let them know that Bishops Andrews, Forbes, Taylor, and many more bishops and doctors of the first English reformation, adored the living flesh of Christ in the Sacrament.

Above all things take care not to give your hearers a definition of the word *Idolatry*, lest some of them might retort the charge of Idolatry against yourselves.

"What," I hear you exclaim with rage and fury in your countenance, "against ourselves? Who will dare accuse us of Idolatry?" Why, gentlemen, did you never read in your Bible the celebrated history of the Golden Calf? No doubt you have. Well, now, suppose that Golden Calf to be melted and being cast into new moulds, to come out of them in the shape of Eagles, half-Eagles, Guineas or Sovereigns &c. &c., would not the Idol in this new form, find a far greater number of worshippers—ay! and more devout ones, more sincere worshippers than the Calf did? Worshippers willing to sacrifice to that Idol their God, their own conscience, the Church and all the holy institutions of Jesus Christ, the souls of millions, and their own souls into the bargain? This you know from EPHES. v. 5, would be real genuine Idolatry.

Now, gentlemen parsons, to prevent your hearers from harboring the least suspicion on that score, speak in glowing terms about your missions: exhibit your missionaries, fearless of dangers, dashing into the midst of Pagan nations, suffering hunger and thirst, poverty, persecutions, torments, and death by Martyrdom for the sake of Christ, and to preserve thousands of souls from eternal damnation. Exhibit before your hearers a faithful list of your missionaries [who] have fallen martyrs in the glorious cause of converting the heathen. Publish a catalogue of the many nations which the immense sums, collected yearly among your hearers, have been the means of converting to Jesus Christ.

Conceal from your hearers the fact that, in the East India Mission alone, the Catholic missionaries are [as we are told by the London papers] to your Protestant missionaries as three hundred to one! Above all things, dont let them know that the Pages of the Bible which you send by millions to all parts of the globe, are (as we are told by a letter from the British Lieutenant Slade, a Protestant) by many of them used as wadding for their guns. Conceal all these things from your hearers, for fear that, growing cool in this work of charity, of throwing pearls before swine, the rivers of dollars would shrink into small rivulets, and perhaps finally dry up altogether.

And now, Gentlemen Parsons, I bid you a final farewell,
    Remaining your very humble servant,
        DEMETRIUS AUGUSTINE GALLITZIN.

CHAPTER XXVII.
AT EVENING TIME.
(1834—1840.)

O good gray head which all men knew,
O iron nerve to true occasion true,
O fall'n at length that tower of strength,
Which stood four-square to all the winds that blew!
(Tennyson.)

In 1834.—First signs of failing strength.—The winter of 1839-40.—Lenten duties.—Easter Sunday.—His last sermon.—Mr. Bradley, Mr. Lemcke, and Mr. Heyden called to Loretto.—Wednesday, May 6th, 1840.

"When I first saw Gallitzin," says Rev. Mr. Lemcke*, "he was certainly very thin and his general appearance fragile, but he was erect, his walk firm and rapid, his voice loud and sonorous, his look keen and decided." He was never absent from his place on Sundays, continuing full of vigor and life, taking the same lively interest in the affairs of the Church, and the welfare of the clergymen of his neighborhood, whose cares and troubles he always knew to understand, even to anticipate, which had always distinguished him, writing in 1838 to Mr. Heyden, who was then in Philadelphia, with his usual vigorous and kindly thought for all:

VERY REV. D. A. GALLITZIN TO REV. THOMAS HEYDEN.
†
Loretto, Jan. 24, 1838.

Rev. and very dear Friend,

Your favor of the 16th ult. was about two weeks on the road before it came to my hands. The duties of the holidays together with a little spell of sickness which kept me con-

---

* Page 355.

fined for about eight or nine days are my apology for not replying sooner to your friendly letter. Your appointment for Philadelphia was fully anticipated by me, and affords an ample field for the display of your zeal and talents in the cause of God. In consequence of your promise to render me any office of friendship in your power, I beg of you, my dear friend, to reject as a temptation the wish to see me appointed to an episcopal see. Could I even deceive myself so far as to suppose (which God forbid) that I really possess the necessary qualifications, my age (I am since Dec. 22, in my 68th year), and my inability to travel, are insuperable obstacles to the discharge of episcopal functions. The only object of my ambition is to give the finishing stroke to my undertaking in this flourishing Catholic establishment, by building a large and permanent church, as soon as a favorable change of times will justify so costly an undertaking. This being accomplished, I shall then, (if I live to see it accomplished), consider it my duty to resign my Trust into my bishop's hands, to enable him to transfer it into better hands. Permit me now, dear friend, to add (principally for the bishop's perusal) some observations I wish to present to his consideration on the subject of the Synod contemplated by him to be held in May next.

1st, One of the priests who attended the late Diocesan Synod, who lives about two hundred and forty miles from Philadelphia, complained to me, or told me, that attending the Synod put him to the expense of nearly one hundred dollars. Those priests who live in the westernmost parts of Pennsylvania have a far greater distance to travel, say from three hundred miles, and are, of course, put to a far greater expense. This it must be confessed, is a very heavy tax which falls exclusively upon those who have nothing to spare, while the city priests, who receive handsome salaries, besides no inconsiderable amount in perquisites, are (by attending the Synod) not put to any expense whatever.

To illustrate my general position, I will only mention the case of my friend the Rev. P. Lemcke (and I doubt not but there are more of the country clergy in a similar situation).

Since last spring the said Mr. Lemcke with the view of forming a permanent church establishment, hath purchased some improved land, for which he paid the first installment; on the first of April he is obliged to pay two hundred dollars, as the former owner is going to remove to Illinois, and cannot possibly do without his money, unfortunately.... I am not able to assist my friend Lemcke.

....Under such circumstances to be obliged to attend the Synod, would prove ruinous to him.

2nd, With regard to the time appointed for the Synod, it happens to be the very busiest part of Paschal time. Although the time for Easter confessions begins on the first Sunday in Lent, by far the greater number of our congregation always put off that sacred duty until after Easter, in consequence of which we are from Easter until Trinity quite overwhelmed with confessions. This, at least as far as women and children are concerned, is, no doubt, owing to the excessive badness of the roads in the early part of the spring, of which you can hardly form an idea.

The objections above mentioned could be in a great measure obviated if the Synod could be put off until after the division of the diocese, which (if I am not misinformed) is to take place before very long.

My dear friend, following your edifying example I have held my retreat, and made my general confession the last week in Advent. May the residue of our lives be a continual retreat from this wicked world, and a constant preparation for a better.

Present my humble respects to our good and worthy bishop, together with my sincere wishes for an abundance of the blessings of the season for both him and yourself.

Later, when some reports of the doctor's failing health alarmed his friend, he wrote:

SAME TO THE SAME.

Loretto, Aug. 27, 1839.

My RIGHT Rev. and dear friend!

The account you had of my illness was not founded in fact. What may have given rise to it is that I was, (by pains in the lower joints), for one Sunday only, prevented from appearing at the holy altar, which, perhaps, alarmed some of those who being in the habit of seeing me there every Sunday, concluded that I must be very ill. In Chambersburg they had me dead and buried.

* * *

Give my respect to your venerable parents, my affectionate compliments to Mr. and Mrs. Lyon, and accept for yourself (together with hopes of seeing a mitre on your head), my sincere wishes for your temporal and spiritual welfare.

Your most hble servt and friend,

Demetrius Aug. Gallitzin.

In the winter following, a very severe one, it was noticed with forebodings instantly repressed as too painful for consideration, that he no longer carried himself as formerly, that the once ringing step all knew so well, was at times slow and uncertain; his voice failed him in preaching, and in his exhortations tears would fall from the beautiful eyes which once flashed accompaniment to his thrilling words,— tears and a look more touching than the most powerful sermon of his youth.—"Sometimes in the course of these sermons," one who heard them relates,* "he became truly eloquent. At such times he would lean forward a little, his face would light up, and his eyes shine with heavenly radiance; but this would last only a few minutes, being repressed as soon as he perceived it, as if it were against his calmer judgment, and after a few sentences he would resume his conversational tone; his sermons, if such they could be called, did not last quite thirty minutes." Those who observed him closely, or saw him but seldom could not doubt that he who had never cared for the world, was now more than ever detached from it, that he who had waited so long for heaven was looking wistfully to the promised rest, as an old general who sees the ravages of war disappearing, the conquered country settling into loyalty and peace, young officers rising

---

* Rev. Mr. Lemcke, p. 356.

to eminence, looks towards his native land, and his sovereign's recall. The burden of debt had nearly disappeared, all that remained could be dissolved at any moment; the children whom he had adopted were for the most part married and settled, portioned by him as they would have been by a prosperous father in their rank of life. He would have wished to have a larger church built for his people before he left them, and been glad to see the diocese divided, but this gave him no anxiety for he knew all that was needful would come in God's own time.

The severe mountain winter [1839—40] was still lingering in excessive cold, broken only by dreary storms of mingled rain and snow, while the roads were fast assuming their spring form of snow, mud and melting ice, when Lent with its multiplied duties, and the increasing sick calls of the unhealthy season, came to exhaust his failing strength. "He was so evidently weak and suffering", says Mr. Lemcke,* "that I begged him to spare himself and leave the rest to me, but of this he would hear nothing. Indeed, with the best of intentions and even with his indomitable will, Mr Lemcke could not have assisted him much, for his own special charge claimed his fullest attention, as was the case with the other priests in their more distant stations. The trouble resulting from the fall from his horse one night, years before, when returning from a sick-call, which had prevented his ever riding again, now assumed a very serious form always painful and at times excruciatingly so; Dr. Rodrigue, his physician, an excellent one, his friends, his brother priests urged him to rest, but as long as it pleased his master to leave him at his post, he refused to consider himself incompetent to fulfill its duties let the result be what it would; all they could say was met by a smile that tenderly acknowledged their solicitude, but put aside all hope of compliance with their wishes.

Towards the end of Lent, happening to meet Dr. Rodrigue he asked his advice and was counselled to go at once to his room, keeping warm and quiet, avoiding all care and exer-

---

* Page 360.

tion; but this he regarded as impossible, for the duties of Holy Week were at hand, and so far from going to his room he would be obliged to spend the greater part of his time in the cold church, hearing confessions, after Easter he thought he might consider the doctor's advice. He went through all the services of Holy Week, heard confessions for half a day at a time, at what cost can never be told. Early Easter morning he was in the confessional again, but was so exhausted by ten o'clock that he could only say a low Mass, and give a short exhortation on the Resurrection, which he ended with the words spoken on the cross: *It is consummated.* They were his last to his congregation.

Scarcely able to reach his room he made no further resistance, and the next day, Easter Monday, the news of his illness passing from one to another, became known to Mr. Lemcke, the nearest priest, who was, unhappily, suffering from an accident and unable to leave home; he knew Dr. Gallitzin would not have given up unless forced to it, and sent a trusty messenger to find exactly how he was. This person returning reported that he had found the doctor in bed, looking miserably and as if in great distress, but insisting that Mr. Lemcke should not risk coming to him at present, and that if there was danger notice would be given him; a friend present followed the messenger out of the room, told him it was a critical case, and that Mr. Lemcke would do well to lose no time.

A messenger was soon sent for Mr. Bradley who came at once, and April 28th wrote hastily to Mr. Heyden: "that our dear and much revered Dr. Gallitzin is fast approaching his last end; it is the opinion of all who see him that he cannot survive this day, in which opinion his attending physician, Dr. Roderick [Rodrigue] full concurs. I therefore request you by that love and charity we all owe to each other, and by that tender regard we all owe to our beloved Dr. Gallitzin to come with all speed to assist me.... Mr. Lemcke is not able to attend on account of some unfortunate accident, and Mr. Rattigan is gone to Pittsburg."

The sled had been sent for Mr. Lemcke and now returned with him. Dr. Rodrigue thought an operation if successful would relieve the sufferer, and give him a few days more to live, and requested Mr. Lemcke to prepare him for it; he expressed himself perfectly submissive to God's will, to go at this time or that as it pleased him best." "My will," he said, "is made. I trust as far as that is concerned I can depart in peace, that no one will lose anything through me, that there may even be something over. Now I wish first of all to receive the Last Sacraments, and then do with me as you will." As soon as midnight had passed Mr. Lemcke said Mass in the sick room, all the household being present, and gave him Holy Communion.

Soon afterwards Dr. Rodrigue performed the operation, to which the doctor submitted with heroic fortitude; but for it the physician had no hope that he could survive the night. During the following nights Dr. Rodrigue scarcely left his side; after riding all day to attend to his other patients he would hasten back over the wretched roads, to watch all night with the dying priest. On the 4th of May Mr. Heyden arrived, but the doctor was only able to welcome him with a faint smile and a few whispered, broken words. The people from far and near pressed about the doors, and when they were admitted to his presence, for the dear sufferer would let none be refused, they were so unwilling to leave they had often to be forced from the room. About the time of Mr. Heyden's arrival the pains seemed less, and Dr. Gallitzin lay as one peacefully sleeping, an expression of serenest repose on his countenance; nature was exhausted, the life spent in toil and sacrifice was slipping away, and the real life, the great, boundless life of perfect joy, was already on the other side to receive him.

We who have no such saintly cheerfulness as his shrink in the bitterness of our hearts from a few years more, but when patient virtue thus passes into holy rest, how beautiful and to be envied the longest and saddest life appears! How little now his three score and ten beside the eternal happiness!

So he lay there resting until the evening of the 6th of May, between six and seven o'clock. When the hour came for the laborers to go home from their work, they saw that he was going, too. Mr. Heyden read the prayers for the dying, the room doors were opened, the crowds in the house and chapel prayed with tears and sobs, and in a few minutes, without any perceptible sign, all was over, the heavens were open,. all their joybells were ringing a welcoming peal; he had gone home to his own country.

CONCLUSION.

The souls of the Just are in the hands of God.—(Wis. iii. 2, 4.)

Grief of the people.—The funeral procession.—The Requiem Mass.—His last will and testament.—His successor.—Division of the diocese.—The new church at Loretto.—Dr. Gallitzin's monument.—Influence of his memory.

That damp, dreary night, in every home in Loretto, and far into the country around it, there was sorrow and desolation; save that here was no passionate, bitter grief, no wild despair, one might have been reminded of that awful night in Egypt, when the Angel passed by, and in every house he breathed upon there was death. But in the midst of the most heart-broken sorrow there was here a certain undertone of thought, ready to rise into exultation, as the souls of the mourners recognized their own destiny delayed in his fulfilled. "What a happiness for him that he listened to the voice of God, and gathered up his strength and courage to leave all and run that race, which gained for him that brilliant and unfading crown of a true and faithful priest of Jesus Christ, who had brought thousands of souls into the way of justice; and had practised himself that Christian perfection which he preached to others?"* "Does he not look like an old warrior taking his rest," said one, looking at that which remained to show where once he had lived, that empty house from which the noble soul had moved away. There was no light to answer those who loved him, in that quiet face which for so many years had shed benedictions with

---

* *Memoir of Rev. F. A. Baker* by Rev. A. F. Hewit, page 204.

every glance, but the "great glory," which gleamed through the golden gates opened to admit him, "Shone still upon the watcher's face."

But as the hours passed on and human weakness showed itself weary of looking upward, the grief of the people appeared uncontrollable; that which had once been their idolized pastor was laid, clothed in the vestments his mother had made him, in the chapel attached to the house, and crowds filled the grounds awaiting their turn to enter the chapel and watch by his side.

The funeral was set for Saturday, May 9th, by that time, notwithstanding the bad roads, and that no invitations or public anouncement was given, the entire population, for a hundred miles around had gathered in Loretto. It was but a few steps from the chapel to the church, and the only direction in regard to the funeral he himself had given was that he might be laid between the two, where he had passed a thousand times from his home to the altar, where his children gone before would be around him, but as so many contended for the honor of bearing him to the church, and then to his resting place, it was decided the procession should pass from the chapel to the village, past the honest homes, around the church he left in place of the howling wilderness he found, and there where the patient feet had made their toilsome journey, where the folded hands had given countless blessings, where the heavenly eyes had illumined the darkest hour, sacred and dear as the relics of a saint he was carried, slowly and solemnly, the cross he had borne faithfully through life, before him, his children, young and old, in weeping procession behind him. Although the route extended over a half a mile, and the pall bearers were changed every few minutes, many had not been able to obtain place, when they reached the church. Rev. Mr. Heyden sang the requiem Mass, assisted by Rev. Messrs. Bradley, McGirr, Lemcke, and Rattigan. Rev. Mr. Heyden preached a funeral sermon in English from the text: *The Just shall live in everlasting remembrance*, and Rev. Mr. Lemcke made some remarks in German, taking his text from the eleventh chapter of Hebrews: *Of whom the world was not worthy; wandering in deserts, in mountains, and in dens, and in caves of the earth.* The people were forced from the coffin, and the lid closed. It was placed in one of zinc and amid heartrending prayers and wails lowered into the earth.

In his will Dr. Gallitzin directed that his debts and funeral expenses should be paid as soon after his decease as possible; he left the farm upon which St. Michael's church was built, and the lands belonging to it, to the Bishop of Philadelphia, or to his successor who might be appointed for the Western diocese of Pennsylvania, and his successors, in trust forever for the support and use of the Roman Catholic clergy duly appointed to officiate at St. Micheal's church; also to the same a square of six lots in the town of Loretto, upon which to erect a new church. The remainder of his estate was to be appropriated for the relief of poor widows and orphans; for Masses for the faithful departed; to aid in the erection of a Catholic church in Loretto upon the lots mentioned, and for legacies to several persons who had been brought up in his house.

The little furniture his house contained was eagerly bought by his parishioners, who cherish with pride and affection and transmit as a sacred inheritance to their children the least thing that had once been his. "I remember," writes Mr. Gibson,* "finding in one of the rooms a discipline and an iron chain with sharp points for attaching round the waist, both covered with his blood."

The news of his death reached Bishop Kenrick while attending the Council in Baltimore, and was communicated to the bishops assembled there, who expressed the deepest grief at the loss of the venerated Apostle of the Alleghanies. Mr. Heyden was appointed to remain in charge of the Loretto congregation for the present, but not wishing to be separated from his own parish, he declined the appointment, a step he afterwards bitterly regretted, for by that means Dr. Gallitzin's letters and papers, which were of the great-

---

* Who was ordained in 1814, and said his first Mass in Gallitzin's church in Loretto on the eighth of September in the same year.

est literary and historical, as well as personal value, were suffered to become scattered and lost, to the very great embarrassment of those who would wish to preserve the memory of one of the greatest and saintliest men who ever came to sanctify the soil of our beloved country, or to write the story of the most fascinating period of our Church history. "It was the doctor's custom," says Rev. Mr. Lemcke,* who remained in charge at Loretto, Mr. Heyden declining, "to preserve not merely all the letters he received, but copies of all he wrote, if of the least importance; more than this, he kept every paper in which there was any notice of events, even the most ordinary, which had any interest for him; in one large chest there were papers and letters of every description from the memoirs of his mother to his last tailor's bill; notes from the princess to his tutors, to her children, in a word the accummulation of half a century." Among these were said to be "letters from Russia and all parts of Europe, from bishops, and even prominent statesmen of America, for he was a well known and prominent character." Mr. Lemcke sometime after visited Europe taking with him such letters and manuscripts as he considered of interest for the purpose, and in 1861 published at Muenster his *Leben und Wirken des Prinzen Demetrius Augustin Gallitzin.*

The divison of the Philadelphia diocese did not take place until three years after the great missionary's death; in 1843 the diocese of Pittsburg was formed from the western division of Pennsylvania, and in 1852 was itself divided, and the northwestern counties made to constitute the diocese of Erie. Loretto remains in the diocese of Pittsburg; the new church Gallitzin so desired to see there was built a few years after the first division; the Sisters of Mercy have a large and handsome building for a boarding school near it, and not far distant the Franciscan brothers a college. Ten years after his death Dr. Gallizin's remains were disinterred and placed in a vault in front of the church, and a monument† erected

* Page 11.

† Which the pastor and people of Loretto are making efforts to replace with one more suitable to his cherished memory.

over the spot; with an inscription composed by Archbishop Kenrick:

Sacrum Memoriae.

Dem. A. E. Principibus Gallitzin,—nat. xxii Decemb. A. D. MDCCLXX.

Qui Schismate ejurato Ad. Sacerdotium. erectus. Sacro. Ministerio. per. tot. hauc. reg. perfunctus, Fide, Zelo, Charitate, insignis. Heic. Obiit Dei VI Maii A. D. MDCCCXL.

Sacred to the Memory

Of Dem. A. Prince of Gallitzin,—born Dec 22 1770 who having renounced Schism was raised to the Priesthood,

Exercised the sacred ministry through the whole of this region,

. And distinguished for faith, zeal, charity,
Died May 6 1840.

The sadness with which the people for the first time saw another standing in his place did not lessen as the days advanced, however honored his sucessors, but almost every hour, and certainly every religious duty required of them, pressed home to them some new phase of their immeasurable loss; their desolation, and soul-weariness, could be in a measure controlled even when they passed his little cabin where he no longer sat, silent and alone, under the great trees, or came with shining eyes to welcome them at his garden gate, but when the sorrows of life darkened their doors, and the hand of the Lord lay heavy upon them, a wail of misery forced itself from their inmost soul, aching for the ringing step nearing their doorway, the low toned words of heavenly comfort, with which in days of old he had taken the load from their hearts. In the confessional it was still harder, and for years many of his penitents found it almost impossible to confess at all, so overpowering were the recollections of the lovely ways by which he had led their souls to God. But though the silence was never to be broken by that comforting step, he was not absent. In the darkest hour of their sin and sorrow the most forsaken of them all, had sudden glimpses of heavenly hope and faith, rousing them to incomprehensible courage; it is no irreverence to say death had lost half its terrors since he had passed so tranquilly through them, the promised reward seemed no longer vague and afar off since all things told them he had surely reached it. From far and wide others have come to learn of that holy life, and to bless the day they first heard his name. Looking upon his life and abroad to all the world can offer, it is seen that virtue and truth, the desire of heaven, and loving labor for other's souls, for Christ's sake, are the only clear cut and vivid things in this world, all else is cold and gray, vague, shadowy and insecure. *He being dead, yet speaketh.*

THE END.

www.ingramcontent.com/pod-product-compliance
Lightning Source LLC
Chambersburg PA
CBHW022059300426
44117CB00007B/514